Good
Manufacturing
Practice
(GMP) Guidelines

---

*The Rules Governing Medicinal
Products in the European Union*

EudraLex Volume 4
Concise Reference

Good Manufacturing Practice (GMP) Guidelines

The Rules
Governing Medicinal Products
in the European Union

EudraLex Volume 4
Concise Reference

Good Manufacturing Practice (GMP) Guidelines: The Rules Governing
Medicinal Products in the European Union EudraLex Volume 4 Concise
Reference

PharmaLogika, Inc.
PO Box 461
Willow Springs, NC 27592

www.pharmalogika.com

Author / Editor: Mindy J. Allport-Settle

Published by PharmaLogika, Inc.

Printed in the United States of America. First Printing.

ISBN 0-9821476-0-0
ISBN-13 978-0-9821476-0-3

Contents

Procedures Related to Rapid Alerts............... 413

Handling of Reports of Suspected Quality Defects in Medicinal Products 415

Procedure for Handling Rapid Alerts and Recalls Arising from Quality Defects 425

Preface

About this Book

This book is first, and foremost, a unified reference source for the European Commission's Good Manufacturing Practice (GMP) Guidelines, Volume 4 of the EudraLex (The Rules Governing Medicinal Products in the European Union). In addition to the regulations defining the GMPs, the European Medicines Agency's (EMEA) procedures, guidance documents and forms have also been collected.

The included *Overview and Orientation* (Chapter 2 of this book) is designed to provide a foundation for understanding the background of the European Union's regulations and its relationship with the individual regulations of each Member State.

This book was designed to be used both as a reference for experienced industry representatives and as a training resource for those new to the industry.

Included Documents and Features

European Union Regulations and Associated Guidance:

- Overview and Orientation
- Introduction
- Commission Directive 2003/94/EC
- Part I: Basic Requirements for Medicinal Products
- Part II: Basic Requirements for Active Substances used as Starting Materials
- Annexes 1 – 20 and the European Commission Glossary

EMEA (European Medicines Agency) GMP Documents:

- Inspections - Good Manufacturing Practice
- Quality Systems Framework for GMP Inspectorates

Procedures Related to Rapid Alerts:

- Handling of Reports of Suspected Quality Defects in Medicinal Products
- Procedure for Handling Rapid Alerts and Recalls Arising from Quality Defects
- Procedure for Handling Rapid Alerts and Recalls Arising from Quality Defects [Pending Adoption]

Procedures Related to GMP Inspections:

- Procedure for Dealing with Serious GMP Noncompliance or Voiding/Suspension of CEPs thus Requiring Coordinated Administrative Action
- Conduct of Inspections of Pharmaceutical Manufacturers
- Outline of a Procedure for Co-ordinating the Verification of the GMP Status of Manufacturers in Third Countries
- Guideline on Training and Qualifications of GMP Inspectors
- Exchange of Information on Manufacturers and Manufacturing or Wholesale Distribution Authorisations between Competent Authorities in the European Economic Area
- Guidance on the Occasions when it is Appropriate for Competent Authorities to Conduct Inspections at the Premises of Manufacturers of Active Substances used as Starting Materials
- The Issue and Update of GMP Certificates
- A Model for Risk Based Planning for Inspections of Pharmaceutical Manufacturers
- GMP Inspection Report - Community Format
- Community Basic Format for Manufacturers Authorisation

Forms Used by Regulators:

- GMP Inspection Report - Community Format
- Community Basic Format for Manufacturers Authorisation
- Community Format for a GMP Certificate

Procedures Related to Centralised Procedures:

- Procedure for Co-ordinating Foreign and Community Pre-Authorisation Inspections during the Assessment of Applications

- Guideline on the Preparation of Reports on GMP Inspections Requested by Either the CPMP or CVMP in Connection with Applications for Marketing Authorisations and with Products Authorised under the Centralised System
- Delegation of Responsibilities for GMP Inspections for Products covered under the Centralised Procedure

Reference Tools

- Glossaries for each included part and procedure combined in one location
- Combined Index for all standards and guidance documents

About the Reference Tools

EU Overview and Orientation

This overview provides the reader with a brief history of the European Union's European Commission and explains not only what good manufacturing practice is, but why we have it and how it came to be.

The overview also lists all of the titles within EudraLex.

Combined Glossary

The Combined Glossary includes all of the glossaries from each regulation and guidance listed alphabetically rather than by document.

When a word or term appears multiple times in the regulation and guidance documents, the word will appear multiple times in the Combined Glossary. Each duplicate entry is indented to highlight that it is a duplicate and the earliest reference to the entry is listed first. The source for each entry is bracketed (i.e., [Part II: Annex 20]) for ease of reference. While the definitions are similar from one regulatory or guidance document to the next, they are not always identical.

Combined Index for all standards and guidance documents

The index is composed of a list of both words and terms specific to good manufacturing practice. It is a tool that assists in cross-referencing the various regulations and guidance documents (rather than having to rely on reading and comparing each document individually).

Pharmaceutical, biotechnology, and medical device companies use terminology that combines scientific and technical jargon with legal phrases and concepts.

The index provides keywords and terminology as a tool to easily locate specific references across all documents rather than having to rely on memory or paging through the entire regulation.

Overview and Orientation

Pharmaceuticals in in the European Union[1]

The role of the EU

The basic rules defining the framework for pharmaceutical medicinal products in the EU date back to 1965. Since the first Community Directive was adopted a score of Community legislation has followed with the aim of achieving a single EU-wide market for pharmaceuticals. This single market should help not only to enhance the health of European citizens, but also to strengthen the competitiveness and research capability of the European pharmaceutical industry for generations to come.

Much of the impetus behind the first Community legislation in this sector, Directive 65/65/EEC, stemmed from the determination to prevent the recurrence of the thalidomide disaster of the early 1960s, when thousands of babies were born with limb deformities as a result of their mothers taking thalidomide as a sedative during pregnancy. This experience, which shook public health authorities and the general public, made it clear that to safeguard public health, no medicinal product must ever again be marketed without prior authorisation.

Today the pharmaceutical sector is extensively regulated at the European Union's level in the dual interest of ensuring the highest possible level of public health and patient confidence in safe, effective and high-quality medicinal products, while continuing to develop a single EU-wide market for pharmaceuticals in order to strengthen European pharmaceutical industry's competitiveness and research capability.

---

[1]

http://ec.europa.eu/enterprise/pharmaceuticals/pharmacos/pharmeu_en.htm

Evaluation of medicinal products and marketing authorisations

To guarantee the highest possible level of public health and to secure the availability of medicinal products to citizens across the European Union all medicinal products for human and animal use have to be authorised either at the Member States or at Community level.

Special rules exist for the authorisation of medicinal products for paediatric use, orphan drugs, herbal medicinal products, vaccines and clinical trials.

Good manufacturing practice (GMP) and inspection

To ensure that medicinal products are consistently produced and controlled against the quality standards appropriate to their intended use, the European Union has set quality standards known as Good Manufacturing Practice (GMP). Compliance with these principles and guidelines is mandatory within the European Economic Area.

Pharmacovigilance

Once medicinal products have been authorised in the Community and are placed on the market, the supervision and in particular the intensive monitoring of adverse reactions to those medicinal products and the rapid withdrawal from the market of any medicinal product, which presents an unacceptable level of risk under normal conditions of use, is done through the Community's pharmacovigilance system.

Veterinary medicinal products

The principles of quality, safety and efficacy apply as well to veterinary medicines. Particular special rules are applied to ensure consumer protection from residue limits from pharmacologically active substances used in food-producing animals. These rules contribute to guaranteeing a high level of animal health and welfare in Europe.

European Medicines Agency - EMEA

In order to help the European Union ensure the highest possible level of public health the European Medicines Agency (EMEA) was established in 1994 with the main task of coordinating the scientific evaluation of the quality, safety and efficacy of medicinal products which undergo an authorisation procedure, and of providing scientific advice of the highest possible quality.

An environment conducive to innovation and competitiveness

There is a general consensus among decision makers that Europe needs to preserve a vibrant pharmaceutical sector as an essential pre-condition for the well-being and high level of public health of Europe's citizens and a competitive knowledge-based economy.

The pharmaceutical industry provides by far the largest contribution to European production, employment and share of global exports.

However, over the last decade Europe has been facing numerous challenges and has gradually lost its leadership in the pharmaceutical sector with a steady transfer of research and development to its global competitors. This relative decline in competitiveness has a number of causes including distortions created by diverging pricing and reimbursement policies at Member States' level. Therefore, the Commission has taken the initiative to address some of the most pressing issues by creating the Pharmaceutical Forum.

Established in June 2005, the Forum brings together, for the first time, senior decision makers in Member States, industry and other stakeholders. Based on previous work, the G10 Medicines process, it will take forward three sensitive and important issues "Information to Patients, Relative Effectiveness of Medicines and Pricing/Reimbursement". In particular, the two latter issues have been the source of unintended distortions in the Single Market for pharmaceuticals in the EU with different national pricing/reimbursement decisions and the diverging requirements to measure relative effectiveness.

The European Union is also addressing the issue of information on medicinal products available to its citizens. EU citizens have the right to high-quality, reliable and validated information about diseases, prevention, treatments and medicines available in order to be more actively involved in decisions about their health.

The objective of the Forum is to find a way forward which will ensure patients' access to new medicines at affordable costs and create a predictable environment for business with economic rewards for innovators. Creating an environment conducive to innovation will foster the competitiveness of the industry. Based on the deliberations in this framework, concrete actions will have to follow at EU, and particularly at Member States' level, in order to regenerate Europe as a world centre of pharmaceutical innovation.

Herbal Medicinal Products[2]

EU legislation on pharmaceutical products for human use also applies in general to traditional herbal medicines. However, in order to overcome difficulties encountered by Member States in applying pharmaceutical legislation to traditional herbal medicinal products in a uniform manner, a simplified registration procedure was introduced in 2004.

The simplified procedure was introduced by Directive 2004/24/EC of the European Parliament and of the Council of 31 March 2004 amending, as regards traditional herbal medicinal products, Directive 2001/83/EC on the Community code relating to medicinal products for human use.

A brief description of the procedure is available under point 3.4 of the Notice to Applicants Volume 2A - Procedures for marketing authorisation, Chapter 1 - Marketing Authorisation

The simplified registration procedure aims to safeguard public health, remove the differences and uncertainties about the status of traditional herbal medicinal products that existed in the past in the Member States, and facilitate the free movement of such products by introducing harmonised rules in this area.

Herbal medicinal products are defined as any medicinal product, exclusively containing as active ingredients one or more herbal substances or one or more herbal preparations, or one or more such herbal substances in combination with one or more such herbal preparations.

This simplified registration procedure is intended for herbal medicinal products with a long tradition, which do not fulfil the requirements for a marketing authorisation, in particular those requirements whereby an applicant can demonstrate by detailed references to published scientific literature that the constituent or the constituents of the medicinal products has or have a well-established medicinal use with recognised efficacy and level of safety (so called "well established use").

The simplified procedure allows the registration of herbal medicinal products without requiring particulars and documents on tests and trials on safety and efficacy, provided that there is sufficient evidence of the medicinal use of the product

---

[2] http://ec.europa.eu/enterprise/pharmaceuticals/herbal/herbal_en.htm

throughout a period of at least 30 years, including at least 15 years in the Community.

With regard to the manufacturing of these products and their quality, applications for registration of traditional herbal medicinal products have to fulfil the same requirements as applications for a marketing authorisation.

In view of the particularities of herbal medicinal products, a Committee for Herbal Medicinal Products (HMPC) has been established at the European Medicines Agency. A major task for the HMPC is to establish Community monographs for traditional herbal medicinal products, and, with the objective of further facilitating the registration and the harmonisation in the field of traditional herbal medicinal products, prepare a draft list of herbal substances which have been in medicinal use for a sufficiently long time, and hence are considered not to be harmful under normal conditions of use.

List of herbal substances, preparations and combinations thereof for use in traditional herbal medicinal products

With a view to further facilitating the registration of certain traditional herbal medicinal products in the EU, a list of herbal substances, preparations and combinations thereof for use in traditional herbal medicinal products has been established on the basis of the scientific opinion of the HMPC. As regards the safety and efficacy of a traditional herbal medicinal product, applicants can refer to the list. However they would still need to demonstrate the quality of the medicinal products they seek to register.

The list was established by Commission Decision 2008/911/EC of 21 November 2008. The decision will be amended based on new scientific opinions of the HMPC to include new herbal substances.

The Rules Governing Medicinal Products in the European Union

Introduction[3]

The body of European Union legislation in the pharmaceutical sector is compiled in Volume 1 and Volume 5 of the publication

---

[3] These documents are each available on the EudraLex website at http://ec.europa.eu/enterprise/pharmaceuticals/eudralex/eudralex_en.htm

"The rules governing medicinal products in the European Union".

- Volume 1 – EU pharmaceutical legislation for medicinal products for human use
- Volume 5 – EU pharmaceutical legislation for medicinal products for veterinary use

The basic legislation is supported by a series of guidelines that are also published in the following volumes of "The rules governing medicinal products in the European Union":

- Volume 2 - Notice to applicants and regulatory guidelines for medicinal products for human use
- Volume 3 - Scientific guidelines for medicinal products for human use
- Volume 4 – Guidelines for good manufacturing practices for medicinal products for human and veterinary use
- Volume 6 - Notice to applicants and regulatory guidelines for medicinal products for veterinary use
- Volume 7 - Scientific guidelines for medicinal products for veterinary use
- Volume 8 - Maximum residue limits
- Volume 9 – Guidelines for pharmacovigilance for medicinal products for human and veterinary use
- Volume 10 – Guidelines for clinical trial

Medicinal products for paediatric use, orphan, herbal medicinal products and advanced therapies are governed by specific rules.

Reference documents[4]

The objective of the work of Directorate-General for Enterprise and Industry in the pharmaceutical sector is to develop and maintain a favourable environment for medicinal products in the European Union which guarantees a high level of protection of public health, contributes to the completion of the Single Market in pharmaceuticals and fosters a stable and predictable environment for pharmaceutical innovation and competitiveness.

---

[4] http://ec.europa.eu/enterprise/sectors/pharmaceuticals/documents/index_en.htm

This section of the Europa website provides links to the following:

- Communication on the future of the Pharmaceutical sector

- On 10 December 2008, the European Commission adopted a communication on the future of the pharmaceutical sector as part of the pharmaceutical package. The Communication sets out a vision for the future of the pharmaceutical sector, addresses the main challenges that lie ahead and proposes concrete deliverables for the years to come.

- The volumes of "The rules governing medicinal products in the European Union" (EUDRALEX) which contain all Community legislation in the areas of medicinal products for human and veterinary use.

- The Community Register which is a register that contains a listing of all medicinal products for human and veterinary use, as well as orphan medicinal products, that have received a marketing authorisation through the centralised procedure.

- The reports of the Pharmaceutical Committee, which is an advisory Committee made of senior experts from the Member States, entrusted with the task of examining all questions relating to proprietary medicinal products, and in particular, the preparation of proposals for Directives.

- A listing of the judgements of the European Court of Justice of particular interest for the pharmaceutical sector.

- The news archives which include all major news related to pharmaceuticals published in the past on this website.

- G10 Medicines - Report 2002

  High-Level Group on Innovation and the Provision of Medicines

  The G10 Group was assigned to explore different ways to enhance pharmaceutical industry competitiveness in Europe. The G10 report, issued in 2002, contains a total of fourteen wide-ranging recommendations.

- In response to the G10 report, the European Commission adopted on 1 July 2003 the Communication "A stronger European-based pharmaceutical industry for the benefit of the patient - a call for action" which outlines the Commission's proposals to advance the G10 recommendations.

- Pharmaceutical Forum 2005-2008: Conclusions and Recommendations

The Pharmaceutical Forum was set up in 2005 as a three-year process by Vice-President Verheugen and former Commissioner Kyprianou, in order to find relevant solutions to public health considerations regarding pharmaceuticals, while ensuring the competitiveness of the industry and the sustainability of the national healthcare systems.

- Transparency Directive 89/105/EEC lays down harmonised provisions to ensure the transparency of national provisions regulating the pricing and reimbursement of medicinal products. It is commonly referred to as the "Transparency Directive" and was adopted at the end of the 1980s.

Community Register[5]

The Community Register lists all medicinal products for human and veterinary use as well as orphan medicinal products that have received a marketing authorisation through the centralised procedure.

The information provided in the Register can be accessed either by searching for the name of the product, the name of the active substance (INN) or the EU registration number.

This information includes: the name of the medicinal product, the EU registration number, the name and address of the marketing authorisation holder, the active substance, the international non-proprietary name, the ATC code, the therapeutic indication and the date of issue of the marketing authorisation valid throughout the EU. Detailed information on the European Commission procedures is also available together with relevant documents.

In addition to medicinal products that are currently on the EU market, a listing of medicinal products that were suspended or withdrawn and a listing of medicinal products for which a marketing authorisation was refused are also available.

The Register also provides information on medicinal products for human and veterinary use adopted nationally for which a Commission decision was necessary. These medicinal products, listed by the name of their active substance, as the commercial name may vary from State to State, are listed under the heading EU Referrals. In addition to details concerning the

---

[5]

http://ec.europa.eu/enterprise/sectors/pharmaceuticals/documents/community-register/index_en.htm

---

products, information on the European Commission procedures and the relevant documents are also available.

Information on traditional herbal medicinal products for human use, is also available in the Register. This includes: the marketing authorisation number, a list of Member States in which the product is authorised, the name of the medicinal product, the marketing authorisation holder and relevant address, and the date of issue of the marketing authorisation.

Other information that can be found in the Register includes a listing of the Commission decisions adopted in the last six months; a general index of active substances adopted in the EU and a general index of medicinal products listed by the brand name adopted in the EU.

Pharmaceutical Committee[6]

The Pharmaceutical Committee is an advisory Committee which was set up by Council Decision 75/320/EEC

of 20 May 1975 with the task of examining all questions relating to proprietary medicinal products and, in particular, the preparation of proposals for Directives.

When taking decisions in the pharmaceutical field, the Commission also consults the Veterinary Pharmaceutical Committee for issues related to medicinal products for veterinary use.

These advisory Committees consist of senior experts in public health matters from the Member States' administrations and are chaired by a Commission representative.

European Union Assistance Groups[7]

EU services and agencies

- European Commission - Enterprise and Industry Directorate General

  Medical Devices Sector
  Cosmetics
  Bio- and Nanotechnology

- European Commission - Research Directorate General

---

[6] http://ec.europa.eu/enterprise/sectors/pharmaceuticals/documents/pharmaceutical-committee/index_en.htm
[7] http://ec.europa.eu/enterprise/sectors/pharmaceuticals/links/index_en.htm

Innovative Medicines Initiative

- European Commission - Health and Consumer Protection Directorate General
- Health-EU - The Public Health Portal of the European Union
- EMEA - European Medicines Evaluation Agency

Pharmaceuticals associations and organisations

- European Directorate for the Quality of Medicines
- European Federation of Pharmaceutical Industries and Associations, representing the innovative pharmaceutical manufacturers (EFPIA)
- European Generics Association, representing the generic pharmaceutical manufacturers (EGA)
- European Self-Medication Industry (AESGP)
- The Heads of Medicines Agencies website

Human Medicines Agencies
Veterinary Medicines Agencies

Pharmaceuticals in the European Union[8]

The pharmaceutical industry makes an important contribution to Europe's and the world's well-being. It is a strategic sector due to its economic as well as its public health dimension.

Europe needs to preserve a vibrant pharmaceutical sector as an essential precondition to ensure a high level of public health protection and a competitive knowledge-based economy.

Since the adoption of the first Community Directive (Directive 65/65/EEC) in 1965, a score of Community legislation, which led to the creation of the European Medicines Agency, has followed with the aim of achieving a single market for pharmaceuticals.

Today, the pharmaceutical sector is extensively regulated at EU level in the dual interest of ensuring the highest possible level of public health and patient confidence in safe, effective and high-quality medicinal products, while continuing to develop a single EU market for pharmaceuticals in order to strengthen the European pharmaceutical industry's competitiveness and research capability.

---

[8] http://ec.europa.eu/enterprise/sectors/pharmaceuticals/index_en.htm

European standards[9]

Standardisation is the voluntary process of developing technical specifications based on consensus among all interested parties (industry including Small and Medium-sized Enterprises (SMEs), consumers, trade unions, environmental Non Governmental Organisations (NGO), public authorities, etc). It is carried out by independent standards bodies, acting at national, European and international level.

While the use of standards remains voluntary, the European Union has, since the mid-1980s, made an increasing use of standards in support of its policies and legislation.

Standardisation has contributed significantly to the completion of the Internal Market in the context of 'New Approach' legislation, which refers to European standards developed by the European standards organisations.

Furthermore, European standardisation supports European policies in the areas of competitiveness, Information and Communication Technologies (ICT), innovation, interoperability, environment, transport, energy, consumer protection, etc.

Standardisation is an excellent tool to facilitate international trade, competition and the acceptance of innovations by markets. A key challenge for European standardisation is to strengthen its contribution to the competitiveness of Small and Medium-sized Enterprises (SMEs).

Medicinal products for human use[10]

To guarantee the highest possible level of public health and to secure the availability of medicinal products to citizens across the European Union, all medicinal products for human use have to be authorised either at Member State or Community level before they can be placed on the EU market. Special rules exist for the authorisation of medicinal products for paediatric use, orphan medicines, traditional herbal medicines, vaccines and clinical trials.

Furthermore, to ensure that medicinal products are consistently produced and controlled against the quality standards appropriate to their intended use, the European Union has set

---

[9] http://ec.europa.eu/enterprise/policies/european-standards/index_en.htm#top

[10] http://ec.europa.eu/enterprise/sectors/pharmaceuticals/human-use/index_en.htm

quality standards known as 'good manufacturing practice'. Compliance with these principles and guidelines is mandatory within the European Economic Area.

In addition, once a medicinal product has been authorised in the Community and placed on the market, its safety is monitored throughout its entire lifespan to ensure that, in case of adverse reactions that present an unacceptable level of risk under normal conditions of use, it is rapidly withdrawn from the market. This is done through the EU system of pharmacovigilance.

In order to help the European Union ensure the highest possible level of public health protection, in 1994 the EU established the European Medicines Agency (EMEA) with the main task of coordinating the scientific evaluation of the quality, safety and efficacy of medicinal products which undergo an authorisation procedure, and providing scientific advice of the highest possible quality.

Authorisation Procedures for medicinal products[11]

Procedures for evaluating medicinal products and granting marketing authorisation

The European system for the authorisation of medicinal products for human and animal use was introduced in January 1995 with the objective of ensuring that safe, effective and high quality medicines could quickly be made available to citizens across the European Union.

The European system offers several routes for the authorisation of medicinal products:

- The centralised procedure, which is compulsory for products derived from biotechnology, for orphan medicinal products and for medicinal products for human use which contain an active substance authorised in the Community after 20 May 2004 (date of entry into force of Regulation (EC) No 726/2004) and which are intended for the treatment of AIDS, cancer, neurodegenerative disorders or diabetes. The centralised procedure is also mandatory for veterinary medicinal products intended primarily for use as performance enhancers in order to promote growth or to increase yields from treated animals.

---

[11] http://ec.europa.eu/enterprise/sectors/pharmaceuticals/authorisation-procedures_en.htm

Applications for the centralised procedure are made directly to the European Medicines Agency (EMEA) and lead to the granting of a European marketing authorisation by the Commission which is binding in all Member States.

- The mutual recognition procedure, which is applicable to the majority of conventional medicinal products, is based on the principle of recognition of an already existing national marketing authorisation by one or more Member States.

- The decentralised procedure, which was introduced with the legislative review of 2004, is also applicable to the majority of conventional medicinal products. Through this procedure an application for the marketing authorisation of a medicinal product is submitted simultaneously in several Member States, one of them being chosen as the "Reference Member State". At the end of the procedure national marketing authorisations are granted in the reference and in the concerned Member States.

Purely national authorisations are still available for medicinal products to be marketed in one Member State only.

Special rules exist for the authorisation of medicinal products for paediatric use, orphan drugs, traditional herbal medicinal products, vaccines and clinical trials.

The EMEA and the authorisation procedure

In 1993 the European Medicines Agency (EMEA) was founded with the primary task of providing scientific advice of the highest possible quality to the Community Institutions on all matters relating to medicinal products for human and veterinary use. EMEA's main task is to co-ordinate the scientific evaluation of the safety, efficacy and quality of medicinal products which undergo either procedure. All scientific questions arising in these procedures are dealt with by the EMEA.

The agency has today established itself as a world-leading agency for the evaluation of medicinal products. It constitutes a major asset in making Europe an attractive location for new pharmaceuticals and allows for speedy and robust authorisation of new innovative medicines.

EMEA's key tasks are to:

- provide Member States and Community institutions with the best possible scientific advice on questions about the quality, safety and efficacy of medicinal products for human and veterinary use;

- establish a pool of multinational scientific expertise (by mobilising existing national resources) in order to achieve a single evaluation via the centralised or mutual recognition marketing authorisation procedures;

- organise speedy, transparent and efficient procedures for the authorisation, surveillance and where appropriate, withdrawal of medicinal products in the EU;

- advise companies on the conduct of pharmaceutical research;

- reinforce the supervision of existing medicinal products (by co-ordinating national pharmacovigilance and inspection activities);

- create databases and electronic communication facilities as necessary to promote the rational use of medicines.

Manufacturing and Importation: Good Manufacturing Practice (GMP)[12]

The manufacturing or importation of medicinal products, including investigational medicinal products, is subject to a manufacturing or import authorisation. The holder of such an authorisation is obliged to comply with the principles and guidelines of good manufacturing practice for medicinal products and to use as starting materials only active substances (active pharmaceutical ingredients), which have been manufactured in accordance with GMP Part II. (Title IV of Directive 2001/83/EC); Article 13 of Directive 2001/20/EC, Title IV of Directive 2001/82/EC).

The Commission has adopted the principles and guidelines of GMP for medicinal products in form of Commission Directive 2003/94/EC concerning medicinal products for human use and investigational medicinal products and Commission Directive 91/412/EEC for veterinary medicinal products. In addition, the Commission has published detailed GMP guidelines in line with those principles in EudraLex Volume 4.

Currently, the legal basis for GMP on excipients is subject to further discussions.

---

[12] http://ec.europa.eu/enterprise/sectors/pharmaceuticals/human-use/quality/manufacturing-practices/index_en.htm

International Agreements and Collaboration

Mutual Recognition Agreement (MRA)

The Community has concluded MRAs covering the sector of GMP with Switzerland, Canada, Australia, New Zealand and Japan . In line with the scope of each MRA the EMEA has made public areas, including product categories, for which the MRAs have become operational. On the basis of equivalent provisions for GMP and supervision by competent authorities, the EU and the third country mutually accept results of inspections of manufacturers. Furthermore, the qualified person of the importer in the EU may be relieved of his responsibility to carry out the so-called re-testing.

For more information consult:

- International activities
- EMEA

Agreement on Conformity Assessment and Acceptance of Industrial Products (ACAA)

As a protocol to the Euro-Mediterranean Agreement establishing an Association between the European Communities and their Member States and the State of Israel an ACAA with Israel is currently being discussed with the Member States in the Council. A specific Sectoral Annex will include provisions for the area of GMP. On the basis of implementation of relevant Community legislation for manufacture, importation, official batch release, supervision and inspections results of inspections and official batch release are expected to be mutually recognised by both parties.

Priorities for the Pharmaceutical sector[13]

The pharmaceutical sector is extensively regulated in the dual interest of protecting public health while completing the single market for pharmaceuticals.

Our mission is to develop and maintain a favourable environment for medicinal products in the European Union which ensures a high level of protection of public health, contributes to the completion of the single market in pharmaceuticals and fosters a stable and predictable environment for pharmaceutical innovation.

---

[13]

http://ec.europa.eu/enterprise/pharmaceuticals/pharmacos/priorities_en.htm

Our responsibilities cover:

Regulatory policy

Our main tasks are:

- to maintain, update and simplify EU pharmaceutical legislation whenever feasible;
- to grant marketing authorisations for medicinal products for the EU market;
- to support Member States in the mutual recognition and decentralised procedures and in operating national mutual authorisations; and
- to provide guidance on pharmaceutical legislation and ensure that it is properly implemented within the EU.

Industrial policy

Our main tasks are:

- to support pharmaceutical innovation in the EU;
- to facilitate the market access of new medicines; and
- to meet the health needs of European citizens.

International cooperation

Our main tasks are:

- to promote international harmonisation within the International Conference on Harmonisation of technical requirements for registration of pharmaceuticals for human use (ICH), and the International Conference on Harmonisation of technical requirements for registration of veterinary medicinal products (VICH);
- to negotiate and apply mutual recognition agreements with third countries;
- to establish bilateral dialogues with third countries, including cooperation between regulators through confidentiality arrangements; and
- to cooperate with European and international organisations to address issues related to medicinal products.

Introduction

EudraLex

The Rules Governing Medicinal Products in the European Union

Volume 4

EU Guidelines to Good Manufacturing Practice Medicinal Products for Human and Veterinary Use

Document History	
The *first edition* of the Guide was published, including an annex on the manufacture of sterile medicinal products.	1989
The *second edition* was published; implementing Commission Directives 91/356 of 13 June 1991 and 91/412 of 23 July 1991 laying down the principles and guidelines on good manufacturing practice for medicinal products for human use as well as for veterinary medicinal products. The second edition also included 12 additional annexes.	January 1992
An update of legal references was made. In the meantime, the guide is updated as needed on the website of the European Commission, several additional annexes added.	August 2004
Re-structuring of GMP guide, consisting of Part I for medicinal products for human and veterinary use and Part II for active substances used as starting materials, implementing Directives 2004/27/EC and 2004/28/EC. The current guide includes 17 Annexes, the former Annex 18 being replaced.	October 2005
Implementation of ICH Q9 guideline as GMP Annex 20	March 2008

The pharmaceutical industry of the European Union maintains high standards of quality assurance in the development, manufacture and control of medicinal products. A system of marketing authorisations ensures that all medicinal products are assessed by a competent authority to ensure compliance with contemporary requirements of safety, quality and efficacy. A system of manufacturing authorisations ensures that all products authorised on the European market are manufactured only by authorised manufacturers, whose activities are regularly inspected by the competent authorities. Manufacturing authorisations are required by all pharmaceutical manufacturers in the European Community whether the products are sold within or outside of the Community.

Two directives laying down principles and guidelines of good manufacturing practice (GMP) for medicinal products were adopted by the Commission. Directive 2003/94/EC applies to medicinal products for human use and Directive 91/412/EEC for veterinary use. Detailed guidelines in accordance with those principles are published in the Guide to Good Manufacturing Practice which will be used in assessing applications for manufacturing authorisations and as a basis for inspection of manufacturers of medicinal products.

The principles of GMP and the detailed guidelines are applicable to all operations which require the authorisation referred to in Article 40 of Directive 2001/83/EC and in Article 44 of Directive 2001/82/EC, as amended by Directives 2004/27/EC and 2004/28/EC, respectively. They are also relevant for all other large scale pharmaceutical manufacturing processes, such as that undertaken in hospitals, and for the preparation of products for use in clinical trials.

All Member States and the industry agreed that the GMP requirements applicable to the manufacture of veterinary medicinal products are the same as those applicable to the manufacture of medicinal products for human use. Certain detailed adjustments to the GMP guidelines are set out in two annexes specific to veterinary medicinal products and to immunological veterinary medicinal products.

The Guide is presented in two parts of basic requirements and specific annexes. Part I covers GMP principles for the manufacture of medicinal products. Part II covers GMP for active substances used as starting materials.

Chapters of Part I on "basic requirements" are headed by principles as defined in Directives 2003/94/EC and 91/412/EEC. Chapter 1 on Quality Management outlines the fundamental concept of quality assurance as applied to the manufacture of medicinal products. Thereafter, each chapter has a principle outlining the quality assurance objectives of that chapter and a text which provides sufficient detail for manufacturers to be made aware of the essential matters to be considered when implementing the principle.

Part II was newly established on the basis of a guideline developed on the level of ICH and published as ICH Q7a on "active pharmaceutical ingredients", which was implemented as GMP Annex 18 for voluntary application in 2001. According to the revised Article 47 and Article 51, respectively, of the Directive 2001/83/EC and Directive 2001/82/EC, as amended, detailed guidelines on the principles of GMP for active substances used as starting materials shall be adopted and published by the Commission. The former Annex 18 has been replaced by the new Part II of the GMP guide, which has an extended application both for the human and the veterinary sector.

In addition to the general matters of Good Manufacturing Practice outlined in Part I and II, a series of annexes providing detail about specific areas of activity is included. For some manufacturing processes, different annexes will apply simultaneously (e.g. annex on sterile preparations and on radiopharmaceuticals and/or on biological medicinal products).

GMP Part I, Chapter 1 on Quality Management, has been revised to include aspects of quality risk management within the quality system framework. In future revisions of the guide the opportunity will be taken to introduce quality risk management elements when appropriate.

The new GMP Annex 20, which corresponds to the ICH Q9 guideline, provides guidance on a systematic approach to quality risk management leading to compliance with GMP and other quality requirements. It includes principles to be used and options for processes, methods and tools which may be used when applying a formal quality risk management approach. While the GMP guide is primarily addressed to manufacturers, the ICH Q9 guideline, has relevance for other quality guidelines and includes specific sections for regulatory agencies. However, for reasons of coherence and completeness the ICH Q9 guideline has been transferred completely into GMP Annex 20.

A glossary of some terms used in the Guide has been incorporated after the annexes.

The Guide is not intended to cover security aspects for the personnel engaged in manufacture. This may be particularly important in the manufacture of certain medicinal products such as highly active, biological and radioactive medicinal products. However, those aspects are governed by other provisions of Community or national law.

Throughout the Guide it is assumed that the requirements of the Marketing Authorisation relating to the safety, quality and efficacy of the products, are systematically incorporated into all the manufacturing, control and release for sale arrangements of the holder of the Manufacturing Authorisation.

The manufacture of medicinal products has for many years taken place in accordance with guidelines for Good Manufacturing Practice and the manufacture of medicinal products is not governed by CEN/ISO standards. Harmonised standards as adopted by the European standardisation organisations CEN/ISO may be used at industry's discretion as a tool for implementing a quality system in the pharmaceutical sector. The CEN/ISO standards have been considered but the terminology of these standards has not been implemented in this edition. It is recognised that there are acceptable methods, other than those described in the Guide, which are capable of achieving the principles of Quality Assurance. The Guide is not intended to place any restraint upon the development of any new concepts or new technologies which have been validated and which provide a level of Quality Assurance at least equivalent to those set out in this Guide. With its principles, methods and tools Annex 20 provides a systematic approach, which may be used to demonstrate such equivalence.

The GMP guide will be regularly revised. Revisions will be made publicly available on the website of the European Commission:

http://ec.europa.eu/enterprise/pharmaceuticals/eudralex/homev 4.htm.

Commission Directive 2003/94/EC

Commission Directive 2003/94/EC

of 8 October 2003 laying down the principles and guidelines of good manufacturing practice in respect of medicinal products for human use and investigational medicinal products for human use

(Text with EEA relevance)

[Cite: Directive 2003/94/EC]

THE COMMISSION OF THE EUROPEAN COMMUNITIES,

Having regard to the Treaty establishing the European Community,

Having regard to Directive 2001/83/EC of the European Parliament and of the Council of 6 November 2001 on the Community code relating to medicinal products for human use (1), as last amended by Commission Directive 2003/63/EC (2), and in particular Article 47 thereof,

Whereas:

(1) All medicinal products for human use manufactured or imported into the Community, including medicinal products intended for export, are to be manufactured in accordance with the principles and guidelines of good manufacturing practice.

(2) Those principles and guidelines are set out in Commission Directive 91/356/EEC of 13 June 1991 laying down the principles and guidelines of good manufacturing practice for medicinal products for human use (3).

(3) Article 13(3) of Directive 2001/20/EC of the European Parliament and of the Council of 4 April 2001 on the approximation of the laws, regulations and administrative

provisions of the Member States relating to the implementation of good clinical practice in the conduct of clinical trials on medicinal products for human use (4) requires that detailed guidance be drawn up, in accordance with the guidelines on good manufacturing practice, on the elements to be taken into account when evaluating investigational medicinal products for human use with the object of releasing batches within the Community.

(4) It is therefore necessary to extend and adapt the provisions of Directive 91/356/EEC to cover good manufacturing practice of investigational medicinal products.

(5) Since most of the provisions of Directive 91/356/EEC need to be adjusted, for the sake of clarity that Directive should be replaced.

(6) In order to ensure conformity with the principles and guidelines of good manufacturing practice, it is necessary to lay down detailed provisions on inspections by the competent authorities and on certain obligations of the manufacturer.

(1) OJ L 311, 28.11.2001, p. 67.

(2) OJ L 159, 27.6.2003, p. 46.

(3) OJ L 193, 17.7.1991, p. 30.

(4) OJ L 121, 1.5.2001, p. 34.

(7) All manufacturers should operate an effective quality management system of their manufacturing operations, which requires the implementation of a pharmaceutical quality assurance system.

(8) Principles and guidelines of good manufacturing practice should be set out in relation to quality management, personnel, premises and equipment, documentation, production, quality control, contracting out, complaints and product recall, and self-inspection.

(9) In order to protect the human beings involved in clinical trials and to ensure that investigational medicinal products can be traced, specific provisions on the labelling of those products are necessary.

(10)   The measures provided for in this Directive are in accordance with the opinion of the Standing Committee on Medicinal Products for Human Use, set up under Article 121 of Directive 2001/83/EC,

HAS ADOPTED THIS DIRECTIVE:

Article 1

Scope

This Directive lays down the principles and guidelines of good manufacturing practice in respect of medicinal products for human use whose manufacture requires the authorisation referred to in Article 40 of Directive 2001/83/EC and in respect of investigational medicinal products for human use whose manufacture requires the authorisation referred to in Article 13 of Directive 2001/20/EC.

Article 2

Definitions

For the purposes of this Directive, the following definitions shall apply:

1. 'medicinal product' means any product as defined in Article 1(2) of Directive 2001/83/EC;

2. 'investigational medicinal product' means any product as defined in Article 2(d) of Directive 2001/20/EC;

3. 'manufacturer' means any person engaged in activities for which the authorisation referred to in Article 40(1) and (3) of Directive 2001/83/EC or the authorisation referred to in Article 13(1) of Directive 2001/20/EC is required;

4. 'qualified person' means the person referred to in Article 48 of Directive 2001/83/EC or in Article 13(2) of Directive 2001/20/EC;

5. 'pharmaceutical quality assurance'   means the total sum of the organised arrangements made with the object of ensuring that medicinal products or investigational medicinal products are of the quality required for their intended use;

6. 'good manufacturing practice' means the part of quality assurance which ensures that products are consistently produced and controlled in accordance with the quality standards appropriate to their intended use;

7. 'blinding' means the deliberate disguising of the identity of an investigational medicinal product in accordance with the instructions of the sponsor;

8. 'unblinding' means the disclosure of the identity of a blinded product.

Article 3

Inspections

1. By means of the repeated inspections referred to in Article 111(1) of Directive 2001/83/EC and by means of the inspections referred to in Article 15(1) of Directive 2001/20/EC, the Member States shall ensure that manufacturers respect the principles and guidelines of good manufacturing practice laid down by this Directive. Member States shall also take into account the compilation, published by the Commission, of Community procedures on inspections and exchange of information.

2. For the interpretation of the principles and guidelines of good manufacturing practice, the manufacturers and the competent authorities shall take into account the detailed guidelines referred to in the second paragraph of Article 47 of Directive 2001/83/EC, published by the Commission in the 'Guide to good manufacturing practice for medicinal products and for investigational medicinal products'.

Article 4

Conformity with good manufacturing practice

1. The manufacturer shall ensure that manufacturing operations are carried out in accordance with good manufacturing practice and with the manufacturing authorisation. This provision shall also apply to medicinal products intended only for export.

2. For medicinal products and investigational medicinal products imported from third countries, the importer shall

ensure that the products have been manufactured in accordance with standards which are at least equivalent to the good manufacturing practice standards laid down by the Community.

In addition, an importer of medicinal products shall ensure that such products have been manufactured by manufacturers duly authorised to do so. An importer of investigational medicinal products shall ensure that such products have been manufactured by a manufacturer notified to the competent authorities and accepted by them for that purpose.

Article 5

Compliance with marketing authorisation

1. The manufacturer shall ensure that all manufacturing operations for medicinal products subject to a marketing authorisation are carried out in accordance with the information provided in the application for marketing authorisation as accepted by the competent authorities.

   In the case of investigational medicinal products, the manufacturer shall ensure that all manufacturing operations are carried out in accordance with the information provided by the sponsor pursuant to Article 9(2) of Directive 2001/20/EC as accepted by the competent authorities.

2. The manufacturer shall regularly review his manufacturing methods in the light of scientific and technical progress and the development of the investigational medicinal product.

   If a variation to the marketing authorisation dossier or an amendment to the request referred to in Article 9(2) of Directive 2001/20/EC is necessary, the application for modification shall be submitted to the competent authorities.

Article 6

Quality assurance system

The manufacturer shall establish and implement an effective pharmaceutical quality assurance system, involving the active participation of the management and personnel of the different departments.

Article 7

Personnel

1. At each manufacturing site, the manufacturer shall have a sufficient number of competent and appropriately qualified personnel at his disposal to achieve the pharmaceutical quality assurance objective.

2. The duties of the managerial and supervisory staff, including the qualified persons, responsible for implementing and operating good manufacturing practice, shall be defined in job descriptions. Their hierarchical relationships shall be defined in an organisation chart. Organisation charts and job descriptions shall be approved in accordance with the manufacturer's internal procedures.

3. The staff referred to in paragraph 2 shall be given sufficient authority to discharge their responsibility correctly.

4. The personnel shall receive initial and ongoing training, the effectiveness of which shall be verified, covering in particular the theory and application of the concept of quality assurance and good manufacturing practice, and, where appropriate, the particular requirements for the manufacture of investigational medicinal products.

5. Hygiene programmes adapted to the activities to be carried out shall be established and observed. These programmes shall, in particular, include procedures relating to health, hygiene practice and clothing of personnel.

Article 8

Premises and equipment

1. Premises and manufacturing equipment shall be located, designed, constructed, adapted and maintained to suit the intended operations.

2. Premises and manufacturing equipment shall be laid out, designed and operated in such a way as to minimise the risk of error and to permit effective cleaning and maintenance in order to avoid contamination, cross contamination and, in general, any adverse effect on the quality of the product.

3. Premises and equipment to be used for manufacturing operations, which are critical to the quality of the products, shall be subjected to appropriate qualification and validation.

Article 9

Documentation

1. The manufacturer shall establish and maintain a documentation system based upon specifications, manufacturing formulae and processing and packaging instructions, procedures and records covering the various manufacturing operations performed. Documents shall be clear, free from error and kept up to date. Pre-established procedures for general manufacturing operations and conditions shall be kept available, together with specific documents for the manufacture of each batch. That set of documents shall enable the history of the manufacture of each batch and the changes introduced during the development of an investigational medicinal product to be traced.

   For a medicinal product, the batch documentation shall be retained for at least one year after the expiry date of the batches to which it relates or at least five years after the certification referred to in Article 51(3) of Directive 2001/83/EC, whichever is the longer period.

   For an investigational medicinal product, the batch documentation shall be retained for at least five years after the completion or formal discontinuation of the last clinical trial in which the batch was used. The sponsor or marketing authorisation holder, if different, shall be responsible for ensuring that records are retained as required for marketing authorisation in accordance with the Annex I to Directive 2001/83/EC, if required for a subsequent marketing authorisation.

2. When electronic, photographic or other data processing systems are used instead of written documents, the manufacturer shall first validate the systems by showing that the data will be appropriately stored during the anticipated period of storage. Data stored by those systems shall be made readily available in legible form and shall be provided to the competent authorities at their request. The electronically stored data shall be protected, by methods

such as duplication or back-up and transfer on to another storage system, against loss or damage of data, and audit trails shall be maintained.

Article 10

Production

1. The different production operations shall be carried out in accordance with pre-established instructions and procedures and in accordance with good manufacturing practice. Adequate and sufficient resources shall be made available for the in-process controls. All process deviations and product defects shall be documented and thoroughly investigated.

2. Appropriate technical or organisational measures shall be taken to avoid cross contamination and mix-ups. In the case of investigational medicinal products, particular attention shall be paid to the handling of products during and after any blinding operation.

3. For medicinal products, any new manufacture or important modification of a manufacturing process of a medicinal product shall be validated. Critical phases of manufacturing processes shall be regularly re-validated.

4. For investigational medicinal products, the manufacturing process shall be validated in its entirety in so far as is appropriate, taking into account the stage of product development. At least the critical process steps, such as sterilisation, shall be validated. All steps in the design and development of the manufacturing process shall be fully documented.

Article 11

Quality control

1. The manufacturer shall establish and maintain a quality control system placed under the authority of a person who has the requisite qualifications and is independent of production.

   That person shall have at his disposal, or shall have access to, one or more quality control laboratories appropriately staffed and equipped to carry out the necessary examination and testing of the starting materials and packaging materials and the testing of intermediate and finished products.

2. For medicinal products, including those imported from third countries, contract laboratories may be used if authorised in accordance with Article 12 of this Directive and point (b) of Article 20 of Directive 2001/83/EC.

   For investigational medicinal products, the sponsor shall ensure that the contract laboratory complies with the content of the request referred to in Article 9(2) of Directive 2001/20/EC, as accepted by the competent authority. When the products are imported from third countries, analytical control shall not be mandatory.

3. During the final control of the finished product before its release for sale or distribution or for use in clinical trials, the quality control system shall take into account, in addition to analytical results, essential information such as the production conditions, the results of in-process controls, the examination of the manufacturing documents and the conformity of the product to its specifications, including the final finished pack.

4. Samples of each batch of finished medicinal product shall be retained for at least one year after the expiry date.

   For an investigational medicinal product, sufficient samples of each batch of bulk formulated product and of key packaging components used for each finished product batch shall be retained for at least two years after completion or formal discontinuation of the last clinical trial in which the batch was used, whichever period is the longer.

   Unless a longer period is required under the law of the Member State of manufacture, samples of starting materials, other than solvents, gases or water, used in the manufacturing process shall be retained for at least two years after the release of product. That period may be shortened if the period of stability of the material, as indicated in the relevant specification, is shorter. All those samples shall be maintained at the disposal of the competent authorities.

Other conditions may be defined, by agreement with the competent authority, for the sampling and retaining of starting materials and certain products manufactured individually or in small quantities, or when their storage could raise special problems.

Article 12

Work contracted out

1. Any manufacturing operation or operation linked thereto which is carried out under contract shall be the subject of a written contract.

2. The contract shall clearly define the responsibilities of each party and shall define, in particular, the observance of good manufacturing practice to be followed by the contract-acceptor and the manner in which the qualified person responsible for certifying each batch is to discharge his responsibilities.

3. The contract-acceptor shall not subcontract any of the work entrusted to him under the contract without written authorisation from the contract-giver.

4. The contract-acceptor shall comply with the principles and guidelines of good manufacturing practice and shall submit to inspections carried out by the competent authorities pursuant to Article 111 of Directive 2001/83/EC and Article 15 of Directive 2001/20/EC.

Article 13

Complaints, product recall and emergency unblinding

1. In the case of medicinal products, the manufacturer shall implement a system for recording and reviewing complaints together with an effective system for recalling, promptly and at any time, medicinal products in the distribution network. Any complaint concerning a defect shall be recorded and investigated by the manufacturer. The manufacturer shall inform the competent authority of any defect that could result in a recall or abnormal restriction on supply and, in so far as is possible, indicate the countries of destination.

Any recall shall be made in accordance with the

requirements referred to in Article 123 of Directive 2001/83/EC.

2. In the case of investigational medicinal products, the manufacturer shall, in cooperation with the sponsor, implement a system for recording and reviewing complaints together with an effective system for recalling promptly and at any time investigational medicinal products which have already entered the distribution network. The manufacturer shall record and investigate any complaint concerning a defect and shall inform the competent authority of any defect that could result in a recall or abnormal restriction on supply.

In the case of investigational medicinal products, all trial sites shall be identified and, in so far as is possible, the countries of destination shall be indicated.

In the case of an investigational medicinal product for which a marketing authorisation has been issued, the manufacturer of the investigational medicinal product shall, in cooperation with the sponsor, inform the marketing authorisation holder of any defect that could be related to the authorised medicinal product.

3. The sponsor shall implement a procedure for the rapid unblinding of blinded products, where this is necessary for a prompt recall as referred to in paragraph 2. The sponsor shall ensure that the procedure discloses the identity of the blinded product only in so far as is necessary.

Article 14

Self-inspection

The manufacturer shall conduct repeated self-inspections as part of the quality assurance system in order to monitor the implementation and respect of good manufacturing practice and to propose any necessary corrective measures. Records shall be maintained of such self-inspections and any corrective action subsequently taken.

Article 15

Labelling

In the case of an investigational medicinal product, labelling shall be such as to ensure protection of the subject and traceability, to enable identification of the product and trial, and to facilitate proper use of the investigational medicinal product.

Article 16

Repeal of Directive 91/356/EEC

Directive 91/356/EEC is repealed.

References to the repealed Directive shall be construed as references to this Directive.

Article 17

Transposition

1. Member States shall bring into force the laws, regulations and administrative provisions necessary to comply with this Directive by 30 April 2004 at the latest. They shall forthwith communicate to the Commission the text of the provisions and correlation table between those provisions and the provisions of this Directive.

   When Member States adopt those provisions, they shall contain a reference to this Directive or be accompanied by such a reference on the occasion of their official publication. The Member States shall determine how such reference is to be made.

2. Member States shall communicate to the Commission the text of the main provisions of national law which they adopt in the field covered by this Directive.

Article 18

Entry into force

This Directive shall enter into force on the 20th day following that of its publication in the Official Journal of the European Union.

Article 19

Addressees

This Directive is addressed to the Member States.

Done at Brussels, 8 October 2003.

For the Commission

Erkki LIIKANEN

Member of the Commission

Part I

Basic Requirements
for Medicinal Products

Chapter 1:
Quality Management

EudraLex

The Rules Governing Medicinal Products in the European Union

Volume 4

EU Guidelines to Good Manufacturing Practice Medicinal Products for Human and Veterinary Use

Document History	
Revision to include concept of Product Quality Review	25 October 2005
Date of revised version coming into operation and superseding previous version dated	25 October 2005

Principle

The holder of a Manufacturing Authorisation must manufacture medicinal products so as to ensure that they are fit for their intended use, comply with the requirements of the

Marketing Authorisation and do not place patients at risk due to inadequate safety, quality or efficacy. The attainment of this quality objective is the responsibility of senior management and requires the participation and commitment by staff in many different departments and at all levels within the company, by the company's suppliers and by the distributors. To achieve the quality objective reliably there must be a comprehensively designed and correctly implemented system of Quality Assurance incorporating Good Manufacturing Practice, Quality Control and Quality Risk Management. It should be fully documented and its effectiveness monitored. All parts of the Quality Assurance system should be adequately resourced with competent personnel, and suitable and sufficient premises, equipment and facilities. There are additional legal responsibilities for the holder of the Manufacturing Authorisation and for the Qualified Person(s).

The basic concepts of Quality Assurance, Good Manufacturing Practice, Quality Control and Quality Risk Management are inter-related. They are described here in order to emphasise their relationships and their fundamental importance to the production and control of medicinal products.

Quality Assurance

1.1 Quality Assurance is a wide-ranging concept, which covers all matters, which individually or collectively influence the quality of a product. It is the sum total of the organised arrangements made with the objective of ensuring that medicinal products are of the quality required for their intended use. Quality Assurance therefore incorporates Good Manufacturing Practice plus other factors outside the scope of this Guide.

The system of Quality Assurance appropriate for the manufacture of medicinal products should ensure that:

(i) medicinal products are designed and developed in a way that takes account of the requirements of Good Manufacturing Practice;

(ii) production and control operations are clearly specified and Good Manufacturing Practice adopted;

(iii) managerial responsibilities are clearly specified;

(iv) arrangements are made for the manufacture, supply and use of the correct starting and packaging materials;

(v) all necessary controls on intermediate products, and any other in-process controls and validations are carried out;

(vi) the finished product is correctly processed and checked, according to the defined procedures;

(vii) medicinal products are not sold or supplied before a Qualified Person has certified that each production batch has been produced and controlled in accordance with the requirements of the Marketing Authorisation and any other regulations relevant to the production, control and release of medicinal products;

(viii) satisfactory arrangements exist to ensure, as far as possible, that the medicinal products are stored, distributed and subsequently handled so that quality is maintained throughout their shelf life;

(ix) there is a procedure for Self-Inspection and/or quality audit, which regularly appraises the effectiveness and applicability of the Quality Assurance system.

Good Manufacturing Practice for Medicinal Products (GMP)

1.2 Good Manufacturing Practice is that part of Quality Assurance which ensures that products are consistently produced and controlled to the quality standards appropriate to their intended use and as required by the Marketing Authorisation or product specification.

Good Manufacturing Practice is concerned with both production and quality control.

The basic requirements of GMP are that:

(i) all manufacturing processes are clearly defined, systematically reviewed in the light of experience and shown to be capable of consistently manufacturing medicinal products of the required quality and complying with their specifications;

(ii) critical steps of manufacturing processes and significant changes to the process are validated;

(iii) all necessary facilities for GMP are provided including:

- appropriately qualified and trained personnel;

- adequate premises and space;

- suitable equipment and services;

- correct materials, containers and labels;

- approved procedures and instructions;

- suitable storage and transport;

(iv) instructions and procedures are written in an instructional form in clear and unambiguous language, specifically applicable to the facilities provided;

(v) operators are trained to carry out procedures correctly;

(vi) records are made, manually and/or by recording instruments, during manufacture which demonstrate that all the steps required by the defined procedures and instructions were in fact taken and that the quantity and quality of the product was as expected. Any significant deviations are fully recorded and investigated;

(vii) records of manufacture including distribution which enable the complete history of a batch to be traced, are retained in a comprehensible and accessible form;

(viii) the distribution (wholesaling) of the products minimises any risk to their quality;

(ix) a system is available to recall any batch of product, from sale or supply;

(x) complaints about marketed products are examined, the causes of quality defects investigated and appropriate measures taken in respect of the defective products and to prevent reoccurrence.

Quality Control

1.3 Quality Control is that part of Good Manufacturing Practice which is concerned with sampling, specifications and testing, and with the organisation, documentation and release procedures which ensure that the necessary and relevant tests are actually carried out and that materials are not released for use, nor products released for sale or supply, until their quality has been judged to be satisfactory.

The basic requirements of Quality Control are that:

(i) adequate facilities, trained personnel and approved procedures are available for sampling, inspecting and testing starting materials, packaging materials, intermediate, bulk, and finished products, and where appropriate for monitoring environmental conditions for GMP purposes;

(ii)   samples of starting materials, packaging materials, intermediate products, bulk products and finished products are taken by personnel and by methods approved by Quality Control;

(iii)   test methods are validated;

(iv)   records are made, manually and/or by recording instruments, which demonstrate that all the required sampling, inspecting and testing procedures were actually carried out. Any deviations are fully recorded and investigated;

(v)   the finished products contain active ingredients complying with the qualitative and quantitative composition of the Marketing Authorisation, are of the purity required, and are enclosed within their proper containers and correctly labelled;

(vi)   records are made of the results of inspection and that testing of materials, intermediate, bulk, and finished products is formally assessed against specification. Product assessment includes a review and evaluation of relevant production documentation and an assessment of deviations from specified procedures;

(vii)   no batch of product is released for sale or supply prior to certification by a Qualified Person that it is in accordance with the requirements of the relevant authorisations;

(viii) sufficient reference samples of starting materials and products are retained to permit future examination of the product if necessary and that the product is retained in its final pack unless exceptionally large packs are produced.

Product Quality Review

1.4   Regular periodic or rolling quality reviews of all licensed medicinal products, including export only products, should be conducted with the objective of verifying the consistency of the existing process, the appropriateness of current specifications for both starting materials and finished product to highlight any trends and to identify product and process improvements. Such reviews should normally be conducted and documented annually, taking into account previous reviews, and should include at least:

(i)   A review of starting materials including packaging materials used in the product, especially those from new sources.

(ii)   A review of critical in-process controls and finished product results.

(iii)   A review of all batches that failed to meet established specification(s) and their investigation.

(iv)   A review of all significant deviations or non-conformances, their related investigations, and the effectiveness of resultant corrective and preventative actions taken.

(v)   A review of all changes carried out to the processes or analytical methods.

(vi)   A review of Marketing Authorisation variations submitted/granted/refused, including those for third country (export only) dossiers.

(vii)   A review of the results of the stability monitoring programme and any adverse trends.

(viii)   A review of all quality-related returns, complaints and recalls and the investigations performed at the time.

(ix)   A review of adequacy of any other previous product process or equipment corrective actions.

(x)   For new marketing authorisations and variations to marketing authorisations, a review of post-marketing commitments.

(xi)   The qualification status of relevant equipment and utilities, e.g. HVAC, water, compressed gases, etc.

(xii)   A review of any contractual arrangements as defined in Chapter 7 to ensure that they are up to date.

The manufacturer and marketing authorisation holder should evaluate the results of this review, where different, and an assessment made of whether corrective and preventative action or any revalidation should be undertaken. Reasons for such corrective actions should be documented. Agreed corrective and preventative actions should be completed in a timely and effective manner. There should be management procedures for the ongoing management and review of these actions and the effectiveness of these procedures verified during selfinspection. Quality reviews may be grouped by product type, e.g. solid dosage forms, liquid dosage forms, sterile products, etc. where scientifically justified.

Where the marketing authorisation holder is not the manufacturer, there should be a technical agreement in place between the various parties that defines their respective responsibilities in producing the quality review. The Qualified Person responsible for final batch certification together with the marketing authorisation holder should ensure that the quality review is performed in a timely manner and is accurate.

Quality Risk Management

1.5 Quality risk management is a systematic process for the assessment, control, communication and review of risks to the quality of the medicinal product. It can be applied both proactively and retrospectively.

1.6 The quality risk management system should ensure that:

— the evaluation of the risk to quality is based on scientific knowledge, experience with the process and ultimately links to the protection of the patient

— the level of effort, formality and documentation of the quality risk management process is commensurate with the level of risk

Examples of the processes and applications of quality risk management can be found inter alia in Annex 20.

Chapter 2: Personnel

Principle

The establishment and maintenance of a satisfactory system of quality assurance and the correct manufacture of medicinal products relies upon people. For this reason there must be sufficient qualified personnel to carry out all the tasks which are the responsibility of the manufacturer. Individual responsibilities should be clearly understood by the individuals and recorded. All personnel should be aware of the principles of Good Manufacturing Practice that affect them and receive initial and continuing training, including hygiene instructions, relevant to their needs.

General

2.1   The manufacturer should have an adequate number of personnel with the necessary qualifications and practical experience. The responsibilities placed on any one individual should not be so extensive as to present any risk to quality.

2.2   The manufacturer must have an organisation chart. People in responsible positions should have specific duties recorded in written job descriptions and adequate authority to carry out their responsibilities. Their duties may be delegated to designated deputies of a satisfactory qualification level. There should be no gaps or unexplained overlaps in the responsibilities of those personnel concerned with the application of Good Manufacturing Practice.

Key Personnel

2.3   Key Personnel include the head of Production, the head of Quality Control, and if at least one of these persons is

not responsible for the duties described in Article 51 of
Directive 2001/83/EC[14], the Qualified Person(s)
designated for the purpose. Normally key posts should
be occupied by full-time personnel. The heads of
Production and Quality Control must be independent
from each other. In large organisations, it may be
necessary to delegate some of the functions listed in 2.5,
2.6 and 2.7.

2.4   The duties of the Qualified Person(s) are fully described
in Article 51 of Directive 2001/83/EC, and can be
summarised as follows:

a)   for medicinal products manufactured within the
European Community, a Qualified Person must
ensure that each batch has been produced and
tested/checked in accordance with the directives
and the marketing authorisation[15];

(b)   for medicinal products manufactured outside the
European Community, a Qualified Person must
ensure that each imported batch has undergone, in
the importing country, the testing specified in
paragraph 1(b) of Article 51;

(c)   a Qualified Person must certify in a register or
equivalent document, as operations are carried out
and before any release, that each production batch
satisfies the provisions of Article 51.

The persons responsible for these duties must
meet the qualification requirements laid down in
Article 49[16] of the same Directive, they shall be
permanently and continuously at the disposal of
the holder of the Manufacturing Authorisation to
carry out their responsibilities. Their responsibilities
may be delegated, but only to other Qualified
Person(s).

---

[14] Article 55 of Directive 2001/82/EC
[15] According to Directive 75/319/EEC (now codified Directive
2001/83/EC) and the Ruling (Case 247/81) of the Court of Justice of the
European Commununities, medicinal products which have been properly
controlled in the EU by a Qualified Person do not have to be recontrolled or
rechecked in any other Member State of the Community.
[16] Article 53 of Directive 2001/82/EC

2.5   The head of the Production Department generally has the following responsibilities:

    i.   to ensure that products are produced and stored according to the appropriate documentation in order to obtain the required quality;

    ii.   to approve the instructions relating to production operations and to ensure their strict implementation;

    iii.   to ensure that the production records are evaluated and signed by an authorised person before they are sent to the Quality Control Department;

    iv.   to check the maintenance of his department, premises and equipment;

    v.   to ensure that the appropriate validations are done;

    vi.   to ensure that the required initial and continuing training of his department personnel is carried out and adapted according to need.

2.6   The head of the Quality Control Department generally has the following responsibilities:

    i.   to approve or reject, as he sees fit, starting materials, packaging materials, and intermediate, bulk and finished products;

    ii.   to evaluate batch records;

    iii.   to ensure that all necessary testing is carried out;

    iv.   to approve specifications, sampling instructions, test methods and other Quality Control procedures;

    v.   to approve and monitor any contract analysts;

    vi.   to check the maintenance of his department, premises and equipment;

    vii.   to ensure that the appropriate validations are done;

    viii.   to ensure that the required initial and continuing training of his department personnel is carried out and adapted according to need.

Other duties of the Quality Control Department are summarised in Chapter 6.

C.2 Personnel

2.7 The heads of Production and Quality Control generally have some shared, or jointly exercised, responsibilities relating to quality. These may include, subject to any national regulations:

— the authorisation of written procedures and other documents, including amendments;

— the monitoring and control of the manufacturing environment;

— plant hygiene;

— process validation;

— training;

— the approval and monitoring of suppliers of materials;

— the approval and monitoring of contract manufacturers;

— the designation and monitoring of storage conditions for materials and products;

— the retention of records;

— the monitoring of compliance with the requirements of Good Manufacturing Practice;

— the inspection, investigation, and taking of samples, in order to monitor factors which may affect product quality.

Training

2.8 The manufacturer should provide training for all the personnel whose duties take them into production areas or into control laboratories (including the technical, maintenance and cleaning personnel), and for other personnel whose activities could affect the quality of the product.

2.9 Besides the basic training on the theory and practice of Good Manufacturing Practice, newly recruited personnel should receive training appropriate to the duties assigned to them. Continuing training should also be given, and its practical effectiveness should be periodically assessed. Training programmes should be available, approved by either the head of Production or the head of Quality Control, as appropriate. Training records should be kept.

2.10 Personnel working in areas where contamination is a hazard, e.g. clean areas or areas where highly active, toxic, infectious or sensitising materials are handled, should be given specific training.

2.11 Visitors or untrained personnel should, preferably, not be taken into the production and quality control areas. If this is unavoidable, they should be given information in advance, particularly about personal hygiene and the prescribed protective clothing. They should be closely supervised.

2.12 The concept of Quality Assurance and all the measures capable of improving its understanding and implementation should be fully discussed during the training sessions.

Personnel Hygiene

2.13 Detailed hygiene programmes should be established and adapted to the different needs within the factory. They should include procedures relating to the health, hygiene practices and clothing of personnel. These procedures should be understood and followed in a very strict way by every person whose duties take him into the production and control areas. Hygiene programmes should be promoted by management and widely discussed during training sessions.

2.14 All personnel should receive medical examination upon recruitment. It must be the manufacturer's responsibility that there are instructions ensuring that health conditions that can be of relevance to the quality of products come to the manufacturer's knowledge. After the first medical examination, examinations should be carried out when necessary for the work and personal health.

2.15 Steps should be taken to ensure as far as is practicable that no person affected by an infectious disease or having open lesions on the exposed surface of the body is engaged in the manufacture of medicinal products.

C.2 Personnel

2.16   Every person entering the manufacturing areas should wear protective garments appropriate to the operations to be carried out.

2.17   Eating, drinking, chewing or smoking, or the storage of food, drink, smoking materials or personal medication in the production and storage areas should be prohibited. In general, any unhygienic practice within the manufacturing areas or in any other area where the product might be adversely affected, should be forbidden.

2.18   Direct contact should be avoided between the operator's hands and the exposed product as well as with any part of the equipment that comes into contact with the products.

2.19   Personnel should be instructed to use the hand-washing facilities.

2.20   Any specific requirements for the manufacture of special groups of products, for example sterile preparations, are covered in the annexes.

Chapter 3:
Premises and Equipment

Principle

Premises and equipment must be located, designed, constructed, adapted and maintained to suit the operations to be carried out. Their layout and design must aim to minimise the risk of errors and permit effective cleaning and maintenance in order to avoid crosscontamination, build up of dust or dirt and, in general, any adverse effect on the quality of products.

Premises

General

3.1 Premises should be situated in an environment which, when considered together with measures to protect the manufacture, presents minimal risk of causing contamination of materials or products.

3.2 Premises should be carefully maintained, ensuring that repair and maintenance operations do not present any hazard to the quality of products. They should be cleaned and, where applicable, disinfected according to detailed written procedures.

3.3 Lighting, temperature, humidity and ventilation should be appropriate and such that they do not adversely affect, directly or indirectly, either the medicinal products during their manufacture and storage, or the accurate functioning of equipment.

3.4 Premises should be designed and equipped so as to afford maximum protection against the entry of insects or other animals.

3.5 Steps should be taken in order to prevent the entry of unauthorised people. Production, storage and quality

control areas should not be used as a right of way by
personnel who do not work in them.

Production Area

3.6   In order to minimise the risk of a serious medical hazard
       due to cross-contamination, dedicated and self contained
       facilities must be available for the production of particular
       medicinal products, such as highly sensitising materials
       (e.g. penicillins) or biological preparations (e.g. from live
       micro-organisms). The production of certain additional
       products, such as certain antibiotics, certain hormones,
       certain cytotoxics, certain highly active drugs and non-
       medicinal products should not be conducted in the same
       facilities. For those products, in exceptional cases, the
       principle of campaign working in the same facilities can
       be accepted provided that specific precautions are taken
       and the necessary validations are made. The
       manufacture of technical poisons, such as pesticides and
       herbicides, should not be allowed in premises used for
       the manufacture of medicinal products.

3.7   Premises should preferably be laid out in such a way as
       to allow the production to take place in areas connected
       in a logical order corresponding to the sequence of the
       operations and to the requisite cleanliness levels.

3.8   The adequacy of the working and in-process storage
       space should permit the orderly and logical positioning of
       equipment and materials so as to minimise the risk of
       confusion between different medicinal products or their
       components, to avoid cross-contamination and to
       minimise the risk of omission or wrong application of any
       of the manufacturing or control steps.

3.9   Where starting and primary packaging materials,
       intermediate or bulk products are exposed to the
       environment, interior surfaces (walls, floors and ceilings)
       should be smooth, free from cracks and open joints, and
       should not shed particulate matter and should permit
       easy and effective cleaning and, if necessary,
       disinfection.

3.10   Pipework, light fittings, ventilation points and other
       services should be designed and sited to avoid the
       creation of recesses which are difficult to clean. As far as

possible, for maintenance purposes, they should be accessible from outside the manufacturing areas.

3.11 Drains should be of adequate size, and have trapped gullies. Open channels should be avoided where possible, but if necessary, they should be shallow to facilitate cleaning and disinfection.

3.12 Production areas should be effectively ventilated, with air control facilities (including temperature and, where necessary, humidity and filtration) appropriate both to the products handled, to the operations undertaken within them and to the external environment.

3.13 Weighing of starting materials usually should be carried out in a separate weighing room designed for that use.

3.14 In cases where dust is generated (e.g. during sampling, weighing, mixing and processing operations, packaging of dry products), specific provisions should be taken to avoid crosscontamination and facilitate cleaning.

3.15 Premises for the packaging of medicinal products should be specifically designed and laid out so as to avoid mix-ups or cross-contamination.

3.16 Production areas should be well lit, particularly where visual on-line controls are carried out.

3.17 In-process controls may be carried out within the production area provided they do not carry any risk for the production.

Storage Areas

3.18 Storage areas should be of sufficient capacity to allow orderly storage of the various categories of materials and products: starting and packaging materials, intermediate, bulk and finished products, products in quarantine, released, rejected, returned or recalled.

3.19 Storage areas should be designed or adapted to ensure good storage conditions. In particular, they should be clean and dry and maintained within acceptable temperature limits. Where special storage conditions are required (e.g. temperature, humidity) these should be provided, checked and monitored.

C.3 Premises and Equipment

3.20   Receiving and dispatch bays should protect materials and products from the weather.

Reception areas should be designed and equipped to allow containers of incoming materials to be cleaned where necessary before storage.

3.21   Where quarantine status is ensured by storage in separate areas, these areas must be clearly marked and their access restricted to authorised personnel. Any system replacing the physical quarantine should give equivalent security.

3.22   There should normally be a separate sampling area for starting materials. If sampling is performed in the storage area, it should be conducted in such a way as to prevent contamination or cross-contamination.

3.23   Segregated areas should be provided for the storage of rejected, recalled or returned materials or products.

3.24   Highly active materials or products should be stored in safe and secure areas.

3.25   Printed packaging materials are considered critical to the conformity of the medicinal product and special attention should be paid to the safe and secure storage of these materials.

Quality Control Areas

3.26   Normally, Quality Control laboratories should be separated from production areas. This is particularly important for laboratories for the control of biologicals, microbiologicals and radioisotopes, which should also be separated from each other.

3.27   Control laboratories should be designed to suit the operations to be carried out in them.

Sufficient space should be given to avoid mix-ups and cross-contamination. There should be adequate suitable storage space for samples and records.

3.28   Separate rooms may be necessary to protect sensitive instruments from vibration, electrical interference, humidity, etc.

3.29 Special requirements are needed in laboratories handling particular substances, such as biological or radioactive samples.

Ancillary Areas

3.30 Rest and refreshment rooms should be separate from other areas.

3.31 Facilities for changing clothes, and for washing and toilet purposes should be easily accessible and appropriate for the number of users. Toilets should not directly communicate with production or storage areas.

3.32 Maintenance workshops should as far as possible be separated from production areas.

Whenever parts and tools are stored in the production area, they should be kept in rooms or lockers reserved for that use.

3.33 Animal houses should be well isolated from other areas, with separate entrance (animal access) and air handling facilities.

Equipment

3.34 Manufacturing equipment should be designed, located and maintained to suit its intended purpose.

3.35 Repair and maintenance operations should not present any hazard to the quality of the products.

3.36 Manufacturing equipment should be designed so that it can be easily and thoroughly cleaned. It should be cleaned according to detailed and written procedures and stored only in a clean and dry condition.

3.37 Washing and cleaning equipment should be chosen and used in order not to be a source of contamination.

3.38 Equipment should be installed in such a way as to prevent any risk of error or of contamination.

3.39 Production equipment should not present any hazard to the products. The parts of the production equipment that come into contact with the product must not be reactive, additive or absorptive to such an extent that it will affect the quality of the product and thus present any hazard.

3.40   Balances and measuring equipment of an appropriate range and precision should be available for production and control operations.

3.41   Measuring, weighing, recording and control equipment should be calibrated and checked at defined intervals by appropriate methods. Adequate records of such tests should be maintained.

3.42   Fixed pipework should be clearly labelled to indicate the contents and, where applicable, the direction of flow.

3.43   Distilled, deionized and, where appropriate, other water pipes should be sanitised according to written procedures that detail the action limits for microbiological contamination and the measures to be taken.

3.44   Defective equipment should, if possible, be removed from production and quality control areas, or at least be clearly labelled as defective.

Chapter 4: Documentation

Principle

Good documentation constitutes an essential part of the quality assurance system. Clearly written documentation prevents errors from spoken communication and permits tracing of batch history. Specifications, Manufacturing Formulae and instructions, procedures, and records must be free from errors and available in writing. The legibility of documents is of paramount importance.

General

4.1   Specifications describe in detail the requirements with which the products or materials used or obtained during manufacture have to conform. They serve as a basis for quality evaluation.

Manufacturing Formulae, Processing and Packaging Instructions state all the starting materials used and lay down all processing and packaging operations.

Procedures give directions for performing certain operations e.g. cleaning, clothing, environmental control, sampling, testing, equipment operation.

Records provide a history of each batch of product, including its distribution, and also of all other relevant circumstances pertinent to the quality of the final product.

4.2   Documents should be designed, prepared, reviewed and distributed with care. They should comply with the relevant parts of the manufacturing and marketing authorisation dossiers.

4.3   Documents should be approved, signed and dated by appropriate and authorised persons.

4.4   Documents should have unambiguous contents; title,
        nature and purpose should be clearly stated. They should
        be laid out in an orderly fashion and be easy to check.
        Reproduced documents should be clear and legible. The
        reproduction of working documents from master
        documents must not allow any error to be introduced
        through the reproduction process.

4.5   Documents should be regularly reviewed and kept up-to-
        date. When a document has been revised, systems
        should be operated to prevent inadvertent use of
        superseded documents.

4.6   Documents should not be handwritten; although, where
        documents require the entry of data, these entries may
        be made in clear, legible, indelible handwriting. Sufficient
        space should be provided for such entries.

4.7   Any alteration made to the entry on a document should
        be signed and dated; the alteration should permit the
        reading of the original information. Where appropriate,
        the reason for the alteration should be recorded.

4.8   The records should be made or completed at the time
        each action is taken and in such a way that all significant
        activities concerning the manufacture of medicinal
        products are traceable. They should be retained for at
        least one year after the expiry date of the finished
        product.

4.9   Data may be recorded by electronic data processing
        systems, photographic or other reliable means, but
        detailed procedures relating to the system in use should
        be available and the accuracy of the records should be
        checked. If documentation is handled by electronic data
        processing methods, only authorised persons should be
        able to enter or modify data in the computer and there
        should be a record of changes and deletions; access
        should be restricted by passwords or other means and
        the result of entry of critical data should be independently
        checked. Batch records electronically stored should be
        protected by back-up transfer on magnetic tape,
        microfilm, paper or other means. It is particularly
        important that the data are readily available throughout
        the period of retention.

Documents required

Specifications

4.10   There should be appropriately authorised and dated specifications for starting and packaging materials, and finished products; where appropriate, they should be also available for intermediate or bulk products.

Specifications for starting and packaging materials

4.11   Specifications for starting and primary or printed packaging materials should include, if applicable:

     a)   a description of the materials, including:

         —   the designated name and the internal code reference;

         —   the reference, if any, to a pharmacopoeial monograph;

         —   the approved suppliers and, if possible, the original producer of the products;

         —   a specimen of printed materials; b) directions for sampling and testing or reference to procedures; c) qualitative and quantitative requirements with acceptance limits; d) storage conditions and precautions; e) the maximum period of storage before re-examination.

Specifications for intermediate and bulk products

4.12   Specifications for intermediate and bulk products should be available if these are purchased or dispatched, or if data obtained from intermediate products are used for the evaluation of the finished product. The specifications should be similar to specifications for starting materials or for finished products, as appropriate.

Specifications for finished products

4.13   Specifications for finished products should include: a) the designated name of the product and the code reference where applicable; b) the formula or a reference to; c) a description of the pharmaceutical form and package details; d) directions for sampling and testing or a reference to procedures; e) the qualitative and

C.4 Documentation

quantitative requirements, with the acceptance limits; f)
the storage conditions and any special handling
precautions, where applicable; g) the shelf-life.

Manufacturing Formula and Processing Instructions

Formally authorised Manufacturing Formula and Processing
Instructions should exist for each product and batch size to be
manufactured. They are often combined in one document.

4.14 The Manufacturing Formula should include:

a) the name of the product, with a product reference
code relating to its specification;

b) a description of the pharmaceutical form, strength
of the product and batch size;

c) a list of all starting materials to be used, with the
amount of each, described using the designated
name and a reference which is unique to that
material; mention should be made of any
substance that may disappear in the course of
processing;

d) a statement of the expected final yield with the
acceptable limits, and of relevant intermediate
yields, where applicable.

4.15 The Processing Instructions should include:

a) a statement of the processing location and the
principal equipment to be used;

b) the methods, or reference to the methods, to be
used for preparing the critical equipment (e.g.
cleaning, assembling, calibrating, sterilising);

c) detailed stepwise processing instructions (e.g.
checks on materials, pre-treatments, sequence for
adding materials, mixing times, temperatures);

d) the instructions for any in-process controls with
their limits;

e) where necessary, the requirements for bulk
storage of the products; including the container,
labelling and special storage conditions where
applicable;

f)   any special precautions to be observed.

Packaging Instructions

4.16   There should be formally authorised Packaging
        Instructions for each product, pack size and type. These
        should normally include, or have a reference to, the
        following:

a)   name of the product;

b)   description of its pharmaceutical form, and
        strength where applicable;

c)   the pack size expressed in terms of the number,
        weight or volume of the product in the final
        container;

d)   a complete list of all the packaging materials
        required for a standard batch size, including
        quantities, sizes and types, with the code or
        reference number relating to the specifications of
        each packaging material;

e)   where appropriate, an example or reproduction of
        the relevant printed packaging materials, and
        specimens indicating where to apply batch number
        references, and shelf life of the product;

f)   special precautions to be observed, including a
        careful examination of the area and equipment in
        order to ascertain the line clearance before
        operations begin;

g)   a description of the packaging operation, including
        any significant subsidiary operations, and
        equipment to be used;

h)   details of in-process controls with instructions for
        sampling and acceptance limits.

Batch Processing Records

4.17   A Batch Processing Record should be kept for each
        batch processed. It should be based on the relevant parts
        of the currently approved Manufacturing Formula and
        Processing Instructions. The method of preparation of
        such records should be designed to avoid transcription

errors. The record should carry the number of the batch being manufactured.

Before any processing begins, there should be recorded checks that the equipment and work station are clear of previous products, documents or materials not required for the planned process, and that equipment is clean and suitable for use.

During processing, the following information should be recorded at the time each action is taken and, after completion, the record should be dated and signed in agreement by the person responsible for the processing operations:

a) the name of the product;

b) dates and times of commencement, of significant intermediate stages and of completion of production;

c) name of the person responsible for each stage of production;

d) initials of the operator of different significant steps of production and, where appropriate, of the person who checked each of these operations (e.g. weighing);

e) the batch number and/or analytical control number as well as the quantities of each starting material actually weighed (including the batch number and amount of any recovered or reprocessed material added);

f) any relevant processing operation or event and major equipment used;

g) a record of the in-process controls and the initials of the person(s) carrying them out, and the results obtained;

h) the product yield obtained at different and pertinent stages of manufacture;

i) notes on special problems including details, with signed authorisation for any deviation from the Manufacturing Formula and Processing Instructions.

Batch Packaging Records

4.18 A Batch Packaging Record should be kept for each batch or part batch processed. It should be based on the relevant parts of the Packaging Instructions and the method of preparation of such records should be designed to avoid transcription errors. The record should carry the batch number and the quantity of bulk product to be packed, as well as the batch number and the planned quantity of finished product that will be obtained.

Before any packaging operation begins, there should be recorded checks that the equipment and work station are clear of previous products, documents or materials not required for the planned packaging operations, and that equipment is clean and suitable for use.

The following information should be entered at the time each action is taken and, after completion, the record should be dated and signed in agreement by the person(s) responsible for the packaging operations:

a) the name of the product;

b) the date(s) and times of the packaging operations;

c) the name of the responsible person carrying out the packaging operation;

d) the initials of the operators of the different significant steps;

e) records of checks for identity and conformity with the packaging instructions including the results of in-process controls;

f) details of the packaging operations carried out, including references to equipment and the packaging lines used;

g) whenever possible, samples of printed packaging materials used, including specimens of the batch coding, expiry dating and any additional overprinting;

h) notes on any special problems or unusual events including details, with signed authorisation for any deviation from the Manufacturing Formula and Processing Instructions;

C.4 Documentation

i) the quantities and reference number or
identification of all printed packaging materials and
bulk product issued, used, destroyed or returned to
stock and the quantities of obtained product, in
order to provide for an adequate reconciliation.

Procedures and records

Receipt

4.19 There should be written procedures and records for the
receipt of each delivery of each starting and primary and
printed packaging material.

4.20 The records of the receipts should include: a) the name
of the material on the delivery note and the containers; b)
the "in-house" name and/or code of material (if different
from a); c) date of receipt; d) supplier's name and, if
possible, manufacturer's name; e) manufacturer's batch
or reference number; f) total quantity, and number of
containers received; g) the batch number assigned after
receipt; h) any relevant comment (e.g. state of the
containers).

4.21 There should be written procedures for the internal
labelling, quarantine and storage of starting materials,
packaging materials and other materials, as appropriate.

Sampling

4.22 There should be written procedures for sampling, which
include the person(s) authorised to take samples, the
methods and equipment to be used, the amounts to be
taken and any precautions to be observed to avoid
contamination of the material or any deterioration in its
quality (see Chapter 6, item 13).

Testing

4.23 There should be written procedures for testing materials
and products at different stages of manufacture,
describing the methods and equipment to be used. The
tests performed should be recorded (see Chapter 6, item
17).

Other

4.24 Written release and rejection procedures should be available for materials and products, and in particular for the release for sale of the finished product by the Qualified Person(s) in accordance with the requirements of Article 51 of Directive 2001/83/EC[17].

4.25 Records should be maintained of the distribution of each batch of a product in order to facilitate the recall of the batch if necessary (see Chapter 8).

4.26 There should be written procedures and the associated records of actions taken or conclusions reached, where appropriate, for:

— validation;

— equipment assembly and calibration;

— maintenance, cleaning and sanitation;

— personnel matters including training, clothing, hygiene;

— environmental monitoring;

— pest control;

— complaints;

— recalls;

— returns.

4.27 Clear operating procedures should be available for major items of manufacturing and test equipment.

4.28 Log books should be kept for major or critical equipment recording, as appropriate, any validations, calibrations, maintenance, cleaning or repair operations, including the dates and identity of people who carried these operations out.

4.29 Log books should also record in chronological order the use of major or critical equipment and the areas where the products have been processed.

---

[17] Article 55 of Directive 2001/82/EC

C.4 Documentation

Chapter 5:
Production

Principle

Production operations must follow clearly defined procedures; they must comply with the principles of Good Manufacturing Practice in order to obtain products of the requisite quality and be in accordance with the relevant manufacturing and marketing authorisations.

General

5.1 Production should be performed and supervised by competent people.

5.2 All handling of materials and products, such as receipt and quarantine, sampling, storage, labelling, dispensing, processing, packaging and distribution should be done in accordance with written procedures or instructions and, where necessary, recorded.

5.3 All incoming materials should be checked to ensure that the consignment corresponds to the order. Containers should be cleaned where necessary and labelled with the prescribed data.

5.4 Damage to containers and any other problem which might adversely affect the quality of a material should be investigated, recorded and reported to the Quality Control Department.

5.5 Incoming materials and finished products should be physically or administratively quarantined immediately after receipt or processing, until they have been released for use or distribution.

5.6　Intermediate and bulk products purchased as such should be handled on receipt as though they were starting materials.

5.7　All materials and products should be stored under the appropriate conditions established by the manufacturer and in an orderly fashion to permit batch segregation and stock rotation.

5.8　Checks on yields, and reconciliation of quantities, should be carried out as necessary to ensure that there are no discrepancies outside acceptable limits.

5.9　Operations on different products should not be carried out simultaneously or consecutively in the same room unless there is no risk of mix-up or cross-contamination.

5.10　At every stage of processing, products and materials should be protected from microbial and other contamination.

5.11　When working with dry materials and products, special precautions should be taken to prevent the generation and dissemination of dust. This applies particularly to the handling of highly active or sensitising materials.

5.12　At all times during processing, all materials, bulk containers, major items of equipment and where appropriate rooms used should be labelled or otherwise identified with an indication of the product or material being processed, its strength (where applicable) and batch number. Where applicable, this indication should also mention the stage of production.

5.13　Labels applied to containers, equipment or premises should be clear, unambiguous and in the company's agreed format. It is often helpful in addition to the wording on the labels to use colours to indicate status (for example, quarantined, accepted, rejected, clean, ...).

5.14　Checks should be carried out to ensure that pipelines and other pieces of equipment used for the transportation of products from one area to another are connected in a correct manner.

5.15 Any deviation from instructions or procedures should be avoided as far as possible. If a deviation occurs, it should be approved in writing by a competent person, with the involvement of the Quality Control Department when appropriate.

5.16 Access to production premises should be restricted to authorised personnel.

5.17 Normally, the production of non-medicinal products should be avoided in areas and with the equipment destined for the production of medicinal products.

Prevention of cross-contamination in production

5.18 Contamination of a starting material or of a product by another material or product must be avoided. This risk of accidental cross-contamination arises from the uncontrolled release of dust, gases, vapours, sprays or organisms from materials and products in process, from residues on equipment, and from operators' clothing. The significance of this risk varies with the type of contaminant and of product being contaminated. Amongst the most hazardous contaminants are highly sensitising materials, biological preparations containing living organisms, certain hormones, cytotoxics, and other highly active materials. Products in which contamination is likely to be most significant are those administered by injection, those given in large doses and/or over a long time.

5.19 Cross-contamination should be avoided by appropriate technical or organizational measures, for example:

a) production in segregated areas (required for products such as penicillins, live vaccines, live bacterial preparations and some other biologicals), or by campaign (separation in time) followed by appropriate cleaning;

b) providing appropriate air-locks and air extraction;

c) minimising the risk of contamination caused by recirculation or re-entry of untreated or insufficiently treated air;

d)   keeping protective clothing inside areas where products with special risk of crosscontamination are processed;

e)   using cleaning and decontamination procedures of known effectiveness, as ineffective cleaning of equipment is a common source of cross-contamination;

f)   using "closed systems" of production;

g)   testing for residues and use of cleaning status labels on equipment.

5.20   Measures to prevent cross-contamination and their effectiveness should be checked periodically according to set procedures.

Validation

5.21   Validation studies should reinforce Good Manufacturing Practice and be conducted in accordance with defined procedures. Results and conclusions should be recorded.

5.22   When any new manufacturing formula or method of preparation is adopted, steps should be taken to demonstrate its suitability for routine processing. The defined process, using the materials and equipment specified, should be shown to yield a product consistently of the required quality.

5.23   Significant amendments to the manufacturing process, including any change in equipment or materials, which may affect product quality and/or the reproducibility of the process should be validated.

5.24   Processes and procedures should undergo periodic critical re-validation to ensure that they remain capable of achieving the intended results.

Starting materials

5.25   The purchase of starting materials is an important operation which should involve staff who have a particular and thorough knowledge of the suppliers.

5.26   Starting materials should only be purchased from approved suppliers named in the relevant specification and, where possible, directly from the producer. It is recommended that the specifications established by the manufacturer for the starting materials be discussed with the suppliers. It is of benefit that all aspects of the production and control of the starting material in question, including handling, labelling and packaging requirements, as well as complaints and rejection procedures are discussed with the manufacturer and the supplier.

5.27 For each delivery, the containers should be checked for integrity of package and seal and for correspondence between the delivery note and the supplier's labels.

5.28 If one material delivery is made up of different batches, each batch must be considered as separate for sampling, testing and release.

5.29 Starting materials in the storage area should be appropriately labelled (see Chapter 5, item 13). Labels should bear at least the following information:

— the designated name of the product and the internal code reference where applicable;

— a batch number given at receipt;

— where appropriate, the status of the contents (e.g. in quarantine, on test, released, rejected);

— where appropriate, an expiry date or a date beyond which retesting is necessary.

When fully computerised storage systems are used, all the above information need not necessarily be in a legible form on the label.

5.30 There should be appropriate procedures or measures to assure the identity of the contents of each container of starting material. Bulk containers from which samples have been drawn should be identified (see Chapter 6, item 13).

5.31 Only starting materials which have been released by the Quality Control Department and which are within their shelf life should be used.

5.32 Starting materials should only be dispensed by designated persons, following a written procedure, to

C.5 Production

ensure that the correct materials are accurately weighed or measured into clean and properly labelled containers.

5.33 Each dispensed material and its weight or volume should be independently checked and the check recorded.

5.34 Materials dispensed for each batch should be kept together and conspicuously labelled as such.

Processing operations: intermediate and bulk products

5.35 Before any processing operation is started, steps should be taken to ensure that the work area and equipment are clean and free from any starting materials, products, product residues or documents not required for the current operation.

5.36 Intermediate and bulk products should be kept under appropriate conditions.

5.37 Critical processes should be validated (see "VALIDATION" in this Chapter).

5.38 Any necessary in-process controls and environmental controls should be carried out and recorded.

5.39 Any significant deviation from the expected yield should be recorded and investigated.

Packaging materials

5.40 The purchase, handling and control of primary and printed packaging materials shall be accorded attention similar to that given to starting materials.

5.41 Particular attention should be paid to printed materials. They should be stored in adequately secure conditions such as to exclude unauthorised access. Cut labels and other loose printed materials should be stored and transported in separate closed containers so as to avoid mix-ups. Packaging materials should be issued for use only by authorized personnel following an approved and documented procedure.

5.42 Each delivery or batch of printed or primary packaging material should be given a specific reference number or identification mark.

5.43 Outdated or obsolete primary packaging material or printed packaging material should be destroyed and this disposal recorded.

Packaging operations

5.44 When setting up a programme for the packaging operations, particular attention should be given to minimising the risk of cross-contamination, mix-ups or substitutions. Different products should not be packaged in close proximity unless there is physical segregation.

5.45 Before packaging operations are begun, steps should be taken to ensure that the work area, packaging lines, printing machines and other equipment are clean and free from any products, materials or documents previously used, if these are not required for the current operation. The line-clearance should be performed according to an appropriate check-list.

5.46 The name and batch number of the product being handled should be displayed at each packaging station or line.

5.47 All products and packaging materials to be used should be checked on delivery to the packaging department for quantity, identity and conformity with the Packaging Instructions.

5.48 Containers for filling should be clean before filling. Attention should be given to avoiding and removing any contaminants such as glass fragments and metal particles.

5.49 Normally, filling and sealing should be followed as quickly as possible by labelling. If it is not the case, appropriate procedures should be applied to ensure that no mix-ups or mislabelling can occur.

5.50 The correct performance of any printing operation (for example code numbers, expiry dates) to be done

C.5 Production

separately or in the course of the packaging should be
checked and recorded.

Attention should be paid to printing by hand which should
be re-checked at regular intervals.

5.51 Special care should be taken when using cut-labels and
when over-printing is carried out off-line. Roll-feed labels
are normally preferable to cut-labels, in helping to avoid
mix-ups.

5.52 Checks should be made to ensure that any electronic
code readers, label counters or similar devices are
operating correctly.

5.53 Printed and embossed information on packaging
materials should be distinct and resistant to fading or
erasing.

5.54 On-line control of the product during packaging should
include at least checking the following:

a) general appearance of the packages;

b) whether the packages are complete;

c) whether the correct products and packaging
materials are used;

d) whether any over-printing is correct;

e) correct functioning of line monitors.

Samples taken away from the packaging line should not
be returned.

5.55 Products which have been involved in an unusual event
should only be reintroduced into the process after special
inspection, investigation and approval by authorised
personnel.

Detailed record should be kept of this operation.

5.56 Any significant or unusual discrepancy observed during
reconciliation of the amount of bulk product and printed
packaging materials and the number of units produced
should be investigated and satisfactorily accounted for
before release.

5.57 Upon completion of a packaging operation, any unused batch-coded packaging materials should be destroyed and the destruction recorded. A documented procedure should be followed if uncoded printed materials are returned to stock.

Finished products

5.58 Finished products should be held in quarantine until their final release under conditions established by the manufacturer.

5.59 The evaluation of finished products and documentation which is necessary before release of product for sale are described in Chapter 6 (Quality Control).

5.60 After release, finished products should be stored as usable stock under conditions established by the manufacturer.

Rejected, recovered and returned materials

5.61 Rejected materials and products should be clearly marked as such and stored separately in restricted areas. They should either be returned to the suppliers or, where appropriate, reprocessed or destroyed. Whatever action is taken should be approved and recorded by authorised personnel.

5.62 The reprocessing of rejected products should be exceptional. It is only permitted if the quality of the final product is not affected, if the specifications are met and if it is done in accordance with a defined and authorised procedure after evaluation of the risks involved.

Record should be kept of the reprocessing.

5.63 The recovery of all or part of earlier batches which conform to the required quality by incorporation into a batch of the same product at a defined stage of manufacture should be authorised beforehand. This recovery should be carried out in accordance with a defined procedure after evaluation of the risks involved, including any possible effect on shelf life.

The recovery should be recorded.

C.5 Production

5.64 The need for additional testing of any finished product which has been reprocessed, or into which a recovered product has been incorporated, should be considered by the Quality Control Department.

5.65 Products returned from the market and which have left the control of the manufacturer should be destroyed unless without doubt their quality is satisfactory; they may be considered for re-sale, re-labelling or recovery in a subsequent batch only after they have been critically assessed by the Quality Control Department in accordance with a written procedure. The nature of the product, any special storage conditions it requires, its condition and history, and the time elapsed since it was issued should all be taken into account in this assessment. Where any doubt arises over the quality of the product, it should not be considered suitable for re-issue or re-use, although basic chemical reprocessing to recover active ingredient may be possible. Any action taken should be appropriately recorded.

Chapter 6:
Quality Control

Document History	
Revision to include new Chapter on On-going Stability Programme and adjust Section 6.14 on reference samples	October 2005
Date of revised version coming into operation	1 June 2006

Principle

Quality Control is concerned with sampling, specifications and testing as well as the organisation, documentation and release procedures which ensure that the necessary and relevant tests are carried out, and that materials are not released for use, nor products released for sale or supply, until their quality has been judged satisfactory. Quality Control is not confined to laboratory operations, but must be involved in all decisions which may concern the quality of the product. The independence of Quality Control from Production is considered fundamental to the satisfactory operation of Quality Control.

(see also Chapter 1).

General

6.1   Each holder of a manufacturing authorisation should have a Quality Control Department. This department should be independent from other departments, and under the authority of a person with appropriate qualifications and experience, who has one or several control laboratories at his disposal. Adequate resources must be available to ensure that all the Quality Control arrangements are effectively and reliably carried out.

6.2   The principal duties of the head of Quality Control are summarised in Chapter 2. The Quality Control Department as a whole will also have other duties, such as to establish, validate and implement all quality control procedures, keep the reference samples of materials and products, ensure the correct labelling of containers of materials and products, ensure the monitoring of the stability of the products, participate in the investigation of complaints related to the quality of the product, etc. All these operations should be carried out in accordance with written procedures and, where necessary, recorded.

6.3   Finished product assessment should embrace all relevant factors, including production conditions, results of in-process testing, a review of manufacturing (including packaging) documentation, compliance with Finished Product Specification and examination of the final finished pack.

6.4   Quality Control personnel should have access to production areas for sampling and investigation as appropriate.

Good Quality Control Laboratory Practice

6.5   Control laboratory premises and equipment should meet the general and specific requirements for Quality Control areas given in Chapter 3.

6.6   The personnel, premises, and equipment in the laboratories should be appropriate to the tasks imposed by the nature and the scale of the manufacturing operations. The use of outside laboratories, in conformity with the principles detailed in Chapter 7, Contract Analysis, can be accepted for particular reasons, but this should be stated in the Quality Control records.

Documentation

6.7   Laboratory documentation should follow the principles given in Chapter 4. An important part of this documentation deals with Quality Control and the following details should be readily available to the Quality Control Department:

- specifications;

- sampling procedures;

- testing procedures and records (including analytical worksheets and/or laboratory notebooks);

- analytical reports and/or certificates;

- data from environmental monitoring, where required;

- validation records of test methods, where applicable;

- procedures for and records of the calibration of instruments and maintenance of equipment.

6.8 Any Quality Control documentation relating to a batch record should be retained for one year after the expiry date of the batch and at least 5 years after the certification referred to in Article 51(3) of Directive 2001/83/EC.

6.9 For some kinds of data (e.g. analytical tests results, yields, environmental controls) it is recommended that records are kept in a manner permitting trend evaluation.

6.10 In addition to the information which is part of the batch record, other original data such as laboratory notebooks and/or records should be retained and readily available

Sampling

6.11 The sample taking should be done in accordance with approved written procedures that describe:

- the method of sampling;

- the equipment to be used;

- the amount of the sample to be taken;

- instructions for any required sub-division of the sample;

- the type and condition of the sample container to be used;

- the identification of containers sampled;

- any special precautions to be observed, especially with regard to the sampling of sterile or noxious materials;

- the storage conditions;

- instructions for the cleaning and storage of sampling equipment.

6.12 Reference samples should be representative of the batch of materials or products from which they are taken. Other samples may also be taken to monitor the most stressed part of a process (e.g. beginning or end of a process).

6.13 Sample containers should bear a label indicating the contents, with the batch number, the date of sampling and the containers from which samples have been drawn.

6.14 Further guidance on reference and retention samples is given in Annex 19.

Testing

6.15 Analytical methods should be validated. All testing operations described in the marketing authorisation should be carried out according to the approved methods.

6.16 The results obtained should be recorded and checked to make sure that they are consistent with each other. Any calculations should be critically examined.

6.17 The tests performed should be recorded and the records should include at least the following data:

a) name of the material or product and, where applicable, dosage form;

b) batch number and, where appropriate, the manufacturer and/or supplier;

c) references to the relevant specifications and testing procedures;

d) test results, including observations and calculations, and reference to any certificates of analysis;

e) dates of testing;

f) initials of the persons who performed the testing;

g) initials of the persons who verified the testing and the calculations, where appropriate;

h)   a clear statement of release or rejection (or other status decision) and the dated signature of the designated responsible person.

6.18   All the in-process controls, including those made in the production area by production personnel, should be performed according to methods approved by Quality Control and the results recorded.

6.19   Special attention should be given to the quality of laboratory reagents, volumetric glassware and solutions, reference standards and culture media. They should be prepared in accordance with written procedures.

6.20   Laboratory reagents intended for prolonged use should be marked with the preparation date and the signature of the person who prepared them. The expiry date of unstable reagents and culture media should be indicated on the label, together with specific storage conditions. In addition, for volumetric solutions, the last date of standardisation and the last current factor should be indicated.

6.21   Where necessary, the date of receipt of any substance used for testing operations (e.g. reagents and reference standards) should be indicated on the container. Instructions for use and storage should be followed. In certain cases it may be necessary to carry out an identification test and/or other testing of reagent materials upon receipt or before use.

6.22   Animals used for testing components, materials or products, should, where appropriate, be quarantined before use. They should be maintained and controlled in a manner that assures their suitability for the intended use. They should be identified, and adequate records should be maintained, showing the history of their use.

On-going stability programme

6.23   After marketing, the stability of the medicinal product should be monitored according to a continuous appropriate programme that will permit the detection of any stability issue (e.g. changes in levels of impurities or dissolution profile) associated with the formulation in the marketed package.

C.6 Quality Control

6.24 The purpose of the on-going stability programme is to monitor the product over its shelf life and to determine that the product remains, and can be expected to remain, within specifications under the labelled storage conditions.

6.25 This mainly applies to the medicinal product in the package in which it is sold, but consideration should also be given to the inclusion in the programme of bulk product. For example, when the bulk product is stored for a long period before being packaged and/or shipped from a manufacturing site to a packaging site, the impact on the stability of the packaged product should be evaluated and studied under ambient conditions. In addition, consideration should be given to intermediates that are stored and used over prolonged periods. Stability studies on reconstituted product are performed during product development and need not be monitored on an on-going basis. However, when relevant, the stability of reconstituted product can also be monitored.

6.26 The on-going stability programme should be described in a written protocol following the general rules of Chapter 4 and results formalised as a report. The equipment used for the on-going stability programme (stability chambers among others) should be qualified and maintained following the general rules of Chapter 3 and annex 15.

6.27 The protocol for an on-going stability programme should extend to the end of the shelf life period and should include, but not be limited to, the following parameters:

- number of batch(es) per strength and different batch sizes, if applicable

- relevant physical, chemical, microbiological and biological test methods

- acceptance criteria

- reference to test methods

- description of the container closure system(s)

- testing intervals (time points)

- description of the conditions of storage (standardised ICH conditions for long term testing, consistent with the product labelling, should be used)

- other applicable parameters specific to the medicinal product.

6.28 The protocol for the on-going stability programme can be different from that of the initial long-term stability study as submitted in the marketing authorisation dossier provided that this is justified and documented in the protocol (for example the frequency of testing, or when updating to ICH recommendations).

6.29 The number of batches and frequency of testing should provide a sufficient amount of data to allow for trend analysis. Unless otherwise justified, at least one batch per year of product manufactured in every strength and every primary packaging type, if relevant, should be included in the stability programme (unless none are produced during that year). For products where on-going stability monitoring would normally require testing using animals and no appropriate alternative, validated techniques are available, the frequency of testing may take account of a risk-benefit approach. The principle of bracketing and matrixing designs may be applied if scientifically justified in the protocol.

6.30 In certain situations, additional batches should be included in the on-going stability programme. For example, an on-going stability study should be conducted after any significant change or significant deviation to the process or package. Any reworking, reprocessing or recovery operation should also be considered for inclusion.

6.31 Results of on-going stability studies should be made available to key personnel and, in particular, to the Qualified Person(s). Where on-going stability studies are carried out at a site other than the site of manufacture of the bulk or finished product, there should be a written agreement between the parties concerned. Results of on-going stability studies should be available at the site of manufacture for review by the competent authority.

6.32 Out of specification or significant atypical trends should be investigated. Any confirmed out of specification result, or significant negative trend, should be reported to the relevant competent authorities. The possible impact on batches on the market should be considered in accordance with chapter 8 of the GMP Guide and in consultation with the relevant competent authorities.

6.33. A summary of all the data generated, including any interim conclusions on the programme, should be written and maintained. This summary should be subjected to periodic review.

Chapter 7: Contract Manufacture and Analysis

Principle

Contract manufacture and analysis must be correctly defined, agreed and controlled in order to avoid misunderstandings which could result in a product or work of unsatisfactory quality. There must be a written contract between the Contract Giver and the Contract Acceptor which clearly establishes the duties of each party. The contract must clearly state the way in which the Qualified Person releasing each batch of product for sale exercises his full responsibility.

Note: *This Chapter deals with the responsibilities of manufacturers towards the Competent Authorities of the Member States with respect to the granting of marketing and manufacturing authorisations. It is not intended in any way to affect the respective liability of contract acceptors and contract givers to consumers; this is governed by other provisions of Community and national law.*

General

7.1 There should be a written contract covering the manufacture and/or analysis arranged under contract and any technical arrangements made in connection with it.

7.2 All arrangements for contract manufacture and analysis including any proposed changes in technical or other arrangements should be in accordance with the marketing authorisation for the product concerned.

The Contract Giver

7.3   The Contract Giver is responsible for assessing the competence of the Contract Acceptor to carry out successfully the work required and for ensuring by means of the contract that the principles and guidelines of GMP as interpreted in this Guide are followed.

7.4   The Contract Giver should provide the Contract Acceptor with all the information necessary to carry out the contracted operations correctly in accordance with the marketing authorisation and any other legal requirements. The Contract Giver should ensure that the Contract Acceptor is fully aware of any problems associated with the product or the work which might pose a hazard to his premises, equipment, personnel, other materials or other products.

7.5   The Contract Giver should ensure that all processed products and materials delivered to him by the Contract Acceptor comply with their specifications or that the products have been released by a Qualified Person.

The Contract Acceptor

7.6   The Contract Acceptor must have adequate premises and equipment, knowledge and experience, and competent personnel to carry out satisfactorily the work ordered by the Contract Giver. Contract manufacture may be undertaken only by a manufacturer who is the holder of a manufacturing authorisation.

7.7   The Contract Acceptor should ensure that all products or materials delivered to him are suitable for their intended purpose.

7.8   The Contract Acceptor should not pass to a third party any of the work entrusted to him under the contract without the Contract Giver's prior evaluation and approval of the arrangements. Arrangements made between the Contract Acceptor and any third party should ensure that the manufacturing and analytical information is made available in the same way as between the original Contract Giver and Contract Acceptor.

7.9 The Contract Acceptor should refrain from any activity which may adversely affect the quality of the product manufactured and/or analysed for the Contract Giver.

The Contract

7.10 A contract should be drawn up between the Contract Giver and the Contract Acceptor which specifies their respective responsibilities relating to the manufacture and control of the product. Technical aspects of the contract should be drawn up by competent persons suitably knowledgeable in pharmaceutical technology, analysis and Good Manufacturing Practice. All arrangements for manufacture and analysis must be in accordance with the marketing authorisation and agreed by both parties.

7.11 The contract should specify the way in which the Qualified Person releasing the batch for sale ensures that each batch has been manufactured and checked for compliance with the requirements of Marketing Authorisation.

7.12 The contract should describe clearly who is responsible for purchasing materials, testing and releasing materials, undertaking production and quality controls, including in-process controls, and who has responsibility for sampling and analysis. In the case of contract analysis, the contract should state whether or not the Contract Acceptor should take samples at the premises of the manufacturer.

7.13 Manufacturing, analytical and distribution records, and reference samples should be kept by, or be available to, the Contract Giver. Any records relevant to assessing the quality of a product in the event of complaints or a suspected defect must be accessible and specified in the defect/recall procedures of the Contract Giver.

7.14 The contract should permit the Contract Giver to visit the facilities of the Contract Acceptor.

7.15 In the case of contract analysis, the Contract Acceptor should understand that he is subject to Inspection by the competent Authorities.

Chapter 8:
Complaints and Product Recall

Document History	
Revision to include new Points 8.7 on requirements on counterfeit products and transferring the original Points 8.7 into a modified Point 8.8; slight modification of Point 8.16	December 2005
Date of revised version coming into operation	01 February 2006

Principle

All complaints and other information concerning potentially defective products must be reviewed carefully according to written procedures. In order to provide for all contingencies, and in accordance with Article 117 of Directive 2001/83/EC and Article 84 of Directive 2001/82/EC, a system should be designed to recall, if necessary, promptly and effectively products known or suspected to be defective from the market.

Complaints

8.1　A person should be designated responsible for handling the complaints and deciding the measures to be taken together with sufficient supporting staff to assist him. If this person is not the Qualified Person, the latter should be made aware of any complaint, investigation or recall.

8.2　There should be written procedures describing the action to be taken, including the need to consider a recall, in the case of a complaint concerning a possible product defect.

8.3 Any complaint concerning a product defect should be recorded with all the original details and thoroughly investigated. The person responsible for Quality Control should normally be involved in the study of such problems.

8.4 If a product defect is discovered or suspected in a batch, consideration should be given to checking other batches in order to determine whether they are also affected. In particular, other batches which may contain reworks of the defective batch should be investigated.

8.5 All the decisions and measures taken as a result of a complaint should be recorded and referenced to the corresponding batch records.

8.6 Complaints records should be reviewed regularly for any indication of specific or recurring problems requiring attention and possibly the recall of marketed products.

8.7 Special attention should be given to establishing whether a complaint was caused because of counterfeiting.

8.8 The competent authorities should be informed if a manufacturer is considering action following possibly faulty manufacture, product deterioration, detection of counterfeiting or any other serious quality problems with a product

Recalls

8.9 A person should be designated as responsible for execution and co-ordination of recalls and should be supported by sufficient staff to handle all the aspects of the recalls with the appropriate degree of urgency. This responsible person should normally be independent of the sales and marketing organisation. If this person is not the Qualified Person, the latter should be made aware of any recall operation.

8.10 There should be established written procedures, regularly checked and updated when necessary, in order to organise any recall activity.

8.11 Recall operations should be capable of being initiated promptly and at any time.

8.12 All Competent Authorities of all countries to which products may have been distributed should be informed promptly if products are intended to be recalled because they are, or are suspected of being defective.

8.13 The distribution records should be readily available to the person(s) responsible for recalls, and should contain sufficient information on wholesalers and directly supplied customers (with addresses, phone and/or fax numbers inside and outside working hours, batches and amounts delivered), including those for exported products and medical samples.

8.14 Recalled products should be identified and stored separately in a secure area while awaiting a decision on their fate.

8.15 The progress of the recall process should be recorded and a final report issued, including a reconciliation between the delivered and recovered quantities of the products.

8.16 The effectiveness of the arrangements for recalls should be evaluated regularly.

C.8 Complaints and Product Recall

Chapter 9:
Self Inspection

Principle

Self inspections should be conducted in order to monitor the implementation and compliance with Good Manufacturing Practice principles and to propose necessary corrective measures.

9.1   Personnel matters, premises, equipment, documentation, production, quality control, distribution of the medicinal products, arrangements for dealing with complaints and recalls, and self inspection, should be examined at intervals following a pre-arranged programme in order to verify their conformity with the principles of Quality Assurance.

9.2   Self inspections should be conducted in an independent and detailed way by designated competent person(s) from the company. Independent audits by external experts may also be useful.

9.3   All self inspections should be recorded. Reports should contain all the observations made during the inspections and, where applicable, proposals for corrective measures. Statements on the actions subsequently taken should also be recorded.

Part II

Basic Requirements for Active Substances used as Starting Materials

Part II
Basic Requirements for Active Substances used as Starting Materials

Also

Annex 18

Good manufacturing practice for active pharmaceutical ingredients requirements for active substances used as starting materials from October 2005 covered under part II

Document History	
Adoption as ICH Step 4 document	November 2000
Publication as GMP Annex 18 by the European Commission	July 2001
Revision of introduction to comply with Directive 2001/83/EC and Directive 2001/82/EC, as amended by Directives 2004/27/EC and 2004/28/EC, respectively, following consultation of the public, the Ad Hoc Working Group of GMP Inspectors, the Pharmaceutical and the Veterinary Pharmaceutical Committee. After a re-structuring process of the GMP Guide publication of the new guidance as GMP Part II replacing the former Annex 18.	October 2005
Deadline for application by Member States of new legislation for active substances used as starting materials in the manufacture of human and veterinary medicinal products.	30 October 2005

1. Introduction

This guideline was published in November 2000 as Annex 18 to the GMP Guide reflecting the EU's agreement to ICH Q7A and has been used by manufacturers and GMP inspectorates on a voluntary basis. Article 46 (f) of Directive 2001/83/EC and Article 50 (f) of Directive 2001/82/EC; as amended by Directives 2004/27/EC and 2004/28/EC respectively, place new obligations on manufacturing authorisation holders to use only active substances that have been manufactured in accordance with Good Manufacturing Practice for starting materials. The directives go on to say that the principles of Good Manufacturing Practice for active substances are to be adopted as detailed guidelines. Member States have agreed that the text of former Annex 18 should form the basis of the detailed guidelines to create Part II of the GMP Guide.

1.1 Objective

These guidelines are intended to provide guidance regarding Good Manufacturing Practice (GMP) for the manufacture of active substances under an appropriate system for managing quality. It is also intended to help ensure that active substances meet the requirements for quality and purity that they purport or are represented to possess.

In these guidelines "manufacturing" includes all operations of receipt of materials, production, packaging, repackaging, labeling, relabelling, quality control, release, storage and distribution of active substances and the related controls. The term "should" indicates recommendations that are expected to apply unless shown to be inapplicable, modified in any relevant annexes to the GMP Guide, or replaced by an alternative demonstrated to provide at least an equivalent level of quality assurance.

The GMP Guide as a whole does not cover safety aspects for the personnel engaged in manufacture, nor aspects of protection of the environment. These controls are inherent responsibilities of the manufacturer and are governed by other parts of the legislation.

These guidelines are not intended to define registration requirements or modify pharmacopoeial requirements and do not affect the ability of the responsible competent authority to establish specific registration requirements regarding active substances within the context of marketing/manufacturing authorisations. All commitments in registration documents must be met.

1.2 Scope

These guidelines apply to the manufacture of active substances for medicinal products for both human and veterinary use. They apply to the manufacture of sterile active substances only up to the point immediately prior to the active substance being rendered sterile. The sterilisation and aseptic processing of sterile active substances are not covered, but should be performed in accordance with the principles and guidelines of GMP as laid down in Directive 2003/94/EC and interpreted in the GMP Guide including its Annex 1.

In the case of ectoparasiticides for veterinary use, other standards than these guidelines, that ensure that the material is of appropriate quality, may be used.

These guidelines exclude, whole blood and plasma, as Directive 2002/98/EC and the technical requirements supporting that directive lay down the detailed requirements for the collection and testing of blood, however, it does include active substances that are produced using blood or plasma as raw materials. Finally, these guidelines do not apply to bulk-packaged medicinal products. They apply to all other active starting materials subject to any derogations described in the annexes to the GMP Guide, in particular Annexes 2 to 7 where supplementary guidance for certain types of active substance may be found. The annexes will consequently undergo a review but in the meantime and only until this review is complete, manufacturers may choose to continue to use Part I of the basic requirements and the relevant annexes for products covered by those annexes, or may already apply Part II.

Section 19 contains guidance that only applies to the manufacture of active substances used in the production of investigational medicinal products although it should be noted that its application in this case, although recommended, is not required by Community legislation.

An "Active Substance Starting Material" is a raw material, intermediate, or an active substance that is used in the production of an active substance and that is incorporated as a significant structural fragment into the structure of the active substance. An Active Substance Starting Material can be an article of commerce, a material purchased from one or more suppliers under contract or commercial agreement, or produced in-house. Active Substance Starting Materials normally have defined chemical properties and structure.

The manufacturer should designate and document the rationale for the point at which production of the active substance begins.

For synthetic processes, this is known as the point at which "Active Substance Starting Materials" are entered into the process. For other processes (e.g. fermentation, extraction, purification, etc), this rationale should be established on a case-by-case basis. Table 1 gives guidance on the point at which the Active Substance Starting Material is normally introduced into the process. From this point on, appropriate GMP as defined in these guidelines should be applied to these intermediate and/or active substance manufacturing steps. This would include the validation of critical process steps determined to impact the quality of the active substance. However, it should be noted that the fact that a manufacturer chooses to validate a process step does not necessarily define that step as critical. The guidance in this document would normally be applied to the steps shown in grey in Table 1. It does not imply that all steps shown should be completed. The stringency of GMP in active substance manufacturing should increase as the process proceeds from early steps to final steps, purification, and packaging. Physical processing of active substances, such as granulation, coating or physical manipulation of particle size (e.g. milling, micronising), should be conducted at least to the standards of these guidelines. These guidelines do not apply to steps prior to the first introduction of the defined "Active Substance Starting Material".

In the remainder of this guideline the term Active Pharmaceutical Ingredient (API) is used repeatedly and should be considered interchangeable with the term "Active Substance". The glossary in section 20 of Part II should only be applied in the context of Part II. Some of the same terms are already defined in Part I of the GMP guide and these therefore should only be applied in the context of Part I.

Table 1: *Application of this Guide to API Manufacturing*

Type of Manufacturing	Application of this Guide to steps (shown in grey) used in this type of manufacturing				
Chemical Manufacturing	Production of the API Starting Material	Introduction of the API Starting Material into process	Production of Intermediate(s)	Isolation and purification	Physical processing, and packaging
API derived from animal	Collection of organ,	Cutting, mixing,	Introduction of the API Starting	Isolation and	Physical processing,

Type of Manufacturing	Application of this Guide to steps (shown in grey) used in this type of manufacturing				
sources	fluid, or tissue	and/or initial processing	Material into process	purification	and packaging
API extracted from plant sources	Collection of plant	Cutting and initial extraction(s)	Introduction of the API Starting Material into process	Isolation and purification	Physical processing, and packaging
Herbal extracts used as API	Collection of plants	Cutting and initial extraction		Further extraction	Physical processing, and packaging
API consisting of comminuted or powdered herbs	Collection of plants and/or cultivation and harvesting	Cutting/ comminuting			Physical processing, and packaging
Biotechnology: fermentation/ cell culture	Establishment of master cell bank and working cell bank	Maintenance of working cell bank	Cell culture and/or fermentation	Isolation and purification	Physical processing, and packaging
"Classical" Fermentation to produce an API	Establishm ent of cell bank	Maintenance of the cell bank	Introduction of the cells into fermentation	Isolation and purification	Physical processing, and packaging

Increasing GMP requirements

2. *Quality Management*

2.1 Principles

2.10   Quality should be the responsibility of all persons involved in manufacturing.

2.11   Each manufacturer should establish, document, and implement an effective system for managing quality that involves the active participation of management and appropriate manufacturing personnel.

2.12   The system for managing quality should encompass the organisational structure, procedures, processes and resources, as well as activities necessary to ensure confidence that the API will meet its intended specifications for quality and purity. All quality related activities should be defined and documented.

2.13 There should be a quality unit(s) that is independent of production and that fulfills both quality assurance (QA) and quality control (QC) responsibilities. This can be in the form of separate QA and QC units or a single individual or group, depending upon the size and structure of the organization.

2.14 The persons authorised to release intermediates and APIs should be specified.

2.15 All quality related activities should be recorded at the time they are performed.

2.16 Any deviation from established procedures should be documented and explained. Critical deviations should be investigated, and the investigation and its conclusions should be documented.

2.17 No materials should be released or used before the satisfactory completion of evaluation by the quality unit(s) unless there are appropriate systems in place to allow for such use (e.g. release under quarantine as described in Section 10.20 or the use of raw materials or intermediates pending completion of evaluation).

2.18 Procedures should exist for notifying responsible management in a timely manner of regulatory inspections, serious GMP deficiencies, product defects and related actions (e.g. quality related complaints, recalls, regulatory actions, etc.).

2.2 Responsibilities of the Quality Unit(s)

2.20 The quality unit(s) should be involved in all quality-related matters.

2.21 The quality unit(s) should review and approve all appropriate quality-related documents.

2.22 The main responsibilities of the independent quality unit(s) should not be delegated. These responsibilities should be described in writing and should include but not necessarily be limited to:

1. Releasing or rejecting all APIs. Releasing or rejecting intermediates for use outside the control of the manufacturing company;

2. Establishing a system to release or reject raw materials, intermediates, packaging and labelling materials;

3. Reviewing completed batch production and laboratory control records of critical process steps before release of the API for distribution;

4. Making sure that critical deviations are investigated and resolved;

5. Approving all specifications and master production instructions;

6. Approving all procedures impacting the quality of intermediates or APIs;

7. Making sure that internal audits (self-inspections) are performed;

8. Approving intermediate and API contract manufacturers;

9. Approving changes that potentially impact intermediate or API quality;

10. Reviewing and approving validation protocols and reports;

11. Making sure that quality related complaints are investigated and resolved;

12. Making sure that effective systems are used for maintaining and calibrating critical equipment;

13. Making sure that materials are appropriately tested and the results are reported;

14. Making sure that there is stability data to support retest or expiry dates and storage conditions on APIs and/or intermediates where appropriate; and

15. Performing product quality reviews (as defined in Section 2.5)

2.3 Responsibility for Production Activities

The responsibility for production activities should be described in writing, and should include but not necessarily be limited to:

1. Preparing, reviewing, approving and distributing the instructions for the production of intermediates or APIs according to written procedures;

2. Producing APIs and, when appropriate, intermediates according to pre-approved instructions;

3. Reviewing all production batch records and ensuring that these are completed and signed;

4. Making sure that all production deviations are reported and evaluated and that critical deviations are investigated and the conclusions are recorded;

5. Making sure that production facilities are clean and when appropriate disinfected;

6. Making sure that the necessary calibrations are performed and records kept;

7. Making sure that the premises and equipment are maintained and records kept;

8. Making sure that validation protocols and reports are reviewed and approved;

9. Evaluating proposed changes in product, process or equipment; and

10. Making sure that new and, when appropriate, modified facilities and equipment are qualified.

2.4 Internal Audits (Self Inspection)

2.40 In order to verify compliance with the principles of GMP for APIs, regular internal audits should be performed in accordance with an approved schedule.

2.41 Audit findings and corrective actions should be documented and brought to the attention of responsible management of the firm. Agreed corrective actions should be completed in a timely and effective manner.

2.5 Product Quality Review

2.50 Regular quality reviews of APIs should be conducted with the objective of verifying the consistency of the process. Such reviews should normally be conducted and documented annually and should include at least:

— A review of critical in-process control and critical API test results;

— A review of all batches that failed to meet established specification(s);

— A review of all critical deviations or non-conformances and related investigations;

— A review of any changes carried out to the processes or analytical methods;

— A review of results of the stability monitoring program;

— A review of all quality-related returns, complaints and recalls; and

— A review of adequacy of corrective actions.

2.51 The results of this review should be evaluated and an assessment made of whether corrective action or any revalidation should be undertaken. Reasons for such corrective action should be documented. Agreed corrective actions should be completed in a timely and effective manner.

3. Personnel

3.1 Personnel Qualifications

3.10 There should be an adequate number of personnel qualified by appropriate education, training and/or experience to perform and supervise the manufacture of intermediates and APIs.

3.11 The responsibilities of all personnel engaged in the manufacture of intermediates and APIs should be specified in writing.

3.12 Training should be regularly conducted by qualified individuals and should cover, at a minimum, the particular operations that the employee performs and GMP as it relates to the employee's functions. Records of training should be maintained. Training should be periodically assessed.

3.2 Personnel Hygiene

3.20 Personnel should practice good sanitation and health habits.

3.21 Personnel should wear clean clothing suitable for the manufacturing activity with which they are involved and this clothing should be changed when appropriate. Additional protective apparel, such as head, face, hand, and arm coverings, should be worn when necessary, to protect intermediates and APIs from contamination.

3.22 Personnel should avoid direct contact with intermediates or APIs.

3.23 Smoking, eating, drinking, chewing and the storage of food should be restricted to certain designated areas separate from the manufacturing areas.

3.24 Personnel suffering from an infectious disease or having open lesions on the exposed surface of the body should not engage in activities that could result in compromising the quality of APIs. Any person shown at any time (either by medical examination or supervisory observation) to have an apparent illness or open lesions should be excluded from activities where the health condition could adversely affect the quality of the APIs until the condition is corrected or qualified medical personnel determine that the person's inclusion would not jeopardize the safety or quality of the APIs.

3.3 Consultants

3.30 Consultants advising on the manufacture and control of intermediates or APIs should have sufficient education, training, and experience, or any combination thereof, to advise on the subject for which they are retained.

3.31 Records should be maintained stating the name, address, qualifications, and type of service provided by these consultants.

4. Buildings and Facilities

4.1 Design and Construction

4.10 Buildings and facilities used in the manufacture of intermediates and APIs should be located, designed, and constructed to facilitate cleaning, maintenance, and operations as appropriate to the type and stage of manufacture. Facilities should also be designed to minimize potential contamination. Where microbiological specifications have been established for the intermediate or API, facilities should also be designed to limit exposure to objectionable microbiological contaminants as appropriate.

4.11 Buildings and facilities should have adequate space for the orderly placement of equipment and materials to prevent mix-ups and contamination.

4.12 Where the equipment itself (e.g., closed or contained systems) provides adequate protection of the material, such equipment can be located outdoors.

4.13 The flow of materials and personnel through the building or facilities should be designed to prevent mix-ups or contamination.

4.14 There should be defined areas or other control systems for the following activities:

— Receipt, identification, sampling, and quarantine of incoming materials, pending release or rejection;

— Quarantine before release or rejection of intermediates and APIs;

— Sampling of intermediates and APIs;

— Holding rejected materials before further disposition (e.g., return, reprocessing or destruction)

— Storage of released materials;

— Production operations;

— Packaging and labelling operations; and

— Laboratory operations.

4.15 Adequate, clean washing and toilet facilities should be provided for personnel. These washing facilities should be equipped with hot and cold water as appropriate, soap or detergent, air driers or single service towels. The washing and toilet facilities should be separate from, but easily accessible to, manufacturing areas. Adequate facilities for showering and/or changing clothes should be provided, when appropriate.

4.16 Laboratory areas/operations should normally be separated from production areas. Some laboratory areas, in particular those used for in-process controls, can be located in production areas, provided the operations of the production process do not adversely affect the accuracy of the laboratory measurements, and the laboratory and its operations do not adversely affect the production process or intermediate or API.

4.2 Utilities

4.20 All utilities that could impact on product quality (e.g. steam, gases, compressed air, and heating, ventilation and air conditioning) should be qualified and appropriately monitored and action should be taken when limits are exceeded. Drawings for these utility systems should be available.

4.21 Adequate ventilation, air filtration and exhaust systems should be provided, where appropriate. These systems should be designed and constructed to minimise risks of contamination and cross-contamination and should include equipment for control of air pressure, microorganisms (if appropriate), dust, humidity, and temperature, as appropriate to the stage of manufacture. Particular attention should be given to areas where APIs are exposed to the environment.

4.22 If air is recirculated to production areas, appropriate measures should be taken to control risks of contamination and cross-contamination.

4.23 Permanently installed pipework should be appropriately identified. This can be accomplished by identifying individual lines, documentation, computer control systems, or alternative means. Pipework should be located to avoid risks of contamination of the intermediate or API.

4.24 Drains should be of adequate size and should be provided with an air break or a suitable device to prevent back-siphonage, when appropriate.

4.3 Water

4.30 Water used in the manufacture of APIs should be demonstrated to be suitable for its intended use.

4.31 Unless otherwise justified, process water should, at a minimum, meet World Health Organization (WHO) guidelines for drinking (potable) water quality.

4.32 If drinking (potable) water is insufficient to assure API quality, and tighter chemical and/or microbiological water quality specifications are called for, appropriate specifications for physical/chemical attributes, total microbial counts, objectionable organisms and/or endotoxins should be established.

4.33 Where water used in the process is treated by the manufacturer to achieve a defined quality, the treatment process should be validated and monitored with appropriate action limits.

4.34 Where the manufacturer of a non-sterile API either intends or claims that it is suitable for use in further processing to produce a sterile drug (medicinal) product, water used in the final isolation and purification steps should be monitored and controlled for total microbial counts, objectionable organisms, and endotoxins.

4.4 Containment

4.40 Dedicated production areas, which can include facilities, air handling equipment and/or process equipment, should be employed in the production of highly sensitizing materials, such as penicillins or cephalosporins.

4.41 Dedicated production areas should also be considered when material of an infectious nature or high pharmacological activity or toxicity is involved (e.g., certain steroids or cytotoxic anti-cancer agents) unless validated inactivation and/or cleaning procedures are established and maintained.

4.42 Appropriate measures should be established and implemented to prevent cross-contamination from personnel, materials, etc. moving from one dedicated area to another.

4.43 Any production activities (including weighing, milling, or packaging) of highly toxic non-pharmaceutical materials such as herbicides and pesticides should not be conducted using the buildings and/or equipment being used for the production of APIs. Handling and storage of these highly toxic non-pharmaceutical materials should be separate from APIs.

4.5 Lighting

4.50 Adequate lighting should be provided in all areas to facilitate cleaning, maintenance, and proper operations.

4.6 Sewage and Refuse

4.60 Sewage, refuse, and other waste (e.g., solids, liquids, or gaseous by-products from manufacturing) in and from buildings and the immediate surrounding area should be disposed of in a safe, timely, and sanitary manner. Containers and/or pipes for waste material should be clearly identified.

4.7 Sanitation and Maintenance

4.70 Buildings used in the manufacture of intermediates and APIs should be properly maintained and repaired and kept in a clean condition.

4.71 Written procedures should be established assigning responsibility for sanitation and describing the cleaning schedules, methods, equipment, and materials to be used in cleaning buildings and facilities.

4.72 When necessary, written procedures should also be established for the use of suitable rodenticides, insecticides, fungicides, fumigating agents, and cleaning and sanitizing agents to prevent the contamination of equipment, raw materials, packaging/labelling materials, intermediates, and APIs.

5. Process Equipment

5.1 Design and Construction

5.10 Equipment used in the manufacture of intermediates and APIs should be of appropriate design and adequate size, and suitably located for its intended use, cleaning, sanitization (where appropriate), and maintenance.

5.11 Equipment should be constructed so that surfaces that contact raw materials, intermediates, or APIs do not alter the quality of the intermediates and APIs beyond the official or other established specifications.

5.12 Production equipment should only be used within its qualified operating range.

5.13 Major equipment (e.g., reactors, storage containers) and permanently installed processing lines used during the production of an intermediate or API should be appropriately identified.

5.14 Any substances associated with the operation of equipment, such as lubricants, heating fluids or coolants, should not contact intermediates or APIs so as to alter their quality beyond the official or other established specifications. Any deviations from this should be evaluated to ensure that there are no detrimental effects upon the fitness for purpose of the material. Wherever possible, food grade lubricants and oils should be used.

5.15 Closed or contained equipment should be used whenever appropriate. Where open equipment is used, or equipment is opened, appropriate precautions should be taken to minimize the risk of contamination.

5.16 A set of current drawings should be maintained for equipment and critical installations (e.g., instrumentation and utility systems).

5.2 Equipment Maintenance and Cleaning

5.20 Schedules and procedures (including assignment of responsibility) should be established for the preventative maintenance of equipment.

5.21 Written procedures should be established for cleaning of equipment and its subsequent release for use in the manufacture of intermediates and APIs. Cleaning procedures should contain sufficient details to enable operators to clean each type of equipment in a reproducible and effective manner. These procedures should include:

— Assignment of responsibility for cleaning of equipment;

— Cleaning schedules, including, where appropriate, sanitizing schedules;

— A complete description of the methods and materials, including dilution of cleaning agents used to clean equipment;

— When appropriate, instructions for disassembling and reassembling each article of equipment to ensure proper cleaning;

— Instructions for the removal or obliteration of previous batch identification;

— Instructions for the protection of clean equipment from contamination prior to use;

— Inspection of equipment for cleanliness immediately before use, if practical; and

— Establishing the maximum time that may elapse between the completion of processing and equipment cleaning, when appropriate.

5.22 Equipment and utensils should be cleaned, stored, and, where appropriate, sanitized or sterilized to prevent contamination or carry-over of a material that would alter the quality of the intermediate or API beyond the official or other established specifications.

5.23 Where equipment is assigned to continuous production or campaign production of successive batches of the same intermediate or API, equipment should be cleaned at appropriate intervals to prevent build-up and carry-over of contaminants (e.g. degradants or objectionable levels of micro-organisms).

5.24 Non-dedicated equipment should be cleaned between production of different materials to prevent cross-contamination.

5.25 Acceptance criteria for residues and the choice of cleaning procedures and cleaning agents should be defined and justified.

5.26 Equipment should be identified as to its contents and its cleanliness status by appropriate means.

5.3 Calibration

5.30 Control, weighing, measuring, monitoring and test equipment that is critical for assuring the quality of intermediates or APIs should be calibrated according to written procedures and an established schedule.

5.31 Equipment calibrations should be performed using standards traceable to certified standards, if existing.

5.32 Records of these calibrations should be maintained.

5.33 The current calibration status of critical equipment should be known and verifiable.

5.34 Instruments that do not meet calibration criteria should not be used.

5.35 Deviations from approved standards of calibration on critical instruments should be investigated to determine if these could have had an impact on the quality of the intermediate(s) or API(s) manufactured using this equipment since the last successful calibration.

5.4 Computerized Systems

5.40 GMP related computerized systems should be validated. The depth and scope of validation depends on the diversity, complexity and criticality of the computerized application.

5.41 Appropriate installation qualification and operational qualification should demonstrate the suitability of computer hardware and software to perform assigned tasks.

5.42 Commercially available software that has been qualified does not require the same level of testing. If an existing system was not validated at time of installation, a retrospective validation could be conducted if appropriate documentation is available.

5.43 Computerized systems should have sufficient controls to prevent unauthorized access or changes to data. There should be controls to prevent omissions in data (e.g. system turned off and data not captured). There should be a record of any data change made, the previous entry, who made the change, and when the change was made.

5.44 Written procedures should be available for the operation and maintenance of computerized systems.

5.45 Where critical data are being entered manually, there should be an additional check on the accuracy of the entry. This can be done by a second operator or by the system itself.

5.46 Incidents related to computerized systems that could affect the quality of intermediates or APIs or the reliability of records or test results should be recorded and investigated.

5.47 Changes to the computerized system should be made according to a change procedure and should be formally authorized, documented and tested. Records should be kept of all changes, including modifications and enhancements made to the hardware, software and any other critical component of the system. These records should demonstrate that the system is maintained in a validated state.

5.48 If system breakdowns or failures would result in the permanent loss of records, a back-up system should be provided. A means of ensuring data protection should be established for all computerized systems.

5.49 Data can be recorded by a second means in addition to the computer system.

6. Documentation and Records

6.1 Documentation System and Specifications

6.10 All documents related to the manufacture of intermediates or APIs should be prepared, reviewed, approved and distributed according to written procedures. Such documents can be in paper or electronic form.

6.11 The issuance, revision, superseding and withdrawal of all documents should be controlled with maintenance of revision histories.

6.12 A procedure should be established for retaining all appropriate documents (e.g., development history reports, scale-up reports, technical transfer reports, process validation reports, training records, production records, control records, and distribution records). The retention periods for these documents should be specified.

6.13 All production, control, and distribution records should be retained for at least 1 year after the expiry date of the batch. For APIs with retest dates, records should be retained for at least 3 years after the batch is completely distributed.

6.14 When entries are made in records, these should be made indelibly in spaces provided for such entries, directly after performing the activities, and should identify the person making the entry. Corrections to entries should be dated and signed and leave the original entry still readable.

6.15 During the retention period, originals or copies of records should be readily available at the establishment where the activities described in such records occurred. Records that can be promptly retrieved from another location by electronic or other means are acceptable.

6.16 Specifications, instructions, procedures, and records can be retained either as originals or as true copies such as photocopies, microfilm, microfiche, or other accurate reproductions of the original records. Where reduction techniques such as microfilming or electronic records are used, suitable retrieval equipment and a means to produce a hard copy should be readily available.

6.17 Specifications should be established and documented for raw materials, intermediates where necessary, APIs, and labelling and packaging materials. In addition, specifications may be appropriate for certain other materials, such as process aids, gaskets, or other materials used during the production of intermediates or APIs that could critically impact on quality. Acceptance criteria should be established and documented for in-process controls.

6.18   If electronic signatures are used on documents, they should be authenticated and secure.

6.2 Equipment Cleaning and Use Record

6.20   Records of major equipment use, cleaning, sanitization and/or sterilization and maintenance should show the date, time (if appropriate), product, and batch number of each batch processed in the equipment, and the person who performed the cleaning and maintenance.

6.21   If equipment is dedicated to manufacturing one intermediate or API, then individual equipment records are not necessary if batches of the intermediate or API follow in traceable sequence. In cases where dedicated equipment is employed, the records of cleaning, maintenance, and use can be part of the batch record or maintained separately.

6.3 Records of Raw Materials, Intermediates, API Labelling and Packaging Materials

6.30   Records should be maintained including:

—   The name of the manufacturer, identity and quantity of each shipment of each batch of raw materials, intermediates or labelling and packaging materials for API's; the name of the supplier; the supplier's control number(s), if known, or other identification number; the number allocated on receipt; and the date of receipt;

—   The results of any test or examination performed and the conclusions derived from this; -Records tracing the use of materials; -Documentation of the examination and review of API labelling and packaging materials for conformity with established specifications; and -The final decision regarding rejected raw materials, intermediates or API labelling and packaging materials.

6.31   Master (approved) labels should be maintained for comparison to issued labels.

6.4 Master Production Instructions (Master Production and Control Records)

6.40 To ensure uniformity from batch to batch, master production instructions for each intermediate and API should be prepared, dated, and signed by one person and independently checked, dated, and signed by a person in the quality unit(s).

6.41 Master production instructions should include:

— The name of the intermediate or API being manufactured and an identifying document reference code, if applicable;

— A complete list of raw materials and intermediates designated by names or codes sufficiently specific to identify any special quality characteristics;

— An accurate statement of the quantity or ratio of each raw material or intermediate to be used, including the unit of measure. Where the quantity is not fixed, the calculation for each batch size or rate of production should be included. Variations to quantities should be included where they are justified;

— The production location and major production equipment to be used;

— Detailed production instructions, including the:

— sequences to be followed,

— ranges of process parameters to be used,

— sampling instructions and in-process controls with their acceptance criteria, where appropriate,

— time limits for completion of individual processing steps and/or the total process, where appropriate; and

— expected yield ranges at appropriate phases of processing or time;

— Where appropriate, special notations and precautions to be followed, or cross references to these; and

— The instructions for storage of the intermediate or API to assure its suitability for use, including the labelling and packaging materials and special storage conditions with time limits, where appropriate.

6.5 Batch Production Records (Batch Production and Control Records)

6.50 Batch production records should be prepared for each intermediate and API and should include complete information relating to the production and control of each batch. The batch production record should be checked before issuance to assure that it is the correct version and a legible accurate reproduction of the appropriate master production instruction. If the batch production record is produced from a separate part of the master document, that document should include a reference to the current master production instruction being used.

6.51 These records should be numbered with a unique batch or identification number, dated and signed when issued. In continuous production, the product code together with the date and time can serve as the unique identifier until the final number is allocated.

6.52 Documentation of completion of each significant step in the batch production records (batch production and control records) should include:

— Dates and, when appropriate, times;

— Identity of major equipment (e.g., reactors, driers, mills, etc.) used;

— Specific identification of each batch, including weights, measures, and batch numbers of raw materials, intermediates, or any reprocessed materials used during manufacturing;

— Actual results recorded for critical process parameters;

— Any sampling performed;

— Signatures of the persons performing and directly supervising or checking each critical step in the operation;

— In-process and laboratory test results;

— Actual yield at appropriate phases or times;

— Description of packaging and label for intermediate or API;

— Representative label of API or intermediate if made commercially available;

— Any deviation noted, its evaluation, investigation conducted (if appropriate) or reference to that investigation if stored separately; and

— Results of release testing.

6.53 Written procedures should be established and followed for investigating critical deviations or the failure of a batch of intermediate or API to meet specifications. The investigation should extend to other batches that may have been associated with the specific failure or deviation.

6.6 Laboratory Control Records

6.60 Laboratory control records should include complete data derived from all tests conducted to ensure compliance with established specifications and standards, including examinations and assays, as follows:

— A description of samples received for testing, including the material name or source, batch number or other distinctive code, date sample was taken, and, where appropriate, the quantity and date the sample was received for testing;

— A statement of or reference to each test method used;

— A statement of the weight or measure of sample used for each test as described by the method; data on or cross-reference to the preparation and testing of reference standards, reagents and standard solutions,

— A complete record of all raw data generated during each test, in addition to graphs, charts, and spectra from laboratory instrumentation, properly identified to show the specific material and batch tested;

— A record of all calculations performed in connection with the test, including, for example,

units of measure, conversion factors, and
equivalency factors;

— A statement of the test results and how they
compare with established acceptance criteria;

— The signature of the person who performed each
test and the date(s) the tests were performed; and

— The date and signature of a second person
showing that the original records have been
reviewed for accuracy, completeness, and
compliance with established standards.

6.61 Complete records should also be maintained for:

— Any modifications to an established analytical
method,

— Periodic calibration of laboratory instruments,
apparatus, gauges, and recording devices;

— All stability testing performed on APIs; and

— Out-of-specification (OOS) investigations.

6.7 Batch Production Record Review

6.70 Written procedures should be established and followed
for the review and approval of batch production and
laboratory control records, including packaging and
labelling, to determine compliance of the intermediate or
API with established specifications before a batch is
released or distributed.

6.71 Batch production and laboratory control records of critical
process steps should be reviewed and approved by the
quality unit(s) before an API batch is released or
distributed. Production and laboratory control records of
non-critical process steps can be reviewed by qualified
production personnel or other units following procedures
approved by the quality unit(s).

6.72 All deviation, investigation, and OOS reports should be
reviewed as part of the batch record review before the
batch is released.

6.73 The quality unit(s) can delegate to the production unit the
responsibility and authority for release of intermediates,

except for those shipped outside the control of the manufacturing company.

7. Materials Management

7.1 General Controls

7.10 There should be written procedures describing the receipt, identification, quarantine, storage, handling, sampling, testing, and approval or rejection of materials.

7.11 Manufacturers of intermediates and/or APIs should have a system for evaluating the suppliers of critical materials.

7.12 Materials should be purchased against an agreed specification, from a supplier or suppliers approved by the quality unit(s).

7.13 If the supplier of a critical material is not the manufacturer of that material, the name and address of that manufacturer should be known by the intermediate and/or API manufacturer.

7.14 Changing the source of supply of critical raw materials should be treated according to Section 13, Change Control.

7.2 Receipt and Quarantine

7.20 Upon receipt and before acceptance, each container or grouping of containers of materials should be examined visually for correct labelling (including correlation between the name used by the supplier and the in-house name, if these are different), container damage, broken seals and evidence of tampering or contamination. Materials should be held under quarantine until they have been sampled, examined or tested as appropriate, and released for use.

7.21 Before incoming materials are mixed with existing stocks (e.g., solvents or stocks in silos), they should be identified as correct, tested, if appropriate, and released. Procedures should be available to prevent discharging incoming materials wrongly into the existing stock.

7.22 If bulk deliveries are made in non-dedicated tankers, there should be assurance of no cross-contamination from the tanker. Means of providing this assurance could include one or more of the following:

— certificate of cleaning

— testing for trace impurities

— audit of the supplier.

7.23 Large storage containers, and their attendant manifolds, filling and discharge lines should be appropriately identified.

7.24 Each container or grouping of containers (batches) of materials should be assigned and identified with a distinctive code, batch, or receipt number. This number should be used in recording the disposition of each batch. A system should be in place to identify the status of each batch.

7.3 Sampling and Testing of Incoming Production Materials

7.30 At least one test to verify the identity of each batch of material should be conducted, with the exception of the materials described below in 7.32. A supplier's Certificate of Analysis can be used in place of performing other tests, provided that the manufacturer has a system in place to evaluate suppliers.

7.31 Supplier approval should include an evaluation that provides adequate evidence (e.g., past quality history) that the manufacturer can consistently provide material meeting specifications. Full analyses should be conducted on at least three batches before reducing in-house testing. However, as a minimum, a full analysis should be performed at appropriate intervals and compared with the Certificates of Analysis. Reliability of Certificates of Analysis should be checked at regular intervals.

7.32 Processing aids, hazardous or highly toxic raw materials, other special materials, or materials transferred to another unit within the company's control do not need to be tested if the manufacturer's Certificate of Analysis is obtained, showing that these raw materials conform to established specifications. Visual examination of containers, labels, and recording of batch numbers should help in establishing the identity of these materials. The lack of on-site testing for these materials should be justified and documented.

7.33 Samples should be representative of the batch of material from which they are taken. Sampling methods should specify the number of containers to be sampled, which part of the container to sample, and the amount of material to be taken from each container. The number of containers to sample and the sample size should be based upon a sampling plan that takes into consideration the criticality of the material, material variability, past quality history of the supplier, and the quantity needed for analysis.

7.34 Sampling should be conducted at defined locations and by procedures designed to prevent contamination of the material sampled and contamination of other materials.

7.35 Containers from which samples are withdrawn should be opened carefully and subsequently reclosed. They should be marked to indicate that a sample has been taken.

7.4 Storage

7.40 Materials should be handled and stored in a manner to prevent degradation, contamination, and cross-contamination.

7.41 Materials stored in fiber drums, bags, or boxes should be stored off the floor and, when appropriate, suitably spaced to permit cleaning and inspection.

7.42 Materials should be stored under conditions and for a period that have no adverse affect on their quality, and should normally be controlled so that the oldest stock is used first.

7.43 Certain materials in suitable containers can be stored outdoors, provided identifying labels remain legible and containers are appropriately cleaned before opening and use.

7.44 Rejected materials should be identified and controlled under a quarantine system designed to prevent their unauthorised use in manufacturing.

7.5 Re-evaluation

7.50   Materials should be re-evaluated as appropriate to determine their suitability for use (e.g., after prolonged storage or exposure to heat or humidity).

8. *Production and In-Process Controls*

8.1 Production Operations

8.10   Raw materials for intermediate and API manufacturing should be weighed or measured under appropriate conditions that do not affect their suitability for use. Weighing and measuring devices should be of suitable accuracy for the intended use.

8.11   If a material is subdivided for later use in production operations, the container receiving the material should be suitable and should be so identified that the following information is available:

—   Material name and/or item code;

—   Receiving or control number;

—   Weight or measure of material in the new container; and

—   Re-evaluation or retest date if appropriate.

8.12   Critical weighing, measuring, or subdividing operations should be witnessed or subjected to an equivalent control. Prior to use, production personnel should verify that the materials are those specified in the batch record for the intended intermediate or API.

8.13   Other critical activities should be witnessed or subjected to an equivalent control.

8.14   Actual yields should be compared with expected yields at designated steps in the production process. Expected yields with appropriate ranges should be established based on previous laboratory, pilot scale, or manufacturing data. Deviations in yield associated with critical process steps should be investigated to determine their impact or potential impact on the resulting quality of affected batches.

8.15 Any deviation should be documented and explained. Any critical deviation should be investigated.

8.16 The processing status of major units of equipment should be indicated either on the individual units of equipment or by appropriate documentation, computer control systems, or alternative means.

8.17 Materials to be reprocessed or reworked should be appropriately controlled to prevent unauthorized use.

8.2 Time Limits

8.20 If time limits are specified in the master production instruction (see 6.41), these time limits should be met to ensure the quality of intermediates and APIs. Deviations should be documented and evaluated. Time limits may be inappropriate when processing to a target value (e.g., pH adjustment, hydrogenation, drying to predetermined specification) because completion of reactions or processing steps are determined by in-process sampling and testing.

8.21 Intermediates held for further processing should be stored under appropriate conditions to ensure their suitability for use.

8.3 In-process Sampling and Controls

8.30 Written procedures should be established to monitor the progress and control the performance of processing steps that cause variability in the quality characteristics of intermediates and APIs. In-process controls and their acceptance criteria should be defined based on the information gained during the development stage or historical data.

8.31 The acceptance criteria and type and extent of testing can depend on the nature of the intermediate or API being manufactured, the reaction or process step being conducted, and the degree to which the process introduces variability in the product's quality. Less stringent in-process controls may be appropriate in early processing steps, whereas tighter controls may be appropriate for later processing steps (e.g., isolation and purification steps).

8.32 Critical in-process controls (and critical process monitoring), including the control points and methods, should be stated in writing and approved by the quality unit(s).

8.33 In-process controls can be performed by qualified production department personnel and the process adjusted without prior quality unit(s) approval if the adjustments are made within pre-established limits approved by the quality unit(s). All tests and results should be fully documented as part of the batch record.

8.34 Written procedures should describe the sampling methods for in-process materials, intermediates, and APIs. Sampling plans and procedures should be based on scientifically sound sampling practices.

8.35 In-process sampling should be conducted using procedures designed to prevent contamination of the sampled material and other intermediates or APIs. Procedures should be established to ensure the integrity of samples after collection.

8.36 Out-of-specification (OOS) investigations are not normally needed for in-process tests that are performed for the purpose of monitoring and/or adjusting the process.

8.4 Blending Batches of Intermediates or APIs

8.40 For the purpose of this document, blending is defined as the process of combining materials within the same specification to produce a homogeneous intermediate or API. In-process mixing of fractions from single batches (e.g., collecting several centrifuge loads from a single crystallization batch) or combining fractions from several batches for further processing is considered to be part of the production process and is not considered to be blending.

8.41 Out-Of-Specification batches should not be blended with other batches for the purpose of meeting specifications. Each batch incorporated into the blend should have been manufactured using an established process and should have been individually tested and found to meet appropriate specifications prior to blending.

8.42 Acceptable blending operations include but are not limited to:

— Blending of small batches to increase batch size

— Blending of tailings (i.e., relatively small quantities of isolated material) from batches of the same intermediate orAPItoforma single batch.

8.43 Blending processes should be adequately controlled and documented and the blended batch should be tested for conformance to established specifications where appropriate.

8.44 The batch record of the blending process should allow traceability back to the individual batches that make up the blend.

8.45 Where physical attributes of the API are critical (e.g., APIs intended for use in solid oral dosage forms or suspensions), blending operations should be validated to show homogeneity of the combined batch. Validation should include testing of critical attributes (e.g., particle size distribution, bulk density, and tap density) that may be affected by the blending process.

8.46 If the blending could adversely affect stability, stability testing of the final blended batches should be performed.

8.47 The expiry or retest date of the blended batch should be based on the manufacturing date of the oldest tailings or batch in the blend.

8.5 Contamination Control

8.50 Residual materials can be carried over into successive batches of the same intermediate or API if there is adequate control. Examples include residue adhering to the wall of a micronizer, residual layer of damp crystals remaining in a centrifuge bowl after discharge, and incomplete discharge of fluids or crystals from a processing vessel upon transfer of the material to the next step in the process. Such carryover should not result in the carryover of degradants or microbial contamination that may adversely alter the established API impurity profile.

8.51 Production operations should be conducted in a manner that will prevent contamination of intermediates or APIs by other materials.

8.52 Precautions to avoid contamination should be taken when APIs are handled after purification.

9. Packaging and Identification Labelling of APIs and Intermediates

9.1 General

9.10 There should be written procedures describing the receipt, identification, quarantine, sampling, examination and/or testing and release, and handling of packaging and labelling materials.

9.11 Packaging and labelling materials should conform to established specifications. Those that do not comply with such specifications should be rejected to prevent their use in operations for which they are unsuitable.

9.12 Records should be maintained for each shipment of labels and packaging materials showing receipt, examination, or testing, and whether accepted or rejected.

9.2 Packaging Materials

9.20 Containers should provide adequate protection against deterioration or contamination of the intermediate or API that may occur during transportation and recommended storage.

9.21 Containers should be clean and, where indicated by the nature of the intermediate or API, sanitized to ensure that they are suitable for their intended use. These containers should not be reactive, additive, or absorptive so as to alter the quality of the intermediate or API beyond the specified limits.

9.22 If containers are re-used, they should be cleaned in accordance with documented procedures and all previous labels should be removed or defaced.

9.3 Label Issuance and Control

9.30   Access to the label storage areas should be limited to authorised personnel.

9.31   Procedures should be used to reconcile the quantities of labels issued, used, and returned and to evaluate discrepancies found between the number of containers labelled and the number of labels issued. Such discrepancies should be investigated, and the investigation should be approved by the quality unit(s).

9.32   All excess labels bearing batch numbers or other batch-related printing should be destroyed. Returned labels should be maintained and stored in a manner that prevents mix-ups and provides proper identification.

9.33   Obsolete and out-dated labels should be destroyed.

9.34   Printing devices used to print labels for packaging operations should be controlled to ensure that all imprinting conforms to the print specified in the batch production record.

9.35   Printed labels issued for a batch should be carefully examined for proper identity and conformity to specifications in the master production record. The results of this examination should be documented.

9.36   A printed label representative of those used should be included in the batch production record.

9.4 Packaging and Labelling Operations

9.40   There should be documented procedures designed to ensure that correct packaging materials and labels are used.

9.41   Labelling operations should be designed to prevent mix-ups. There should be physical or spatial separation from operations involving other intermediates or APIs.

9.42   Labels used on containers of intermediates or APIs should indicate the name or identifying code, the batch number of the product, and storage conditions, when such information is critical to assure the quality of intermediate or API.

9.43 If the intermediate or API is intended to be transferred outside the control of the manufacturer's material management system, the name and address of the manufacturer, quantity of contents, and special transport conditions and any special legal requirements should also be included on the label. For intermediates or APIs with an expiry date, the expiry date should be indicated on the label and Certificate of Analysis. For intermediates or APIs with a retest date, the retest date should be indicated on the label and/or Certificate of Analysis.

9.44 Packaging and labelling facilities should be inspected immediately before use to ensure that all materials not needed for the next packaging operation have been removed. This examination should be documented in the batch production records, the facility log, or other documentation system.

9.45 Packaged and labelled intermediates or APIs should be examined to ensure that containers and packages in the batch have the correct label. This examination should be part of the packaging operation. Results of these examinations should be recorded in the batch production or control records.

9.46 Intermediate or API containers that are transported outside of the manufacturer's control should be sealed in a manner such that, if the seal is breached or missing, the recipient will be alerted to the possibility that the contents may have been altered.

10. Storage and Distribution

10.1 Warehousing Procedures

10.10 Facilities should be available for the storage of all materials under appropriate conditions (e.g. controlled temperature and humidity when necessary). Records should be maintained of these conditions if they are critical for the maintenance of material characteristics.

10.11 Unless there is an alternative system to prevent the unintentional or unauthorised use of quarantined, rejected, returned, or recalled materials, separate storage areas should be assigned for their temporary storage until the decision as to their future use has been taken.

10.2 Distribution Procedures

10.20 APIs and intermediates should only be released for distribution to third parties after they have been released by the quality unit(s). APIs and intermediates can be transferred under quarantine to another unit under the company's control when authorized by the quality unit(s) and if appropriate controls and documentation are in place.

10.21 APIs and intermediates should be transported in a manner that does not adversely affect their quality.

10.22 Special transport or storage conditions for an API or intermediate should be stated on the label.

10.23 The manufacturer should ensure that the contract acceptor (contractor) for transportation of the API or intermediate knows and follows the appropriate transport and storage conditions.

10.24 A system should be in place by which the distribution of each batch of intermediate and/or API can be readily determined to permit its recall.

11. *Laboratory Controls*

11.1 General Controls

11.10 The independent quality unit(s) should have at its disposal adequate laboratory facilities.

11.11 There should be documented procedures describing sampling, testing, approval or rejection of materials, and recording and storage of laboratory data. Laboratory records should be maintained in accordance with Section 6.6.

11.12 All specifications, sampling plans, and test procedures should be scientifically sound and appropriate to ensure that raw materials, intermediates, APIs, and labels and packaging materials conform to established standards of quality and/or purity. Specifications and test procedures should be consistent with those included in the registration/filing. There can be specifications in addition to those in the registration/filing. Specifications, sampling plans, and test procedures, including changes to them, should be drafted by the appropriate organizational unit and reviewed and approved by the quality unit(s).

11.13 Appropriate specifications should be established for APIs in accordance with accepted standards and consistent with the manufacturing process. The specifications should include a control of the impurities (e.g. organic impurities, inorganic impurities, and residual solvents). If the API has a specification for microbiological purity, appropriate action limits for total microbial counts and objectionable organisms should be established and met. If the API has a specification for endotoxins, appropriate action limits should be established and met.

11.14 Laboratory controls should be followed and documented at the time of performance. Any departures from the above described procedures should be documented and explained.

11.15 Any out-of-specification result obtained should be investigated and documented according to a procedure. This procedure should require analysis of the data, assessment of whether a significant problem exists, allocation of the tasks for corrective actions, and conclusions. Any re-sampling and/or retesting after OOS results should be performed according to a documented procedure.

11.16 Reagents and standard solutions should be prepared and labelled following written procedures. "Use by" dates should be applied as appropriate for analytical reagents or standard solutions.

11.17 Primary reference standards should be obtained as appropriate for the manufacture of APIs. The source of each primary reference standard should be documented. Records should be maintained of each primary reference standard's storage and use in accordance with the supplier's recommendations. Primary reference standards obtained from an officially recognised source are normally used without testing if stored under conditions consistent with the supplier's recommendations.

11.18 Where a primary reference standard is not available from an officially recognized source, an "in-house primary standard" should be established. Appropriate testing should be performed to establish fully the identity and purity of the primary reference standard. Appropriate documentation of this testing should be maintained.

11.19 Secondary reference standards should be appropriately prepared, identified, tested, approved, and stored. The suitability of each batch of secondary reference standard should be determined prior to first use by comparing against a primary reference standard. Each batch of secondary reference standard should be periodically requalified in accordance with a written protocol.

11.2 Testing of Intermediates and APIs

11.20 For each batch of intermediate and API, appropriate laboratory tests should be conducted to determine conformance to specifications.

11.21 An impurity profile describing the identified and unidentified impurities present in a typical batch produced by a specific controlled production process should normally be established for each API. The impurity profile should include the identity or some qualitative analytical designation (e.g. retention time), the range of each impurity observed, and classification of each identified impurity (e.g. inorganic, organic, solvent). The impurity profile is normally dependent upon the production process and origin of the API. Impurity profiles are normally not necessary for APIs from herbal or animal tissue origin. Biotechnology considerations are covered in ICH Guideline Q6B.

11.22 The impurity profile should be compared at appropriate intervals against the impurity profile in the regulatory submission or compared against historical data in order to detect changes to the API resulting from modifications in raw materials, equipment operating parameters, or the production process.

11.23 Appropriate microbiological tests should be conducted on each batch of intermediate and API where microbial quality is specified.

11.3 Validation of Analytical Procedures - see Section 12.

11.4 Certificates of Analysis

11.40 Authentic Certificates of Analysis should be issued for each batch of intermediate or API on request.

11.41 Information on the name of the intermediate or API including where appropriate its grade, the batch number, and the date of release should be provided on the Certificate of Analysis. For intermediates or APIs with an expiry date, the expiry date should be provided on the label and Certificate of Analysis. For intermediates or APIs with a retest date, the retest date should be indicated on the label and/or Certificate of Analysis.

11.42 The Certificate should list each test performed in accordance with compendial or customer requirements, including the acceptance limits, and the numerical results obtained (if test results are numerical).

11.43 Certificates should be dated and signed by authorised personnel of the quality unit(s) and should show the name, address and telephone number of the original manufacturer. Where the analysis has been carried out by a repacker or reprocessor, the Certificate of Analysis should show the name, address and telephone number of the repacker/ reprocessor and a reference to the name of the original manufacturer.

11.44 If new Certificates are issued by or on behalf of repackers/ reprocessors, agents or brokers, these Certificates should show the name, address and telephone number of the laboratory that performed the analysis. They should also contain a reference to the name and address of the original manufacturer and to the original batch Certificate, a copy of which should be attached.

11.5 Stability Monitoring of APIs

11.50 A documented, on-going testing program should be designed to monitor the stability characteristics of APIs, and the results should be used to confirm appropriate storage conditions and retest or expiry dates.

11.51 The test procedures used in stability testing should be validated and be stability indicating.

11.52 Stability samples should be stored in containers that simulate the market container. For example, if the API is marketed in bags within fiber drums, stability samples can be packaged in bags of the same material and in smaller-scale drums of similar or identical material composition to the market drums.

11.53 Normally the first three commercial production batches should be placed on the stability monitoring program to confirm the retest or expiry date. However, where data from previous studies show that the API is expected to remain stable for at least two years, fewer than three batches can be used.

11.54 Thereafter, at least one batch per year of API manufactured (unless none is produced that year) should be added to the stability monitoring program and tested at least annually to confirm the stability.

11.55 For APIs with short shelf-lives, testing should be done more frequently. For example, for those biotechnological/biologic and other APIs with shelf-lives of one year or less, stability samples should be obtained and should be tested monthly for the first three months, and at three month intervals after that. When data exist that confirm that the stability of the API is not compromised, elimination of specific test intervals (e.g. 9 month testing) can be considered.

11.56 Where appropriate, the stability storage conditions should be consistent with the ICH guidelines on stability.

11.6 Expiry and Retest Dating

11.60 When an intermediate is intended to be transferred outside the control of the manufacturer's material management system and an expiry or retest date is assigned, supporting stability information should be available (e.g. published data, test results).

11.61 An API expiry or retest date should be based on an evaluation of data derived from stability studies. Common practice is to use a retest date, not an expiration date.

11.62 Preliminary API expiry or retest dates can be based on pilot scale batches if

(1) the pilot batches employ a method of manufacture and procedure that simulates the final process to be used on a commercial manufacturing scale; and

(2) the quality of the API represents the material to be made on a commercial scale.

11.63 A representative sample should be taken for the purpose of performing a retest.

11.7 Reserve/Retention Samples

11.70 The packaging and holding of reserve samples is for the purpose of potential future evaluation of the quality of batches of API and not for future stability testing purposes.

11.71 Appropriately identified reserve samples of each API batch should be retained for one year after the expiry date of the batch assigned by the manufacturer, or for three years after distribution of the batch, whichever is the longer. For APIs with retest dates, similar reserve samples should be retained for three years after the batch is completely distributed by the manufacturer.

11.72 The reserve sample should be stored in the same packaging system in which the API is stored or in one that is equivalent to or more protective than the marketed packaging system. Sufficient quantities should be retained to conduct at least two full compendial analyses or, when there is no pharmacopoeial monograph, two full specification analyses.

12. Validation

12.1 Validation Policy

12.10 The company's overall policy, intentions, and approach to validation, including the validation of production processes, cleaning procedures, analytical methods, in-process control test procedures, computerized systems, and persons responsible for design, review, approval and documentation of each validation phase, should be documented.

12.11 The critical parameters/attributes should normally be identified during the development stage or from historical data, and the ranges necessary for the reproducible operation should be defined. This should include:

— Defining the API in terms of its critical product attributes;

— Identifying process parameters that could affect the critical quality attributes of the API;

— Determining the range for each critical process parameter expected to be used during routine manufacturing and process control.

12.12 Validation should extend to those operations determined to be critical to the quality and purity of the API.

12.2 Validation Documentation

12.20 A written validation protocol should be established that specifies how validation of a particular process will be conducted. The protocol should be reviewed and approved by the quality unit(s) and other designated units.

12.21 The validation protocol should specify critical process steps and acceptance criteria as well as the type of validation to be conducted (e.g. retrospective, prospective, concurrent) and the number of process runs.

12.22 A validation report that cross-references the validation protocol should be prepared, summarising the results obtained, commenting on any deviations observed, and drawing the appropriate conclusions, including recommending changes to correct deficiencies.

12.23 Any variations from the validation protocol should be documented with appropriate justification.

12.3 Qualification

12.30 Before starting process validation activities, appropriate qualification of critical equipment and ancillary systems should be completed. Qualification is usually carried out by conducting the following activities, individually or combined:

— Design Qualification (DQ): documented verification that the proposed design of the facilities, equipment, or systems is suitable for the intended purpose.

— Installation Qualification (IQ): documented verification that the equipment or systems, as installed or modified, comply with the approved design, the manufacturer's recommendations and/or user requirements.

— Operational Qualification (OQ): documented verification that the equipment or systems, as installed or modified, perform as intended throughout the anticipated operating ranges.

— Performance Qualification (PQ): documented verification that the equipment and ancillary systems, as connected together, can perform effectively and reproducibly based on the approved process method and specifications.

12.4 Approaches to Process Validation

12.40 Process Validation (PV) is the documented evidence that the process, operated within established parameters, can perform effectively and reproducibly to produce an intermediate or API meeting its predetermined specifications and quality attributes.

12.41 There are three approaches to validation. Prospective validation is the preferred approach, but there are exceptions where the other approaches can be used. These approaches and their applicability are listed below.

12.42 Prospective validation should normally be performed for all API processes as defined in 12.12. Prospective validation performed on an API process should be completed before the commercial distribution of the final drug product manufactured from that API.

12.43 Concurrent validation can be conducted when data from replicate production runs are unavailable because only a limited number of API batches have been produced, API batches are produced infrequently, or API batches are produced by a validated process that has been modified. Prior to the completion of concurrent validation, batches can be released and used in final drug product for commercial distribution based on thorough monitoring and testing of the API batches.

12.44 An exception can be made for retrospective validation for well established processes that have been used without significant changes to API quality due to changes in raw materials, equipment, systems, facilities, or the production process. This validation approach may be used where:

(1) Critical quality attributes and critical process parameters have been identified;

(2) Appropriate in-process acceptance criteria and controls have been established;

(3) There have not been significant process/product failures attributable to causes other than operator error or equipment failures unrelated to equipment suitability; and

(4) Impurity profiles have been established for the existing API.

12.45 Batches selected for retrospective validation should be representative of all batches made during the review period, including any batches that failed to meet specifications, and should be sufficient in number to demonstrate process consistency. Retained samples can be tested to obtain data to retrospectively validate the process.

12.5 Process Validation Program

12.50 The number of process runs for validation should depend on the complexity of the process or the magnitude of the process change being considered. For prospective and concurrent validation, three consecutive successful production batches should be used as a guide, but there may be situations where additional process runs are warranted to prove consistency of the process (e.g., complex API processes or API processes with prolonged completion times). For retrospective validation, generally data from ten to thirty consecutive batches should be examined to assess process consistency, but fewer batches can be examined if justified.

12.51 Critical process parameters should be controlled and monitored during process validation studies. Process

parameters unrelated to quality, such as variables
controlled to minimize energy consumption or equipment
use, need not be included in the process validation.

12.52 Process validation should confirm that the impurity profile
for each API is within the limits specified. The impurity
profile should be comparable to or better than historical
data and, where applicable, the profile determined during
process development or for batches used for pivotal
clinical and toxicological studies.

12.6 Periodic Review of Validated Systems

12.60 Systems and processes should be periodically evaluated
to verify that they are still operating in a valid manner.
Where no significant changes have been made to the
system or process, and a quality review confirms that the
system or process is consistently producing material
meeting its specifications, there is normally no need for
revalidation.

12.7 Cleaning Validation

12.70 Cleaning procedures should normally be validated. In
general, cleaning validation should be directed to
situations or process steps where contamination or
carryover of materials poses the greatest risk to API
quality. For example, in early production it may be
unnecessary to validate equipment cleaning procedures
where residues are removed by subsequent purification
steps.

12.71 Validation of cleaning procedures should reflect actual
equipment usage patterns. If various APIs or
intermediates are manufactured in the same equipment
and the equipment is cleaned by the same process, a
representative intermediate or API can be selected for
cleaning validation. This selection should be based on
the solubility and difficulty of cleaning and the calculation
of residue limits based on potency, toxicity, and stability.

12.72 The cleaning validation protocol should describe the
equipment to be cleaned, procedures, materials,
acceptable cleaning levels, parameters to be monitored
and controlled, and analytical methods. The protocol
should also indicate the type of samples to be obtained
and how they are collected and labelled.

12.73 Sampling should include swabbing, rinsing, or alternative methods (e.g., direct extraction), as appropriate, to detect both insoluble and soluble residues. The sampling methods used should be capable of quantitatively measuring levels of residues remaining on the equipment surfaces after cleaning. Swab sampling may be impractical when product contact surfaces are not easily accessible due to equipment design and/or process limitations (e.g., inner surfaces of hoses, transfer pipes, reactor tanks with small ports or handling toxic materials, and small intricate equipment such as micronizers and microfluidizers).

12.74 Validated analytical methods having sensitivity to detect residues or contaminants should be used. The detection limit for each analytical method should be sufficiently sensitive to detect the established acceptable level of the residue or contaminant. The method's attainable recovery level should be established. Residue limits should be practical, achievable, verifiable and based on the most deleterious residue. Limits can be established based on the minimum known pharmacological, toxicological, or physiological activity of the API or its most deleterious component.

12.75 Equipment cleaning/sanitization studies should address microbiological and endotoxin contamination for those processes where there is a need to reduce total microbiological count or endotoxins in the API, or other processes where such contamination could be of concern (e.g., non-sterile APIs used to manufacture sterile products).

12.76 Cleaning procedures should be monitored at appropriate intervals after validation to ensure that these procedures are effective when used during routine production. Equipment cleanliness can be monitored by analytical testing and visual examination, where feasible. Visual inspection can allow detection of gross contamination concentrated in small areas that could otherwise go undetected by sampling and/or analysis.

12.8 Validation of Analytical Methods

12.80 Analytical methods should be validated unless the method employed is included in the relevant pharmacopoeia or other recognised standard reference.

The suitability of all testing methods used should nonetheless be verified under actual conditions of use and documented.

12.81 Methods should be validated to include consideration of characteristics included within the ICH guidelines on validation of analytical methods. The degree of analytical validation performed should reflect the purpose of the analysis and the stage of the API production process.

12.82 Appropriate qualification of analytical equipment should be considered before starting validation of analytical methods.

12.83 Complete records should be maintained of any modification of a validated analytical method. Such records should include the reason for the modification and appropriate data to verify that the modification produces results that are as accurate and reliable as the established method.

13. Change Control

13.10 A formal change control system should be established to evaluate all changes that may affect the production and control of the intermediate or API.

13.11 Written procedures should provide for the identification, documentation, appropriate review, and approval of changes in raw materials, specifications, analytical methods, facilities, support systems, equipment (including computer hardware), processing steps, labelling and packaging materials, and computer software.

13.12 Any proposals for GMP relevant changes should be drafted, reviewed, and approved by the appropriate organisational units, and reviewed and approved by the quality unit(s).

13.13 The potential impact of the proposed change on the quality of the intermediate or API should be evaluated. A classification procedure may help in determining the level of testing, validation, and documentation needed to justify changes to a validated process. Changes can be classified (e.g. as minor or major) depending on the nature and extent of the changes, and the effects these changes may impart on the process. Scientific judgement should determine what additional testing and validation studies are appropriate to justify a change in a validated process.

13.14 When implementing approved changes, measures should be taken to ensure that all documents affected by the changes are revised.

13.15 After the change has been implemented, there should be an evaluation of the first batches produced or tested under the change.

13.16 The potential for critical changes to affect established retest or expiry dates should be evaluated. If necessary, samples of the intermediate or API produced by the modified process can be placed on an accelerated stability program and/or can be added to the stability monitoring program.

13.17 Current dosage form manufacturers should be notified of changes from established production and process control procedures that can impact the quality of the API.

14. Rejection and Re-Use of Materials

14.1 Rejection

14.10 Intermediates and APIs failing to meet established specifications should be identified as such and quarantined. These intermediates or APIs can be reprocessed or reworked as described below. The final disposition of rejected materials should be recorded.

14.2 Reprocessing

14.20 Introducing an intermediate or API, including one that does not conform to standards or specifications, back into the process and reprocessing by repeating a crystallization step or other appropriate chemical or physical manipulation steps (e.g., distillation, filtration, chromatography, milling) that are part of the established manufacturing process is generally considered acceptable. However, if such reprocessing is used for a majority of batches, such reprocessing should be included as part of the standard manufacturing process.

14.21 Continuation of a process step after an in-process control test has shown that the step is incomplete is considered to be part of the normal process. This is not considered to be reprocessing.

14.22 Introducing unreacted material back into a process and repeating a chemical reaction is considered to be reprocessing unless it is part of the established process. Such reprocessing should be preceded by careful evaluation to ensure that the quality of the intermediate or API is not adversely impacted due to the potential formation of by-products and over-reacted materials.

14.3 Reworking

14.30 Before a decision is taken to rework batches that do not conform to established standards or specifications, an investigation into the reason for non-conformance should be performed.

14.31 Batches that have been reworked should be subjected to appropriate evaluation, testing, stability testing if warranted, and documentation to show that the reworked product is of equivalent quality to that produced by the original process. Concurrent validation is often the appropriate validation approach for rework procedures. This allows a protocol to define the rework procedure, how it will be carried out, and the expected results. If there is only one batch to be reworked, then a report can be written and the batch released once it is found to be acceptable.

14.32 Procedures should provide for comparing the impurity profile of each reworked batch against batches manufactured by the established process. Where routine analytical methods are inadequate to characterize the reworked batch, additional methods should be used.

14.4 Recovery of Materials and Solvents

14.40 Recovery (e.g. from mother liquor or filtrates) of reactants, intermediates, or the API is considered acceptable, provided that approved procedures exist for the recovery and the recovered materials meet specifications suitable for their intended use.

14.41 Solvents can be recovered and reused in the same processes or in different processes, provided that the recovery procedures are controlled and monitored to ensure that solvents meet appropriate standards before reuse or co-mingling with other approved materials.

14.42 Fresh and recovered solvents and reagents can be combined if adequate testing has shown their suitability for all manufacturing processes in which they may be used.

14.43 The use of recovered solvents, mother liquors, and other recovered materials should be adequately documented.

14.5 Returns

14.50 Returned intermediates or APIs should be identified as such and quarantined.

14.51 If the conditions under which returned intermediates or APIs have been stored or shipped before or during their return or the condition of their containers casts doubt on their quality, the returned intermediates or APIs should be reprocessed, reworked, or destroyed, as appropriate.

14.52 Records of returned intermediates or APIs should be maintained. For each return, documentation should include:

- — Name and address of the consignee
- — Intermediate or API, batch number, and quantity returned
- — Reason for return
- — Use or disposal of the returned intermediate or API

15. Complaints and Recalls

15.10 All quality related complaints, whether received orally or in writing, should be recorded and investigated according to a written procedure.

15.11 Complaint records should include:

- — Name and address of complainant;

- Name (and, where appropriate, title) and phone number of person submitting the complaint;

- Complaint nature (including name and batch number of the API);

- Date complaint is received;

- Action initially taken (including dates and identity of person taking the action);

- Any follow-up action taken;

- Response provided to the originator of complaint (including date response sent); and

- Final decision on intermediate or API batch or lot.

15.12 Records of complaints should be retained in order to evaluate trends, product-related frequencies, and severity with a view to taking additional, and if appropriate, immediate corrective action.

15.13 There should be a written procedure that defines the circumstances under which a recall of an intermediate or API should be considered.

15.14 The recall procedure should designate who should be involved in evaluating the information, how a recall should be initiated, who should be informed about the recall, and how the recalled material should be treated.

15.15 In the event of a serious or potentially life-threatening situation, local, national, and/or international authorities should be informed and their advice sought.

16. Contract Manufacturers (including Laboratories)

16.10 All contract manufacturers (including laboratories) should comply with the GMP defined in this Guide. Special consideration should be given to the prevention of cross-contamination and to maintaining traceability.

16.11 Contract manufacturers (including laboratories) should be evaluated by the contract giver to ensure GMP compliance of the specific operations occurring at the contract sites.

16.12 There should be a written and approved contract or formal agreement between the contract giver and the contract acceptor that defines in detail the GMP responsibilities, including the quality measures, of each party.

16.13 The contract should permit the contract giver to audit the contract acceptor's facilities for compliance with GMP.

16.14 Where subcontracting is allowed, the contract acceptor should not pass to a third party any of the work entrusted to him under the contract without the contract giver's prior evaluation and approval of the arrangements.

16.15 Manufacturing and laboratory records should be kept at the site where the activity occurs and be readily available.

16.16 Changes in the process, equipment, test methods, specifications, or other contractual requirements should not be made unless the contract giver is informed and approves the changes.

17. Agents, Brokers, Traders, Distributors, Repackers, and Relabellers

17.1 Applicability

17.10 This section applies to any party other than the original manufacturer who may trade and/or take possession, repack, relabel, manipulate, distribute or store an API or intermediate.

17.11 All agents, brokers, traders, distributors, repackers, and relabellers should comply with GMP as defined in this Guide.

17.2 Traceability of Distributed APIs and Intermediates

17.20 Agents, brokers, traders, distributors, repackers, or relabellers should maintain complete traceability of APIs and intermediates that they distribute. Documents that should be retained and available include:

— Identity of original manufacturer

— Address of original manufacturer

— Purchase orders

— Bills of lading (transportation documentation)

— Receipt documents

— Name or designation of API or intermediate

— Manufacturer's batch number

— Transportation and distribution records

— All authentic Certificates of Analysis, including those of the original manufacturer

— Retest or expiry date

17.3 Quality Management

17.30 Agents, brokers, traders, distributors, repackers, or relabellers should establish, document and implement an effective system of managing quality, as specified in Section 2.

17.4 Repackaging, Relabelling and Holding of APIs and Intermediates

17.40 Repackaging, relabelling and holding of APIs and intermediates should be performed under appropriate GMP controls, as stipulated in this Guide, to avoid mix-ups and loss of API or intermediate identity or purity.

17.41 Repackaging should be conducted under appropriate environmental conditions to avoid contamination and cross-contamination.

17.5 Stability

17.50 Stability studies to justify assigned expiration or retest dates should be conducted if the API or intermediate is repackaged in a different type of container than that used by the API or intermediate manufacturer.

17.6 Transfer of Information

17.60 Agents, brokers, distributors, repackers, or relabellers should transfer all quality or regulatory information received from an API or intermediate manufacturer to the customer, and from the customer to the API or intermediate manufacturer.

17.61 The agent, broker, trader, distributor, repacker, or relabeller who supplies the API or intermediate to the customer should provide the name of the original API or intermediate   manufacturer and the batch number(s) supplied.

17.62 The agent should also provide the identity of the original API or intermediate manufacturer to regulatory authorities upon request. The original manufacturer can respond to the regulatory authority directly or through its authorized agents, depending on the legal relationship between the authorized agents and the original API or intermediate manufacturer. (In this context "authorized" refers to authorized by the manufacturer.)

17.63 The specific guidance for Certificates of Analysis included in Section 11.4 should be met.

17.7 Handling of Complaints and Recalls

17.70 Agents, brokers, traders, distributors, repackers, or relabellers should maintain records of complaints and recalls, as specified in Section 15, for all complaints and recalls that come to their attention.

17.71 If the situation warrants, the agents, brokers, traders, distributors, repackers, or relabellers should review the complaint with the original API or intermediate manufacturer in order to determine whether any further action, either with other customers who may have received this API or intermediate or with the regulatory authority, or both, should be initiated. The investigation into the cause for the complaint or recall should be conducted and documented by the appropriate party.

17.72 Where a complaint is referred to the original API or intermediate manufacturer, the record maintained by the agents, brokers, traders, distributors, repackers, or relabellers should include any response received from the original API or intermediate manufacturer (including date and information provided).

17.8 Handling of Returns

17.80 Returns should be handled as specified in Section 14.52. The agents, brokers, traders, distributors, repackers, or relabellers should maintain documentation of returned APIs and intermediates.

18. Specific Guidance for APIs Manufactured by Cell Culture/Fermentation

18.1 General

18.10 Section 18 is intended to address specific controls for APIs or intermediates manufactured by cell culture or fermentation using natural or recombinant organisms and that have not been covered adequately in the previous sections. It is not intended to be a stand-alone Section. In general, the GMP principles in the other sections of this document apply. Note that the principles of fermentation for "classical" processes for production of small molecules and for processes using recombinant and nonrecombinant organisms for production of proteins and/or polypeptides are the same, although the degree of control will differ. Where practical, this section will address these differences. In general, the degree of control for biotechnological processes used to produce proteins and polypeptides is greater than that for classical fermentation processes.

18.11 The term "biotechnological process" (biotech) refers to the use of cells or organisms that have been generated or modified by recombinant DNA, hybridoma or other technology to produce APIs. The APIs produced by biotechnological processes normally consist of high molecular weight substances, such as proteins and polypeptides, for which specific guidance is given in this Section. Certain APIs of low molecular weight, such as antibiotics, amino acids, vitamins, and carbohydrates, can also be produced by recombinant DNA technology. The level of control for these types of APIs is similar to that employed for classical fermentation.

18.12 The term "classical fermentation" refers to processes that use microorganisms existing in nature and/or modified by conventional methods (e.g. irradiation or chemical mutagenesis) to produce APIs. APIs produced by "classical fermentation" are normally low molecular weight products such as antibiotics, amino acids, vitamins, and carbohydrates.

18.13 Production of APIs or intermediates from cell culture or fermentation involves biological processes such as cultivation of cells or extraction and purification of material from living organisms. Note that there may be additional process steps, such as physicochemical modification, that are part of the manufacturing process. The raw materials used (media, buffer components) may provide the potential for growth of microbiological contaminants. Depending on the source, method of preparation, and the intended use of the API or intermediate, control of bioburden, viral contamination, and/or endotoxins during manufacturing and monitoring of the process at appropriate stages may be necessary.

18.14 Appropriate controls should be established at all stages of manufacturing to assure intermediate and/or API quality. While this Guide starts at the cell culture/fermentation step, prior steps (e.g. cell banking) should be performed under appropriate process controls. This Guide covers cell culture/fermentation from the point at which a vial of the cell bank is retrieved for use in manufacturing.

18.15 Appropriate equipment and environmental controls should be used to minimize the risk of contamination. The acceptance criteria for quality of the environment and the frequency of monitoring should depend on the step in production and the production conditions (open, closed, or contained systems).

18.16 In general, process controls should take into account:

— Maintenance of the Working Cell Bank (where appropriate);

— Proper inoculation and expansion of the culture;

— Control of the critical operating parameters during fermentation/cell culture;

— Monitoring of the process for cell growth, viability (for most cell culture processes) and productivity where appropriate;

— Harvest and purification procedures that remove cells, cellular debris and media components while

> protecting the intermediate or API from contamination (particularly of a microbiological nature) and from loss of quality;

— Monitoring of bioburden and, where needed, endotoxin levels at appropriate stages of production; and

— Viral safety concerns as described in ICH Guideline Q5A Quality of Biotechnological Products: Viral Safety Evaluation of Biotechnology Products Derived from Cell Lines of Human or Animal Origin.

18.17 Where appropriate, the removal of media components, host cell proteins, other process-related impurities, product-related impurities and contaminants should be demonstrated.

18.2 Cell Bank Maintenance and Record Keeping

18.20 Access to cell banks should be limited to authorized personnel.

18.21 Cell banks should be maintained under storage conditions designed to maintain viability and prevent contamination.

18.22 Records of the use of the vials from the cell banks and storage conditions should be maintained.

18.23 Where appropriate, cell banks should be periodically monitored to determine suitability for use.

18.24 See ICH Guideline Q5D Quality of Biotechnological Products: Derivation and Characterization of Cell Substrates Used for Production of Biotechnological/Biological Products for a more complete discussion of cell banking.

18.3 Cell Culture/Fermentation

18.30 Where aseptic addition of cell substrates, media, buffers, and gases is needed, closed or contained systems should be used where possible. If the inoculation of the initial vessel or subsequent transfers or additions (media, buffers) are performed in open vessels, there should be controls and procedures in place to minimize the risk of contamination.

18.31 Where the quality of the API can be affected by microbial contamination, manipulations using open vessels should be performed in a biosafety cabinet or similarly controlled environment.

18.32 Personnel should be appropriately gowned and take special precautions handling the cultures.

18.33 Critical operating parameters (for example temperature, pH, agitation rates, addition of gases, pressure) should be monitored to ensure consistency with the established process. Cell growth, viability (for most cell culture processes), and, where appropriate, productivity should also be monitored. Critical parameters will vary from one process to another, and for classical fermentation, certain parameters (cell viability, for example) may not need to be monitored.

18.34 Cell culture equipment should be cleaned and sterilized after use. As appropriate, fermentation equipment should be cleaned, and sanitized or sterilized.

18.35 Culture media should be sterilized before use when appropriate to protect the quality of the API.

18.36 There should be appropriate procedures in place to detect contamination and determine the course of action to be taken. This should include procedures to determine the impact of the contamination on the product and those to decontaminate the equipment and return it to a condition to be used in subsequent batches. Foreign organisms observed during fermentation processes should be identified as appropriate and the effect of their presence on product quality should be assessed, if necessary. The results of such assessments should be taken into consideration in the disposition of the material produced.

18.37 Records of contamination events should be maintained.

18.38 Shared (multi-product) equipment may warrant additional testing after cleaning between product campaigns, as appropriate, to minimize the risk of cross-contamination.

18.4 Harvesting, Isolation and Purification

18.40 Harvesting steps, either to remove cells or cellular components or to collect cellular components after disruption, should be performed in equipment and areas designed to minimize the risk of contamination.

18.41 Harvest and purification procedures that remove or inactivate the producing organism, cellular debris and media components (while minimizing degradation, contamination, and loss of quality) should be adequate to ensure that the intermediate or API is recovered with consistent quality.

18.42 All equipment should be properly cleaned and, as appropriate, sanitized after use. Multiple successive batching without cleaning can be used if intermediate or API quality is not compromised.

18.43 If open systems are used, purification should be performed under environmental conditions appropriate for the preservation of product quality.

18. 44   Additional controls, such as the use of dedicated chromatography resins or additional testing, may be appropriate if equipment is to be used for multiple products.

18.5 Viral Removal/Inactivation steps

18.50 See the ICH Guideline Q5A Quality of Biotechnological Products: Viral Safety Evaluation of Biotechnology Products Derived from Cell Lines of Human or Animal Origin for more specific information.

18.51 Viral removal and viral inactivation steps are critical processing steps for some processes and should be performed within their validated parameters.

18.52 Appropriate precautions should be taken to prevent potential viral contamination from pre-viral to post-viral removal/inactivation steps. Therefore, open processing should be performed in areas that are separate from other processing activities and have separate air handling units.

18.53 The same equipment is not normally used for different purification steps. However, if the same equipment is to be used, the equipment should be appropriately cleaned and sanitized before reuse. Appropriate precautions should be taken to prevent potential virus carry-over (e.g. through equipment or environment) from previous steps.

19. APIs for Use in Clinical Trials

19.1 General

19.10 Not all the controls in the previous sections of this Guide are appropriate for the manufacture of a new API for investigational use during its development. Section 19 provides specific guidance unique to these circumstances.

19.11 The controls used in the manufacture of APIs for use in clinical trials should be consistent with the stage of development of the drug product incorporating the API. Process and test procedures should be flexible to provide for changes as knowledge of the process increases and clinical testing of a drug product progresses from pre-clinical stages through clinical stages. Once drug development reaches the stage where the API is produced for use in drug products intended for clinical trials, manufacturers should ensure that APIs are manufactured in suitable facilities using appropriate production and control procedures to ensure the quality of the API.

19.2 Quality

19.20 Appropriate GMP concepts should be applied in the production of APIs for use in clinical trials with a suitable mechanism of approval of each batch.

19.21 A quality unit(s) independent from production should be established for the approval or rejection of each batch of API for use in clinical trials.

19.22 Some of the testing functions commonly performed by the quality unit(s) can be performed within other organizational units.

19.23 Quality measures should include a system for testing of raw materials, packaging materials, intermediates, and APIs.

19.24 Process and quality problems should be evaluated.

19.25 Labelling for APIs intended for use in clinical trials should be appropriately controlled and should identify the material as being for investigational use.

19.3 Equipment and Facilities

19.30 During all phases of clinical development, including the use of small-scale facilities or laboratories to manufacture batches of APIs for use in clinical trials, procedures should be in place to ensure that equipment is calibrated, clean and suitable for its intended use.

19.31 Procedures for the use of facilities should ensure that materials are handled in a manner that minimizes the risk of contamination and cross-contamination.

19.4 Control of Raw Materials

19.40 Raw materials used in production of APIs for use in clinical trials should be evaluated by testing, or received with a supplier's analysis and subjected to identity testing. When a material is considered hazardous, a supplier's analysis should suffice.

19.41 In some instances, the suitability of a raw material can be determined before use based on acceptability in small-scale reactions (i.e., use testing) rather than on analytical testing alone.

19.5 Production

19.50 The production of APIs for use in clinical trials should be documented in laboratory notebooks, batch records, or by other appropriate means. These documents should include information on the use of production materials, equipment, processing, and scientific observations.

19.51 Expected yields can be more variable and less defined than the expected yields used in commercial processes. Investigations into yield variations are not expected.

19.6 Validation

19.60 Process validation for the production of APIs for use in clinical trials is normally inappropriate, where a single API batch is produced or where process changes during API development make batch replication difficult or inexact. The combination of controls, calibration, and, where appropriate, equipment qualification assures API quality during this development phase.

19.61 Process validation should be conducted in accordance with Section 12 when batches are produced for commercial use, even when such batches are produced on a pilot or small scale.

19.7 Changes

19.70 Changes are expected during development, as knowledge is gained and the production is scaled up. Every change in the production, specifications, or test procedures should be adequately recorded.

19.8 Laboratory Controls

19.80 While analytical methods performed to evaluate a batch of API for clinical trials may not yet be validated, they should be scientifically sound.

19.81 A system for retaining reserve samples of all batches should be in place. This system should ensure that a sufficient quantity of each reserve sample is retained for an appropriate length of time after approval, termination, or discontinuation of an application.

19.82 Expiry and retest dating as defined in Section 11.6 applies to existing APIs used in clinical trials. For new APIs, Section 11.6 does not normally apply in early stages of clinical trials.

19.9 Documentation

19.90 A system should be in place to ensure that information gained during the development and the manufacture of APIs for use in clinical trials is documented and available.

19.91 The development and implementation of the analytical methods used to support the release of a batch of API for use in clinical trials should be appropriately documented.

19.92 A system for retaining production and control records and documents should be used. This system should ensure that records and documents are retained for an appropriate length of time after the approval, termination, or discontinuation of an application.

20. *Glossary*

Acceptance Criteria

Numerical limits, ranges, or other suitable measures for acceptance of test results.

Active Pharmaceutical Ingredient (API) (or Drug Substance)

Any substance or mixture of substances intended to be used in the manufacture of a drug (medicinal) product and that, when used in the production of a drug, becomes an active ingredient of the drug product. Such substances are intended to furnish pharmacological activity or other direct effect in the diagnosis, cure, mitigation, treatment, or prevention of disease or to affect the structure and function of the body.

API Starting Material

A raw material, intermediate, or an API that is used in the production of an API and that is incorporated as a significant structural fragment into the structure of the API. An API Starting Material can be an article of commerce, a material purchased from one or more suppliers under contract or commercial agreement, or produced in-house. API Starting Materials are normally of defined chemical properties and structure.

Batch (or Lot)

A specific quantity of material produced in a process or series of processes so that it is expected to be homogeneous within specified limits. In the case of continuous production, a batch may correspond to a defined fraction of the production. The batch size can be defined either by a fixed quantity or by the amount produced in a fixed time interval.

Batch Number (or Lot Number)

A unique combination of numbers, letters, and/or symbols that identifies a batch (or lot) and from which the production and distribution history can be determined.

Bioburden

The level and type (e.g. objectionable or not) of micro-organisms that can be present in raw materials, API starting materials, intermediates or APIs. Bioburden should not be considered contamination unless the levels have been exceeded or defined objectionable organisms have been detected.

Calibration

The demonstration that a particular instrument or device produces results within specified limits by comparison with those produced by a reference or traceable standard over an appropriate range of measurements.

Computer System

A group of hardware components and associated software, designed and assembled to perform a specific function or group of functions.

Computerized System

A process or operation integrated with a computer system.

Contamination

The undesired introduction of impurities of a chemical or microbiological nature, or of foreign matter, into or onto a raw material, intermediate, or API during production, sampling, packaging or repackaging, storage or transport.

Contract Manufacturer

A manufacturer performing some aspect of manufacturing on behalf of the original manufacturer.

Critical

> Describes a process step, process condition, test
> requirement, or other relevant parameter or item that
> must be controlled within predetermined criteria to ensure
> that the API meets its specification.

Cross-Contamination

> Contamination of a material or product with another
> material or product.

Deviation

> Departure from an approved instruction or established
> standard.

Drug (Medicinal) Product

> The dosage form in the final immediate packaging
> intended for marketing. (Reference Q1A)

Drug Substance

> See *Active Pharmaceutical Ingredient*

Expiry Date (or Expiration Date)

> The date placed on the container/labels of an API
> designating the time during which the API is expected to
> remain within established shelf life specifications if stored
> under defined conditions, and after which it should not be
> used.

Impurity

> Any component present in the intermediate or API that is
> not the desired entity.

Impurity Profile

> A description of the identified and unidentified impurities
> present in an API.

In-Process Control (or Process Control)

Checks performed during production in order to monitor and, if appropriate, to adjust the process and/or to ensure that the intermediate or API conforms to its specifications.

Intermediate

A material produced during steps of the processing of an API that undergoes further molecular change or purification before it becomes an API. Intermediates may or may not be isolated. (Note: this Guide only addresses those intermediates produced after the point that the company has defined as the point at which the production of the API begins.)

Lot

See *Batch*

Lot Number

see *Batch Number*

Manufacture

All operations of receipt of materials, production, packaging, repackaging, labelling, relabelling, quality control, release, storage, and distribution of APIs and related controls.

Material

A general term used to denote raw materials (starting materials, reagents, solvents), process aids, intermediates, APIs and packaging and labelling materials.

Mother Liquor

The residual liquid which remains after the crystallization or isolation processes. A mother liquor may contain unreacted materials, intermediates, levels of the API and/or impurities. It may be used for further processing.

Packaging Material

Any material intended to protect an intermediate or API during storage and transport.

Procedure

A documented description of the operations to be performed, the precautions to be taken and measures to be applied directly or indirectly related to the manufacture of an intermediate or API.

Process Aids

Materials, excluding solvents, used as an aid in the manufacture of an intermediate or API that do not themselves participate in a chemical or biological reaction (e.g. filter aid, activated carbon, etc).

Process Control

See *In-Process Control*

Production

All operations involved in the preparation of an API from receipt of materials through processing and packaging of the API.

Qualification

Action of proving and documenting that equipment or ancillary systems are properly installed, work correctly, and actually lead to the expected results. Qualification is part of validation, but the individual qualification steps alone do not constitute process validation.

Quality Assurance (QA)

The sum total of the organised arrangements made with the object of ensuring that all APIs are of the quality required for their intended use and that quality systems are maintained.

Quality Control (QC)

Checking or testing that specifications are met.

Quality Unit(s)

An organizational unit independent of production which fulfills both Quality Assurance and Quality Control responsibilities. This can be in the form of separate QA and QC units or a single individual or group, depending upon the size and structure of the organization.

Quarantine

The status of materials isolated physically or by other effective means pending a decision on their subsequent approval or rejection.

Raw Material

A general term used to denote starting materials, reagents, and solvents intended for use in the production of intermediates or APIs.

Reference Standard, Primary

A substance that has been shown by an extensive set of analytical tests to be authentic material that should be of high purity. This standard can be:

(1)   obtained from an officially recognised source, or

(2)   prepared by independent synthesis, or

(3)   obtained from existing production material of high purity, or

(4)   prepared by further purification of existing production material.

Reference Standard, Secondary

A substance of established quality and purity, as shown by comparison to a primary reference standard, used as a reference standard for routine laboratory analysis.

Reprocessing

> Introducing an intermediate or API, including one that
> does not conform to standards or specifications, back
> into the process and repeating a crystallization step or
> other appropriate chemical or physical manipulation
> steps (e.g., distillation, filtration, chromatography, milling)
> that are part of the established manufacturing process.
> Continuation of a process step after an in-process control
> test has shown that the step is incomplete is considered
> to be part of the normal process, and not reprocessing.

Retest Date

> The date when a material should be re-examined to
> ensure that it is still suitable for use.

Reworking

> Subjecting an intermediate or API that does not conform
> to standards or specifications to one or more processing
> steps that are different from the established
> manufacturing process to obtain acceptable quality
> intermediate or API (e.g., recrystallizing with a different
> solvent).

Signature (signed)

> See definition for *signed*

Signed (signature)

> The record of the individual who performed a particular
> action or review. This record can be initials, full
> handwritten signature, personal seal, or authenticated
> and secure electronic signature.

Solvent

> An inorganic or organic liquid used as a vehicle for the
> preparation of solutions or suspensions in the
> manufacture of an intermediate or API.

Specification

A list of tests, references to analytical procedures, and appropriate acceptance criteria that are numerical limits, ranges, or other criteria for the test described. It establishes the set of criteria to which a material should conform to be considered acceptable for its intended use. "Conformance to specification" means that the material, when tested according to the listed analytical procedures, will meet the listed acceptance criteria.

Validation

A documented program that provides a high degree of assurance that a specific process, method, or system will consistently produce a result meeting pre-determined acceptance criteria.

Validation Protocol

A written plan stating how validation will be conducted and defining acceptance criteria. For example, the protocol for a manufacturing process identifies processing equipment, critical process parameters/operating ranges, product characteristics, sampling, test data to be collected, number of validation runs, and acceptable test results.

Yield, Expected

The quantity of material or the percentage of theoretical yield anticipated at any appropriate phase of production based on previous laboratory, pilot scale, or manufacturing data.

Yield, Theoretical

The quantity that would be produced at any appropriate phase of production, based upon the quantity of material to be used, in the absence of any loss or error in actual production.

Annexes

Annex 1: Manufacture of Sterile Medicinal Products (corrected version)

Brussels, 25 November 2008 (rev.)

Document History	
Previous version dated 30 May 2003, in operation since	September 2003
Revision to align classification table of clean rooms, to include guidance on media simultations, bioburden monitoring and capping of vials	November 2005 to December 2007
Date for coming into operation and superseding	01 March 2009[18]

Please note correction on the implementation of provisions for capping of vials!

Principle

The manufacture of sterile products is subject to special requirements in order to minimize risks of microbiological contamination, and of particulate and pyrogen contamination. Much depends on the skill, training and attitudes of the personnel involved. Quality Assurance is particularly important, and this type of manufacture must strictly follow carefully established and validated methods of preparation and procedure. Sole reliance for sterility or other quality aspects

---

[18] Note: Provisions on capping of vials should be implemented by 01 March 2010.

must not be placed on any terminal process or finished product test.

Note: *This guidance does not lay down detailed methods for determining the microbiological and particulate cleanliness of air, surfaces etc. Reference should be made to other documents such as the EN/ISO Standards.*

General

1. The manufacture of sterile products should be carried out in clean areas entry to which should be through airlocks for personnel and/or for equipment and materials. Clean areas should be maintained to an appropriate cleanliness standard and supplied with air which has passed through filters of an appropriate efficiency.

2. The various operations of component preparation, product preparation and filling should be carried out in separate areas within the clean area. Manufacturing operations are divided into two categories; firstly those where the product is terminally sterilised, and secondly those which are conducted aseptically at some or all stages.

3. Clean areas for the manufacture of sterile products are classified according to the required characteristics of the environment. Each manufacturing operation requires an appropriate environmental cleanliness level in the operational state in order to minimise the risks of particulate or microbial contamination of the product or materials being handled.

In order to meet "in operation" conditions these areas should be designed to reach certain specified air-cleanliness levels in the "at rest" occupancy state. The "at-rest" state is the condition where the installation is installed and operating, complete with production equipment but with no operating personnel present. The "in operation" state is the condition where the installation is functioning in the defined operating mode with the specified number of personnel working.

The "in operation" and "at rest" states should be defined for each clean room or suite of clean rooms.

For the manufacture of sterile medicinal products 4 grades can be distinguished.

Grade A:

> The local zone for high risk operations, e.g. filling zone, stopper bowls, open ampoules and vials, making aseptic connections. Normally such conditions are provided by a laminar air flow work station. Laminar air flow systems should provide a homogeneous air speed in a range of 0.36 – 0.54 m/s (guidance value) at the working position in open clean room applications. The maintenance of laminarity should be demonstrated and validated.
>
> A uni-directional air flow and lower velocities may be used in closed isolators and glove boxes.

Grade B:

> For aseptic preparation and filling, this is the background environment for the grade A zone.

Grade C and D:

> Clean areas for carrying out less critical stages in the manufacture of sterile products.
>
> Clean room and clean air device classification

4.   Clean rooms and clean air devices should be classified in accordance with EN ISO 14644-1.   Classification should be clearly differentiated from operational process environmental monitoring. The maximum permitted airborne particle concentration for each grade is given in the following table.

	Maximum permitted number of particles per m3 equal to or greater than the tabulated size			
	At rest		In operation	
Grade	0.5 µm	5.0µm	0.5 µm	5.0µm
A	3 520	20	3 520	20
B	3 520	29	352 000	2 900
C	352 000	2 900	3 520 000	29 000
D	3 520 000	29 000	Not defined	Not defined

1. For classification purposes in Grade A zones, a minimum sample volume of 1m should be taken per sample location. For Grade A the airborne particle classification is ISO 4.8 dictated by the limit for particles ≥5.0 μm. For Grade B (at rest) the airborne particle classification is ISO 5 for both considered particle sizes. . For Grade C (at rest & in operation) the airborne particle classification is ISO 7 and ISO 8 respectively. For Grade D (at rest) the airborne particle classification is ISO 8. For classification purposes EN/ISO 14644-1 methodology defines both the minimum number of sample locations and the sample size based on the class limit of the largest considered particle size and the method of evaluation of the data collected.

2. Portable particle counters with a short length of sample tubing should be used for classification purposes because of the relatively higher rate of precipitation of particles ≥5.0μm in remote sampling systems with long lengths of tubing. Isokinetic sample heads shall be used in unidirectional airflow systems.

3. "In operation" classification may be demonstrated during normal operations, simulated operations or during media fills as worst-case simulation is required for this. EN ISO 14644-2 provides information on testing to demonstrate continued compliance with the assigned cleanliness classifications.

Clean room and clean air device monitoring

1. Clean rooms and clean air devices should be routinely monitored in operation and the monitoring locations based on a formal risk analysis study and the results obtained during the classification of rooms and/or clean air devices.

2. For Grade A zones, particle monitoring should be undertaken for the full duration of critical processing, including equipment assembly, except where justified by contaminants in the process that would damage the particle counter or present a hazard, e.g. live organisms and radiological hazards. In such cases monitoring during routine equipment set up operations should be undertaken prior to exposure to the risk. Monitoring

during simulated operations should also be performed. The Grade A zone should be monitored at such a frequency and with suitable sample size that all interventions, transient events and any system deterioration would be captured and alarms triggered if alert limits are exceeded. It is accepted that it may not always be possible to demonstrate low levels of ≥5.0 μm particles at the point of fill when filling is in progress, due to the generation of particles or droplets from the product itself.

10. It is recommended that a similar system be used for Grade B zones although the sample frequency may be decreased. The importance of the particle monitoring system should be determined by the effectiveness of the segregation between the adjacent Grade A and B zones. The Grade B zone should be monitored at such a frequency and with suitable sample size that changes in levels of contamination and any system deterioration would be captured and alarms triggered if alert limits are exceeded.

11. Airborne particle monitoring systems may consist of independent particle counters; a network of sequentially accessed sampling points connected by manifold to a single particle counter; or a combination of the two. The system selected must be appropriate for the particle size considered. Where remote sampling systems are used, the length of tubing and the radii of any bends in the tubing must be considered in the context of particle losses in the tubing. The selection of the monitoring system should take account of any risk presented by the materials used in the manufacturing operation, for example those involving live organisms or radiopharmaceuticals.

12. The sample sizes taken for monitoring purposes using automated systems will usually be a function of the sampling rate of the system used. It is not necessary for the sample volume to be the same as that used for formal classification of clean rooms and clean air devices.

13. In Grade A and B zones, the monitoring of the ≥5.0 μm particle concentration count takes on a particular significance as it is an important diagnostic tool for early detection of failure. The occasional indication of ≥5.0 μm

particle counts may be false counts due to electronic noise, stray light, coincidence, etc. However consecutive or regular counting of low levels is an indicator of a possible contamination event and should be investigated. Such events may indicate early failure of the HVAC system, filling equipment failure or may also be diagnostic of poor practices during machine set-up and routine operation.

14. The particle limits given in the table for the "at rest" state should be achieved after a short "clean up" period of 15-20 minutes (guidance value) in an unmanned state after completion of operations.

15. The monitoring of Grade C and D areas in operation should be performed in accordance with the principles of quality risk management. The requirements and alert/action limits will depend on the nature of the operations carried out, but the recommended "clean up period" should be attained.

16. Other characteristics such as temperature and relative humidity depend on the product and nature of the operations carried out. These parameters should not interfere with the defined cleanliness standard.

17. Examples of operations to be carried out in the various grades are given in the table below (see also paragraphs 28 to 35):

Grade	Examples of operations for terminally sterilised products. (see paragraphs 28 – 30)
A	Filling of products, when unusually at risk
C	Preparation of solutions, when unusually at risk. Filling of products
D	Preparation of solutions and components for subsequent filling

Grade	Examples of operations for aseptic preparations. (see paragraphs 31 – 35)
A	Aseptic preparation and filling.
C	Preparation of solutions to be filtered.
D	Handling of components after washing.

18. Where aseptic operations are performed monitoring should be frequent using methods such as settle plates, volumetric air and surface sampling (e.g. swabs and contact plates). Sampling methods used in operation should not interfere with zone protection. Results from monitoring should be considered when reviewing batch documentation for finished product release. Surfaces and personnel should be monitored after critical operations. Additional microbiological monitoring is also required outside production operations, e.g. after validation of systems, cleaning and sanitisation.

19. Recommended limits for microbiological monitoring of clean areas during operation:

Grade	Recommended limits for microbial contamination (a)			
	air sample cfu/m3	settle plates (diameter 90 mm) cfu/4 hours (b)	contact plates (diameter 55 mm) cfu/plate	glove print 5 fingers cfu/glove
A	< 1	< 1	< 1	< 1
B	10	5	5	5
C	100	50	25	-
D	200	100	50	-

Notes: (a) These are average values.

(b) Individual settle plates may be exposed for less than 4 hours.

20. Appropriate alert and action limits should be set for the results of particulate and microbiological monitoring. If

these limits are exceeded operating procedures should
prescribe corrective action.

Isolator technology

21.   The utilisation of isolator technology to minimize human
        interventions in processing areas may result in a
        significant decrease in the risk of microbiological
        contamination of aseptically manufactured products from
        the environment. There are many possible designs of
        isolators and transfer devices. The isolator and the
        background environment should be designed so that the
        required air quality for the respective zones can be
        realised. Isolators are constructed of various materials
        more or less prone to puncture and leakage. Transfer
        devices may vary from a single door to double door
        designs to fully sealed systems incorporating sterilisation
        mechanisms.

22.   The transfer of materials into and out of the unit is one of
        the greatest potential sources of contamination. In
        general the area inside the isolator is the local zone for
        high risk manipulations, although it is recognised that
        laminar air flow may not exist in the working zone of all
        such devices.

23.   The air classification required for the background
        environment depends on the design of the isolator and its
        application. It should be controlled and for aseptic
        processing it should be at least grade D.

24.   Isolators should be introduced only after appropriate
        validation. Validation should take into account all critical
        factors of isolator technology, for example the quality of
        the air inside and outside (background) the isolator,
        sanitisation of the isolator, the transfer process and
        isolator integrity.

25.   Monitoring should be carried out routinely and should
        include frequent leak testing of the isolator and
        glove/sleeve system.

Blow/fill/seal technology

26.   Blow/fill/seal units are purpose built machines in which, in
        one continuous operation, containers are formed from a
        thermoplastic granulate, filled and then sealed, all by the

one automatic machine. Blow/fill/seal equipment used for aseptic production which is fitted with an effective grade A air shower may be installed in at least a grade C environment, provided that grade A/B clothing is used. The environment should comply with the viable and non viable limits at rest and the viable limit only when in operation. Blow/fill/seal equipment used for the production of products which are terminally sterilised should be installed in at least a grade D environment.

27.   Because of this special technology particular attention should be paid to, at least the following:

- equipment design and qualification

- validation and reproducibility of cleaning-in-place and sterilisation-in-place

- background clean room environment in which the equipment is located

- operator training and clothing

- interventions in the critical zone of the equipment including any aseptic assembly prior to the commencement of filling.

Terminally sterilised products

1.   Preparation of components and most products should be done in at least a grade D environment in order to give low risk of microbial and particulate contamination, suitable for filtration and sterilisation. Where the product is at a high or unusual risk of microbial contamination, (for example, because the product actively supports microbial growth or must be held for a long period before sterilisation or is necessarily processed not mainly in closed vessels), then preparation should be carried out in a grade C environment.

2.   Filling of products for terminal sterilisation should be carried out in at least a grade C environment.

3.   Where the product is at unusual risk of contamination from the environment, for example because the filling operation is slow or the containers are wide-necked or are necessarily exposed for more than a few seconds before sealing, the filling should be done in a grade A zone with at least a grade C background. Preparation

and filling of ointments, creams, suspensions and emulsions should generally be carried out in a grade C environment before terminal sterilisation.

Aseptic preparation

1. Components after washing should be handled in at least a grade D environment. Handling of sterile starting materials and components, unless subjected to sterilisation or filtration through a micro-organism-retaining filter later in the process, should be done in a grade A environment with grade B background.

2. Preparation of solutions which are to be sterile filtered during the process should be done in a grade C environment; if not filtered, the preparation of materials and products should be done in a grade A environment with a grade B background.

3. Handling and filling of aseptically prepared products should be done in a grade A environment with a grade B background.

4. Prior to the completion of stoppering, transfer of partially closed containers, as used in freeze drying should be done either in a grade A environment with grade B background or in sealed transfer trays in a grade B environment.

5. Preparation and filling of sterile ointments, creams, suspensions and emulsions should be done in a grade A environment, with a grade B background, when the product is exposed and is not subsequently filtered.

Personnel

36. Only the minimum number of personnel required should be present in clean areas; this is particularly important during aseptic processing. Inspections and controls should be conducted outside the clean areas as far as possible.

37. All personnel (including those concerned with cleaning and maintenance) employed in such areas should receive regular training in disciplines relevant to the correct manufacture of sterile products. This training should include reference to hygiene and to the basic

elements of microbiology. When outside staff who have not received such training (e.g. building or maintenance contractors) need to be brought in, particular care should be taken over their instruction and supervision.

38. Staff who have been engaged in the processing of animal tissue materials or of cultures of micro-organisms other than those used in the current manufacturing process should not enter sterile-product areas unless rigorous and clearly defined entry procedures have been followed.

39. High standards of personal hygiene and cleanliness are essential. Personnel involved in the manufacture of sterile preparations should be instructed to report any condition which may cause the shedding of abnormal numbers or types of contaminants; periodic health checks for such conditions are desirable. Actions to be taken about personnel who could be introducing undue microbiological hazard should be decided by a designated competent person.

40. Wristwatches, make-up and jewellery should not be worn in clean areas.

41. Changing and washing should follow a written procedure designed to minimize contamination of clean area clothing or carry-through of contaminants to the clean areas.

42. The clothing and its quality should be appropriate for the process and the grade of the working area. It should be worn in such a way as to protect the product from contamination.

43. The description of clothing required for each grade is given below:

- *Grade D:* Hair and, where relevant, beard should be covered. A general protective suit and appropriate shoes or overshoes should be worn. Appropriate measures should be taken to avoid any contamination coming from outside the clean area.

- *Grade C:* Hair and where relevant beard and moustache should be covered. A single or two-piece trouser suit, gathered at the wrists and with high neck and appropriate shoes or overshoes should be worn. They should shed virtually no fibres or particulate matter.

- *Grade A/B:* Headgear should totally enclose hair and, where relevant, beard and moustache; it should be tucked into the neck of the suit; a face mask should be worn to prevent the shedding of droplets. Appropriate sterilised, non-powdered rubber or plastic gloves and sterilised or disinfected footwear should be worn. Trouser-legs should be tucked inside the footwear and garment sleeves into the gloves. The protective clothing should shed virtually no fibres or particulate matter and retain particles shed by the body.

44. Outdoor clothing should not be brought into changing rooms leading to grade B and C rooms. For every worker in a grade A/B area, clean sterile (sterilised or adequately sanitised) protective garments should be provided at each work session. Gloves should be regularly disinfected during operations. Masks and gloves should be changed at least for every working session.

45. Clean area clothing should be cleaned and handled in such a way that it does not gather additional contaminants which can later be shed. These operations should follow written procedures. Separate laundry facilities for such clothing are desirable. Inappropriate treatment of clothing will damage fibres and may increase the risk of shedding of particles.

Premises

46. In clean areas, all exposed surfaces should be smooth, impervious and unbroken in order to minimize the shedding or accumulation of particles or micro-organisms and to permit the repeated application of cleaning agents, and disinfectants where used.

47. To reduce accumulation of dust and to facilitate cleaning there should be no uncleanable recesses and a minimum of projecting ledges, shelves, cupboards and equipment. Doors should be designed to avoid those uncleanable recesses; sliding doors may be undesirable for this reason.

48. False ceilings should be sealed to prevent contamination from the space above them.

49. Pipes and ducts and other utilities should be installed so that they do not create recesses, unsealed openings and surfaces which are difficult to clean.

50. Sinks and drains should be prohibited in grade A/B areas used for aseptic manufacture. In other areas air breaks should be fitted between the machine or sink and the drains. Floor drains in lower grade clean rooms should be fitted with traps or water seals to prevent back-flow.

51. Changing rooms should be designed as airlocks and used to provide physical separation of the different stages of changing and so minimize microbial and particulate contamination of protective clothing. They should be flushed effectively with filtered air. The final stage of the changing room should, in the at-rest state, be the same grade as the area into which it leads. The use of separate changing rooms for entering and leaving clean areas is sometimes desirable. In general hand washing facilities should be provided only in the first stage of the changing rooms.

52. Both airlock doors should not be opened simultaneously. An interlocking system or a visual and/or audible warning system should be operated to prevent the opening of more than one door at a time.

53. A filtered air supply should maintain a positive pressure and an air flow relative to surrounding areas of a lower grade under all operational conditions and should flush the area effectively. Adjacent rooms of different grades should have a pressure differential of 10 - 15 pascals (guidance values). Particular attention should be paid to the protection of the zone of greatest risk, that is, the immediate environment to which a product and cleaned components which contact the product are exposed. The various recommendations regarding air supplies and pressure differentials may need to be modified where it becomes necessary to contain some materials, e.g. pathogenic, highly toxic, radioactive or live viral or bacterial materials or products. Decontamination of facilities and treatment of air leaving a clean area may be necessary for some operations.

54. It should be demonstrated that air-flow patterns do not present a contamination risk, e.g. care should be taken to ensure that air flows do not distribute particles from a particle-generating person, operation or machine to a zone of higher product risk.

55. A warning system should be provided to indicate failure in the air supply. Indicators of pressure differences should be fitted between areas where these differences are important. These pressure differences should be recorded regularly or otherwise documented.

Equipment

56. A conveyor belt should not pass through a partition between a grade A or B area and a processing area of lower air cleanliness, unless the belt itself is continually sterilised (e.g. in a sterilising tunnel).

57. As far as practicable equipment, fittings and services should be designed and installed so that operations, maintenance and repairs can be carried out outside the clean area. If sterilisation is required, it should be carried out, wherever possible, after complete reassembly.

58. When equipment maintenance has been carried out within the clean area, the area should be cleaned, disinfected and/or sterilised where appropriate, before processing recommences if the required standards of cleanliness and/or asepsis have not been maintained during the work.

59. Water treatment plants and distribution systems should be designed, constructed and maintained so as to ensure a reliable source of water of an appropriate quality. They should not be operated beyond their designed capacity. Water for injections should be produced, stored and distributed in a manner which prevents microbial growth, for example by constant circulation at a temperature above 70°C.

60. All equipment such as sterilisers, air handling and filtration systems, air vent and gas filters, water treatment, generation, storage and distribution systems should be subject to validation and planned maintenance; their return to use should be approved.

Sanitation

61. The sanitation of clean areas is particularly important. They should be cleaned thoroughly in accordance with a written programme. Where disinfectants are used, more than one type should be employed. Monitoring should be undertaken regularly in order to detect the development of resistant strains.

62. Disinfectants and detergents should be monitored for microbial contamination; dilutions should be kept in previously cleaned containers and should only be stored for defined periods unless sterilised. Disinfectants and detergents used in Grades A and B areas should be sterile prior to use.

63. Fumigation of clean areas may be useful for reducing microbiological contamination in inaccessible places.

Processing

64. Precautions to minimize contamination should be taken during all processing stages including the stages before sterilisation.

65. Preparations of microbiological origin should not be made or filled in areas used for the processing of other medicinal products; however, vaccines of dead organisms or of bacterial extracts may be filled, after inactivation, in the same premises as other sterile medicinal products.

66. Validation of aseptic processing should include a process simulation test using a nutrient medium (media fill).Selection of the nutrient medium should be made based on dosage form of the product and selectivity, clarity, concentration and suitability for sterilisation of the nutrient medium.

67. The process simulation test should imitate as closely as possible the routine aseptic manufacturing process and include all the critical subsequent manufacturing steps. It should also take into account various interventions known to occur during normal production as well as worst-case situations.

68. Process simulation tests should be performed as initial validation with three consecutive satisfactory simulation tests per shift and repeated at defined intervals and after any significant modification to the HVAC-system, equipment, process and number of shifts. Normally process simulation tests should be repeated twice a year per shift and process.

69. The number of containers used for media fills should be sufficient to enable a valid evaluation. For small batches, the number of containers for media fills should at least equal the size of the product batch. The target should be zero growth and the following should apply:

- When filling fewer than 5000 units, no contaminated units should be detected.

- When filling 5,000 to 10,000 units:

   a) One (1) contaminated unit should result in an investigation, including consideration of a repeat media fill;

   b) Two (2) contaminated units are considered cause for revalidation, following investigation.

- When filling more than 10,000 units:

   a) One (1) contaminated unit should result in an investigation;

   b) Two (2) contaminated units are considered cause for revalidation, following investigation.

70. For any run size, intermittent incidents of microbial contamination may be indicative of low-level contamination that should be investigated. Investigation of gross failures should include the potential impact on the sterility assurance of batches manufactured since the last successful media fill.

71. Care should be taken that any validation does not compromise the processes.

72. Water sources, water treatment equipment and treated water should be monitored regularly for chemical and biological contamination and, as appropriate, for endotoxins. Records should be maintained of the results of the monitoring and of any action taken.

73. Activities in clean areas and especially when aseptic operations are in progress should be kept to a minimum and movement of personnel should be controlled and methodical, to avoid excessive shedding of particles and organisms due to over-vigorous activity. The ambient temperature and humidity should not be uncomfortably high because of the nature of the garments worn.

74. Microbiological contamination of starting materials should be minimal. Specifications should include requirements for microbiological quality when the need for this has been indicated by monitoring.

75. Containers and materials liable to generate fibres should be minimised in clean areas.

76. Where appropriate, measures should be taken to minimize the particulate contamination of the end product.

77. Components, containers and equipment should be handled after the final cleaning process in such a way that they are not recontaminated.

78. The interval between the washing and drying and the sterilisation of components, containers and equipment as well as between their sterilisation and use should be minimised and subject to a time-limit appropriate to the storage conditions.

79. The time between the start of the preparation of a solution and its sterilisation or filtration through a micro-organism-retaining filter should be minimised. There should be a set maximum permissible time for each product that takes into account its composition and the prescribed method of storage.

80. The bioburden should be monitored before sterilisation. There should be working limits on contamination immediately before sterilisation, which are related to the efficiency of the method to be used. Bioburden assay should be performed on each batch for both aseptically filled product and terminally sterilised products. Where overkill sterilisation parameters are set for terminally sterilised products, bioburden might be monitored only at suitable scheduled intervals. For parametric release systems, bioburden assay should be performed on each

batch and considered as an in-process test. Where appropriate the level of endotoxins should be monitored. All solutions, in particular large volume infusion fluids, should be passed through a micro-organism-retaining filter, if possible sited immediately before filling.

81. Components, containers, equipment and any other article required in a clean area where aseptic work takes place should be sterilised and passed into the area through double-ended sterilisers sealed into the wall, or by a procedure which achieves the same objective of not introducing contamination. Non-combustible gases should be passed through micro-organism retentive filters.

82. The efficacy of any new procedure should be validated, and the validation verified at scheduled intervals based on performance history or when any significant change is made in the process or equipment.

Sterilisation

83. All sterilisation processes should be validated. Particular attention should be given when the adopted sterilisation method is not described in the current edition of the European Pharmacopoeia, or when it is used for a product which is not a simple aqueous or oily solution. Where possible, heat sterilisation is the method of choice. In any case, the sterilisation process must be in accordance with the marketing and manufacturing authorisations.

84. Before any sterilisation process is adopted its suitability for the product and its efficacy in achieving the desired sterilising conditions in all parts of each type of load to be processed should be demonstrated by physical measurements and by biological indicators where appropriate. The validity of the process should be verified at scheduled intervals, at least annually, and whenever significant modifications have been made to the equipment. Records should be kept of the results.

85. For effective sterilisation the whole of the material must be subjected to the required treatment and the process should be designed to ensure that this is achieved.

86. Validated loading patterns should be established for all sterilisation processes.

87. Biological indicators should be considered as an additional method for monitoring the sterilisation. They should be stored and used according to the manufacturer's instructions, and their quality checked by positive controls. If biological indicators are used, strict precautions should be taken to avoid transferring microbial contamination from them.

88. There should be a clear means of differentiating products which have not been sterilised from those which have. Each basket, tray or other carrier of products or components should be clearly labelled with the material name, its batch number and an indication of whether or not it has been sterilised. Indicators such as autoclave tape may be used, where appropriate, to indicate whether or not a batch (or sub-batch) has passed through a sterilisation process, but they do not give a reliable indication that the lot is, in fact, sterile.

89. Sterilisation records should be available for each sterilisation run. They should be approved as part of the batch release procedure.

Sterilisation by heat

90. Each heat sterilisation cycle should be recorded on a time/temperature chart with a sufficiently large scale or by other appropriate equipment with suitable accuracy and precision. The position of the temperature probes used for controlling and/or recording should have been determined during the validation, and where applicable also checked against a second independent temperature probe located at the same position.

91. Chemical or biological indicators may also be used, but should not take the place of physical measurements.

92. Sufficient time must be allowed for the whole of the load to reach the required temperature before measurement of the sterilising time-period is commenced. This time must be determined for each type of load to be processed.

93. After the high temperature phase of a heat sterilisation cycle, precautions should be taken against contamination of a sterilised load during cooling. Any cooling fluid or gas in contact with the product should be sterilised unless it can be shown that any leaking container would not be approved for use.

Moist heat

94. Both temperature and pressure should be used to monitor the process. Control instrumentation should normally be independent of monitoring instrumentation and recording charts. Where automated control and monitoring systems are used for these applications they should be validated to ensure that critical process requirements are met. System and cycle faults should be registered by the system and observed by the operator. The reading of the independent temperature indicator should be routinely checked against the chart recorder during the sterilisation period. For sterilisers fitted with a drain at the bottom of the chamber, it may also be necessary to record the temperature at this position, throughout the sterilisation period. There should be frequent leak tests on the chamber when a vacuum phase is part of the cycle.

95. The items to be sterilised, other than products in sealed containers, should be wrapped in a material which allows removal of air and penetration of steam but which prevents recontamination after sterilisation. All parts of the load should be in contact with the sterilizing agent at the required temperature for the required time.

96. Care should be taken to ensure that steam used for sterilisation is of suitable quality and does not contain additives at a level which could cause contamination of product or equipment.

Dry heat

97. The process used should include air circulation within the chamber and the maintenance of a positive pressure to prevent the entry of non-sterile air. Any air admitted should be passed through a HEPA filter. Where this process is also intended to remove pyrogens, challenge tests using endotoxins should be used as part of the validation.

Sterilisation by radiation

98. Radiation sterilisation is used mainly for the sterilisation of heat sensitive materials and products. Many medicinal products and some packaging materials are radiation-sensitive, so this method is permissible only when the absence of deleterious effects on the product has been confirmed experimentally. Ultraviolet irradiation is not normally an acceptable method of sterilisation.

99. During the sterilisation procedure the radiation dose should be measured. For this purpose, dosimetry indicators which are independent of dose rate should be used, giving a quantitative measurement of the dose received by the product itself. Dosimeters should be inserted in the load in sufficient number and close enough together to ensure that there is always a dosimeter in the irradiator. Where plastic dosimeters are used they should be used within the time-limit of their calibration. Dosimeter absorbances should be read within a short period after exposure to radiation.

100. Biological indicators may be used as an additional control

101. Validation procedures should ensure that the effects of variations in density of the packages are considered.

102. Materials handling procedures should prevent mix-up between irradiated and non-irradiated materials. Radiation sensitive colour disks should also be used on each package to differentiate between packages which have been subjected to irradiation and those which have not.

103. The total radiation dose should be administered within a predetermined time span.

Sterilisation with ethylene oxide

104. This method should only be used when no other method is practicable. During process validation it should be shown that there is no damaging effect on the product and that the conditions and time allowed for degassing are such as to reduce any residual gas and reaction products to defined acceptable limits for the type of product or material.

---

105. Direct contact between gas and microbial cells is essential; precautions should be taken to avoid the presence of organisms likely to be enclosed in material such as crystals or dried protein. The nature and quantity of packaging materials can significantly affect the process.

106. Before exposure to the gas, materials should be brought into equilibrium with the humidity and temperature required by the process. The time required for this should be balanced against the opposing need to minimize the time before sterilisation.

107. Each sterilisation cycle should be monitored with suitable biological indicators, using the appropriate number of test pieces distributed throughout the load. The information so obtained should form part of the batch record.

108. For each sterilisation cycle, records should be made of the time taken to complete the cycle, of the pressure, temperature and humidity within the chamber during the process and of the gas concentration and of the total amount of gas used. The pressure and temperature should be recorded throughout the cycle on a chart. The record(s) should form part of the batch record.

109. After sterilisation, the load should be stored in a controlled manner under ventilated conditions to allow residual gas and reaction products to reduce to the defined level. This process should be validated.

Filtration of medicinal products which cannot be sterilised in their final container

110. Filtration alone is not considered sufficient when sterilisation in the final container is possible. With regard to methods currently available, steam sterilisation is to be preferred. If the product cannot be sterilised in the final container, solutions or liquids can be filtered through a sterile filter of nominal pore size of 0.22 micron (or less), or with at least equivalent micro-organism retaining properties, into a previously sterilised container. Such filters can remove most bacteria and moulds, but not all viruses or mycoplasmas. Consideration should be given to complementing the filtration process with some degree of heat treatment.

111. Due to the potential additional risks of the filtration method as compared with other sterilization processes, a second filtration via a further sterilised micro-organism retaining filter, immediately prior to filling, may be advisable. The final sterile filtration should be carried out as close as possible to the filling point.

112. Fibre-shedding characteristics of filters should be minimal.

113. The integrity of the sterilised filter should be verified before use and should be confirmed immediately after use by an appropriate method such as a bubble point, diffusive flow or pressure hold test. The time taken to filter a known volume of bulk solution and the pressure difference to be used across the filter should be determined during validation and any significant differences from this during routine manufacturing should be noted and investigated. Results of these checks should be included in the batch record. The integrity of critical gas and air vent filters should be confirmed after use. The integrity of other filters should be confirmed at appropriate intervals.

114. The same filter should not be used for more than one working day unless such use has been validated.

115. The filter should not affect the product by removal of ingredients from it or by release of substances into it.

Finishing of sterile products

116. Partially stoppered freeze drying vials should be maintained under Grade A conditions at all times until the stopper is fully inserted.

117. Containers should be closed by appropriately validated methods. Containers closed by fusion, e.g. glass or plastic ampoules should be subject to 100% integrity testing. Samples of other containers should be checked for integrity according to appropriate procedures.

118. The container closure system for aseptically filled vials is not fully integral until the aluminium cap has been crimped into place on the stoppered vial. Crimping of the cap should therefore be performed as soon as possible after stopper insertion.

119. As the equipment used to crimp vial caps can generate large quantities of non-viable particulates, the equipment should be located at a separate station equipped with adequate air extraction.

120. Vial capping can be undertaken as an aseptic process using sterilised caps or as a clean process outside the aseptic core. Where this latter approach is adopted, vials should be protected by Grade A conditions up to the point of leaving the aseptic processing area, and thereafter stoppered vials should be protected with a Grade A air supply until the cap has been crimped.

121. Vials with missing or displaced stoppers should be rejected prior to capping. Where human intervention is required at the capping station, appropriate technology should be used to prevent direct contact with the vials and to minimise microbial contamination.

122. Restricted access barriers and isolators may be beneficial in assuring the required conditions and minimising direct human interventions into the capping operation.

123. Containers sealed under vacuum should be tested for maintenance of that vacuum after an appropriate, pre-determined period.

124. Filled containers of parenteral products should be inspected individually for extraneous contamination or other defects. When inspection is done visually, it should be done under suitable and controlled conditions of illumination and background. Operators doing the inspection should pass regular eye-sight checks, with spectacles if worn, and be allowed frequent breaks from inspection. Where other methods of inspection are used, the process should be validated and the performance of the equipment checked at intervals. Results should be recorded.

Quality control

125. The sterility test applied to the finished product should only be regarded as the last in a series of control measures by which sterility is assured. The test should be validated for the product(s) concerned.

126. In those cases where parametric release has been authorised, special attention should be paid to the validation and the monitoring of the entire manufacturing process.

127. Samples taken for sterility testing should be representative of the whole of the batch, but should in particular include samples taken from parts of the batch considered to be most at risk of contamination, e.g.:

   — for products which have been filled aseptically, samples should include containers filled at the beginning and end of the batch and after any significant intervention,

   — or products which have been heat sterilised in their final containers, consideration should be given to taking samples from the potentially coolest part of the load.

Annex 1

Annex 2:
Manufacture of Biological Medicinal Products for Human Use

Scope

The methods employed in the manufacture of biological medicinal products are a critical factor in shaping the appropriate regulatory control. Biological medicinal products can be defined therefore largely by reference to their method of manufacture. Biological medicinal products prepared by the following methods of manufacture will fall under the scope of this annex[19]. Biological medicinal products manufactured by these methods include: vaccines, immunosera, antigens, hormones, cytokines, enzymes and other products of fermentation (including monoclonal antibodies and products derived from r-DNA).

a)   Microbial cultures, excluding those resulting from r-DNA techniques;

b)   Microbial and cell cultures, including those resulting from recombinant DNA or hybridoma techniques;

c)   Extraction from biological tissues

d)   Propagation of live agents in embryos or animals

(Not all of the aspects of this annex may necessarily apply to products in category a).

---

[19] Biological medicinal products manufactured by these methods include: vaccines, immunosera, antigens, hormones, cytokines, enzymes and other products of fermentation (including monoclonal antibodies and products derived from r-DNA).

Note   *In drawing up this guidance, due consideration has been given to the general requirements for manufacturing establishments and control laboratories proposed by the WHO.*

The present guidance does not lay down detailed requirements for specific classes of biological products, and attention is therefore directed to other guidelines issued by the Committee for Proprietary Medicinal Products (CPMP), for example the note for guidance on monoclonal antibodies and the note for guidance on products of recombinant DNA technology ("The rules governing medicinal product in the European Community", Volume 3).

Principle

The manufacture of biological medicinal products involves certain specific considerations arising from the nature of the products and the processes. The way in which biological medicinal products are produced, controlled and administered make some particular precautions necessary.

Unlike conventional medicinal products, which are reproduced using chemical and physical techniques capable of a high degree of consistency, the production of biological medicinal products involves biological processes and materials, such as cultivation of cells or extraction of material from living organisms. These biological processes may display inherent variability, so that the range and nature of by-products are variable. Moreover, the materials used in these cultivation processes provide good substrates for growth of microbial contaminants.

Control of biological medicinal products usually involves biological analytical techniques which have a greater variability than physico-chemical determinations. In-process controls therefore take on a great importance in the manufacture of biological medicinal products.

Personnel

1.   All personnel (including those concerned with cleaning, maintenance or quality control) employed in areas where biological medicinal products are manufactured should receive additional training specific to the products manufactured and to their work. Personnel should be given relevant information and training in hygiene and microbiology.

2. Persons responsible for production and quality control should have an adequate background in relevant scientific disciplines, such as bacteriology, biology, biometry, chemistry, medicine, pharmacy, pharmacology, virology, immunology and veterinary medicine, together with sufficient practical experience to enable them to exercise their management function for the process concerned.

3. The immunological status of personnel may have to be taken into consideration for product safety. All personnel engaged in production, maintenance, testing and animal care (and inspectors) should be vaccinated where necessary with appropriate specific vaccines and have regular health checks. Apart from the obvious problem of exposure of staff to infectious agents, potent toxins or allergens, it is necessary to avoid the risk of contamination of a production batch with infectious agents. Visitors should generally be excluded from production areas.

4. Any changes in the immunological status of personnel which could adversely affect the quality of the product should preclude work in the production area. Production of BCG vaccine and tuberculin products should be restricted to staff who are carefully monitored by regular checks of immunological status or chest X-ray.

5. In the course of a working day, personnel should not pass from areas where exposure to live organisms or animals is possible to areas where other products or different organisms are handled. If such passage is unavoidable, clearly defined decontamination measures, including change of clothing and shoes and, where necessary, showering should be followed by staff involved in any such production.

Premises and equipment

6. The degree of environmental control of particulate and microbial contamination of the production premises should be adapted to the product and the production step, bearing in mind the level of contamination of the starting materials and the risk to the finished product.

7. The risk of cross-contamination between biological medicinal products, especially during those stages of the

Annex 2

manufacturing process in which live organisms are used, may require additional precautions with respect to facilities and equipment, such as the use of dedicated facilities and equipment, production on a campaign basis and the use of closed systems. The nature of the product as well as the equipment used will determine the level of segregation needed to avoid cross-contamination.

8. In principle, dedicated facilities should be used for the production of BCG vaccine and for the handling of live organisms used in production of tuberculin products.

9. Dedicated facilities should be used for the handling of Bacillus anthracis, of Clostridium botulinum and of Clostridium tetani until the inactivation process is accomplished.

10. Production on a campaign basis may be acceptable for other spore forming organisms provided that the facilities are dedicated to this group of products and not more than one product is processed at any one time.

11. Simultaneous production in the same area using closed systems of biofermenters may be acceptable for products such as monoclonal antibodies and products prepared by DNA techniques.

12. Processing steps after harvesting may be carried out simultaneously in the same production area provided that adequate precautions are taken to prevent cross contamination. For killed vaccines and toxoids, such parallel processing should only be performed after inactivation of the culture or after detoxification.

13. Positive pressure areas should be used to process sterile products but negative pressure in specific areas at point of exposure of pathogens is acceptable for containment reasons.

    Where negative pressure areas or safety cabinets are used for aseptic processing of pathogens, they should be surrounded by a positive pressure sterile zone.

14. Air filtration units should be specific to the processing area concerned and recirculation of air should not occur from areas handling live pathogenic organisms.

15. The layout and design of production areas and equipment should permit effective cleaning and decontamination (e.g. by fumigation). The adequacy of cleaning and decontamination procedures should be validated.

16. Equipment used during handling of live organisms should be designed to maintain cultures in a pure state and uncontaminated by external sources during processing.

17. Pipework systems, valves and vent filters should be properly designed to facilitate cleaning and sterilisation. The use of 'clean in place' and 'sterilise in place' systems should be encouraged. Valves on fermentation vessels should be completely steam sterilisable. Air vent filters should be hydrophobic and validated for their scheduled life span.

18. Primary containment should be designed and tested to demonstrate freedom from leakage risk.

19. Effluents which may contain pathogenic micro-organisms should be effectively decontaminated.

20. Due to the variability of biological products or processes, some additives or ingredients have to be measured or weighed during the production process (e.g. buffers). In these cases, small stocks of these substances may be kept in the production area.

Animal quarters and care

21. Animals are used for the manufacture of a number of biological products, for example polio vaccine (monkeys), snake antivenoms (horses and goats), rabies vaccine (rabbits, mice and hamsters) and serum gonadotropin (horses). In addition, animals may also be used in the quality control of most sera and vaccines, e.g. pertussis vaccine (mice), pyrogenicity (rabbits), BCG vaccine (guinea-pigs).

22. General requirements for animal quarters, care and quarantine are laid down in Directive 86/609/EEC[20].

[20] Directive 2003/65/EC of the European Parliament and of the Council of 22 July 2003 amending Council Directive 86/609/EEC on the

Annex 2

Quarters for animals used in production and control of biological products should be separated from production and control areas. The health status of animals from which some starting materials are derived and of those used for quality control and safety testing should be monitored and recorded. Staff employed in such areas must be provided with special clothing and changing facilities. Where monkeys are used for the production or quality control of biological medicinal products, special consideration is required as laid down in the current WHO Requirements for Biological Substances n° 7.

Documentation

23. Specifications for biological starting materials may need additional documentation on the source, origin, method of manufacture and controls applied, particularly microbiological controls.

24. Specifications are routinely required for intermediate and bulk biological medicinal products.

Production

Starting materials

25. The source, origin and suitability of starting materials should be clearly defined. Where the necessary tests take a long time, it may be permissible to process starting materials before the results of the tests are available. In such cases, release of a finished product is conditional on satisfactory results of these tests.

26. Where sterilisation of starting materials is required, it should be carried out where possible by heat. Where necessary, other appropriate methods may also be used for inactivation of biological materials (e.g. irradiation).

Seed lot and cell bank system

27. In order to prevent the unwanted drift of properties which might ensue from repeated subcultures or multiple generations, the production of biological medicinal

approximation of laws, regulations and administrative provisions of the Member   States regarding the protection of animals used for experimental and other scientific purposes (OJ L 230, 16.09.2003, p. 32- 33) products obtained by microbial culture, cell culture or propagation in embryos and animals should be based on a system of master and working seed lots and/or cell banks.

28. The number of generations (doublings, passages) between the seed lot or cell bank and the finished product should be consistent with the marketing authorisation dossier. Scaling up of the process should not change this fundamental relationship.

29. Seed lots and cell banks should be adequately characterised and tested for contaminants. Their suitability for use should be further demonstrated by the consistency of the characteristics and quality of the successive batches of product. Seed lots and cell banks should be established, stored and used in such a way as to minimise the risks of contamination or alteration.

30. Establishment of the seed lot and cell bank should be performed in a suitably controlled environment to protect the seed lot and the cell bank and, if applicable, the personnel handling it. During the establishment of the seed lot and cell bank, no other living or infectious material (e.g. virus, cell lines or cell strains) should be handled simultaneously in the same area or by the same persons.

31. Evidence of the stability and recovery of the seeds and banks should be documented. Storage containers should be hermetically sealed, clearly labelled and kept at an appropriate temperature. An inventory should be meticulously kept. Storage temperature should be recorded continuously for freezers and properly monitored for liquid nitrogen. Any deviation from set limits and any corrective action taken should be recorded.

32. Only authorised personnel should be allowed to handle the material and this handling should be done under the supervision of a responsible person. Access to stored material should be controlled. Different seed lots or cell banks should be stored in such a way to avoid confusion or cross-contamination. It is desirable to split the seed lots and cell banks and to store the parts at different locations so as to minimise the risks of total loss.

33. All containers of master or working cell banks and seed lots should be treated identically during storage. Once removed from storage, the containers should not be returned to the stock.

Operating principles

34. The growth promoting properties of culture media should be demonstrated.

35. Addition of materials or cultures to fermenters and other vessels and the taking of samples should be carried out under carefully controlled conditions to ensure that absence of contamination is maintained. Care should be taken to ensure that vessels are correctly connected when addition or sampling take place.

36. Centrifugation and blending of products can lead to aerosol formation, and containment of such activities to prevent transfer of live micro-organisms is necessary.

37. If possible, media should be sterilised in situ. In-line sterilising filters for routine addition of gases, media, acids or alkalis, defoaming agents etc. to fermenters should be used where possible.

38. Careful consideration should be given to the validation of any necessary virus removal or inactivation undertaken (see CPMP notes for guidance).

39. In cases where a virus inactivation or removal process is performed during manufacture, measures should be taken to avoid the risk of recontamination of treated products by non-treated products.

40. A wide variety of equipment is used for chromatography, and in general such equipment should be dedicated to the purification of one product and should be sterilised or sanitised between batches. The use of the same equipment at different stages of processing should be discouraged. Acceptance criteria, life span and sanitation or sterilisation method of columns should be defined.

Quality control

41. In-process controls play a specially important role in ensuring the consistency of the quality of biological

medicinal products. Those controls which are crucial for quality (e.g. virus removal) but which cannot be carried out on the finished product, should be performed at an appropriate stage of production.

42. It may be necessary to retain samples of intermediate products in sufficient quantities and under appropriate storage conditions to allow the repetition or confirmation of a batch control.

43. Continuous monitoring of certain production processes is necessary, for example fermentation. Such data should form part of the batch record.

44. Where continuous culture is used, special consideration should be given to the quality control requirements arising from this type of production method.

Annex 2

Annex 3: Manufacture of Radiopharmaceuticals

Brussels, 01 September 2008

The annex has been revised in the light of new GMP requirements for actives substances used as starting materials (GMP Part II) and updated for all relevant aspects of GMP for radiopharmaceuticals.

Document History	
Release for public consultation	December 2006
Deadline for comments	March 2007
Agreed by GMP/GDP Inspectors Working Group	December 2007
Adopted by European Commission	August 2008
Deadline for coming into operation	01 March 2009

Principle

The manufacture of radiopharmaceuticals shall be undertaken in accordance with the principles of Good Manufacturing Practice for Medicinal Products Part I and II. This annex specifically addresses some of the practices, which may be specific for radiopharmaceuticals.

Note i.   Preparation of radiopharmaceuticals in radiopharmacies (hospitals or certain pharmacies), using Generators and Kits with a marketing authorisation or a national licence, is not covered by this guideline, unless covered by national requirement.

Note ii. *According to radiation protection regulations it should be ensured that any medical exposure is under the clinical responsibility of a practitioner. In diagnostic and therapeutic nuclear medicine practices a medical physics expert shall be available.*

Note iii. *This annex is also applicable to radiopharmaceuticals used in clinical trials.*

Note iv. *Transport of radiopharmaceuticals is regulated by the International Atomic Energy Association (IAEA) and radiation protection requirements.*

Note v. *It is recognised that there are acceptable methods, other than those described in this annex, which are capable of achieving the principles of Quality Assurance. Other methods should be validated and provide a level of Quality Assurance at least equivalent to those set out in this annex.*

Introduction

1. The manufacturing and handling of radiopharmaceuticals is potentially hazardous. The level of risk depends in particular upon the types of radiation, the energy of radiation and the half-lives of the radioactive isotopes. Particular attention must be paid to the prevention of cross contamination, to the retention of radionuclide contaminants, and to waste disposal.

2. Due to short shelf-life of their radionuclides, some radiopharmaceuticals may be released before completion of all quality control tests. In this case, the exact and detailed description of the whole release procedure including the responsibilities of the involved personnel and the continuous assessment of the effectiveness of the quality assurance system is essential.

3. This guideline is applicable to manufacturing procedures employed by industrial manufacturers, Nuclear Centres/Institutes and PET Centres for the production and quality control of the following types of products:

    –   Radiopharmaceuticals

    –   Positron Emitting (PET) Radiopharmaceuticals

– Radioactive Precursors for radiopharmaceutical production

– Radionuclide Generators

Type of manufacture	Non - GMP *	GMP part II & I (Increasing) including relevant annexes			
Radiopharmaceuticals PET Radiopharmaceuticals Radioactive Precursors	Reactor / Cyclotron Production	Chemical synthesis	Purification steps	Processing, formulation and dispensing	Aseptic or final sterilization
Radionuclide Generators	Reactor / Cyclotron Production	Processing			

Annex 3

* Target and transfer system from cyclotron to synthesis rig may be considered as the first step of active substance manufacture.

4. The manufacturer of the final radiopharmaceutical should describe and justify the steps for manufacture of the active substance and the final medicinal product and which GMP (part I or II) applies for the specific process/manufacturing steps.

5. Preparation of radiopharmaceuticals involves adherence to regulations on radiation protection.

6. Radiopharmaceuticals to be administered parenterally should comply with sterility requirements for parenterals and, where relevant, aseptic working conditions for the manufacture of sterile medicinal products, which are covered in Eudralex Volume 4, Annex 1.

7. Specifications and quality control testing procedures for the most commonly used radiopharmaceuticals are specified in the European Pharmacopoeia or in the marketing authorisation.

Clinical Trials

8. Radiopharmaceuticals intended for use in clinical trials as investigational medicinal products should in addition be produced in accordance with the principles in Eudralex Volume 4, annex 13.

Quality assurance

9.   Quality assurance is of even greater importance in the manufacture of radiopharmaceuticals because of their particular characteristics, low volumes and in some circumstances the need to administer the product before testing is complete.

10.   As with all pharmaceuticals, the products must be well protected against contamination and cross-contamination. However, the environment and the operators must also be protected against radiation. This means that the role of an effective quality assurance system is of the utmost importance.

11.   It is important that the data generated by the monitoring of premises and processes are rigorously recorded and evaluated as part of the release process.

12.   The principles of qualification and validation should be applied to the manufacturing of radiopharmaceuticals and a risk management approach should be used to determine the extent of qualification/validation, focusing on a combination of Good Manufacturing Practice and Radiation Protection.

Personnel

13.   All manufacturing operations should be carried out under the responsibility of personnel with additional competence in radiation protection. Personnel involved in production, analytical control and release of radiopharmaceuticals should be appropriately trained in radiopharmaceutical specific aspects of the quality management system. The QP should have the overall responsibility for release of the products.

14.   All personnel (including those concerned with cleaning and maintenance) employed in areas where radioactive products are manufactured should receive appropriate additional training specific to these types of procedures and products

15.   Where production facilities are shared with research institutions, the research personnel must be adequately trained in GMP regulations and the QA function must review and approve the research activities to ensure that

they do not pose any hazard to the manufacturing of radiopharmaceuticals.

Premises and equipment

General

16. Radioactive products should be manufactured in controlled (environmental and radioactive) areas. All manufacturing steps should take place in self-contained facilities dedicated to radio-pharmaceuticals

17. Measures should be established and implemented to prevent cross-contamination from personnel, materials, radionuclides etc. Closed or contained equipment should be used whenever appropriate. Where open equipment is used, or equipment is opened, precautions should be taken to minimize the risk of contamination. The risk assessment should demonstrate that the environmental cleanliness level proposed is suitable for the type of product being manufactured.

18. Access to the manufacturing areas should be via a gowning area and should be restricted to authorised personnel.

19. Workstations and their environment should be monitored with respect to radioactivity, particulate and microbiological quality as established during performance qualification (PQ).

20. Preventive maintenance, calibration and qualification programmes should be operated to ensure that all facilities and equipment used in the manufacture of radiopharmaceutical are suitable and qualified. These activities should be carried out by competent personnel and records and logs should be maintained.

21. Precautions should be taken to avoid radioactive contamination within the facility. Appropriate controls should be in place to detect any radioactive contamination, either directly through the use of radiation detectors or indirectly through a swabbing routine.

22. Equipment should be constructed so that surfaces that come into contact with the product are not reactive,

Annex 3

additive or absorptive so as to alter the quality of the radiopharmaceutical.

23. Re-circulation of air extracted from area where radioactive products are handled should be avoided unless justified. Air outlets should be designed to minimize environmental contamination by radioactive particles and gases and appropriate measures should be taken to protect the controlled areas from particulate and microbial contamination.

24. In order to contain radioactive particles, it may be necessary for the air pressure to be lower where products are exposed, compared with the surrounding areas. However, it is still necessary to protect the product from environmental contamination. This may be achieved by, for example, using barrier technology or airlocks, acting as pressure sinks.

Sterile production

25. Sterile radiopharmaceuticals may be divided into those, which are manufactured aseptically, and those, which are terminally sterilised. The facility should maintain the appropriate level of environmental cleanliness for the type of operation being performed. For manufacture of sterile products the working zone where products or containers may be exposed to the environment, the cleanliness requirements should comply with the requirements described in the Eudralex Volume 4, Annex 1.

26. For manufacture of radiopharmaceuticals a risk assessment may be applied to determine the appropriate pressure differences, air flow direction and air quality.

27. In case of use of closed and automated systems (chemical synthesis, purification, on-line sterile filtration) a grade C environment (usually "Hot-cell") will be suitable. Hot-cells should meet a high degree of air cleanliness, with filtered feed air, when closed. Aseptic activities must be carried out in a grade A area.

28. Prior to the start of manufacturing, assembly of sterilised equipment and consumables (tubing, sterilised filters and sterile closed and sealed vials to a sealed fluid path) must be performed under aseptic conditions

Documentation

29. All documents related to the manufacture of radiopharmaceuticals should be prepared, reviewed, approved and distributed according to written procedures.

30. Specifications should be established and documented for raw materials, labelling and packaging materials, critical intermediates and the finished radiopharmaceutical. Specifications should also be in place for any other critical items used in the manufacturing process, such as process aids, gaskets, sterile filtering kits, that could critically impact on quality.

31. Acceptance criteria should be established for the radiopharmaceutical including criteria for release and shelf life specifications (examples: chemical identity of the isotope, radioactive concentration, purity, and specific activity).

32. Records of major equipment use, cleaning, sanitisation or sterilisation and maintenance should show the product name and batch number, where appropriate, in addition to the date and time and signature for the persons involved in these activities.

33. Records should be retained for at least 3 years unless another timeframe is specified in national requirements.

Production

34. Production of different radioactive products in the same working area (i.e. hot-cell, LAF unit), at the same time should be avoided in order to minimise the risk of radioactive cross-contamination or mix-up.

35. Special attention should be paid to validation including validation of computerised systems which should be carried out in accordance in compliance with Eudralex Volume 4, annex 11. New manufacturing processes should be validated prospectively.

36. The critical parameters should normally be identified before or during validation and the ranges necessary for reproducible operation should be defined.

37. Integrity testing of the membrane filter should be performed for aseptically filled products, taking into account the need for radiation protection and maintenance of filter sterility.

38. Due to radiation exposure it is accepted that most of the labelling of the direct container, is done prior to manufacturing. Sterile empty closed vials may be labelled with partial information prior to filling providing that this procedure does not compromise sterility or prevent visual control of the filled vial.

Quality control

39. Some radiopharmaceuticals may have to be distributed and used on the basis of an assessment of batch documentation and before all chemical and microbiology tests have been completed. Radiopharmaceutical product release may be carried out in two or more stages, before and after full analytical testing:

   a) Assessment by a designated person of batch processing records, which should cover production conditions and analytical testing performed thus far, before allowing transportation of the radiopharmaceutical under quarantine status to the clinical department.

   b) Assessment of the final analytical data, ensuring all deviations from normal procedures are documented, justified and appropriately released prior to documented certification by the Qualified Person. Where certain test results are not available before use of the product, the Qualified Person should conditionally certify the product before it is used and should finally certify the product after all the test results are obtained.

40. Most radiopharmaceuticals are intended for use within a short time and the period of validity with regard to the radioactive shelf-life, must be clearly stated.

41. Radiopharmaceuticals having radionuclides with long half-lives should be tested to show, that they meet all relevant acceptance criteria before release and certification by the QP.

42. Before testing is performed samples can be stored to allow sufficient radioactivity decay. All tests including the sterility test should be performed as soon as possible.

43. A written procedure detailing the assessment of production and analytical data, which should be considered before the batch is dispatched, should be established.

44. Products that fail to meet acceptance criteria should be rejected. If the material is reprocessed, preestablished procedures should be followed and the finished product should meet acceptance criteria before release. Returned products may not be reprocessed and must be stored as radioactive waste.

45. A procedure should also describe the measures to be taken by the Qualified Person if unsatisfactory test results (Out-of-Specification) are obtained after dispatch and before expiry. Such events should be investigated to include the relevant corrective and preventative actions taken to prevent future events. This process must be documented.

46. Information should be given to the clinical responsible persons, if necessary. To facilitate this, a traceability system should be implemented for radiopharmaceuticals.

47. A system to verify the quality of starting materials should be in place. Supplier approval should include an evaluation that provides adequate assurance that the material consistently meets specifications. The starting materials, packaging materials and critical process aids should be purchased from approved suppliers.

Reference and Retention samples

48. For radiopharmaceuticals sufficient samples of each batch of bulk formulated product shall be retained for at least six months after expiry of the finished medicinal product unless otherwise justified through risk management.

49. Samples of starting materials, other than solvents gases or water used in the manufacturing process shall be retained for at least two years after the release of the product. That period may be shortened if the period of

stability of the material as indicated in the relevant specification is shorter.

50.   Other conditions may be defined by agreement with the competent authority, for the sampling and retaining of starting materials and products manufactured individually or in small quantities or when their storage could raise special problems.

Distribution

51.   Distribution of the finished product under controlled conditions, before all appropriate test results are available, is acceptable for radiopharmaceuticals, providing the product is not administered by the receiving institute until satisfactory test results has been received and assessed by a designated person.

10.   Glossary

Preparation:

handling and radiolabelling of kits with radionuclide eluted from generators or radioactive precursors within a hospital. Kits, generators and precursors should have a marketing authorisation or a national licence.

Manufacturing:

production, quality control and release and delivery of radiopharmaceuticals from the active substance and starting materials.

Hot –cells:

shielded workstations for manufacture and handling of radioactive materials. Hot-cells are not necessarily designed as an isolator.

Qualified person:

QP as described in Directives 2001/83/EC and 2001/82/EC. QP responsibilities are elaborated in Eudralex Volume 4, annex 16.

Annex 4: Manufacture of Veterinary Medicinal Products other than Immunological Veterinary Medicinal Products

Note   This annex applies to all veterinary medicinal products falling within the scope of Directive 2001/82/EC other than immunological veterinary medicinal products, which are the subject of a separate annex.

Manufacture of premixes for medicated feedingstuffs

For the purposes of these paragraphs,

— a *medicated feedingstuff* is any mixture of a veterinary medicinal product or products and feed or feeds which is ready prepared for marketing and intended to be fed to animals without further processing because of its curative or preventative properties or other properties as a medicinal product covered by Article 1 (2) of Directive 2001/82/EC;

— a *pre-mix for medicated feedingstuffs* is any veterinary medicinal product prepared in advance with a view to the subsequent manufacture of medicated feedingstuffs.

1.   The manufacture of premixes for medicated feedingstuffs requires the use of large quantities of vegetable matter which is likely to attract insects and rodents. Premises should be designed, equipped and operated to minimise

this risk (point 3.4.) and should also be subject to a regular pest control programme.

2. Because of the large volume of dust generated during the production of bulk material for premixes, specific attention should be given to the need to avoid cross contamination and facilitate cleaning (point 3.14), for example through the installation of sealed transport systems and dust extraction, whenever possible. The installation of such systems does not, however, eliminate the need for regular cleaning of production areas.

3. Parts of the process likely to have a significant adverse influence on the stability of the active ingredient(s) (e.g. use of steam in pellet manufacture) should be carried out in an uniform manner from batch to batch.

4. Consideration should be given to undertake the manufacture of premixes in dedicated areas which, if at all possible, do not form part of a main manufacturing plant. Alternatively, such dedicated areas should be surrounded by a buffer zone in order to minimise the risk of contamination of other manufacturing areas.

Manufacture of ectoparasiticides

5. In derogation from point 3.6, ectoparasiticides for external application to animals, which are veterinary medicinal products, and subject to marketing authorisation, may be produced and filled on a campaign basis in pesticide specific areas. However other categories of veterinary medicinal products should not be produced in such areas.

6. Adequate validated cleaning procedures should be employed to prevent cross contamination, and steps should be taken to ensure the secure storage of the veterinary medicinal product in accordance with the guide.

Manufacture of veterinary medicinal products containing penicillins

7. The use of penicillins in veterinary medicine does not present the same risks of hypersensitivity in animals as in humans. Although incidents of hypersensitivity have been recorded in horses and dogs, there are other materials

which are toxic to certain species, e.g. the ionophore antibiotics in horses. Although desirable, the requirements that such products be manufactured in dedicated, self-contained facilities (point 3.6) may be dispensed with in the case of facilities dedicated to the manufacture of veterinary medicinal products only. However, all necessary measures should be taken to avoid cross contamination and any risk to operator safety in accordance with the guide. In such circumstances, penicillin-containing products should be manufactured on a campaign basis and should be followed by appropriate, validated decontamination and cleaning procedures.

Retention of samples (point 1.4 viii and point 6.14)

8.   It is recognised that because of the large volume of certain veterinary medicinal products in their final packaging, in particular premixes, it may not be feasible for manufacturers to retain samples from each batch in its final packaging. However, manufacturers should ensure that sufficient representative samples of each batch are retained and stored in accordance with the guide.

9.   In all cases, the container used for storage should be composed of the same material as the market primary container in which the product is marketed.

Sterile veterinary medicinal products

10.   Where this has been accepted by the competent authorities, terminally sterilised veterinary medicinal products may be manufactured in a clean area of a lower grade than the grade required in the annex on "Sterile preparations", but at least in a grade D environment.

Annex 4

Annex 5: Manufacture of Immunological Veterinary Medicinal Products

Principle

The manufacture of immunological veterinary medicinal products has special characteristics which should be taken into consideration when implementing and assessing the quality assurance system.

Due to the large number of animal species and related pathogenic agents, the variety of products manufactured is very wide and the volume of manufacture is often low; hence, work on a campaign basis is common. Moreover, because of the very nature of this manufacture (cultivation steps, lack of terminal sterilisation, etc.), the products must be particularly well-protected against contamination and cross-contamination. The environment also must be protected especially when the manufacture involves the use of pathogenic or exotic biological agents and the worker must be particularly well-protected when the manufacture involves the use of biological agents pathogenic to man.

These factors, together with the inherent variability of immunological products and the relative inefficiency in particular of final product quality control tests in providing adequate information about products, means that the role of the quality assurance system is of the utmost importance. The need to maintain control over all of the following aspects of GMP, as well as those outlined in this Guide, cannot be overemphasised. In particular, it is important that the data generated by the monitoring of the various aspects of GMP (equipment, premises, product etc.) are rigorously assessed and informed decisions, leading to appropriate action, are made and recorded.

Personnel

1. All personnel (including those concerned with cleaning and maintenance) employed in areas where immunological products are manufactured should be given training in and information on hygiene and microbiology. They should receive additional training specific to the products with which they work.

2. Responsible personnel should be formally trained in some or all of the following fields: bacteriology, biology, biometry, chemistry, immunology, medicine, parasitology, pharmacy, pharmacology, virology and veterinary medicine and should also have an adequate knowledge of environmental protection measures.

3. Personnel should be protected against possible infection with the biological agents used in manufacture. In the case of biological agents known to cause disease in humans, adequate measures should be taken to prevent infection of personnel working with the agent or with experimental animals.

    Where relevant, the personnel should be vaccinated and subject to medical examination.

4. Adequate measures should be taken to prevent biological agents being taken outside the manufacturing plant by personnel acting as a carrier. Dependent on the type of biological agent, such measures may include complete change of clothes and compulsory showering before leaving the production area.

5. For immunological products, the risk of contamination or cross-contamination by personnel is particularly important.

    Prevention of contamination by personnel should be achieved by a set of measures and procedures to ensure that appropriate protective clothing is used during the different stages of the production process.

    Prevention of cross-contamination by personnel involved in production should be achieved by a set of measures and procedures to ensure that they do not pass from one area to another unless they have taken appropriate measures to eliminate the risk of contamination. In the course of a working day, personnel should not pass from areas where contamination with live micro-organisms is likely or where animals are housed to premises where other products or organisms are handled. If such passage is unavoidable, clearly defined decontamination procedures, including change of clothing and shoes, and, where necessary, showering, should be followed by staff involved in any such production.

Personnel entering a contained area where organisms had not been handled in open circuit operations in the previous twelve hours to check on cultures in sealed, surface decontaminated flasks would not be regarded as being at risk of contamination, unless the organism involved was an exotic.

Premises

6.   Premises should be designed in such a way as to control both the risk to the product and to the environment.

This can be achieved by the use of containment, clean, clean/contained or controlled areas.

7.   Live biological agents should be handled in contained areas. The level of containment should depend on the pathogenicity of the micro-organism and whether it has been classified as exotic. (Other relevant legislation, such as Directives 90/219/EEC[21] and 90/220/EEC[22], also applies).

8.   Inactivated biological agents should be handled in clean areas. Clean areas should also be used when handling non-infected cells isolated from multicellular organisms and, in some cases, filtration-sterilised media.

Annex 5

[21] Council Directive 98/81/EC of 26 October 1998 amending Directive 90/219/EEC on the contained use of genetically modified micro-organisms (OJ L 330, 05.12.1998, p. 13-31)
[22] 2 Directive 2001/18/EC of the European Parliament and of the Council of 12 March 2001 on the deliberate release into the environment of genetically modified organisms and repealing Council Directive 90/220/EEC – Commission Declaration (OJ L 106, 17.04.2001, p. 01-39)

9. Open circuit operations involving products or components not subsequently sterilised should be carried out within a laminar air flow work station (grade A) in a grade B area.

10. Other operations where live biological agents are handled (quality control, research and diagnostic services, etc.) should be appropriately contained and separated if production operations are carried out in the same building. The level of containment should depend on the pathogenicity of the biological agent and whether they have been classified as exotic. Whenever diagnostic activities are carried out, there is the risk of introducing highly pathogenic organisms. Therefore, the level of containment should be adequate to cope with all such risks. Containment may also be required if quality control or other activities are carried out in buildings in close proximity to those used for production.

11. Containment premises should be easily disinfected and should have the following characteristics:

    a) the absence of direct venting to the outside;

    b) a ventilation with air at negative pressure. Air should be extracted through HEPA filters and not be re circulated except to the same area, and provided further HEPA filtration is used (normally this condition would be met by routing the re circulated air through the normal supply HEPAs for that area). However, recycling of air between areas may be permissible provided that it passes through two exhaust HEPAs, the first of which is continuously monitored for integrity, and there are adequate measures for safe venting of exhaust air should this filter fail;

    c) air from manufacturing areas used for the handling of exotic organisms should be vented through 2 sets of HEPA filters in series, and that from production areas not re-circulated;

    d) a system for the collection and disinfection of liquid effluents including contaminated condensate from sterilizers, biogenerators, etc. Solid wastes, including animal carcasses, should be disinfected, sterilized or incinerated as appropriate. Contaminated filters should be removed using a safe method;

e) changing rooms designed and used as air locks, and equipped with washing and showering facilities if appropriate. Air pressure differentials should be such that there is no flow of air between the work area and the external environment or risk of contamination of outer clothing worn outside the area;

f) an air lock system for the passage of equipment, which is constructed so that there is no flow of contaminated air between the work area and the external environment or risk of contamination of equipment within the lock. The air lock should be of a size which enables the effective surface decontamination of materials being passed through it. Consideration should be given to having a timing device on the door interlock to allow sufficient time for the decontamination process to be effective.

g) in many instances, a barrier double-door autoclave for the secure removal of waste materials and introduction of sterile items.

12. Equipment passes and changing rooms should have an interlock mechanism or other appropriate system to prevent the opening of more than one door at a time. Changing rooms should be supplied with air filtered to the same standard as that for the work area, and equipped with air extraction facilities to produce an adequate air circulation independent of that of the work area. Equipment passes should normally be ventilated in the same way, but unventilated passes, or those equipped with supply air only, may be acceptable.

13. Production operations such as cell maintenance, media preparation, virus culture, etc. likely to cause contamination should be performed in separate areas. Animals and animal products should be handled with appropriate precautions.

14. Production areas where biological agents particularly resistant to disinfection (e.g. spore-forming bacteria) are handled should be separated and dedicated to that particular purpose until the biological agents have been inactivated.

15. With the exception of blending and subsequent filling operations, one biological agent only should be handled at a time within an area.

16. Production areas should be designed to permit disinfection between campaigns, using validated methods.

17. Production of biological agents may take place in controlled areas provided it is carried out in totally enclosed and heat sterilised equipment, all connections being also heat sterilised after making and before breaking. It may be acceptable for connections to be made under local laminar air flow provided these are few in number and proper aseptic techniques are used and there is no risk of leakage. The sterilisation parameters used before breaking the connections must be validated for the organisms being used. Different products may be placed in different biogenerators, within the same area, provided that there is no risk of accidental cross-contamination. However, organisms generally subject to special requirements for containment should be in areas dedicated to such products.

18. Animal houses where animals intended or used for production are accommodated, should be provided with the appropriate containment and/or clean area measures, and should be separate from other animal accommodation.

    Animal houses where animals used for quality control, involving the use of pathogenic biological agents, are accommodated, should be adequately contained.

19. Access to manufacturing areas should be restricted to authorised personnel. Clear and concise written procedures should be posted as appropriate.

20. Documentation relating to the premises should be readily available in a plant master file.

    The manufacturing site and buildings should be described in sufficient detail (by means of plans and written explanations) so that the designation and conditions of use of all the rooms are correctly identified as well as the biological agents which are handled in them. The flow of people and product should also be clearly marked.

The animal species accommodated in the animal houses or otherwise on the site should be identified.

The activities carried out in the vicinity of the site should also be indicated.

Plans of contained and/or clean area premises, should describe the ventilation system indicating inlets and outlets, filters and their specifications, the number of air changes per hour, and pressure gradients. They should indicate which pressure gradients are monitored by pressure indicator.

Equipment

21. The equipment used should be designed and constructed so that it meets the particular requirements for the manufacture of each product.

    Before being put into operation the equipment should be qualified and validated and subsequently be regularly maintained and validated.

22. Where appropriate, the equipment should ensure satisfactory primary containment of the biological agents.

    Where appropriate, the equipment should be designed and constructed as to allow easy and effective decontamination and/or sterilisation.

23. Closed equipment used for the primary containment of the biological agents should be designed and constructed as to prevent any leakage or the formation of droplets and aerosols.

    Inlets and outlets for gases should be protected so as to achieve adequate containment e.g. by the use of sterilising hydrophobic filters.

    The introduction or removal of material should take place using a sterilisable closed system, or possibly in an appropriate laminar air flow.

24. Equipment where necessary should be properly sterilised before use, preferably by pressurised dry steam. Other methods can be accepted if steam sterilisation cannot be used because of the nature of the equipment. It is important not to overlook such individual items as bench centrifuges and water baths.

Equipment used for purification, separation or concentration should be sterilised or disinfected at least between use for different products. The effect of the sterilisation methods on the effectiveness and validity of the equipment should be studied in order to determine the life span of the equipment.

All sterilisation procedures should be validated.

25. Equipment should be designed so as to prevent any mix-up between different organisms or products. Pipes, valves and filters should be identified as to their function.

Separate incubators should be used for infected and non infected containers and also generally for different organisms or cells. Incubators containing more than one organism or cell type will only be acceptable if adequate steps are taken to seal, surface decontaminate and segregate the containers. Culture vessels, etc. should be individually labelled. The cleaning and disinfection of the items can be particularly difficult and should receive special attention.

Equipment used for the storage of biological agents or products should be designed and used in such a manner as to prevent any possible mix-up. All stored items should be clearly and unambiguously labelled and in leak-proof containers. Items such as cells and organisms seed stock should be stored in dedicated equipment.

26. Relevant equipment, such as that requiring temperature control, should be fitted with recording and/or alarm systems.

To avoid breakdowns, a system of preventive maintenance, together with trend analysis of recorded data, should be implemented.

27. The loading of freeze dryers requires an appropriate clean/contained area.

Unloading freeze dryers contaminates the immediate environment. Therefore, for single-ended freeze dryers, the clean room should be decontaminated before a further manufacturing batch is introduced into the area, unless this contains the same organisms, and double door freeze dryers should be sterilised after each cycle unless opened in a clean area.

Sterilisation of freeze dryers should be done in accordance with item 24. In case of campaign working, they should at least be sterilised after each campaign.

Animals and animal houses

28. General requirements for animal quarters, care and quarantine are laid down in Directive 86/609/EEC[23].

29. Animal houses should be separated from the other production premises and suitably designed.

30. The sanitary status of the animals used for production should be defined, monitored, and recorded. Some animals should be handled as defined in specific monographs (e.g. Specific Pathogens Free flocks).

31. Animals, biological agents, and tests carried out should be the subject of an identification system so as to prevent any risk of confusion and to control all possible hazards.

Disinfection – Waste disposal

32. Disinfection and/or wastes and effluents disposal may be particularly important in the case of manufacture of immunological products. Careful consideration should therefore be given to procedures and equipment aiming at avoiding environmental contamination as well as to their validation or qualification.

---

[23] Directive 2003/65/EC of the European Parliament and of the Council of 22 July 2003 amending Council Directive 86/609/EEC on the approximation of laws, regulations and administrative provisions of the Member States regarding the protection of animals used for experimental and other scientific purposes (OJ L 230 , 16.09.2003, p. 32-33)

Annex 5

Production

33. Because of the wide variety of products, the frequently large number of stages involved in the manufacture of immunological veterinary medicinal products and the nature of the biological processes, careful attention must be paid to adherence to validated operating procedures, to the constant monitoring of production at all stages and to in-process controls.

    Additionally, special consideration should be given to starting materials, media and the use of a seed lot system.

Starting materials

34. The suitability of starting materials should be clearly defined in written specifications. These should include details of the supplier, the method of manufacture, the geographical origin and the animal species from which the materials are derived. The controls to be applied to starting materials must be included. Microbiological controls are particularly important.

35. The results of tests on starting materials must comply with the specifications. Where the tests take a long time (e.g. eggs from SPF flocks) it may be necessary to process starting materials before the results of analytical controls are available. In such cases, the release of a finished product is conditional upon satisfactory results of the tests on starting materials.

36. Special attention should be paid to a knowledge of the supplier's quality assurance system in assessing the suitability of a source and the extent of quality control testing required.

37. Where possible, heat is the preferred method for sterilising starting materials. If necessary, other validated methods, such as irradiation, may be used.

Media

38. The ability of media to support the desired growth should be properly validated in advance.

39. Media should preferably be sterilised in situ or in line. Heat is the preferred method. Gases, media, acids, alkalis, defoaming agents and other materials introduced into sterile biogenerators should themselves be sterile.

Seed lot and cell bank system

40. In order to prevent the unwanted drift of properties which might ensue from repeated subcultures or multiple generations, the production of immunological veterinary medicinal products obtained by microbial, cell or tissue culture, or propagation in embryos and animals, should be based on a system of seed lots or cell banks.

41. The number of generations (doublings, passages) between the seed lot or cell bank and the finished product should be consistent with the dossier of authorisation for marketing.

42. Seed lots and cell banks should be adequately characterised and tested for contaminants. Acceptance criteria for new seed lots should be established. Seed lots and cell banks shall be established, stored and used in such a way as to minimise the risks of contamination, or any alteration. During the establishment of the seed lot and cell bank, no other living or infectious material (e.g. virus or cell lines) shall be handled simultaneously in the same area or by the same person.

43. Establishment of the seed lot and cell bank should be performed in a suitable environment to protect the seed lot and the cell bank and, if applicable, the personnel handling it and the external environment.

44. The origin, form and storage conditions of seed material should be described in full. Evidence of the stability and recovery of the seeds and cells should be provided. Storage containers should be hermetically sealed, clearly labelled and stored at an appropriate temperature. Storage conditions shall be properly monitored. An inventory should be kept and each container accounted for.

45. Only authorised personnel should be allowed to handle the material and this handling should be done under the supervision of a responsible person. Different seed lots or cell banks shall be stored in such a way to avoid

Annex 5

confusion or cross-contamination errors. It is desirable to split the seed lots and cell banks and to store the parts at different locations so as to minimise the risk of total loss.

Operating principles

46.   The formation of droplets and the production of foam should be avoided or minimised during manufacturing processes. Centrifugation and blending procedures which can lead to droplet formation should be carried out in appropriate contained or clean/contained areas to prevent transfer of live organisms.

47.   Accidental spillages, especially of live organisms, must be dealt with quickly and safely. Validated decontamination measures should be available for each organism. Where different strains of single bacteria species or very similar viruses are involved, the process need be validated against only one of them, unless there is reason to believe that they may vary significantly in their resistance to the agent(s) involved.

48.   Operations involving the transfer of materials such as sterile media, cultures or product should be carried out in pre-sterilised closed systems wherever possible. Where this is not possible, transfer operations must be protected by laminar airflow work stations.

49.   Addition of media or cultures to biogenerators and other vessels should be carried out under carefully controlled conditions to ensure that contamination is not introduced. Care must be taken to ensure that vessels are correctly connected when addition of cultures takes place.

50.   Where necessary, for instance when two or more fermenters are within a single area, sampling and addition ports, and connectors (after connection, before the flow of product, and again before disconnection) should be sterilised with steam. In other circumstances, chemical disinfection of ports and laminar air flow protection of connections may be acceptable.

51.   Equipment, glassware, the external surfaces of product containers and other such materials must be disinfected before transfer from a contained area using a validated method (see 47 above). Batch documentation can be a particular problem. Only the absolute minimum required

to allow operations to GMP standards should enter and leave the area. If obviously contaminated, such as by spills or aerosols, or if the organism involved is an exotic, the paperwork must be adequately disinfected through an equipment pass, or the information transferred out by such means as photocopy or fax.

52. Liquid or solid wastes such as the debris after harvesting eggs, disposable culture bottles, unwanted cultures or biological agents, are best sterilised or disinfected before transfer from a contained area. However, alternatives such as sealed containers or piping may be appropriate in some cases.

53. Articles and materials, including documentation, entering a production room should be carefully controlled to ensure that only articles and materials concerned with production are introduced. There should be a system which ensures that articles and materials entering a room are reconciled with those leaving so that their accumulation within the room does not occur.

54. Heat stable articles and materials entering a clean area or clean/contained area should do so through a double-ended autoclave or oven. Heat labile articles and materials should enter through an air-lock with interlocked doors where they are disinfected. Sterilisation of articles and materials elsewhere is acceptable provided that they are double wrapped and enter through an airlock with the appropriate precautions.

55. Precautions must be taken to avoid contamination or confusion during incubation. There should be a cleaning and disinfection procedure for incubators. Containers in incubators should be carefully and clearly labelled.

56. With the exception of blending and subsequent filling operations (or when totally enclosed systems are used) only one live biological agent may be handled within a production room at any given time. Production rooms must be effectively disinfected between the handling of different live biological agents.

57. Products should be inactivated by the addition of inactivant accompanied by sufficient agitation. The mixture should then be transferred to a second sterile vessel, unless the container is of such a size and shape

Annex 5

as to be easily inverted and shaken so as to wet all internal surfaces with the final culture/inactivant mixture.

58. Vessels containing inactivated products should not be opened or sampled in areas containing live biological agents. All subsequent processing of inactivated products should take place in clean areas grade A-B or enclosed equipment dedicated to inactivated products.

59. Careful consideration should be given to the validation of methods for sterilisation, disinfection, virus removal and inactivation.

60. Filling should be carried out as soon as possible following production. Containers of bulk product prior to filling should be sealed, appropriately labelled and stored under specified conditions of temperature.

61. There should be a system to assure the integrity and closure of containers after filling.

62. The capping of vials containing live biological agents must be performed in such a way that ensures that contamination of other products or escape of the live agents into other areas or the external environment does not occur.

63. For various reasons there may be a delay between the filling of final containers and their labelling and packaging. Procedures should be specified for the storage of unlabelled containers in order to prevent confusion and to ensure satisfactory storage conditions. Special attention should be paid to the storage of heat labile or photosensitive products. Storage temperatures should be specified.

64. For each stage of production, the yield of product should be reconciled with that expected from that process. Any significant discrepancies should be investigated.

Quality control

65. In-process controls play a specially important role in ensuring the consistency of the quality of biological medicinal products. Those controls which are crucial for the quality (e.g. virus removal) but which cannot be

carried out on the finished product, should be performed at an appropriate stage of production.

66. It may be necessary to retain samples of intermediate products in sufficient amount and under appropriate storage conditions to allow repetition or confirmation of a batch control.

67. There may be a requirement for the continuous monitoring of data during a production process, for example monitoring of physical parameters during fermentation.

68. Continuous culture of biological products is a common practice and special consideration needs to be given to the quality control requirements arising from this type of production method.

Annex 6:
Manufacture of Medicinal Gases

Brussels, April 2001

Working Party on Control of Medicines and Inspections

Final Version of Annex 6 to the EU Guide to Good Manufacturing Practice

Document History	
First discussions within PIC/S framework	June 1998- August 1999
Consultation with Ad-hoc meeting of GMP Inspection services	September – December 1999
Revised version	February 2000
Pharmaceutical Committee (for release for industry consultation)	23 March 2000
Proposed Deadline for comments	31 August 2000
Final draft after consultation in parallel with PIC/S	29 March 2001
Discussion in Inspectors working party	May 2001
Circulation to Pharmaceutical Committee	July 2001
Proposed Date for coming into operation	September 2001

Note that this document is based in the PICS/S recommendations

1. Principle

This annex deals with industrial manufacturing of medicinal gases, which is aspecialised industrial process not normally undertaken by pharmaceutical companies.It does not cover manufacturing and handling of medicinal gases in hospitals, whichwill be subject to national legislation. However relevant parts of this annex may beused as a basis for such activities.

The manufacture of medicinal gases is generally carried out in closed equipment. Consequently, environmental contamination of the product is minimal. However, there is a risk of cross-contamination with other gases.

Manufacture of medicinal gases should comply with the basic requirements of GMP, with applicable annexes, Pharmacopoeial standards and the following detailedguidelines.

2. Personnel

2.1. The qualified person responsible for release of medicinal gases should have athorough knowledge of the production and control of medicinal gases.

2.2. All personnel involved in the manufacture of medicinal gases should understand theGMP requirements relevant to medicinal gases and should be aware of the criticallyimportant aspects and potential hazards for patients from products in the form ofmedicinal gases.

3. Premises and equipment

3.1. Premises

3.1.1. Medicinal gases should be filled in a separate area from non-medicinal gases andthere should be no exchange of containers between these areas. In exceptional cases,the principal of campaign filling in the same area can be accepted provided thatspecific precautions are taken and necessary validation is done.

3.1.2. Premises should provide sufficient space for manufacturing, testing and storageoperations to avoid the risk of mix-up. Premises should be clean and tidy toencourage orderly working and adequate storage.

3.1.3. Filling areas should be of sufficient size and have an orderly layout to provide:

a.)   separate marked areas for different gases

b.)   clear identification and segregation of empty cylinders and cylinders at various stages of processing (e.g. "awaiting filling", "filled", "quarantine", "approved" "rejected ").

The method used to achieve these various levels of segregation will depend on thenature, extent and complexity of the overall operation, but marked-out floor areas,partitions, barriers and signs could be used or other appropriate means.

3.2. Equipment

3.2.1. All equipment for manufacture and analyses should be qualified and calibrated regularly as appropriate.

3.2.2. It is necessary to ensure that the correct gas is put into the correct container. Except for validated automated filling processes there should be no interconnections between pipelines carrying different gases. The manifolds should be equipped withfill connections that correspond only to the valve for that particular gas or particularmixture of gases so that only the correct containers can be attached to the manifold.(The use of manifold and container valve connections may be subject tointernational or national standards.)

3.2.3. Repair and maintenance operations should not affect the quality of the medicinal gases.

3.2.4. Filling of non-medicinal gases should be avoided in areas and with equipmentdestined for the production of medicinal gases. Exceptions can be acceptable if thequality of the gas used for non-medicinal purposes is at least equal to the quality ofthe medicinal gas and GMP-standards are maintained. There should be a validated method of backflow prevention in the line supplying the filling area for non-medicinal gases to prevent contamination of the medicinal gas.

3.2.5. Storage tanks and mobile delivery tanks should be dedicated to one gas and a well-defined quality of this gas. However liquefied medicinal gases may be stored

Annex 6

ortransported in the same tanks as the same non-medicinal gas provided that thequality of the latter is at least equal to the quality of the medicinal gas.

4. Documentation

4.1. Data included in the records for each batch of cylinders filled must ensure that each filled cylinder is traceable to significant aspects of the relevant filling operations. As appropriate, the following should be entered:

— the name of the product;

— the date and the time of the filling operations;

— a reference to the filling station used;

— equipment used;

— name and reference to the specification of the gas or each gas in a mixture

— pre filling operations performed (see point 7.3.5);

— the quantity and size of cylinders before and after filling;

— the name of the person carrying out the filling operation;

— the initials of the operators for each significant step (line clearance, receipt of cylinders, emptying of cylinders etc);

— key parameters that are needed to ensure correct fill at standard conditions;

— the results of quality control tests and where test equipment is calibrated before each test, the reference gas specification and calibration check results;

— results of appropriate checks to ensure the containers have been filled

— a sample of the batch code label;

— details of any problems or unusual events, and signed authorisation for any deviation from filling instructions; -to indicate agreement, the date and signature of the supervisor responsible for the filling operation.

5. Production

5.1. All critical steps in the different manufacturing processes should be subject to validation.

5.2. Bulk production

5.2.1. Bulk gases intended for medicinal use could be prepared by chemical synthesis orobtained from natural resources followed by purification steps if necessary (as forexample in an air separation plant). These gases could be regarded as ActivePharmaceutical Ingredients (API) or as bulk pharmaceutical products as decided bythe national competent authority.

5.2.2. Documentation should be available specifying the purity, other components andpossible impurities that may be present in the source gas and at purification steps, asapplicable. Flow charts of each different process should be available.

5.2.3. All separation and purification steps should be designed to operate at optimaleffectiveness. For example, impurities that may adversely affect a purification stepshould be removed before this step is reached.

5.2.4. Separation and purification steps should be validated for effectiveness and monitored according to the results of the validation. Where necessary, in-process controls should include continuous analysis to monitor the process. Maintenance and replacement of expendable equipment components, e.g. purification filters, should be based on the results of monitoring and validation.

5.2.5. If applicable, limits for process temperatures should be documented and in-process monitoring should include temperature measurement.

5.2.6. Computer systems used in controlling or monitoring processes should be validated.

5.2.7. For continuous processes, a definition of a batch should be documented and related to the analysis of the bulk gas.

5.2.8. Gas production should be continuously monitored for quality and impurities.

Annex 6

5.2.9. Water used for cooling during compression of air should be monitored for microbiological quality when in contact with the medicinal gas.

5.2.10. All the transfer operations, including controls before transfers, of liquefied gases from primary storage should be in accordance with written procedures designed to avoid any contamination. The transfer line should be equipped with a non-return valve or other suitable alternative. Particular attention should be paid to purge the flexible connections and to coupling hoses and connectors.

5.2.11. Deliveries of gas may be added to bulk storage tanks containing the same gas from previous deliveries. The results of a sample must show that the quality of the delivered gas is acceptable. Such a sample could be taken from

— the delivered gas before the delivery is added; or

— from the bulk tank after adding and mixing

5.2.12 Bulk gases intended for medicinal use should be defined as a batch, controlled in accordance with relevant Pharmacopoeial monographs and released for filling.

5.3. Filling and labelling

5.3.1. For filling of medicinal gases the batch should be defined.

5.3.2. Containers for medicinal gases should conform to appropriate technical specifications. Valve outlets should be equipped with tamper-evident seals afterfilling. Cylinders should preferably have minimum retention valves in order to getadequate protection against contamination.

5.3.3. The medicinal gases filling manifold as well as the cylinders should be dedicated toa single medicinal gas or to a given mixture of medicinal gases (see also 3.2.2).There should be a system in place ensuring traceability of cylinders and valves.

5.3.4. Cleaning and purging of filling equipment and pipelines should be carried outaccording to written procedures. This is especially important after maintenance orbreaches of system integrity. Checks for the absence of contaminants should be carried out before the line is released for use. Records should be maintained.

5.3.5. Cylinders should be subject to an internal visual inspection when

— they are new

— in connection with any hydrostatic pressure test or equivalent test

After fitting of the valve, the valve should be maintained in a closed position toprevent any contamination from entering the cylinder.

5.3.6. Checks to be performed before filling should include:

— a check to determine the residual pressure (>3 to 5 bar) to ensure that the cylinder is not emptied

— Cylinders with no residual pressure should be put aside for additional measures to make sure they are not contaminated with water or other contaminants. These could include cleaning with validated methods or visual inspection as justified.

— Assuring that all batch labels and other labels if damaged have been removed

— visual external inspection of each valve and container for dents, arc burns,debris, other damage and contamination with oil or grease; Cylinders shouldbe cleaned, tested and maintained in an appropriate manner.

— a check of each cylinder or cryogenic vessel valve connection to determinethat it is the proper type for the particular medicinal gas involved;

— a check of the cylinder "test code date" to determine that the hydrostaticpressure test or equivalent test has been conducted and still is valid asrequired by national or international guidelines.

— a check to determine that each container is colour-coded according to therelevant standard

5.3.7. Cylinders which have been returned for refilling should be prepared with great carein order to minimise risks for contamination. For compressed gases a

Annex 6

maximumtheoretical impurity of 500 ppm v/v should be obtained for a filling pressure of 200bar (and equivalent for other filling pressures).

Cylinders could be prepared as follows: -any gas remaining in the cylinders should be removed by evacuating the container [at least to a remaining absolute pressure of 150 millibar] or -by blowing down each container, followed by purging using validated methods (partial pressurisation at least to 7 bar and then blowing down)

For cylinders equipped with residual (positive) pressure valves, one evacuation under vacuum at 150 millibar is sufficient if the pressure is positive. As an alternative, full analysis of the remaining gas should be carried out for each individual container.

5.3.8. There should be appropriate checks to ensure that containers have been filled. Anindication that it is filling properly could be to ensure that the exterior of the cylinderis warm by touching it lightly during filling.

5.3.9. Each cylinder should be labelled and colour-coded. The batch number and/or filling date and expiry date may be on a separate label.

6. Quality Control

6.1. Water used for hydrostatic pressure testing should be at least of drinking waterquality and monitored routinely for microbiological contamination.

6.2. Each medicinal gas should be tested and released according to its specifications. Inaddition, each medicinal gas should be tested to full relevant pharmacopoeialrequirements at sufficient frequency to assure ongoing compliance.

6.3. The bulk gas supply should be released for filling. (see 5.2.12)

6.4. In the case of a single medicinal gas filled via a multi-cylinder manifold, at least onecylinder of product from each manifold filling should be tested for identity, assayand if necessary water content each time the cylinders are changed on the manifold.

6.5. In the case of a single medicinal gas filled put into cylinders one at a time byindividual filling operations, at least one cylinder of each uninterrupted filling cycleshould be tested for identity and assay. An example of an uninterrupted filling operation cycle is one shift's production using the same personnel, equipment, and batch of bulk gas.

6.6. In the case of a medicinal gas produced by mixing two or more different gases in acylinder from the same manifold, at least one cylinder from each manifold fillingoperation cycle should be tested for identity, assay and if necessary water content ofall of the component gases and for identity of the balance gas in the mixture. Whencylinders are filled individually, every cylinder should be tested for identity andassay of all of the component gases and at least one cylinder of each uninterruptedfilling cycle should be tested for identity of the balance gas in the mixture.

6.7. When gases are mixed in-line before filling (e.g. nitrous oxide/oxygen mixture)continuous analysis of the mixture being filled is required.

6.8. When a cylinder is filled with more than one gas, the filling process must ensure thatthe gases are correctly mixed in every cylinder and are fully homogeneous.

6.9. Each filled cylinder should be tested for leaks using an appropriate method, prior tofitting the tamper evident seal. Where sampling and testing is carried out the leaktest should be completed after testing.

6.10. In the case of cryogenic gas filled into cryogenic home vessels for delivery to users,each vessel should be tested for identity and assay.

6.11. Cryogenic vessels which are retained by customers and where the medicinal gas isrefilled in place from dedicated mobile delivery tanks need not be sampled afterfilling provided the filling company delivers a certificate of analysis for a sampletaken from the mobile delivery tank. Cryogenic vessels retained by customers shouldbe

Annex 6

periodically tested to confirm that the contents comply
with Pharmacopoeialrequirements.

6.12. Retained samples are not required, unless otherwise
specified.

7. Storage and release

7.1. Filled cylinders should be held in quarantine until
released by the qualified person.

7.2. Gas cylinders should be stored under cover and not be
subjected to extremes of temperature. Storage areas
should be clean, dry, well ventilated and free of
combustible materials to ensure that cylinders remain
clean up to the time of use.

7.3. Storage arrangements should permit segregation of
different gases and of full/emptycylinders and permit
rotation of stock on a first in – first out basis.

7.4. Gas cylinders should be protected from adverse weather
conditions during transportation. Specific conditions for
storage and transportation should beemployed for gas
mixtures for which phase separation occurs on freezing.

Glossary

Definition of terms relating to manufacture of medicinal gases,
which are not given in the glossary of the current PIC/S Guide
to GMP, but which are used in this Annex are given below.

Air separation plant

Air separation plants take atmospheric air and through
processes of purification, cleaning, compression, cooling,
liquefaction and distillation separates the air into the gases
oxygen, nitrogen and argon

Area

Part of premises that is specific to the manufacture of medicinal
gases

Blowing down

Blow the pressure down to atmospheric pressure

Bulk gas

Any gas intended for medicinal use, which has completed all processing up to but not including final packaging

Compressed gas

A gas which when packaged under pressure is entirely gaseous at −50 0 C. (ISO 10286)

Container

A container is a cryogenic vessel, a tank, a tanker, a cylinder, a cylinder bundle or any other package that is in direct contact with the medicinal gas.

Cryogenic gas

Gas which liquefies at 1.013 bar at temperature below −1500 C.

Cryogenic vessel

A static or mobile thermally insulated container designed to contain liquefied or cryogenic gases. The gas is removed in gaseous or liquid form.

Cylinder

A transportable, pressure container with a water capacity not exceeding 150 litres. In this document when using the word cylinder it includes cylinder bundle (or cylinder pack) when appropriate.

Cylinder bundle

A set assembly of cylinders, which are fastened together in a frame and interconnected by a manifold, transported and used as a unit.

Evacuate

To remove the residual gas in a container by pulling a vacuum on it.

Gas

A substance or a mixture of substances that is completely gaseous at 1,013 bar (101,325 kPa) and +15 0 C or has a vapour pressure exceeding 3 bar (300 kPa) at + 50 0 C. (ISO 10286)

Annex 6

Hydrostatic pressure test
Test performed for safety reasons as required by national or international guideline in order to make sure that cylinders or tanks can withhold high pressures.

Liquefied gas
A gas which when packaged under pressure, is partially liquid (gas over a liquid) at −50 0 C.

Manifold
Equipment or apparatus designed to enable one or more gas containers to be emptied and filled at a time.

Maximum theoretical residual impurity
Gaseous impurity coming from a possible retropollution and remaining after the cylinders pre-treatment before filling. The calculation of the maximum theoretical impurity is only relevant for compressed gases and supposes that these gases act as perfect gases.

Medicinal gas
Any gas or mixture of gases intended to be administered to patients for therapeutic, diagnostic or prophylactic purposes using pharmacological action and classified as a medicinal product.

Minimum pressure retention valve
Valve equipped with a non-return system which maintains a definite pressure (about 3 to 5 bars over atmospheric pressure) in order to prevent contamination during use.

Non-return valve
Valve which permits flow in one direction only.

Purge
To empty and clean a cylinder

– by blowing down and evacuating or

– by blowing down, partial pressurisation with the gas in question and then blowing down.

Tank
Static container for the storage of liquefied or cryogenic gas.

Tanker

Container fixed on a vehicle for the transport of liquefied or cryogenic gas.

Valve

Device for opening and closing containers.

Annex 7: Manufacture of Herbal Medicinal Products

Brussels, 01 September 2008

Document History	
Revision to specify application of GMP provisions for active substances used as starting materials (Part II) for the manufacture of herbal medicinal products. Additional changes are in particular related to the new Directive 2004/24/EC on traditional herbal medicinal products. Collaboration between GMDP Inspectors Working Group (formerly Ad Hoc GMP Inspection Services Working Group) and Committee of Herbal Medicinal Products (HMPC).	May 2005 – March 2006
Public consultation	May - July 2006
Date of revised version coming into operation	01 September 2009

Principle

Because of their often complex and variable nature, control of starting materials, storage and processing assume particular importance in the manufacture of herbal medicinal products.

The "starting material" in the manufacture of a herbal medicinal product[24] can be a medicinal plant, a herbal substance or a

---

[24] Throughout the annex and unless otherwise specified, the term "herbal medicinal product/ preparation" includes "traditional herbal medicinal product/ preparation".

herbal preparation[25]. The herbal substance shall be of suitable quality and supporting data should be provided to the manufacturer of the herbal preparation/herbal medicinal product. Ensuring consistent quality of the herbal substance may require more detailed information on its agricultural production. The selection of seeds, cultivation and harvesting conditions represent important aspects of the quality of the herbal substance and can influence the consistency of the finished product. Recommendations on an appropriate quality assurance system for good agricultural and collection practice are provided in the HMPC guidance document: "Guideline on Good Agricultural and Collection Practice for starting materials of herbal origin".

This Annex applies to all herbal starting materials: medicinal plants, herbal substances or herbal preparations.

Table 1: Table illustrating the application of Good Practices to the manufacture of herbal medicinal products[26].

Activity	Good Agricultural and Collection Practice (GACP)[27]	Part II of the GMP Guide†	Part I of the GMP Guide †
Cultivation, collection and harvesting of plants, algae, fungi and lichens, and collection of exudates	▓		
Cutting, and drying of plants, algae, fungi, lichens and exudates *	▓	▓	
Expression from plants and distillation **		▓	
Comminution, processing of exudates, extraction from plants, fractionation, purification, concentration or fermentation of herbal substances		▓	▓

---

[25] The terms herbal substance and herbal preparation as defined in Directive 2004/24/EC are considered to be equivalent to the Ph. Eur. terms herbal drug and herbal drug preparation respectively.

[26] This table expands in detail the herbal section of Table 1 in part II of the GMP Guide.

[27] as published by the European Medicines Agency EMEA

Activity	Good Agricultural and Collection Practice (GACP)[27]	Part II of the GMP Guide†	Part I of the GMP Guide †
Further processing into a dosage form including packaging as a medicinal product			

† Explanatory Note.

The GMP classification of the herbal material is dependent upon the use made of it by the manufacturing authorisation holder. The material may be classified as an active substance, an intermediate or a finished product. It is the responsibility of the manufacturer of the medicinal product to ensure that the appropriate GMP classification is applied.

* Manufacturers should ensure that these steps are carried out in accordance with the marketing authorisation/registration. For those initial steps that take place in the field, as justified in the marketing authorisation/registration, the standards of Good Agricultural and Collection Practice for starting materials of herbal origin (GACP) is applicable. GMP is applicable to further cutting and drying steps.

** Regarding the expression from plants and distillation, if it is necessary for these activities to be an integral part of harvesting to maintain the quality of the product within the approved specifications, it is acceptable that they are performed in the field, provided that the cultivation is in compliance with GACP. These circumstances should be regarded as exceptional and justified in the relevant marketing authorisation/ registration documentation. For activities carried out in the field, appropriate documentation, control, and validation according to the GMP principles should be assured. Regulatory authorities may carry out GMP inspections of these activities in order to assess compliance.

Premises & Equipment

Storage areas

1. Herbal substances should be stored in separate areas. The storage area should be equipped in such a way as to give

Annex 7

protection against the entry of insects or other animals, especially rodents. Effective measures should be taken to prevent the spread of any such animals and micro-organisms brought in with the herbal substance, to prevent fermentation or mould growth and to prevent cross-contamination. Different enclosed areas should be used to quarantine incoming herbal substances and for the approved herbal substances.

2. The storage area should be well aerated and the containers should be located in such a way so as to allow free circulation of air.

3. Special attention should be paid to the cleanliness and maintenance of the storage areas particularly when dust is generated.

4. Storage of herbal substances and herbal preparations may require special conditions of humidity, temperature or light protection; these conditions should be provided and monitored.

Production area

5. Specific provisions should be made during sampling, weighing, mixing and processing operations of herbal substances and herbal preparations whenever dust is generated, to facilitate cleaning and to avoid cross-contamination, as for example, dust extraction, dedicated premises, etc.

Equipment

6. The equipment, filtering materials etc. used in the manufacturing process must be compatible with the extraction solvent, in order to prevent any release or undesirable absorption of substance that could affect the product.

Documentation

Specifications for starting materials

7. Herbal medicinal product manufacturers must ensure that they use only herbal starting materials manufactured in accordance with GMP and the Marketing Authorisation dossier. Comprehensive documentation on audits of the

herbal starting material suppliers carried out by, or on behalf of the herbal medicinal product manufacturer should be made available. Audit trails for the active substance are fundamental to the quality of the starting material. The manufacturer should ensure that the suppliers of the herbal substance/preparation are in compliance with Good Agricultural and Collection Practice.

8. To fulfil the specification requirements described in the basic requirements of the Guide (chapter 4), documentation for herbal substances/preparations should include:

— the binomial scientific name of plant (genus, species, subspecies/variety and author (e.g. Linnaeus); other relevant information such as the cultivar name and the chemotype should also be provided, as appropriate;

— details of the source of the plant (country or region of origin, and where applicable, cultivation, time of harvesting, collection procedures, possible pesticides used, possible radioactive contamination etc.);

— which part(s) of the plant is/are used;

— when a dried plant is used, the drying system should be specified;

— a description of the herbal substance and its macro and microscopic examination;

— suitable identification tests including, where appropriate, identification tests for constituents with known therapeutic activity, or markers. Specific distinctive tests are required where an herbal substance is liable to be adulterated/ substituted. A reference authentic specimen should be available for identification purposes;

— the water content for herbal substances, determined in accordance with the European Pharmacopoeia;

— assay of constituents of known therapeutic activity or, where appropriate, of markers; the methods suitable to determine possible pesticide contamination and limits accepted, in accordance with European Pharmacopoeia methods or, in absence thereof, with an appropriate validated method, unless otherwise justified;

— tests to determine fungal and/or microbial contamination, including aflatoxins, other mycotoxins, pest-infestations and limits accepted, as appropriate;

Annex 7

— tests for toxic metals and for likely contaminants and adulterants, as appropriate;

— tests for foreign materials, as appropriate;

— any other additional test according to the European Pharmacopoeia general monograph on herbal substances or to the specific monograph of the herbal substance, as appropriate.

Any treatment used to reduce fungal/microbial contamination or other infestation should be documented. Specifications and procedures should be available and should include details of process, tests and limits for residues.

Processing instructions

9. The processing instructions should describe the different operations carried out upon the herbal substance such as cleaning, drying, crushing and sifting, and include drying time and temperatures, and methods used to control cut size or particle size.

10. In particular, there should be written instructions and records, which ensure that each container of herbal substance is carefully examined to detect any adulteration/substitution or presence of foreign matter, such as metal or glass pieces, animal parts or excrement, stones, sand, etc., or rot and signs of decay.

11. The processing instructions should also describe security sieving or other methods of removing foreign materials and appropriate procedures for cleaning/selection of plant material before the storage of the approved herbal substance or before the start of manufacturing.

12. For the production of an herbal preparation, instructions should include details of solvent, time and temperature of extraction, details of any concentration stages and methods used.

Quality control

Sampling

13. Due to the fact that medicinal plant/herbal substances are heterogeneous in nature, their sampling should be carried

out with special care by personnel with particular expertise. Each batch should be identified by its own documentation.

14. A reference sample of the plant material is necessary, especially in those cases where the herbal substance is not described in the European Pharmacopoeia or in another Pharmacopoeia of a Member State. Samples of unmilled plant material are required if powders are used.

15. Quality Control personnel should have particular expertise and experience in herbal substances, herbal preparations and/or herbal medicinal products in order to be able to carry out identification tests and recognise adulteration, the presence of fungal growth, infestations, non-uniformity within a delivery of crude material, etc.

16. The identity and quality of herbal substances, herbal preparations and of herbal medicinal products should be determined in accordance with the relevant current European guidance on quality and specifications of herbal medicinal products and traditional herbal medicinal products and, where relevant, to the specific Ph. Eur. Monographs.

Annex 7

Annex 8:
Sampling of Starting and Packaging Materials

Principle

Sampling is an important operation in which only a small fraction of a batch is taken. Valid conclusions on the whole cannot be based on tests which have been carried out on nonrepresentative samples. Correct sampling is thus an essential part of a system of Quality Assurance.

Note   *Sampling is dealt with in Chapter 6 of the Guide, items 6.11. to 6.14. This annex gives additional guidance on the sampling of starting and packaging materials.*

Personnel

1. Personnel who take samples should receive initial and on-going regular training in the disciplines relevant to correct sampling. This training should include:

    — sampling plans,

    — written sampling procedures,

    — the techniques and equipment for sampling,

    — the risks of cross-contamination,

    — the precautions to be taken with regard to unstable and/or sterile substances,

    — the importance of considering the visual appearance of materials, containers and labels,

    — the importance of recording any unexpected or unusual circumstances.

Starting materials

2. The identity of a complete batch of starting materials can normally only be ensured if individual samples are taken from all the containers and an identity test performed on each sample. It is permissible to sample only a proportion of the containers where a validated procedure has been established to ensure that no single container of starting material has been incorrectly labelled.

3. This validation should take account of at least the following aspects:

   — the nature and status of the manufacturer and of the supplier and their understanding of the GMP requirements of the Pharmaceutical Industry;

   — the Quality Assurance system of the manufacturer of the starting material;

   — the manufacturing conditions under which the starting material is produced and controlled;

   — the nature of the starting material and the medicinal products in which it will be used.

   Under such a system, it is possible that a validated procedure exempting identity testing of each incoming container of starting material could be accepted for:

   — starting materials coming from a single product manufacturer or plant;

   — starting materials coming directly from a manufacturer or in the manufacturer's sealed container where there is a history of reliability and regular audits of the manufacturer's Quality Assurance system are conducted by the purchaser (the manufacturer of the medicinal product) or by an officially accredited body.

   It is improbable that a procedure could be satisfactorily validated for:

   — starting materials supplied by intermediaries such as brokers where the source of manufacture is unknown or not audited;

   — starting materials for use in parenteral products.

4. The quality of a batch of starting materials may be assessed by taking and testing a representative sample. The samples taken for identity testing could be used for this purpose. The number of samples taken for the preparation of a representative sample should be determined statistically and specified in a sampling plan. The number of individual samples which may be blended to form a composite sample should also be defined, taking into account the nature of the material, knowledge of the supplier and the homogeneity of the composite sample.

Packaging material

5. The sampling plan for packaging materials should take account of at least the following: the quantity received, the quality required, the nature of the material (e.g. primary packaging materials and/or printed packaging materials), the production methods, and what is known of the Quality Assurance system of the packaging materials manufacturer based on audits. The number of samples taken should be determined statistically and specified in a sampling plan.

Annex 9: Manufacture of Liquids, Creams and Ointments

Principle

Liquids, creams and ointments may be particularly susceptible to microbial and other contamination during manufacture. Therefore special measures must be taken to prevent any contamination.

Premises and equipment

1. The use of closed systems for processing and transfer is recommended in order to protect the product from contamination. Production areas where the products or open clean containers are exposed should normally be effectively ventilated with filtered air.

2. Tanks, containers, pipework and pumps should be designed and installed so that they may be readily cleaned and if necessary sanitised. In particular, equipment design should include a minimum of dead-legs or sites where residues can accumulate and promote microbial proliferation.

3. The use of glass apparatus should be avoided wherever possible. High quality stainless steel is often the material of choice for parts coming into contact with product.

Production

4. The chemical and microbiological quality of water used in production should be specified and monitored. Care should be taken in the maintenance of water systems in order to avoid the risk of microbial proliferation. After any chemical sanitisation of the water systems, a validated flushing procedure should be followed to ensure that the sanitising agent has been effectively removed.

5. The quality of materials received in bulk tankers should be checked before they are transferred to bulk storage tanks.

6. Care should be taken when transferring materials via pipelines to ensure that they are delivered to their correct destination.

7. Materials likely to shed fibres or other contaminants, like cardboard or wooden pallets, should not enter the areas where products or clean containers are exposed.

8. Care should be taken to maintain the homogeneity of mixtures, suspensions, etc. during filling. Mixing and filling processes should be validated. Special care should be taken at the beginning of a filling process, after stoppages and at the end of the process to ensure that homogeneity is maintained.

9. When the finished product is not immediately packaged, the maximum period of storage and the storage conditions should be specified and adhered to.

Annex 10:
Manufacture of Pressurised Metered Dose Aerosol Preparations for Inhalation

Principle

The manufacture of pressurised aerosol products for inhalation with metering valves requires special consideration because of the particular nature of this form of product. It should be done under conditions which minimise microbial and particulate contamination.

Assurance of the quality of the valve components and, in the case of suspensions, of uniformity is also of particular importance.

General

1. There are presently two common manufacturing and filling methods as follows:

    a. Two-shot system (pressure filling). The active ingredient is suspended in a high boiling point propellant, the dose is put into the container, the valve is crimped on and the lower boiling point propellant is injected through the valve stem to make up the finished product. The suspension of active ingredient in propellant is kept cool to reduce evaporation loss.

    b. One-shot process (cold filling). The active ingredient is suspended in a mixture of propellants and held either under high pressure or at a low temperature, or both.

    The suspension is then filled directly into the container in one shot.

Premises and equipment

2. Manufacture and filling should be carried out as far as possible in a closed system.

3. Where products or clean components are exposed, the area should be fed with filtered air, should comply with the requirements of at least a Grade D environment and should be entered through airlocks.

Production and quality control

4. Metering valves for aerosols are more complex pieces of engineering than most items used in pharmaceutical production. Their specifications, sampling and testing should recognize this. Auditing the Quality Assurance system of the valve manufacturer is of particular importance.

5. All fluids (e.g. liquid or gaseous propellants) should be filtered to remove particles greater than 0.2 micron. An additional filtration where possible immediately before filling is desirable.

6. Containers and valves should be cleaned using a validated procedure appropriate to the use of the product to ensure the absence of any contaminants such as fabrication aids (e.g. lubricants) or undue microbiological contaminants. After cleaning, valves should be kept in clean, closed containers and precautions taken not to introduce contamination during subsequent handling, e.g. taking samples. Containers should be fed to the filling line in a clean condition or cleaned on line immediately before filling.

7. Precautions should be taken to ensure uniformity of suspensions at the point of fill throughout the filling process.

8. When a two-shot filling process is used, it is necessary to ensure that both shots are of the correct weight in order to achieve the correct composition. For this purpose, 100% weight checking at each stage is often desirable.

9. Controls after filling should ensure the absence of undue leakage. Any leakage test should be performed in a way which avoids microbial contamination or residual moisture.

Annex 11:
Computerised Systems

Principle

The introduction of computerised systems into systems of manufacturing, including storage, distribution and quality control does not alter the need to observe the relevant principles given elsewhere in the Guide. Where a computerised system replaces a manual operation, there should be no resultant decrease in product quality or quality assurance.

Consideration should be given to the risk of losing aspects of the previous system which could result from reducing the involvement of operators.

Personnel

1. It is essential that there is the closest co-operation between key personnel and those involved with computer systems. Persons in responsible positions should have the appropriate training for the management and use of systems within their field of responsibility which utilises computers. This should include ensuring that appropriate expertise is available and used to provide advice on aspects of design, validation, installation and operation of computerised system.

Validation

2. The extent of validation necessary will depend on a number of factors including the use to which the system is to be put, whether the validation is to be prospective or retrospective and whether or not novel elements are incorporated. Validation should be considered as part of the complete life cycle of a computer system. This cycle includes the stages of planning, specification, programming, testing, commissioning, documentation, operation, monitoring and modifying.

System

3. Attention should be paid to the siting of equipment in suitable conditions where extraneous factors cannot interfere with the system.

4. A written detailed description of the system should be produced (including diagrams as appropriate) and kept up to date. It should describe the principles, objectives, security measures and scope of the system and the main features of the way in which the computer is used and how it interacts with other systems and procedures.

5. The software is a critical component of a computerised system. The user of such software should take all reasonable steps to ensure that it has been produced in accordance with a system of Quality Assurance.

6. The system should include, where appropriate, built-in checks of the correct entry and processing of data.

7. Before a system using a computer is brought into use, it should be thoroughly tested and confirmed as being capable of achieving the desired results. If a manual system is being replaced, the two should be run in parallel for a time, as a part of this testing and validation.

8. Data should only be entered or amended by persons authorised to do so. Suitable methods of deterring unauthorised entry of data include the use of keys, pass cards, personal codes and restricted access to computer terminals. There should be a defined procedure for the issue, cancellation, and alteration of authorisation to enter and amend data, including the changing of personal passwords. Consideration should be given to systems allowing for recording of attempts to access by unauthorised persons.

9. When critical data are being entered manually (for example the weight and batch number of an ingredient during dispensing), there should be an additional check on the accuracy of the record which is made. This check may be done by a second operator or by validated electronic means.

10. The system should record the identity of operators entering or confirming critical data. Authority to amend entered data

should be restricted to nominated persons. Any alteration to an entry of critical data should be authorised and recorded with the reason for the change. Consideration should be given to building into the system the creation of a complete record of all entries and amendments (an "audit trail").

11. Alterations to a system or to a computer program should only be made in accordance with a defined procedure which should include provision for validating, checking, approving and implementing the change. Such an alteration should only be implemented with the agreement of the person responsible for the part of the system concerned, and the alteration should be recorded. Every significant modification should be validated.

12. For quality auditing purposes, it should be possible to obtain clear printed copies of electronically stored data.

13. Data should be secured by physical or electronic means against wilful or accidental damage, in accordance with item 4.9 of the Guide. Stored data should be checked for accessibility, durability and accuracy. If changes are proposed to the computer equipment or its programs, the above mentioned checks should be performed at a frequency appropriate to the storage medium being used.

14. Data should be protected by backing-up at regular intervals. Back-up data should be stored as long as necessary at a separate and secure location.

15. There should be available adequate alternative arrangements for systems which need to be operated in the event of a breakdown. The time required to bring the alternative arrangements into use should be related to the possible urgency of the need to use them. For example, information required to effect a recall must be available at short notice.

16. The procedures to be followed if the system fails or breaks down should be defined and validated. Any failures and remedial action taken should be recorded.

17. A procedure should be established to record and analyse errors and to enable corrective action to be taken.

18. When outside agencies are used to provide a computer service, there should be a formal agreement including a clear statement of the responsibilities of that outside agency (see Chapter 7).

19. When the release of batches for sale or supply is carried out using a computerised system, the system should allow for only a Qualified Person to release the batches and it should clearly identify and record the person releasing the batches.

Annex 12: Use of Ionising Radiation in the Manufacture of Medicinal Products

Note   *The holder of, or applicant for, a marketing authorisation for a product which includes irradiation as part of its processing should also refer to the note produced by the Committee for Proprietary Medicinal Products giving guidance on "Ionising radiation in the manufacture of medicinal products".*

Introduction

Ionising radiation may be used during the manufacturing process for various purposes including the reduction of bioburden and the sterilisation of starting materials, packaging components or products and the treatment of blood products.

There are two types of irradiation process: Gamma Irradiation from a radioactive source and high energy Electron Irradiation (Beta radiation) from an accelerator.

Gamma Irradiation: two different processing modes may be employed:

(i) *Batch mode:* the product is arranged at fixed locations around the radiation source and cannot be loaded or unloaded while the radiation source is exposed.

(ii) *Continuous mode:* an automatic system conveys the products into the radiation cell, past the exposed radiation source along a defined path and at an appropriate speed, and out of the cell.

Electron Irradiation: the product is conveyed past a continuous or pulsed beam of high energy electrons (Beta radiation) which is scanned back and forth across the product pathway.

Responsibilities

1. Treatment by irradiation may be carried out by the pharmaceutical manufacturer or by an operator of a radiation facility under contract (a "contract manufacturer"), both of whom must hold an appropriate manufacturing authorisation.

2. The pharmaceutical manufacturer bears responsibility for the quality of the product including the attainment of the objective of irradiation. The contract operator of the radiation facility bears responsibility for ensuring that the dose of radiation required by the manufacturer is delivered to the irradiation container (i.e. the outermost container in which the products are irradiated).

3. The required dose including justified limits will be stated in the marketing authorization for the product.

Dosimetry

4. Dosimetry is defined as the measurement of the absorbed dose by the use of dosimeters. Both understanding and correct use of the technique is essential for the validation, commissioning and control of the process.

5. The calibration of each batch of routine dosimeters should be traceable to a national or international standard. The period of validity of the calibration should be stated, justified and adhered to.

6. The same instrument should normally be used to establish the calibration curve of the routine dosimeters and to measure the change in their absorbance after irradiation. If a different instrument is used, the absolute absorbance of each instrument should be established.

7. Depending on the type of dosimeter used, due account should be taken of possible causes of inaccuracy including the change in moisture content, change in temperature, time elapsed between irradiation and measurement, and the dose rate.

8. The wavelength of the instrument used to measure the change in absorbance of dosimeters and the instrument used to measure their thickness should be subject to

regular checks of calibration at intervals established on the basis of stability, purpose and usage.

Validation of the process

9. Validation is the action of proving that the process, i.e. the delivery of the intended absorbed dose to the product, will achieve the expected results. The requirements for validation are given more fully in the note for guidance on "the use of ionising radiation in the manufacture of medicinal products".

10. Validation should include dose mapping to establish the distribution of absorbed dose within the irradiation container when packed with product in a defined configuration.

11. An irradiation process specification should include at least the following:

    a. details of the packaging of the product;

    b. the loading pattern(s) of product within the irradiation container. Particular care needs to be taken, when a mixture of products is allowed in the irradiation container, that there is no underdosing of dense product or shadowing of other products by dense product. Each mixed product arrangement must be specified and validated;

    c. the loading pattern of irradiation containers around the source (batch mode) or the pathway through the cell (continuous mode);

    d. maximum and minimum limits of absorbed dose to the product [and associated routine dosimetry];

    e. maximum and minimum limits of absorbed dose to the irradiation container and associated routine dosimetry to monitor this absorbed dose;

    f. other process parameters, including dose rate, maximum time of exposure, number of exposures, etc.

    When irradiation is supplied under contract at least parts (d) and (e) of the irradiation process specification should form part of that contract.

Commissioning of the plant

General

12. Commissioning is the exercise of obtaining and documenting evidence that the irradiation plant will perform consistently within predetermined limits when operated according to the process specification. In the context of this annex, predetermined limits are the maximum and minimum doses designed to be absorbed by the irradiation container. It must not be possible for variations to occur in the operation of the plant which give a dose to the container outside these limits without the knowledge of the operator.

13. Commissioning should include the following elements:

   a) Design;

   b) Dose mapping;

   c) Documentation;

   d) Requirement for re-commissioning.

Gamma irradiators

Design

14. The absorbed dose received by a particular part of an irradiation container at any specific point in the irradiator depends primarily on the following factors:

   a) the activity and geometry of the source;

   b) the distance from source to container;

   c) The duration of irradiation controlled by the timer setting or conveyor speed;

   d) The composition and density of material, including other products, between the source and the particular part of the container.

15. The total absorbed dose will in addition depend on the path of containers through a continuous irradiator or the loading pattern in a batch irradiator, and on the number of exposure cycles.

16. For a continuous irradiator with a fixed path or a batch irradiator with a fixed loading pattern, and with a given source strength and type of product, the key plant parameter controlled by the operator is conveyor speed or timer setting.

Dose Mapping

17. For the dose mapping procedure, the irradiator should be filled with irradiation containers packed with dummy products or a representative product of uniform density. Dosimeters should be placed throughout a minimum of three loaded irradiation containers which are passed through the irradiator, surrounded by similar containers or dummy products. If the product is not uniformly packed, dosimeters should be placed in a larger number of containers.

18. The positioning of dosimeters will depend on the size of the irradiation container. For example, for containers up to 1 x 1 x 0.5 m, a three-dimensional 20 cm grid throughout the container including the outside surfaces might be suitable. If the expected positions of the minimum and maximum dose are known from a previous irradiator performance characterisation, some dosimeters could be removed from regions of average dose and replaced to form a 10 cm grid in the regions of extreme dose.

19. The results of this procedure will give minimum and maximum absorbed doses in the product and on the container surface for a given set of plant parameters, product density and loading pattern.

20. Ideally, reference dosimeters should be used for the dose mapping exercise because of their greater precision. Routine dosimeters are permissible but it is advisable to place reference dosimeters beside them at the expected positions of minimum and maximum dose and at the routine monitoring position in each of the replicate irradiation containers. The observed values of dose will have an associated random uncertainty which can be estimated from the variations in replicate measurements.

21. The minimum observed dose, as measured by the routine dosimeters, necessary to ensure that all irradiation containers receive the minimum required dose will be set in

Annex 12

the knowledge of the random variability of the routine dosimeters used.

22. Irradiator parameters should be kept constant, monitored and recorded during dose mapping. The records, together with the dosimetry results and all other records generated, should be retained.

Electron beam irradiators

Design

23. The absorbed dose received by a particular portion of an irradiated product depends primarily on the following factors:

   a) the characteristics of the beam, which are: electron energy, average beam current, scan width and scan uniformity;

   b) the conveyor speed;

   c) the product composition and density;

   d) the composition, density and thickness of material between the output window and the particular portion of product;

   e) the output window to container distance.

24. Key parameters controlled by the operator are the characteristics of the beam and the conveyor speed.

Dose Mapping

25. For the dose mapping procedure, dosimeters should be placed between layers of homogeneous absorber sheets making up a dummy product, or between layers of representative products of uniform density, such that at least ten measurements can be made within the maximum range of the electrons. Reference should also be made to sections 18 to 21.

26. Irradiator parameters should be kept constant, monitored and recorded during dose mapping. The records, together with the dosimetry results and all other records generated, should be retained.

Re-commissioning

27. Commissioning should be repeated if there is a change to the process or the irradiator which could affect the dose distribution to the irradiation container (e.g. change of source pencils). The extent to re-commissioning depends on the extent of the change in the irradiator or the load that has taken place. If in doubt, re-commission.

Premises

28. Premises should be designed and operated to segregate irradiated from non-irradiated containers to avoid their cross-contamination. Where materials are handled within closed irradiation containers, it may not be necessary to segregate pharmaceutical from nonpharmaceutical materials, provided there is no risk of the former being contaminated by the latter.

    Any possibility of contamination of the products by radionuclide from the source must be excluded.

Processing

29. Irradiation containers should be packed in accordance with the specified loading pattern(s) established during validation.

30. During the process, the radiation dose to the irradiation containers should be monitored using validated dosimetry procedures. The relationship between this dose and the dose absorbed by the product inside the container must have been established during process validation and plant commissioning.

31. Radiation indicators should be used as an aid to differentiating irradiated from nonirradiated containers. They should not be used as the sole means of differentiation or as an indication of satisfactory processing.

32. Processing of mixed loads of containers within the irradiation cell should only be done when it is known from commissioning trials or other evidence that the radiation dose received by individual containers remains within the limits specified.

Annex 12

33. When the required radiation dose is by design given during more than one exposure or passage through the plant, this should be with the agreement of the holder of the marketing authorisation and occur within a predetermined time period. Unplanned interruptions during irradiation should be notified to the holder of the marketing authorisation if this extends the irradiation process beyond a previously agreed period.

34. Non-irradiated products must be segregated from irradiated products at all times. Methods of doing this include the use of radiation indicators (31.) and appropriate design of premises (28.).

Gamma irradiators

35. For continuous processing modes, dosimeters should be placed so that at least two are exposed in the irradiation at all times.

36. For batch modes, at least two dosimeters should be exposed in positions related to the minimum dose position.

37. For continuous process modes, there should be a positive indication of the correct position of the source and an interlock between source position and conveyor movement. Conveyor speed should be monitored continuously and recorded.

38. For batch process modes source movement and exposure times for each batch should be monitored and recorded.

39. For a given desired dose, the timer setting or conveyor speed requires adjustment for source decay and source additions. The period of validity of the setting or speed should be recorded and adhered to.

Electron Beam Irradiators

40. A dosimeter should be placed on every container.

41. There should be continuous recording of average beam current, electron energy, scan-width and conveyor speed. These variables, other than conveyor speed, need to be controlled within the defined limits established during commissioning since they are liable to instantaneous change.

Documentation

42. The numbers of containers received, irradiated and dispatched should be reconciled with each other and with the associated documentation. Any discrepancy should be reported and resolved.

43. The irradiation plant operator should certify in writing the range of doses received by each irradiated container within a batch or delivery.

44. Process and control records for each irradiation batch should be checked and signed by a nominated responsible person and retained. The method and place of retention should be agreed between the plant operator and the holder of the marketing authorisation.

45. The documentation associated with the validation and commissioning of the plant should be retained for one year after the expiry date or at least five years after the release of the last product processed by the plant, whichever is the longer.

Microbiological monitoring

46. Microbiological monitoring is the responsibility of the pharmaceutical manufacturer. It may include environmental monitoring where product is manufactured and pre-irradiation monitoring of the product as specified in the marketing authorisation.

Annex 12

Annex 13: Manufacture of Investigational Medicinal Products

Brussles, July 2003

Revision 1

Principle

Investigational medicinal products should be produced in accordance with the principles and the detailed guidelines of Good Manufacturing Practice for Medicinal Products (The Rules Governing Medicinal Products in The European Community, Volume IV). Other guidelines published by the European Commission should be taken into account where relevant and as appropriate to the stage of development of the product. Procedures need to be flexible to provide for changes as knowledge of the process increases, and appropriate to the stage of development of the product. In clinical trials there may be added risk to participating subjects compared to patients treated with marketed products. The application of GMP to the manufacture of investigational medicinal products is intended to ensure that trial subjects are not placed at risk, and that the results of clinical trials are unaffected by inadequate safety, quality or efficacy arising from unsatisfactory manufacture. Equally, it is intended to ensure that there is consistency between batches of the same investigational medicinal product used in the same or different clinical trials, and that changes during the development of an investigational medicinal product are adequately documented and justified. The production of investigational medicinal products involves added complexity in comparison to marketed products by virtue of the lack of fixed routines, variety of clinical trial designs, consequent packaging designs, the need, often, for randomisation and blinding and increased risk of product cross-contamination and mix up. Furthermore, there may be incomplete knowledge of the potency and toxicity of the product and a lack of full process validation, or, marketed products may be used which have been re-packaged or modified in some way. These challenges require personnel with a thorough understanding of, and training in, the application of GMP to investigational medicinal products. Co-operation is required with trial sponsors who undertake the ultimate responsibility for all aspects of the clinical trial including the quality of investigational medicinal products.

The increased complexity in manufacturing operations requires a highly effective quality system.

The annex also includes guidance on ordering, shipping, and returning clinical supplies, which are at the interface with, and complementary to, guidelines on Good Clinical Practice.

Note   *Products other than the test product, placebo or comparator may be supplied to subjects participating in a trial. Such products may be used as support or escape medication for preventative, diagnostic or therapeutic reasons and/or needed to ensure that adequate medical care is provided for the subject. They may also be used in accordance with the protocol to induce a physiological response. These products do not fall within the definition of investigational medicinal products and may be supplied by the sponsor, or the investigator. The sponsor should ensure that they are in accordance with the notification/request for authorisation to conduct the trial and that they are of appropriate quality for the purposes of the trial taking into account the source of the materials, whether or not they are the subject of a marketing authorisation and whether they have been repackaged. The advice and involvement of a Qualified Person is recommended in this task.*

Glossary

Blinding

A procedure in which one or more parties to the trial are kept unaware of the treatment assignment(s). Single-blinding usually refers to the subject(s) being unaware, and double-blinding usually refers to the subject(s), investigator(s), monitor, and, in some cases, data analyst(s) being unaware of the treatment assignment(s). In relation to an investigational medicinal product, blinding shall mean the deliberate disguising of the identity of the product in accordance with the instructions of the sponsor. Unblinding shall mean the disclosure of the identity of blinded products.

Clinical trial

Any investigation in human subjects intended to discover or verify the clinical, pharmacological and/or other pharmacodynamic effects of an investigational product(s) and/or to identify any adverse reactions to an investigational product(s), and/or to study absorption, distribution, metabolism, and excretion of one or more investigational medicinal product(s) with the object of ascertaining its/their safety and/or efficacy.

Comparator product

An investigational or marketed product (i.e. active control), or placebo, used as a reference in a clinical trial.

Investigational medicinal product

A pharmaceutical form of an active substance or placebo being tested or used as a reference in a clinical trial, including a product with a marketing authorisation when used or assembled (formulated or packaged) in a way different from the authorised form, or when used for an unauthorised indication, or when used to gain further information about the authorised form.

Immediate packaging

The container or other form of packaging immediately in contact with the medicinal or investigational medicinal product.

Investigator

A person responsible for the conduct of the clinical trial at a trial site. If a trial is conducted by a team of individuals at a trial site, the investigator is the responsible leader of the team and may be called the principal investigator.

Manufacturer/importer of Investigational Medicinal Products

Any holder of the authorisation to manufacture/import referred to in Article 13.1 of Directive 2001/20/EC.

Order

Instruction to process, package and/or ship a certain number of units of investigational medicinal product(s).

Outer packaging

The packaging into which the immediate container is placed.

Annex 13

Product Specification File

A reference file containing, or referring to files containing, all the information necessary to draft the detailed written instructions on processing, packaging, quality control testing, batch release and shipping of an investigational medicinal product.

Randomisation

The process of assigning trial subjects to treatment or control groups using an element of chance to determine the assignments in order to reduce bias.

Randomisation Code

A listing in which the treatment assigned to each subject from the randomisation process is identified.

Shipping

The operation of packaging for shipment and sending of ordered medicinal products for clinical trials.

Sponsor

An individual, company, institution or organisation which takes responsibility for the initiation, management and/or financing of a clinical trial.

Quality Management

1. The Quality System, designed, set up and verified by the manufacturer or importer, should be described in written procedures available to the sponsor, taking into account the GMP principles and guidelines applicable to investigational medicinal products.

2. The product specifications and manufacturing instructions may be changed during development but full control and traceability of the changes should be maintained.

Personnel

3. All personnel involved with investigational medicinal products should be appropriately trained in the requirements specific to these types of product.

4. The Qualified Person should in particular be responsible for ensuring that there are systems in place that meet the requirements of this Annex and should therefore have a

broad knowledge of pharmaceutical development and clinical trial processes. Guidance for the Qualified Person in connection with the certification of investigational medicinal products is given in paragraphs 38 to 41.

Premises and Equipment

5. The toxicity, potency and sensitising potential may not be fully understood for investigational medicinal products and this reinforces the need to minimise all risks of cross-contamination. The design of equipment and premises, inspection / test methods and acceptance limits to be used after cleaning should reflect the nature of these risks. Consideration should be given to campaign working where appropriate. Account should be taken of the solubility of the product in decisions about the choice of cleaning solvent.

Documentation

Specifications and instructions

6. Specifications (for starting materials, primary packaging materials, intermediate, bulk products and finished products), manufacturing formulae and processing and packaging instructions should be as comprehensive as possible given the current state of knowledge. They should be periodically re-assessed during development and updated as necessary. Each new version should take into account the latest data, current technology used, regulatory and pharmacopoeial requirements, and should allow traceability to the previous document. Any changes should be carried out according to a written procedure, which should address any implications for product quality such as stability and bio equivalence.

7. Rationales for changes should be recorded and the consequences of a change on product quality and on any on-going clinical trials should be investigated and documented.

Order

8. The order should request the processing and/or packaging of a certain number of units and/or their shipping and be given by or on behalf of the sponsor to the manufacturer. It should be in writing (though it may be transmitted by electronic means), and precise enough to avoid any

Annex 13

ambiguity. It should be formally authorised and refer to the Product Specification File and the relevant clinical trial protocol as appropriate.

Product Specification File

9. The Product Specification File (see glossary) should be continually updated as development of the product proceeds, ensuring appropriate traceability to the previous versions. It should include, or refer to, the following documents:

   – Specifications and analytical methods for starting materials, packaging materials, intermediate, bulk and finished product.

   – Manufacturing methods.

   – In-process testing and methods.

   – Approved label copy.

   – Relevant clinical trial protocols and randomisation codes, as appropriate.

   – Relevant technical agreements with contract givers, as appropriate.

   – Stability data.

   – Storage and shipment conditions.

   The above listing is not intended to be exclusive or exhaustive. The contents will vary depending on the product and stage of development. The information should form the basis for assessment of the suitability for certification and release of a particular batch by the Qualified Person and should therefore be accessible to him/her. Where different manufacturing steps are carried out at different locations under the responsibility of different Qualified Persons, it is acceptable to maintain separate files limited to information of relevance to the activities at the respective locations.

Manufacturing Formulae and Processing Instructions

10. For every manufacturing operation or supply there should be clear and adequate written instructions and written records. Where an operation is not repetitive it may not be necessary to produce Master Formulae and Processing Instructions. Records are particularly important for the preparation of the final version of the documents to be used

in routine manufacture once the marketing authorisation is granted.

11. The information in the Product Specification File should be used to produce the detailed written instructions on processing, packaging, quality control testing, storage conditions and shipping.

Packaging Instructions

12. Investigational medicinal products are normally packed in an individual way for each subject included in the clinical trial. The number of units to be packaged should be specified prior to the start of the packaging operations, including units necessary for carrying out quality control and any retention samples to be kept. Sufficient reconciliations should take place to ensure the correct quantity of each product required has been accounted for at each stage of processing.

Processing, testing and packaging batch records

13. Batch records should be kept in sufficient detail for the sequence of operations to be accurately determined. These records should contain any relevant remarks which justify the procedures used and any changes made, enhance knowledge of the product and develop the manufacturing operations.

14. Batch manufacturing records should be retained at least for the periods specified in Directive 91/356 as amended for investigational medicinal products.

Production

Packaging materials

15. Specifications and quality control checks should include measures to guard against unintentional unblinding due to changes in appearance between different batches of packaging materials.

Manufacturing operations

16. During development critical parameters should be identified and in-process controls primarily used to control the process. Provisional production parameters and in-process

Annex 13

controls may be deduced from prior experience, including that gained from earlier development work. Careful consideration by key personnel is called for in order to formulate the necessary instructions and to adapt them continually to the experience gained in production. Parameters identified and controlled should be justifiable based on knowledge available at the time.

17. Production processes for investigational medicinal products are not expected to be validated to the extent necessary for routine production but premises and equipment are expected to be validated. For sterile products, the validation of sterilising processes should be of the same standard as for products authorised for marketing. Likewise, when required, virus inactivation/removal and that of other impurities of biological origin should be demonstrated, to assure the safety of biotechnologically derived products, by following the scientific principles and techniques defined in the available guidance in this area.

18. Validation of aseptic processes presents special problems when the batch size is small; in these cases the number of units filled may be the maximum number filled in production. If practicable, and otherwise consistent with simulating the process, a larger number of units should be filled with media to provide greater confidence in the results obtained. Filling and sealing is often a manual or semi-automated operation presenting great challenges to sterility so enhanced attention should be given to operator training, and validating the aseptic technique of individual operators.

Principles applicable to comparator product

19. If a product is modified, data should be available (e.g. stability, comparative dissolution, bioavailability) to demonstrate that these changes do not significantly alter the original quality characteristics of the product.

20. The expiry date stated for the comparator product in its original packaging might not be applicable to the product where it has been repackaged in a different container that may not offer equivalent protection, or be compatible with the product. A suitable use-by date, taking into account the nature of the product, the characteristics of the container and the storage conditions to which the article may be subjected, should be determined by or on behalf of the sponsor. Such a date should be justified and must not be

later than the expiry date of the original package. There should be compatibility of expiry dating and clinical trial duration.

Blinding operations

21. Where products are blinded, systems should be in place to ensure that the blind is achieved and maintained while allowing for identification of "blinded" products when necessary, including the batch numbers of the products before the blinding operation. Rapid identification of product should also be possible in an emergency.

Randomisation code

22. Procedures should describe the generation, security, distribution, handling and retention of any randomisation code used for packaging investigational products, and code-break mechanisms. Appropriate records should be maintained.

Packaging

23. During packaging of investigational medicinal products, it may be necessary to handle different products on the same packaging line at the same time. The risk of product mix up must be minimised by using appropriate procedures and/or, specialised equipment as appropriate and relevant staff training.

24. Packaging and labelling of investigational medicinal products are likely to be more complex and more liable to errors (which are also harder to detect) than for marketed products, particularly when "blinded" products with similar appearance are used. Precautions against mis-labelling such as label reconciliation, line clearance, in-process control checks by appropriately trained staff should accordingly be intensified.

25. The packaging must ensure that the investigational medicinal product remains in good condition during transport and storage at intermediate destinations. Any opening or tampering of the outer packaging during transport should be readily discernible.

Annex 13

Labelling

26. Table 1 summarises the contents of articles 26-30 that follow. Labelling should comply with the requirements of Directive 91/356 as amended for Investigational Medicinal Products. The following information should be included on labels, unless its absence can be justified, e.g. use of a centralised electronic randomisation system:

   (a) name, address and telephone number of the sponsor, contract research organisation or investigator (the main contact for information on the product, clinical trial and emergency unblinding);

   (b) pharmaceutical dosage form, route of administration, quantity of dosage units, and in the case of open trials, the name/identifier and strength/potency;

   (c) the batch and/or code number to identify the contents and packaging operation;

   (d) a trial reference code allowing identification of the trial, site, investigator and sponsor if not given elsewhere;

   (e) the trial subject identification number/treatment number and where relevant, the visit number;

   (f) the name of the investigator (if not included in (a) or (d));

   (g) directions for use (reference may be made to a leaflet or other explanatory document intended for the trial subject or person administering the product);

   (h) "For clinical trial use only" or similar wording;

   (i) the storage conditions;

   (j) period of use (use-by date, expiry date or re-test date as applicable), in month/year format and in a manner that avoids any ambiguity.

   (k) "keep out of reach of children" except when the product is for use in trials where the product is not taken home by subjects.

27. The address and telephone number of the main contact for information on the product, clinical trial and for emergency unblinding need not appear on the label where the subject has been given a leaflet or card which provides these details and has been instructed to keep this in their possession at all times.

---

28. Particulars should appear in the official language(s) of the country in which the investigational medicinal product is to be used. The particulars listed in Article 26 should appear on the immediate container and on the outer packaging (except for immediate containers in the cases described in Articles 29 and 30). The requirements with respect to the contents of the label on the immediate container and outer packaging are summarised in table 1. Other languages may be included.

29. When the product is to be provided to the trial subject or the person administering the medication within an immediate container together with outer packaging that is intended to remain together, and the outer packaging carries the particulars listed in paragraph 26, the following information shall be included on the label of the immediate container (or any sealed dosing device that contains the immediate container):

   a) name of sponsor, contract research organisation or investigator;

   b) pharmaceutical dosage form, route of administration (may be excluded for oral solid dose forms), quantity of dosage units and in the case of open label trials, the name/identifier and strength/potency;

   c) batch and/or code number to identify the contents and packaging operation;

   d) a trial reference code allowing identification of the trial, site, investigator and sponsor if not given elsewhere;

   e) the trial subject identification number/treatment number and where relevant, the visit number.

30. If the immediate container takes the form of blister packs or small units such as ampoules on which the particulars required in paragraph 26 cannot be displayed, outer packaging should be provided bearing a label with those particulars. The immediate container should nevertheless contain the following:

   a) name of sponsor, contract research organisation or investigator;

   b) route of administration (may be excluded for oral solid dose forms) and in the case of open label trials, the name/identifier and strength/potency;

Annex 13

   c) batch and/or code number to identify the contents and packaging operation; d) a trial reference code allowing identification of the trial, site, investigator and sponsor if not given elsewhere; e) the trial subject identification number/treatment number and where relevant, the visit number;

31. Symbols or pictograms may be included to clarify certain information mentioned above. Additional information, warnings and/or handling instructions may be displayed.

32. For clinical trials with the characteristics identified in Article 14 of Directive 2001/20/EC, the following particulars should be added to the original container but should not obscure the original labelling:

   i) name of sponsor, contract research organisation or investigator;

   ii) trial reference code allowing identification of the trial site, investigator and trial subject.

33. If it becomes necessary to change the use-by date, an additional label should be affixed to the investigational medicinal product. This additional label should state the new use-by date and repeat the batch number. It may be superimposed on the old use-by date, but for quality control reasons, not on the original batch number. This operation should be performed at an appropriately authorised manufacturing site. However, when justified, it may be performed at the investigational site by or under the supervision of the clinical trial site pharmacist, or other health care professional in accordance with national regulations. Where this is not possible, it may be performed by the clinical trial monitor(s) who should be appropriately trained. The operation should be performed in accordance with GMP principles, specific and standard operating procedures and under contract, if applicable, and should be checked by a second person. This additional labelling should be properly documented in both the trial documentation and in the batch records.

Quality Control

34. As processes may not be standardised or fully validated, testing takes on more importance in ensuring that each batch meets its specification.

35. Quality control should be performed in accordance with the Product Specification File and in accordance with the information notified pursuant to Article 9(2) of Directive 2001/20/EC. Verification of the effectiveness of blinding should be performed and recorded.

36. Samples of each batch of investigational medicinal product, including blinded product should be retained for the periods specified in Directive 91/356 as amended for investigational medicinal products.

37. Consideration should be given to retaining samples from each packaging run/trial period until the clinical report has been prepared to enable confirmation of product identity in the event of, and as part of an investigation into inconsistent trial results.

Release of Batches

38. Release of investigational medicinal products (see paragraph 43) should not occur until after the Qualified Person has certified that the requirements of Article 13.3 of Directive 2001/20/EC have been met (see paragraph 39). The Qualified Person should take into account the elements listed in paragraph 40 as appropriate.

39. The duties of the Qualified Person in relation to investigational medicinal products are affected by the different circumstances that can arise and are referred to below. Table 2 summarises the elements that need to be considered for the most common circumstances:

    a)i) Product manufactured within EU but not subject to an EU marketing authorisation: the duties are laid down in article 13.3(a) of Directive 2001/20/EC.

    a)ii) Product sourced from the open market within EU in accordance with Article 80(b) of Directive 2001/83/EC and subject to an EU marketing authorisation, regardless of manufacturing origin: the duties are as described above, however, the scope of certification can be limited to assuring that the products are in accordance with the notification/request for authorisation to conduct the trial and any subsequent processing for the purpose of blinding, trial-specific packaging and labelling. The Product Specification File will be similarly restricted in scope (see 9).

Annex 13

b) Product imported directly from a 3rd country: the duties are laid down in article 13.3(b) of Directive 2001/20/EC. Where investigational medicinal products are imported from a 3rd country and they are subject to arrangements concluded between the Community and that country, such as a Mutual Recognition Agreement (MRA), equivalent standards of Good Manufacturing Practice apply provided any such agreement is relevant to the product in question. In the absence of an MRA, the Qualified Person should determine that equivalent standards of Good Manufacturing Practice apply through knowledge of the quality system employed at the manufacturer. This knowledge is normally acquired through participation in audit of the manufacturer's quality systems. In either case, the Qualified Person may then certify on the basis of documentation supplied by the 3rd country manufacturer (see 40).

c) For imported comparator products where adequate assurance cannot be obtained in order to certify that each batch has been manufactured to equivalent standards of Good Manufacturing Practice, the duty of the Qualified Person is defined in article 13.3(c) of Directive 2001/20/EC.

40. Assessment of each batch for certification prior to release may include as appropriate:

- batch records, including control reports, in-process test reports and release reports demonstrating compliance with the product specification file, the order, protocol and randomisation code. These records should include all deviations or planned changes, and any consequent additional checks or tests, and should be completed and endorsed by the staff authorised to do so according to the quality system;

- production conditions;

- the validation status of facilities, processes and methods;

- examination of finished packs;

- where relevant, the results of any analyses or tests performed after importation;

- stability reports;

- the source and verification of conditions of storage and shipment;

- audit reports concerning the quality system of the manufacturer;

- Documents certifying that the manufacturer is authorised to manufacture investigational medicinal products or comparators for export by the appropriate authorities in the country of export;

- where relevant, regulatory requirements for marketing authorisation, GMP standards applicable and any official verification of GMP compliance;

- all other factors of which the QP is aware that are relevant to the quality of the batch.

- The relevance of the above elements is affected by the country of origin of the product, the manufacturer, and the marketed status of the product (with or without a marketing authorisation, in the EU or in a third country) and its phase of development.

The sponsor should ensure that the elements taken into account by the qualified person when certifying the batch are consistent with the information notified pursuant to Article 9(2) of Directive 2001/20/EC. See also 44.

41. Where investigational medicinal products are manufactured and packaged at different sites under the supervision of different Qualified Persons, the recommendations listed in Annex 16 to the GMP Guide should be followed as applicable.

42. Where, permitted in accordance with local regulations, packaging or labelling is carried out at the investigator site by, or under the supervision of a clinical trials pharmacist, or other health care professional as allowed in those regulations, the Qualified Person is not required to certify the activity in question. The sponsor is nevertheless responsible for ensuring that the activity is adequately documented and carried out in accordance with the principles of GMP and should seek the advice of the Qualified Person in this regard.

Shipping

43. Shipping of investigational products should be conducted according to instructions given by or on behalf of the sponsor in the shipping order.

44. Investigational medicinal products should remain under the control of the Sponsor until after completion of a two-step release procedure: certification by the Qualified Person; and release following fulfilment of the requirements of Article 9 (Commencement of a clinical trial) of Directive 2001/20/EC. The sponsor should ensure that these are consistent with the details actually considered by the Qualified Person. Both releases should be recorded and retained in the relevant trial files held by or on behalf of the sponsor.

45. De-coding arrangements should be available to the appropriate responsible personnel before investigational medicinal products are shipped to the investigator site.

46. A detailed inventory of the shipments made by the manufacturer or importer should be maintained. It should particularly mention the addressees' identification.

47. Transfers of investigational medicinal products from one trial site to another should remain the exception. Such transfers should be covered by standard operating procedures. The product history while outside of the control of the manufacturer, through for example, trial monitoring reports and records of storage conditions at the original trial site should be reviewed as part of the assessment of the product's suitability for transfer and the advice of the Qualified person should be sought. The product should be returned to the manufacturer, or another authorised manufacturer for re-labelling, if necessary, and certification by a Qualified Person. Records should be retained and full traceability ensured.

Complaints

48. The conclusions of any investigation carried out in relation to a complaint which could arise from the quality of the product should be discussed between the manufacturer or importer and the sponsor (if different). This should involve the Qualified Person and those responsible for the relevant clinical trial in order to assess any potential impact on the trial, product development and on subjects.

Recalls and Returns

Recalls

49. Procedures for retrieving investigational medicinal products and documenting this retrieval should be agreed by the sponsor, in collaboration with the manufacturer or importer where different. The investigator and monitor need to understand their obligations under the retrieval procedure.

50. The Sponsor should ensure that the supplier of any comparator or other medication to be used in a clinical trial has a system for communicating to the Sponsor the need to recall any product supplied.

Returns

51. Investigational medicinal products should be returned on agreed conditions defined by the sponsor, specified in approved written procedures.

52. Returned investigational medicinal products should be clearly identified and stored in an appropriately controlled, dedicated area. Inventory records of the returned medicinal products should be kept.

Destruction

53. The Sponsor is responsible for the destruction of unused and/or returned investigational medicinal products. Investigational medicinal products should therefore not be destroyed without prior written authorisation by the Sponsor.

54. The delivered, used and recovered quantities of product should be recorded, reconciled and verified by or on behalf of the sponsor for each trial site and each trial period. Destruction of unused investigational medicinal products should be carried out for a given trial site or a given trial period only after any discrepancies have been investigated and satisfactorily explained and the reconciliation has been accepted. Recording of destruction operations should be carried out in such a manner that all operations may be accounted for. The records should be kept by the Sponsor.

55. When destruction of investigational medicinal products takes place a dated certificate of, or receipt for destruction,

should be provided to the sponsor. These documents should clearly identify, or allow traceability to, the batches and/or patient numbers involved and the actual quantities destroyed.

Table 1. Summary of Labelling Details (§26 To 30)	
a) name, address and telephone number of the sponsor, contract research organisation or investigator (the main contact for information on the product, clinical trial and emergency unblinding);	GENERAL CASE For both the outer packaging and immediate container (§26) **Particulars a[28] to k**
(b) pharmaceutical dosage form, route of administration, quantity of dosage units, and in the case of open trials, the name/identifier and strength/potency;	
(c) the batch and/or code number to identify the contents and packaging operation;	IMMEDIATE CONTAINER Where immediate container and

---

[28] The address and telephone number of the main contact for information on the product, clinical trial
and for emergency unblinding need not appear on the label where the subject has been given a leaflet or card which provides these details and has been instructed to keep this in their possession at all times (§ 27).
[29] When the outer packaging carries the particulars listed in Article 26.
[30] The address and telephone number of the main contact for information on the product, clinical trial and for emergency unblinding need not be included.
[31] Route of administration may be excluded for oral solid dose forms.
[32] When the outer packaging carries the particulars listed in Article 26.
[33] The address and telephone number of the main contact for information on the product, clinical trial and for emergency unblinding need not be included.
[34] Route of administration may be excluded for oral solid dose forms. The pharmaceutical dosage form and quantity of dosage units may be omitted.

(d) a trial reference code allowing identification of the trial, site, investigator and sponsor if not given elsewhere;	outer packaging remain together throughout (§29)[29] $a^{30} \ b^{31} \ c \ d \ e$
(e) the trial subject identification number/treatment number and where relevant, the visit number;	
(f) the name of the investigator (if not included in (a) or (d);	**IMMEDIATE CONTAINER** Blisters or small packaging units (§30)[32]
(g) directions for use (reference may be made to a leaflet or other explanatory document intended for the trial subject or person administering the product	$a^{33} \ b^{34} \ c \ d \ e$
(h) "for clinical trial use only" or similar wording;	
(i) the storage conditions;	
(j) period of use (use-by date, expiry date or re-test date as applicable), in month/year format and in a manner that avoids any ambiguity.	
(k) "keep out of reach of children" except when the product is for use in trials where the product is not taken home by subjects.	

Annex 13

Table 2: Batch Release of Products

ELEMENTS TO BE TAKEN INTO ACCOUNT(3)	PRODUCT AVAILABLE IN THE EU		PRODUCT IMPORTED FROM THIRD COUNTRIES		
	Product manufactured in EU without MA	Product with MA and available on EU market	Product without any EU MA	Product with a EU MA	Comparator where documentation certifying that each batch has been manufactured in conditions at least equivalent to those laid down in Directive 91/356/EEC cannot be obtained
BEFORE CLINICAL TRIAL PROCESSING					
a) Shipping and storage conditions	Yes				
b) All relevant factors (1) showing that each batch has been manufactured and released in accordance with: Directive 91/356/EEC, or GMP standards at least equivalent to those laid down in Directive 91/356/EEC.	Yes -		(2) yes		
c) Documentation showing that each batch has been released within the EU according to EU GMP requirements (see Directive 2001/83/EC, article 51), or documentation showing that the product is available on the EU market and has been procured in accordance with article 80(b) of Directive 2001/83/EC.		Yes			
d) Documentation showing that the product is available on the local market and documentation to					Yes

establish confidence in the local regulatory requirements for marketing authorisation and release for local use.				
e) Results of all analysis, tests and checks performed to assess the quality of the imported batch according to: the requirements of the MA (see Directive 2001/83/EC, article 51b), or the Product Specification File, the Order, article 9.2 submission to the regulatory authorities. Where these analyses and tests are not performed in the EU, this should be justified and the QP must certify that they have been carried out in accordance with GMP standards at least equivalent to those laid down in Directive 91/356/EEC.		- yes yes	yes - yes	- yes yes
AFTER CLINICAL TRIAL PROCESSING				
f) In addition to the assessment before clinical trial processing, all further relevant factors (1) showing that each batch has been processed for the purposes of blinding, trial-specific packaging, labelling and testing in accordance with: Directive 91/356/EEC, or GMP standards at least equivalent to those laid down in Directive 91/356/EEC.	Yes -	(2) yes		

Annex 13

(1)   These factors are summarised in paragraph 40.

(2)   Where an MRA or similar arrangements are in place covering the products in question, equivalent standards of GMP apply.

(3)   In all cases the information notified pursuant to Article 9(2) of Directive 2001/20/EC should be consistent with the elements actually taken into account by the QP who certifies the batch prior to release

Annex 14: Manufacture of Medicinal Products[35] Derived from Human Blood or Plasma

Brussels, 31 March 2000

Working Party on Control of Medicines and Inspections

Revision of Annex 14 to the EU Guide to Good Manufacturing Practice

Document History	
First discussion in drafting group	October 1996
Second discussion in drafting group	January 1998
Pharmaceutical Committee (for information)	16 March 1998
Adoption at the Working Party on Control of Medicines and Inspection for release for consultation	20 March 1998
Released for consultation	29 May 1998
Deadline for comments	31 August 1998
Re-discussed in the drafting group	21 January 1999
Comments from BWP	August 1999

---

[35] Council Directive 89/381/EEC of 14 June 1989 extending the scope of Directives 65/65/EEC and 75/319/EEC on the approximation of provisions laid down by law, regulation or administrative action relating to proprietary medicinal products and laying down special provisions for medicinal products derived from human blood or human plasma (OJ No L 181 of 28.6.1989)

Re-discussed in the drafting group	December 1999
Adopted at the Ad-hoc meeting of GMP Inspection services	11th February 2000
Pharmaceutical Committee (for information)	22-23 March 2000
Date for coming into operation	1st September 2000

Principle

In accordance with Directive 75/318/EEC[36], for biological medicinal products derived from human blood or plasma, starting materials include the source materials such as cells or fluids including blood or plasma. Medicinal products derived from human blood or plasma have certain special features arising from the biological nature of the source material. For example, disease-transmitting agents, especially viruses, may contaminate the source material. The safety of these products relies therefore on the control of source materials and their origin as well as on the subsequent manufacturing procedures, including virus removal and inactivation.

The general chapters of the guide to GMP apply to medicinal products derived from human blood or plasma, unless otherwise stated. Some of the Annexes may also apply, e.g. manufacture of sterile medicinal products, use of ionising radiation in the manufacture of medicinal products, manufacture of biological medicinal products and computerised systems.

Since the quality of the final products is affected by all the steps in their manufacture, including the collection of blood or plasma, all operations should therefore be done in accordance with an appropriate system of Quality Assurance and current Good Manufacturing Practice.

By virtue of Directive 89/381/EEC, the necessary measures shall be taken to prevent the transmission of infectious diseases and the requirements and standards of the European

---

[36] Council Directive 75/318/EEC, of 20 May 1975, on the approximation of the laws of Member States relating to analytical, pharmacotoxicological and clinical standards and protocols in respect of the testing of medicinal products (OJ No L 147 of 9.6.1975, p. 1) as last amended by Council Directive 93/39/EEC (OJ No L 214 of 24.8.1993, p. 22).3 O.J. L 20321.7.1998 p. 14

Pharmacopoeia monographs regarding plasma for fractionation and medicinal products derived from human blood or plasma shall be applicable. These measures shall also comprise the Council Recommendation of 29 June 1998 "On the suitability of blood and plasma donors and the screening of donated blood in the European Community[37] (98/463/EC), the recommendations of the Council of Europe (see "Guide to the preparation, use and quality assurance of blood components", Council of Europe Press) and the World Health Organisation (see report by the WHO Expert Committee on Biological Standardisation, WHO Technical Report Series 840, 1994).

This annex should also be read in conjunction with the guidelines adopted by the CPMP, in particular "Note for guidance on plasma-derived medicinal products (CPMP/BWP/269/95 rev.2)", "Virus validation studies: the design, contribution and interpretation of studies validating the inactivation and removal of viruses" published in Volume 3A of the series "The rules governing medicinal products in the European Community") and "Contribution to part II of the structure of the dossier for applications for marketing authorisation - control of starting materials for the production of blood derivatives"(III/5272/94).

These documents are regularly revised and reference should be made to the latest revisions for current guidance.

The provisions of this annex apply to medicinal products derived from human blood and plasma. They do not cover blood components used in transfusion medicine, since these are presently not covered by EC directives. However many of these provisions may be applicable to such components and competent authorities may require compliance with them.

Glossary

Blood

Whole blood collected from a single donor and processed either for transfusion or further manufacturing

Blood components

Therapeutic components of blood (red cells, white cells, plasma, platelets), that can be prepared by centrifugation, filtration and freezing using conventional blood bank methodology

---

[37] O.J. L 20321.7.1998 p. 14

Medicinal product derived from blood or plasma

Same meaning as that given in Directive 89/381/EEC

Quality Management

1. Quality Assurance should cover all stages leading to the finished product, from collection (including donor selection, blood bags, anticoagulant solutions and test kits) to storage, transport, processing, quality control and delivery of the finished product, all in accordance with the texts referred to under Principle at the beginning of this Annex.

2. Blood or plasma used as a source material for the manufacture of medicinal products should be collected by establishments and be tested in laboratories which are subject to inspection and approved by a competent authority.

3. Procedures to determine the suitability of individuals to donate blood and plasma, used as a source material for the manufacture of medicinal products, and the results of the testing of their donations should be documented by the collection establishment and should be available to the manufacturer of the medicinal product.

4. Monitoring of the quality of medicinal products derived from human blood or plasma should be carried out in such a way that any deviations from the quality specifications can be detected.

5. Medicinal products derived from human blood or plasma which have been returned unused should normally not be re-issued; (see also point 5.65 of the main GMP guide).

Premises and Equipment

6. The premises used for the collection of blood or plasma should be of suitable size, construction and location to facilitate their proper operation, cleaning and maintenance. Collection, processing and testing of blood and plasma should not be performed in the same area. There should be suitable donor interview facilities so that these interviews are carried out in private.

7. Manufacturing, collection and testing equipment should be designed, qualified and maintained to suit its intended

purpose and should not present any hazard. Regular maintenance and calibration should be carried out and documented according to established procedures.

8. In the preparation of plasma-derived medicinal products, viral inactivation or removal procedures are used and steps should be taken to prevent cross contamination of treated with untreated products; dedicated and distinct premises and equipment should be used for treated products.

Blood and Plasma collection

9. A standard contract is required between the manufacturer of the medicinal product derived from human blood or plasma and the blood/plasma collection establishment or organisation responsible for collection. Guidance on the content of the standard contract is provided in "Contribution to part II of the structure of the dossier for applications for marketing authorisation - control of starting materials for the production of blood derivatives"(III/5272/94)

10. Each donor must be positively identified at reception and again before venepuncture; see also Council Recommendation of 29 June 1998 on the suitability of blood and plasma donors and the screening of donated blood in the European Community[38] (98/463/EC).

11. The method used to disinfect the skin of the donor should be clearly defined and shown to be effective. Adherence to that method should then be maintained.

12. Donation number labels must be re-checked independently to ensure that those on blood packs, sample tubes and donation records are identical.

13. Blood bag and apheresis systems should be inspected for damage or contamination before being used to collect blood or plasma. In order to ensure traceability, the batch number of blood bags and apheresis systems should be recorded.

Traceability and post collection measures

14. While fully respecting confidentiality, there must be a system in place which enables the path taken by each

---

[38] O.J. L 20321.7.1998 p. 14

Annex 14

donation to be traced, both forward from the donor and back from the finished medicinal product, including the customer (hospital or health care professional). It is normally the responsibility of this customer to identify the recipient.

15. Post-collection measures: A standard operating procedure describing the mutual information system between the blood/plasma collection establishment and the manufacturing/fractionation facility should be set up so that they can inform each other if, following donation:

- it is found that the donor did not meet the relevant donor health criteria;

- a subsequent donation from a donor previously found negative for viral markers is found positive for any of the viral markers;

- it is discovered that testing for viral markers has not been carried out according to agreed procedures;

- the donor has developed an infectious disease caused by an agent potentially transmissible by plasma-derived products (HBV, HCV, HAV and other non-A, non-B, non-C hepatitis viruses, HIV 1 and 2 and other agents in the light of current knowledge);

- the donor develops Creutzfeldt-Jakob disease (CJD or vCJD);

- the recipient of blood or a blood component develops post-transfusion/infusion infection which implicates or can be traced back to the donor.

The procedures to be followed in the event of any of the above should be documented in the standard operating procedure. Look-back should consist of tracing back of previous donations for at least six months prior to the last negative donation. In the event of any of the above, a re-assessment of the batch documentation should always be carried out. The need for withdrawal of the given batch should be carefully considered, taking into account criteria such as the transmissible agent involved, the size of the pool, the time period between donation and seroconversion, the nature of the product and its manufacturing method. Where there are indications that a donation contributing to a plasma pool was infected with HIV or hepatitis A,B or C, the case should be referred to the relevant competent authority(ies) responsible for the authorisation of the medicinal product and the company's view regarding continued manufacture from the implicated pool or of the possibility of withdrawal of the product(s) should be given. More specific guidance is given in the current version of the CPMP Note for Guidance on plasma-derived medicinal products.

Production and Quality Control

16. Before any blood and plasma donations, or any product derived therefrom, are released for issue and/or fractionation, they should be tested, using a validated test method of suitable sensitivity and specificity, for the following markers of specific disease-transmitting agents:

   - HBsAg;

   - antibodies to HIV 1 and HIV 2;

   - antibodies to HCV.

   If a repeat-reactive result is found in any of these tests, the donation is not acceptable.

   (Additional tests may form part of national requirements)

17. The specified storage temperatures of blood, plasma and intermediate products when stored and during transportation from collection establishments to manufacturers, or between different manufacturing sites, should be checked and validated. The same applies to delivery of these products.

18. The first homogeneous plasma pool (e.g. after separation of the cryoprecipitate) should be tested using a validated test method, of suitable sensitivity and specificity, and found non reactive for the following markers of specific disease-transmitting agents:

   - HBsAg;

   - antibodies to HIV 1 and HIV 2;

   - antibodies to HCV.

   Confirmed positive pools must be rejected.

19. Only batches derived from plasma pools tested and found non-reactive for HCV RNA by nucleic acid amplification

Annex 14

technology (NAT), using a validated test method of suitable sensitivity and specificity, should be released.

20. Testing requirements for viruses, or other infectious agents, should be considered in the light of knowledge emerging as to infectious agents and the availability of appropriate test methods.

21. The labels on single units of plasma stored for pooling and fractionation must comply with the provisions of the European Pharmacopoeia monograph "Human plasma for fractionation" and bear at least the identification number of the donation, the name and address of the collection establishment or the references of the blood transfusion service responsible for preparation, the batch number of the container, the storage temperature, the total volume or weight of plasma, the type of anticoagulant used and the date of collection and/or separation.

22. In order to minimise the microbiological contamination of plasma for fractionation or the introduction of foreign material, the thawing and pooling should be performed at least in a grade D clean area, wearing the appropriate clothing and in addition face masks and gloves should be worn. Methods used for opening bags, pooling and thawing should be regularly monitored, e.g. by testing for bioburden. The cleanroom requirements for all other open manipulations should conform to the requirements of Annex 1 of the EU guide to GMP.

23. Methods for clearly distinguishing between products or intermediates which have undergone a process of virus removal or inactivation, from those which have not, should be in place.

24. Validation of methods used for virus removal or virus inactivation should not be conducted in the production facilities in order not to put the routine manufacture at any risk of contamination with the viruses used for validation.

Retention of samples

25. Where possible, samples of individual donations should be stored to facilitate any necessary look-back procedure. This would normally be the responsibility of the collection establishment. Samples of each pool of plasma should be stored under suitable conditions for at least one year after

the expiry date of the finished product with the longest shelf-life.

Disposal of rejected blood, plasma or intermediates

26. There should be a standard operating procedure for the safe and effective disposal of blood, plasma or intermediates.

Annex 14

Annex 15:
Qualification and Validation

Brussels, July 2001

Working Party on Control of Medicines and Inspections

Final Version of Annex 15 to the EU Guide to Good Manufacturing Practice

Document History	
First discussion in drafting group	
Discussion at the working Party on Control of Medicines and Inspection for release for consultation	16 September 1999
Pharmaceutical Committee	28 September 1999
Released for consultation	30 October 1999
Deadline for comments	28 February 2000
Final approval by Inspector's working party	December 2000
Pharmaceutical Committee (for information)	April 2001
Date for coming into operation	September 2001

Note that this document is based in the PICS/S recommendations

Principle

1. This Annex describes the principles of qualification and validation which are applicable to the manufacture of medicinal products. It is a requirement of GMP that manufacturers identify what validation work is needed to prove control of the critical aspects of their particular operations. Significant changes to the facilities, the equipment and the processes, which may affect the quality of the product, should be validated. A risk assessment approach should be used to determine the scope and extent of validation.

Planning For Validation

2. All validation activities should be planned. The key elements of a validation programme should be clearly defined and documented in a validation master plan (VMP) or equivalent documents.

3. The VMP should be a summary document which is brief, concise and clear.

4. The VMP should contain data on at least the following:

   (a) validation policy;

   (b) organisational structure of validation activities;

   (c) summary of facilities, systems, equipment and processes to be validated;

   (d) documentation format: the format to be used for protocols and reports;

   (e) planning and scheduling;

   (f) change control;

   (g) reference to existing documents.

5. In case of large projects, it may be necessary to create separate validation master plans.

Documentation

6. A written protocol should be established that specifies how qualification and validation will be conducted. The protocol should be reviewed and approved. The protocol should specify critical steps and acceptance criteria.

7. A report that cross-references the qualification and/or validation protocol should be prepared, summarising the results obtained, commenting on any deviations observed, and drawing the necessary conclusions, including recommending changes necessary to correct deficiencies. Any changes to the plan as defined in the protocol should be documented with appropriate justification.

8. After completion of a satisfactory qualification, a formal release for the next step in qualification and validation should be made as a written authorisation.

Qualification

Design Qualification

9. The first element of the validation of new facilities, systems or equipment could be design qualification (DQ).

10. The compliance of the design with GMP should be demonstrated and documented.

Installation Qualification

11. Installation qualification (IQ) should be performed on new or modified facilities, systems and equipment.

12. IQ should include, but not be limited to the following:

(a) installation of equipment, piping, services and instrumentation checked to current engineering drawings and specifications;

(b) collection and collation of supplier operating and working instructions and maintenance requirements;

(c) calibration requirements;

(d) verification of materials of construction.

Operational Qualification

13. Operational qualification (OQ) should follow Installation qualification.

14. OQ should include, but not be limited to the following:

Annex 15

(a) tests that have been developed from knowledge of processes, systems and equipment;

(b) tests to include a condition or a set of conditions encompassing upper and lower operating limits, sometimes referred to as "worst case" conditions.

15. The completion of a successful Operational qualification should allow the finalisation of calibration, operating and cleaning procedures, operator training and preventative maintenance requirements. It should permit a formal "release" of the facilities, systems and equipment.

Performance Qualification

16. Performance qualification (PQ) should follow successful completion of Installation qualification and Operational qualification.

17. PQ should include, but not be limited to the following:

(a) tests, using production materials, qualified substitutes or simulated product, that have been developed from knowledge of the process and the facilities, systems or equipment;

(b) tests to include a condition or set of conditions encompassing upper and lower operating limits.

18. Although PQ is described as a separate activity, it may in some cases be appropriate to perform it in conjunction with OQ.

Qualification of Established (In-Use) Facilities, Systems and Equipment

19. Evidence should be available to support and verify the operating parameters and limits for the critical variables of the operating equipment. Additionally, the calibration, cleaning, preventative maintenance, operating procedures and operator training procedures and records should be documented.

Process Validation

General

20. The requirements and principles outlined in this chapter are applicable to the manufacture of pharmaceutical dosage

forms. They cover the initial validation of new processes, subsequent validation of modified processes and re-validation.

21. Process validation should normally be completed prior to the distribution and sale of the medicinal product (prospective validation). In exceptional circumstances, where this is not possible, it may be necessary to validate processes during routine production (concurrent validation). Processes in use for some time should also be validated (retrospective validation).

22. Facilities, systems and equipment to be used should have been qualified and analytical testing methods should be validated. Staff taking part in the validation work should have been appropriately trained.

23. Facilities, systems, equipment and processes should be periodically evaluated to verify that they are still operating in a valid manner.

Prospective Validation

24. Prospective validation should include, but not be limited to the following:

(a) short description of the process;

(b) summary of the critical processing steps to be investigated;

(c) list of the equipment/facilities to be used (including measuring/monitoring/recording equipment) together with its calibration status

(d) finished product specifications for release;

(e) list of analytical methods, as appropriate;

(f) proposed in-process controls with acceptance criteria;

(g) additional testing to be carried out, with acceptance criteria and analytical validation, as appropriate;

(h) sampling plan;

(i) methods for recording and evaluating results

(j) functions and responsibilities;

(k) proposed timetable.

Annex 15

25. Using this defined process (including specified components) a series of batches of the final product may be produced under routine conditions. In theory the number of process runs carried out and observations made should be sufficient to allow the normal extent of variation and trends to be established and to provide sufficient data for evaluation. It is generally considered acceptable that three consecutive batches/runs within the finally agreed parameters, would constitute a validation of the process.

26. Batches made for process validation should be the same size as the intended industrial scale batches.

27. If it is intended that validation batches be sold or supplied, the conditions under which they are produced should comply fully with the requirements of Good Manufacturing Practice, including the satisfactory outcome of the validation exercise, and with the marketing authorisation.

Concurrent Validation

28. In exceptional circumstances it may be acceptable not to complete a validation programme before routine production starts.

29. The decision to carry out concurrent validation must be justified, documented and approved by authorised personnel.

30. Documentation requirements for concurrent validation are the same as specified for prospective validation.

Retrospective Validation

31. Retrospective validation is only acceptable for well-established processes and will be inappropriate where there have been recent changes in the composition of the product, operating procedures or equipment.

32. Validation of such processes should be based on historical data. The steps involved require the preparation of a specific protocol and the reporting of the results of the data review, leading to a conclusion and a recommendation.

33. The source of data for this validation should include, but not be limited to batch processing and packaging records, process control charts, maintenance log books, records of

personnel changes, process capability studies, finished product data, including trend cards and storage stability results.

34. Batches selected for retrospective validation should be representative of all batches made during the review period, including any batches that failed to meet specifications, and should be sufficient in number to demonstrate process consistency. Additional testing of retained samples may be needed to obtain the necessary amount or type of data to retrospectively validate the process.

35. For retrospective validation, generally data from ten to thirty consecutive batches should be examined to assess process consistency, but fewer batches may be examined if justified.

Cleaning Validation

36. Cleaning validation should be performed in order to confirm the effectiveness of a cleaning procedure. The rationale for selecting limits of carry over of product residues, cleaning agents and microbial contamination should be logically based on the materials involved. The limits should be achievable and verifiable.

37. Validated analytical methods having sensitivity to detect residues or contaminants should be used. The detection limit for each analytical method should be sufficiently sensitive to detect the established acceptable level of the residue or contaminant.

38. Normally only cleaning procedures for product contact surfaces of the equipment need to be validated. Consideration should be given to non-contact parts. The intervals between use and cleaning as well as cleaning and reuse should be validated. Cleaning intervals and methods should be determined.

39. For cleaning procedures for products and processes which are similar, it is considered acceptable to select a representative range of similar products and processes. A single validation study utilising a "worst case" approach can be carried out which takes account of the critical issues.

40. Typically three consecutive applications of the cleaning procedure should be performed and shown to be successful in order to prove that the method is validated.

41. "Test until clean". is not considered an appropriate alternative to cleaning validation.

42. Products which simulate the physicochemical properties of the substances to be removed may exceptionally be used instead of the substances themselves, where such substances are either toxic or hazardous.

Change Control

43. Written procedures should be in place to describe the actions to be taken if a change is proposed to a starting material, product component, process equipment, process environment (or site), method of production or testing or any other change that may affect product quality or reproducibility of the process. Change control procedures should ensure that sufficient supporting data are generated to demonstrate that the revised process will result in a product of the desired quality, consistent with the approved specifications.

44. All changes that may affect product quality or reproducibility of the process should be formally requested, documented and accepted. The likely impact of the change of facilities, systems and equipment on the product should be evaluated, including risk analysis. The need for, and the extent of, re-qualification and re-validation should be determined.

Revalidation

45. Facilities, systems, equipment and processes, including cleaning, should be periodically evaluated to confirm that they remain valid. Where no significant changes have been made to the validated status, a review with evidence that facilities, systems, equipment and processes meet the prescribed requirements fulfils the need for revalidation.

Glossary

Definitions of terms relating to qualification and validation which are not given in the glossary of the current EC Guide to GMP, but which are used in this Annex, are given below.

Change Control

A formal system by which qualified representatives of appropriate disciplines review proposed or actual changes that might affect the validated status of facilities, systems, equipment or processes. The intent is to determine the need for action that would ensure and document that the system is maintained in a validated state.

Cleaning Validation

Cleaning validation is documented evidence that an approved cleaning procedure will provide equipment which is suitable for processing medicinal products.

Concurrent Validation

Validation carried out during routine production of products intended for sale.

Design qualification (DQ)

The documented verification that the proposed design of the facilities, systems and equipment is suitable for the intended purpose.

Installation Qualification (IQ)

The documented verification that the facilities, systems and equipment, as installed or modified, comply with the approved design and the manufacturer's recommendations.

Operational Qualification (OQ)

The documented verification that the facilities, systems and equipment, as installed or modified, perform as intended throughout the anticipated operating ranges.

Performance Qualification (PQ)

The documented verification that the facilities, systems and equipment, as connected together, can perform effectively and reproducibly, based on the approved process method and product specification.

Process Validation

The documented evidence that the process, operated within established parameters, can perform effectively and reproducibly to produce a medicinal product meeting its predetermined specifications and quality attributes.

Annex 15

Prospective Validation

Validation carried out before routine production of products intended for sale.

Retrospective Validation

Validation of a process for a product which has been marketed based upon accumulated manufacturing, testing and control batch data.

Re-Validation

A repeat of the process validation to provide an assurance that changes in the process/equipment introduced in accordance with change control procedures do not adversely affect process characteristics and product quality.

Risk analysis

Method to assess and characterise the critical parameters in the functionality of an equipment or process. .

Simulated Product

A material that closely approximates the physical and, where practical, the chemical characteristics (e.g. viscosity, particle size, pH etc.) of the product under validation. In many cases, these characteristics may be satisfied by a placebo product batch.

System

A group of equipment with a common purpose.

Worst Case

A condition or set of conditions encompassing upper and lower processing limits and circumstances, within standard operating procedures, which pose the greatest chance of product or process failure when compared to ideal conditions. Such conditions do not necessarily induce product or process failure.

Annex 16:
Certification by a Qualified Person and Batch Release

Brussels, July 2001

Working Party on Control of Medicines and Inspections

Final Version of Annex 16 to the EU Guide to Good Manufacturing Practice

Document History	
Discussion in Working group	June to November 1999
Transmission of Draft 3 to the Pharmaceutical Committee	September 1999
Transmission of Draft 4 to Interested Parties	December 1999
Deadline for comments on Draft 4	May 2000
Consideration by drafting group and working party	July to October 2000
Consideration of Draft 5 by Working Party	November 2000
Transmission of Draft 6 to Interested Parties	January 2001
Draft 7 showing comments received by 15 March	April 2001
Pharmaceutical Committee (for information)	April 2001

1. Scope

1.1　This annex to the Guide to Good Manufacturing Practice for Medicinal Products ("the Guide") gives guidance on the certification by a Qualified Person (Q.P.) and batch release within the European Community (EC) or European Economic Area (EEA) of medicinal products holding a marketing authorisation or made for export. The relevant legislative requirements are contained in Article 51 of Directive 2001/83/EC or Article 55 of Directive 2001/82/EC.

1.2　The annex covers in particular those cases where a batch has had different stages of production or testing conducted at different locations or by different manufacturers, and where an intermediate or bulk production batch is divided into more than one finished product batch. It also covers the release of batches which have been imported to the EC/EEA both when there is and is not a mutual recognition agreement between the Community and the third country. The guidance may also be applied to investigational medicinal products, subject to any difference in the legal provisions and more specific guidance in Annex 13 to the Guide.

1.3　This annex does not, of course, describe all possible arrangements which are legally acceptable. Neither does it address the official control authority batch release which may be specified for certain blood and immunological products in accordance with Article 11 point 5.4 and Articles 109[39] and 110 of Directive 2001/83/EC.

1.4　The basic arrangements for batch release for a product are defined by its Marketing Authorisation. Nothing in this annex should be taken as overriding those arrangements.

---

[39] As amended by Directive 2002/98/EC of the European Parliament and of the Council of 27 January 2003 setting standards of   quality and safety for the collection, testing, processing, storage and distribution of human blood and blood components and amending Directive 2001/83/EC (OJ L 33, 8.2.2003, p.30)

2. Principle

2.1   Each batch of finished product must be certified by a
       Q.P. within the EC/EEA before being released for sale or
       supply in the EC/EEA or for export.

2.2   The purpose of controlling batch release in this way is:

       •   to ensure that the batch has been manufactured
            and checked in accordance with the requirements
            of its marketing authorisation, the principles and
            guidelines of EC Good Manufacturing Practice or
            the good manufacturing practice of a third country
            recognised as equivalent under a mutual
            recognition agreement and any other relevant legal
            requirement before it is placed on the market, and

       •   in the event that a defect needs to be investigated
            or a batch recalled, to ensure that the Q.P. who
            certified the batch and the relevant records are
            readily identifiable.

3. Introduction

3.1   Manufacture, including quality control testing, of a batch
       of medicinal products takes place in stages which may be
       conducted at different sites and by different
       manufacturers. Each stage should be conducted in
       accordance with the relevant marketing authorisation,
       Good Manufacturing Practice and the laws of the
       Member State concerned and should be taken into
       account by the Q.P. who certifies the finished product
       batch before release to the market.

3.2   However in an industrial situation it is usually not possible
       for a single Q.P. to be closely involved with every stage
       of manufacture. The Q.P. who certifies a finished product
       batch may need therefore to rely in part on the advice
       and decisions of others. Before doing so he should
       ensure that this reliance is well founded, either from
       personal knowledge or from the confirmation by other
       Q.P.s within a quality system which he has accepted.

3.3   When some stages of manufacture occur in a third
       country it is still a requirement that production and testing
       are in accordance with the marketing authorisation, that
       the manufacturer is authorised according to the laws of
       the country concerned and that manufacture follows good

Annex 16

manufacturing practices at least equivalent to those of the EC.

3.4 Certain words used in this annex have particular meanings attributed to them, as defined in the glossary.

4. General

4.1 One batch of finished product may have different stages of manufacture, importation, testing and storage before release conducted at different sites. Each site should be approved under one or more manufacturing authorisations and should have at its disposal the services of at least one Q.P. However the correct manufacture of a particular batch of product, regardless of how many sites are involved, should be the overall concern of the Q.P. who certifies that finished product batch before release.

4.2 Different batches of a product may be manufactured or imported and released at different sites in the EC/EEA. For example a Community marketing authorisation may name batch release sites in more than one member state, and a national authorisation may also name more than one release site. In this situation the holder of the marketing authorisation and each site authorised to release batches of the product should be able to identify the site at which any particular batch has been released and the Q.P. who was responsible for certifying that batch.

4.3 The Q.P. who certifies a finished product batch before release may do so based on his personal knowledge of all the facilities and procedures employed, the expertise of the persons concerned and of the quality system within which they operate. Alternatively he may rely on the confirmation by one or more other Q.P.s of the compliance of intermediate stages of manufacture within a quality system which he has accepted.

This confirmation by other Q.P.s should be documented and should identify clearly the matters which have been confirmed. The systematic arrangements to achieve this should be defined in a written agreement.

4.4 The agreement mentioned above is required whenever a Q.P. wishes to rely on the confirmation by another Q.P.

The agreement should be in general accordance with Chapter 7 of the Guide. The Q.P. who certifies the finished product batch should ensure the arrangements in the agreement are verified. The form of such an agreement should be appropriate to the relationship between the parties; for example a standard operating procedure within a company or a formal contract between different companies even if within the same group.

4.5   The agreement should include an obligation on the part of the provider of a bulk or intermediate product to notify the recipient(s) of any deviations, out-of-specification results, non-compliance with GMP, investigations, complaints or other matters which should be taken into account by the Q.P. who is responsible for certifying the finished product batch.

4.6   When a computerised system is used for recording certification and batch release, particular note should be taken of the guidance in Annex 11 to this Guide.

4.7   Certification of a finished product batch against a relevant marketing authorisation by a Q.P. in the EC/EEA need not be repeated on the same batch provided the batch has remained within the EC/EEA.

4.8   Whatever particular arrangements are made for certification and release of batches, it should always be possible to identify and recall without delay all products which could be rendered hazardous by a quality defect in the batch.

5. Batch testing and release of products manufactured in EC/EEA

5.1 When all manufacture occurs at a single authorised site

When all production and control stages are carried out at a single site, the conduct of certain checks and controls may be delegated to others but the Q.P. at this site who certifies the finished product batch normally retains personal responsibility for these within a defined quality system. However he may, alternatively, take account of the confirmation of the intermediate stages by other Q.Ps on the site who are responsible for those stages.

Annex 16

5.2   Different stages of manufacture are conducted at
       different sites within the same company

When different stages of the manufacture of a batch are
carried out at different sites within the same company
(which may or may not be covered by the same
manufacturing authorisation) a Q.P. should be
responsible for each stage. Certification of the finished
product batch should be performed by a Q.P. of the
manufacturing authorisation holder responsible for
releasing the batch to the market, who may take personal
responsibility for all stages or may take account of the
confirmation of the earlier stages by the relevant Q.P.s
responsible for those stages.

5.3   Some intermediate stages of manufacture are contracted
       to a different company.

One or more intermediate production and control stages
may be contracted to a holder of a manufacturing
authorisation in another company. A Q.P. of the contract
giver may take account of the confirmation of the relevant
stage by a Q.P. of the contract acceptor but is
responsible for ensuring that this work is conducted
within the terms of a written agreement. The finished
product batch should be certified by a Q.P. of the
manufacturing authorisation holder responsible for
releasing the batch to the market.

5.4   A bulk production batch is assembled at different sites
       into several finished product batches which are released
       under a single marketing authorisation. This could occur,
       for example, under a national marketing authorisation
       when the assembly sites are all within one member state
       or under a Community marketing authorisation when the
       sites are in more than one member state.

       5.4.1 One alternative is for a Q.P. of the manufacturing
              authorisation holder making the bulk production
              batch to certify all the finished product batches
              before release to the market. In doing so he may
              either take personal responsibility for all
              manufacturing stages or take account of the
              confirmation of assembly by the Q.P.s of the
              assembly sites.

5.4.2 Another alternative is for the certification of each finished product batch before release to the market to be performed by a Q.P of the manufacturer who has conducted the final assembly operation. In doing so he may either take personal responsibility for all manufacturing stages or take account of the confirmation of the bulk production batch by a Q.P. of the manufacturer of the bulk batch

5.4.3 In all cases of assembly at different sites under a single marketing authorisation, there should be one person, normally a Q.P. of the manufacturer of the bulk production batch, who has an overall responsibility for all released finished product batches which are derived from one bulk production batch. The duty of this person is to be aware of any quality problems reported on any of the finished product batches and to co-ordinate any necessary action arising from a problem with the bulk batch.

While the batch numbers of the bulk and finished product batches are not necessarily the same, there should be a documented link between the two numbers so that an audit trail can be established.

5.5 A bulk production batch is assembled at different sites into several finished product batches which are released under different marketing authorisations. This could occur, for example, when a multi-national organisation holds national marketing authorisations for a product in several member states or when a generic manufacturer purchases bulk products and assembles and releases them for sale under his own marketing authorisation.

5.5.1 A Q.P. of the manufacturer doing the assembly who certifies the finished product batch may either take personal responsibility for all manufacturing stages or may take account of the confirmation of the bulk production batch by a Q.P. of the bulk product manufacturer.

5.5.2 Any problem identified in any of the finished product batches which may have arisen in the bulk production batch should be communicated to the Q.P. responsible for confirming the bulk production batch, who should then take any necessary action in respect of all finished product batches produced

Annex 16

from the suspected bulk production batch. This arrangement should be defined in a written agreement.

5.6　A finished product batch is purchased and released to the market by a manufacturing authorisation holder in accordance with his own marketing authorisation. This could occur, for example, when a company supplying generic products holds a marketing authorisation for products made by another company, purchases finished products which have not been certified against his marketing authorisation and releases them under his own manufacturing authorisation in accordance with his own marketing authorisation.

In this situation a Q.P. of the purchaser should certify the finished product batch before release. In doing so he may either take personal responsibility for all manufacturing stages or may take account of the confirmation of the batch by a Q.P. of the vendor manufacturer.

5.7　The quality control laboratory and the production site are authorised under different manufacturing authorisations.

A Q.P. certifying a finished product batch may either take personal responsibility for the laboratory testing or may take account of the confirmation by another Q.P. of the testing and results. The other laboratory and Q.P. need not be in the same member state as the manufacturing authorisation holder releasing the batch. In the absence of such confirmation the Q.P. should himself have personal knowledge of the laboratory and its procedures relevant to the finished product to be certified.

6. Batch testing and release of products imported from a third country.

6.1　General

6.1.1 Importation of finished products should be conducted by an importer as defined in the glossary to this annex.

6.1.2 Each batch of imported finished product should be certified by a Q.P. of the importer before release for sale in the EC/EEA.

6.1.3 Unless a mutual recognition agreement is in operation between the Community and the third country (see Section 7), samples from each batch should be tested in the EC/EEA before certification of the finished product batch by a Q.P. Importation and testing need not necessarily be performed in the same member state.

6.1.4 The guidance in this section should also be applied as appropriate to the importation of partially manufactured products.

6.2 A complete batch or the first part of a batch of a medicinal product is imported

The batch or part batch should be certified by a Q.P of the importer before release. This Q.P. may take account of the confirmation of the checking, sampling or testing of the imported batch by a Q.P. of another manufacturing authorisation holder (i.e. within EC/EEA).

6.3 Part of a finished product batch is imported after another part of the same batch has previously been imported to the same or a different site.

6.3.1 A Q.P. of the importer receiving a subsequent part of the batch may take account of the testing and certification by a Q.P. of the first part of the batch. If this is done, the Q.P. should ensure, based on evidence, that the two parts do indeed come from the same batch, that the subsequent part has been transported under the same conditions as the first part and that the samples that were tested are representative of the whole batch.

6.3.2 The conditions in paragraph 6.3.1 is most likely to be met when the manufacturer in the third country and the importer(s) in the EC/EEA belong to the same organisation operating under a corporate system of quality assurance. If the Q.P. cannot ensure that the conditions in paragraph 6.3.1 are met, each part of the batch should be treated as a separate batch.

6.3.3 When different parts of the batch are released under the same marketing authorisation, one person, normally a Q.P. of the importer of the first part of a batch, should take overall responsibility for ensuring that records are kept of the

Annex 16

importation of all parts of the batch and that the distribution of all parts of the batch is traceable within the EC/EEA. He should be made aware of any quality problems reported on any part of the batch and should co-ordinate any necessary action concerning these problems and their resolution.

This should be ensured by a written agreement between all the importers concerned.

6.4 Location of sampling for testing in EC/EEA

6.4.1 Samples should be representative of the batch and be tested in the EC/EEA. In order to represent the batch it may be preferable to take some samples during processing in the third country. For example, samples for sterility testing may best be taken throughout the filling operation. However in order to represent the batch after storage and transportation some samples should also be taken after receipt of the batch in the EC/EEA.

6.4.2 When any samples are taken in a third country, they should either be shipped with and under the same conditions as the batch which they represent, or if sent separately it should be demonstrated that the samples are still representative of the batch, for example by defining and monitoring the conditions of storage and shipment. When the Q.P. wishes to rely on testing of samples taken in a third country, this should be justified on technical grounds.

7. Batch testing and release of products imported from a third country with which the EC has a mutual recognition agreement (MRA).

7.1 Unless otherwise specified in the agreement, an MRA does not remove the requirement for a Q.P. within the EC/EEA to certify a batch before it is released for sale or supply within the EC/EEA. However, subject to details of the particular agreement, the Q.P. of the importer may rely on the manufacturer's confirmation that the batch has been made and tested in accordance with its marketing authorisation and the GMP of the third country. and need not repeat the full testing. The Q.P. may certify the batch for release when he is satisfied with this confirmation and that the batch has been transported under the required conditions and has been received and stored in the EC/EEA by an importer as defined in section 8.

7.2   Other procedures, including those for receipt and certification of part batches at different times and/or at different sites, should be the same as in Section 6.

8. Routine duties of a Qualified Person

8.1   Before certifying a batch prior to release the Q.P. doing so should ensure, with reference to the guidance above, that at least the following requirements have been met:

a)   the batch and its manufacture comply with the provisions of the marketing authorisation (including the authorisation required for importation where relevant);

b)   manufacture has been carried out in accordance with Good Manufacturing Practice or, in the case of a batch imported from a third country, in accordance with good manufacturing practice standards at least equivalent to EC GMP;

c)   the principal manufacturing and testing processes have been validated; account has been taken of the actual production conditions and manufacturing records;

d)   any deviations or planned changes in production or quality control have been authorised by the persons responsible in accordance with a defined system. Any changes requiring variation to the marketing or manufacturing authorisation have been notified to and authorised by the relevant authority;

e)   all the necessary checks and tests have been performed, including any additional sampling, inspection, tests or checks initiated because of deviations or planned changes;

f)   all necessary production and quality control documentation has been completed and endorsed by the staff authorised to do so;

g)   all audits have been carried out as required by the quality assurance system;

Annex 16

h)   the QP should in addition take into account any
     other factors of which he is aware which are
     relevant to the quality of the batch

A Q.P. may have additional duties in accordance with
national legislation or administrative procedures.

8.2   A Q.P. who confirms the compliance of an intermediate
      stage of manufacture, as described in paragraph 4.3, has
      the same obligations as above in relation to that stage
      unless specified otherwise in the agreement between the
      Q.P.s.

8.3   A Q.P. should maintain his knowledge and experience up
      to date in the light of technical and scientific progress and
      changes in quality management relevant to the products
      which he is required to certify.

8.4   If a Q.P. is called upon to certify a batch of a product type
      with which he is unfamiliar, for example because the
      manufacturer for whom he works introduces a new
      product range or because he starts to work for a different
      manufacturer, he should first ensure that he has gained
      the relevant knowledge and experience necessary to fulfil
      this duty. In accordance with national requirements the
      Q.P. may be required to notify the authorities of such a
      change and may be subject to renewed authorisation.

Glossary

Certain words and phrases in this annex are used with the
particular meanings defined below. Reference should also be
made to the Glossary in the main part of the Guide.

Bulk production batch
a batch of product, of a size described in the application for a
marketing authorisation, either ready for assembly into final
containers or in individual containers ready for assembly to final
packs. (A bulk production batch may, for example, consist of a
bulk quantity of liquid product, of solid dosage forms such as
tablets or capsules, or of filled ampoules).

Certification of the finished product batch: the certification in a
register or equivalent document by a Q.P., as defined in Article
51 of Directive 2001/83/EC and Article 55 of Directive
2001/82/EC, before a batch is released for sale or distribution.

Confirmation

a signed statement that a process or test has been conducted in accordance with GMP and the relevant marketing authorisation, as agreed in writing with the Q.P. responsible for certifying the finished product batch before release. Confirm and confirmed have equivalent meanings.

Finished product batch

with reference to the control of the finished product, a finished product batch is defined in Part 1 Module 3 point 3.2.2.5 of Directive 2001/83/EC2 and in Part 2 section F 1 of Directive 2001/82/EC. In the context of this annex the term in particular denotes the batch of product in its final pack for release to the market.

Importer

the holder of the authorisation required by Article 40.3 of Directive 2001/83/EC and Article 44.3 of Directive 2001/82/EC for importing medicinal products from third countries.

Mutual Recognition Agreement (MRA)

the 'appropriate arrangement' between the Community and an exporting third country mentioned in Article 51(2) of Directive 2001/83/EC and Article 55(2) of Directive 2001/82/EC.

Qualified Person (Q.P.)

the person defined in Article 48 of Directive 2001/83/EC and Article 52 of Directive 2001/82/EC

Annex 16

Annex 17:
Parametric Release

Brussels, July 2001

Working Party on Control of Medicines and Inspections

Final Version of Annex 17 to the EU Guide to Good Manufacturing Practice

Document History	
First discussions within PIC/S framework	June 1998- August 1999
Consultation with Ad-hoc meeting of GMP Inspection services	September 1999 – February 2000
Revised version	March 2000
Release for industry consultation	6th April 2000
Proposed Deadline for comments	September 2000
New draft following consultation	January 2001
Final draft following consultaion with Ad-hoc meeting of GMP Inspection services	February 2001
Circulation to Pharmaceutical Committee	July 2001
Proposed date for coming into operation	January 2002

Note   that this document has been prepared in association with PIC/S. It should be read in conjunction with CPMP/QWP/3015/99 Note for Guidance on Parametric Release which was adopted by the CPMP in February 2001. See http://www.emea.eu.int/htms/human/qwp/qwpfin.htm

1. Principle

1.1 The definition of Parametric Release used in this Annex is based on that proposed by the European Organization for Quality: " A system of release that gives the assurance that the product is of the intended quality based on information collected during the manufacturing process and on the compliance with specific GMP requirements related to Parametric Release."

1.2. Parametric release should comply with the basic requirements of GMP, with applicable annexes and the following guidelines.

2. Parametric release

2.1. It is recognised that a comprehensive set of in-process tests and controls may provide greater assurance of the finished product meeting specification than finished product testing.

2.2. Parametric release may be authorised for certain specific parameters as an alternative to routine testing of finished products. Authorisation for parametric release should be given, refused or withdrawn jointly by those responsible for assessing products together with the GMP inspectors.

3. Parametric release for sterile products

3.1. This section is only concerned with that part of Parametric Release which deals with the routine release of finished products without carrying out a sterility test. Elimination of the sterility test is only valid on the basis of successful demonstration that predetermined, validated sterilising conditions have been achieved.

3.2. A sterility test only provides an opportunity to detect a major failure of the sterility assurance system due to statistical limitations of the method.

3.3. Parametric Release can be authorised if the data demonstrating correct processing of the batch provides sufficient assurance, on its own, that the process designed and validated to ensure the sterility of the product has been delivered.

3.4. At present Parametric release can only be approved for products terminally sterilized in their final container.

3.5. Sterilization methods according to European Pharmacopeia requirements using steam, dry heat and ionising radiation may be considered for parametric release.

3.6. It is unlikely that a completely new product would be considered as suitable for Parametric Release because a period of satisfactory sterility test results will form part of the acceptance criteria. There may be cases when a new product is only a minor variation, from the sterility assurance point of view, and existing sterility test data from other products could be considered as relevant.

3.7. A risk analysis of the sterility assurance system focused on an evaluation of releasing non-sterilised products should be performed.

3.8. The manufacturer should have a history of good compliance with GMP.

3.9. The history of non sterility of products and of results of sterility tests carried out on the product in question together with products processed through the same or a similar sterility assurance system should be taken into consideration when evaluating GMP compliance.

3.10. A qualified experienced sterility assurance engineer and a qualified microbiologist should normally be present on the site of production and sterilization.

3.11. The design and original validation of the product should ensure that integrity can be maintained under all relevant conditions.

3.12. The change control system should require review of change by sterility assurance personnel.

3.13. There should be a system to control microbiological contamination in the product before sterilisation.

3.14. There should be no possibility for mix ups between sterilised and non sterilised products. Physical barriers or

Annex 17

validated electronic systems may provide such
assurance.

3.15. The sterilization records should be checked for
compliance to specification by at least two independent
systems. These systems may consist of two people or a
validated computer system plus a person.

3.16. The following additional items should be confirmed prior
to release of each batch of product.

- All planned maintenance and routine checks have
been completed in the sterilizer used.

- All repairs and modifications have been approved by
the sterility assurance engineer and microbiologist.

- All instrumentation was in calibration.

- The sterilizer had a current validation for the product
load processed.

3.17. Once parametric release has been granted, decisions for
release or rejection of a batch should be based on the
approved specifications. Non-compliance with the
specification for parametric release cannot be overruled
by a pass of a sterility test.

4. Glossary

Parametric Release
A system of release that gives the assurance that the product is
of the intended quality based on information collected during
the manufacturing process and on the compliance with specific
GMP requirements related to Parametric Release.

Sterility Assurance System
The sum total of the arrangements made to assure the sterility
of products. For terminally sterilized products these typically
include the following stages:

(a) Product design.

(b) Knowledge of and, if possible, control of the microbiological
condition of starting materials and process aids (e.g. gases
and lubricants).

(c) Control of the contamination of the process of manufacture to avoid the ingress of microorganisms and their multiplication in the product. This is usually accomplished by cleaning and sanitization of product contact surfaces, prevention of aerial contamination by handling in clean rooms, use of process control time limits and, if applicable, filtration stages.

(d) Prevention of mix up between sterile and non sterile product streams.

(e) Maintenance of product integrity.

(f) The sterilization process.

(g) The totality of the Quality System that contains the Sterility Assurance System e.g. change control, training, written procedures, release checks, planned preventative maintenance, failure mode analysis, prevention of human error, validation calibration, etc.

Annex 17

Annex 18

Note: *See Good manufacturing practice for active pharmaceutical*
ingredients requirements for active substances used as starting
materials from October 2005 covered under part II

(Found on page 103)

Annex 19: Reference and Retention Samples

Brussels, 14 December 2005

Document History	
Date for new annex coming into operation	01 June 2006

1. Scope

1.1 This Annex to the Guide to Good Manufacturing Practice for Medicinal Products ("the GMP Guide") gives guidance on the taking and holding of reference samples of starting materials, packaging materials or finished products and retention samples of finished products.

1.2 Specific requirements for investigational medicinal products are given in Annex 13 to the Guide.

1.3 This annex also includes guidance on the taking of retention samples for parallel imported/ distributed medicinal products.

2. Principle

2.1 Samples are retained to fulfil two purposes; firstly to provide a sample for analytical testing and secondly to provide a specimen of the fully finished product. Samples may therefore fall into two categories:

Reference sample: a sample of a batch of starting material, packaging material or finished product which is stored for the purpose of being analysed should the need arise during the shelf life of the batch concerned. Where stability permits, reference samples from critical intermediate stages (e.g. those requiring analytical testing and release) or intermediates, that are transported outside of the manufacturer's control, should be kept.

Retention sample: a sample of a fully packaged unit from a batch of finished product. It is stored for identification purposes. For example, presentation, packaging, labelling, patient information leaflet, batch number, expiry date should the need arise during the shelf life of the batch concerned. There may be exceptional circumstances where this requirement can be met without retention of duplicate samples e.g. where small amounts of a batch are packaged for different markets or in the production of very expensive medicinal products.

For finished products, in many instances the reference and retention samples will be presented identically, i.e. as fully packaged units. In such circumstances, reference and retention samples may be regarded as interchangeable.

2.2 It is necessary for the manufacturer, importer or site of batch release, as specified under section 7 and 8, to keep reference and/or retention samples from each batch of finished product and, for the manufacturer to keep a reference sample from a batch of starting material (subject to certain exceptions – see 3.2 below) and/or intermediate product. Each packaging site should keep reference samples of each batch of primary and printed packaging materials. Availability of printed materials as part of the reference and/or retention sample of the finished product can be accepted.

2.3 The reference and/or retention samples serve as a record of the batch of finished product or starting material and can be assessed in the event of, for example, a dosage form quality complaint, a query relating to compliance with the marketing authorisation, a labelling/packaging query or a pharmacovigilance report.

2.4 Records of traceability of samples should be maintained and be available for review by competent authorities.

3. Duration of Storage

3.1 Reference and retention samples from each batch of
finished product should be retained for at least one year
after the expiry date. The reference sample should be
contained in its finished primary packaging or in
packaging composed of the same material as the primary
container in which the product is marketed (for veterinary
medicinal products other than immunologicals, see also
Annex 4, paragraphs 8 & 9).

3.2 Unless a longer period is required under the law of the
Member State of manufacture, samples of starting
materials (other than solvents, gases or water used in the
manufacturing process) shall be retained for at least two
years after the release of product. That period may be
shortened if the period of stability of the material, as
indicated in the relevant specification, is shorter.
Packaging materials should be retained for the duration
of the shelf life of the finished product concerned.

4. Size of Reference and Retention Samples

4.1 The reference sample should be of sufficient size to
permit the carrying out, on, at least, two occasions, of the
full analytical controls on the batch in accordance with
the Marketing Authorisation File which has been
assessed and approved by the relevant Competent
Authority / Authorities. Where it is necessary to do so,
unopened packs should be used when carrying out each
set of analytical controls. Any proposed exception to this
should be justified to, and agreed with, the relevant
competent authority.

4.2 Where applicable, national requirements relating to the
size of reference samples and, if necessary, retention
samples, should be followed.

4.3 Reference samples should be representative of the batch
of starting material, intermediate product or finished
product from which they are taken. Other samples may
also be taken to monitor the most stressed part of a
process (e.g. beginning or end of a process). Where a
batch is packaged in two, or more, distinct packaging
operations, at least one retention sample should be taken
from each individual packaging operation. Any proposed

exception to this should be justified to, and agreed with, the relevant competent authority.

4.4 It should be ensured that all necessary analytical materials and equipment are still available, or are readily obtainable, in order to carry out all tests given in the specification until one year after expiry of the last batch manufactured.

5. Storage Conditions

5.1 Storage of reference samples of finished products and active substances should be in accordance with the current version of the Note for Guidance on Declaration of Storage Conditions for Medicinal Products and Active Substances.

5.2 Storage conditions should be in accordance with the marketing authorisation (e.g. refrigerated storage where relevant).

6. Written Agreements

6.1 Where the marketing authorisation holder is not the same legal entity as the site(s) responsible for batch release within the EEA, the responsibility for taking and storage of reference/retention samples should be defined in a written agreement between the two parties in accordance with Chapter 7 of the EC Guide to Good Manufacturing Practice. This applies also where any manufacturing or batch release activity is carried out at a site other than that with overall responsibility for the batch on the EEA market and the arrangements between each different site for the taking and keeping of reference and retention samples should be defined in a written agreement.

6.2 The Qualified Person who certifies a batch for sale should ensure that all relevant reference and retention samples are accessible at all reasonable times. Where necessary, the arrangements for such access should be defined in a written agreement.

6.3 Where more than one site is involved in the manufacture of a finished product, the availability of written agreements is key to controlling the taking and location of reference and retention samples.

7. Reference Samples – General Points

7.1 Reference samples are for the purpose of analysis and, therefore, should be conveniently available to a laboratory with validated methodology. For starting materials used for medicinal products manufactured within the EEA, this is the original site of manufacture of the finished product. For finished products manufactured within the EEA, this is the original site of manufacture.

7.2 For finished products manufactured by a manufacturer in a country outside the EEA;

7.2.1 where an operational Mutual Recognition Agreement (MRA) is in place, the reference samples may be taken and stored at the site of manufacture. This should be covered in a written agreement (as referred to in section 6 above) between the importer/site of batch release and the manufacturer located outside the EEA.

7.2.2 where an operational MRA is not in place, reference samples of the finished medicinal product should be taken and stored at an authorised manufacturer located within the EEA. These samples should be taken in accordance with written agreement(s) between all of the parties concerned. The samples should, preferably, be stored at the location where testing on importation has been performed.

7.2.3 reference samples of starting materials and packaging materials should be kept at the original site at which they were used in the manufacture of the medicinal product.

8. Retention Samples – General Points

8.1 A retention sample should represent a batch of finished products as distributed in the EEA and may need to be examined in order to confirm non-technical attributes for compliance with the marketing authorisation or EU legislation. Therefore, retention samples should in all cases be located within the EEA. These should preferably be stored at the site where the Qualified Person (QP) certifying the finished product batch is located.

8.2 In accordance with 8.1 above, where an operational MRA is in place and reference samples are retained at a manufacturer located in a country outside the EEA (section 7.2.2 above), separate retention samples should be kept within the EEA.

8.3 Retention samples should be stored at the premises of an authorised manufacturer in order to permit ready access by the Competent Authority.

8.4 Where more than one manufacturing site within the EEA is involved in the manufacture importation/packaging/testing/batch release, as appropriate of a product, the responsibility for taking and storage of retention samples should be defined in a written agreement(s) between the parties concerned.

9. Reference and Retention Samples for Parallel Imported/Parallel Distributed Products.

9.1 Where the secondary packaging is not opened, only the packaging material used needs to be retained, as there is no, or little, risk of product mix up.

9.2 Where the secondary packaging is opened, for example, to replace the carton or patient information leaflet, then one retention sample, per packaging operation, containing the product should be taken, as there is a risk of product mix-up during the assembly process. It is important to be able to identify quickly who is responsible in the event of a mix-up (original manufacturer or parallel import assembler), as it would affect the extent of any resulting recall.

10. Reference and Retention Samples in the Case of Closedown of a Manufacturer

10.1 Where a manufacturer closes down and the manufacturing authorisation is surrendered, revoked, or ceases to exist, it is probable that many unexpired batches of medicinal products manufactured by that manufacturer remain on the market. In order for those batches to remain on the market, the manufacturer should make detailed arrangements for transfer of reference and retention samples (and relevant GMP documentation) to an authorised storage site. The manufacturer should satisfy the Competent Authority that the arrangements for storage are satisfactory and that the samples can, if necessary, be readily accessed and analysed.

10.2 If the manufacturer is not in a position to make the necessary arrangements this may be delegated to another manufacturer. The Marketing Authorisation holder (MAH) is responsible for such delegation and for the provision of all necessary information to the Competent Authority. In addition, the MAH should, in relation to the suitability of the proposed arrangements for storage of reference and retention samples, consult with the competent authority of each Member State in which any unexpired batch has been placed on the market.

10.3 These requirements apply also in the event of the closedown of a manufacture located outside the EEA. In such instances, the importer has a particular responsibility to ensure that satisfactory arrangements are put in place and that the competent authority/authorities is/are consulted.

Annex 20: Quality Risk Management

Brussels, 14 February 2008

Document History	
Adoption as ICH Q9 guideline Step 4	November 2005
Deadline for coming into operation	01 March 2008

Foreword and Scope of Application

The new GMP Annex 20 corresponds to ICH Q9 guideline on Quality Risk Management. It provides guidance on a systematic approach to quality risk management facilitating compliance with GMP and other quality requirements. It includes principles to be used and options for processes, methods and tools which may be used when applying a formal quality risk management approach.

To ensure coherence, GMP Part I, Chapter 1 on Quality Management, has been revised to include aspects of quality risk management within the quality system framework. A similar revision is planned for Part II of the Guide. Other sections of the GMP guide may be adjusted to include aspects of quality risk management in future broader revisions of those sections.

With the revision of the chapters on quality management in GMP Parts I and II quality risk management becomes an integral part of a manufacturer's quality system. Annex 20 itself is not intended, however, to create any new regulatory expectations; it provides an inventory of internationally acknowledged risk management methods and tools together with a list of potential applications at the discretion of manufacturers.

It is understood that the ICH Q9 guideline was primarily developed for quality risk management of medicinal products for human use. With the implementation in Annex 20 benefits of the guideline, such as processes, methods and tools for quality risk management are also made available to the veterinary sector.

While the GMP guide is primarily addressed to manufacturers, the ICH Q9 guideline, has relevance for other quality guidelines and includes specific sections for regulatory agencies. However, for reasons of coherence and completeness, the ICH Q9 guideline has been transferred completely into GMP Annex 20.

Further consideration of regulatory aspects, such as with the revision of the "Compilation of Community Procedures on Inspections and Exchange of Information" and in some quality guidelines, as published by the EMEA, will follow in a step-by-step approach.

1. *Introduction*

Risk management principles are effectively utilized in many areas of business and government including finance, insurance, occupational safety, public health, pharmacovigilance, and by agencies regulating these industries. Although there are some examples of the use of quality risk management in the pharmaceutical industry today, they are limited and do not represent the full contributions that risk management has to offer. In addition, the importance of quality systems has been recognized in the pharmaceutical industry and it is becoming evident that quality risk management is a valuable component of an effective quality system.

It is commonly understood that risk is defined as the combination of the probability of occurrence of harm and the severity of that harm. However, achieving a shared understanding of the application of risk management among diverse stakeholders is difficult because each stakeholder might perceive different potential harms, place a different probability on each harm occurring and attribute different severities to each harm. In relation to pharmaceuticals, although there are a variety of stakeholders, including patients and medical practitioners as well as government and industry, the protection of the patient by managing the risk to quality should be considered of prime importance.

The manufacturing and use of a drug (medicinal) product, including its components, necessarily entail some degree of risk. The risk to its quality is just one component of the overall risk. It is important to understand that product quality should be maintained throughout the product lifecycle such that the attributes that are important to the quality of the drug (medicinal) product remain consistent with those used in the clinical studies. An effective quality risk management approach can further ensure the high quality of the drug (medicinal) product to the patient by providing a proactive means to identify and control potential quality issues during development and manufacturing. Additionally, use of quality risk management can improve the decision making if a quality problem arises. Effective quality risk management can facilitate better and more informed decisions, can provide regulators with greater assurance of a company's ability to deal with potential risks and can beneficially affect the extent and level of direct regulatory oversight.

The purpose of this document is to offer a systematic approach to quality risk management. It serves as a foundation or resource document that is independent of, yet supports, other ICH Quality documents and complements existing quality practices, requirements, standards, and guidelines within the pharmaceutical industry and regulatory environment. It specifically provides guidance on the principles and some of the tools of quality risk management that can enable more effective and consistent risk based decisions, both by regulators and industry, regarding the quality of drug substances and drug (medicinal) products across the product lifecycle. It is not intended to create any new expectations beyond the current regulatory requirements.

It is neither always appropriate nor always necessary to use a formal risk management process (using recognized tools and/ or internal procedures e.g. standard operating procedures). The use of informal risk management processes (using empirical tools and/ or internal procedures) can also be considered acceptable. Appropriate use of quality risk management can facilitate but does not obviate industry's obligation to comply with regulatory requirements and does not replace appropriate communications between industry and regulators.

2. Scope

This guideline provides principles and examples of tools for quality risk management that can be applied to different aspects of pharmaceutical quality. These aspects include development, manufacturing, distribution, and the inspection and submission/review processes throughout the lifecycle of drug substances, drug (medicinal) products, biological and biotechnological products (including the use of raw materials, solvents, excipients, packaging and labeling materials in drug (medicinal) products, biological and biotechnological products).

3. Principles of Quality Risk Management

Two primary principles of quality risk management are:

- The evaluation of the risk to quality should be based on scientific knowledge and ultimately link to the protection of the patient; and

- The level of effort, formality and documentation of the quality risk management process should be commensurate with the level of risk.

4. General Quality Risk Management Process

Quality risk management is a systematic process for the assessment, control, communication and review of risks to the quality of the drug (medicinal) product across the product lifecycle. A model for quality risk management is outlined in the diagram (Figure 1). Other models could be used. The emphasis on each component of the framework might differ from case to case but a robust process will incorporate consideration of all the elements at a level of detail that is commensurate with the specific risk.

Figure 1: Overview of a typical quality risk management process

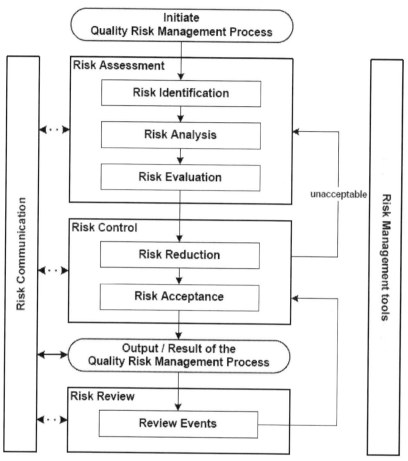

Decision nodes are not shown in the diagram above because decisions can occur at any point in the process. These decisions might be to return to the previous step and seek further information, to adjust the risk models or even to terminate the risk management process based upon information that supports such a decision. Note: "unacceptable" in the flowchart does not only refer to statutory, legislative or regulatory requirements, but also to the need to revisit the risk assessment process.

4.1 Responsibilities

Quality risk management activities are usually, but not always, undertaken by interdisciplinary teams. When teams are formed, they should include experts from the appropriate areas (e.g. quality unit, business development, engineering, regulatory affairs, production operations, sales and marketing, legal, statistics and clinical) in addition to individuals who are knowledgeable about the quality risk management process.

Decision *makers* should

- take responsibility for coordinating quality risk management across various functions and departments of their organization; and

- assure that a quality risk management process is defined, deployed and reviewed and that adequate resources are available.

4.2 Initiating a Quality Risk Management Process

Quality risk management should include systematic processes designed to coordinate, facilitate and improve science-based decision making with respect to risk. Possible steps used to initiate and plan a quality risk management process might include the following:

- Define the problem and/or risk question, including pertinent assumptions identifying the potential for risk

- Assemble background information and/ or data on the potential hazard, harm or human health impact relevant to the risk assessment

- Identify a leader and necessary resources

- Specify a timeline, deliverables and appropriate level of decision making for the risk management process

4.3 Risk Assessment

Risk assessment consists of the identification of hazards and the analysis and evaluation of risks associated with exposure to those hazards (as defined below). Quality risk assessments begin with a well-defined problem description or risk question. When the risk in question is well defined, an appropriate risk management tool (see examples in section 5) and the types of information needed to address the risk question will be more readily identifiable. As an aid to clearly defining the risk(s) for risk assessment purposes, three fundamental questions are often helpful:

1. What might go wrong?

2. What is the likelihood (probability) it will go wrong?

3. What are the consequences (severity)?

Risk identification is a systematic use of information to identify hazards referring to the risk question or problem description. Information can include historical data, theoretical analysis, informed opinions, and the concerns of stakeholders. Risk identification addresses the "What might go wrong?" question, including identifying the possible consequences. This provides the basis for further steps in the quality risk management process.

Risk analysis is the estimation of the risk associated with the identified hazards. It is the qualitative or quantitative process of linking the likelihood of occurrence and severity of harms. In some risk management tools, the ability to detect the harm (detectability) also factors in the estimation of risk.

Risk evaluation compares the identified and analyzed risk against given risk criteria. Risk evaluations consider the strength of evidence for all three of the fundamental questions.

In doing an effective risk assessment, the robustness of the data set is important because it determines the quality of the output. Revealing assumptions and reasonable sources of uncertainty will enhance confidence in this output and/or help identify its limitations. Uncertainty is due to combination of incomplete knowledge about a process and its expected or unexpected variability. Typical sources of uncertainty include gaps in knowledge gaps in pharmaceutical science and process understanding, sources of harm (e.g., failure modes of a process, sources of variability), and probability of detection of problems.

The output of a risk assessment is either a quantitative estimate of risk or a qualitative *description* of a range of risk. When risk is expressed quantitatively, a numerical probability is used. Alternatively, risk can be expressed using qualitative descriptors, such as "high", "medium", or "low", which should be defined in as much detail as possible. Sometimes a "risk score" is used to further define descriptors in risk ranking. In quantitative risk assessments, a risk estimate provides the likelihood of a specific consequence, given a set of risk-generating circumstances. Thus, quantitative risk estimation is useful for one particular consequence at a time. Alternatively, some risk management tools use a relative risk measure to combine multiple levels of severity and probability into an overall estimate of relative risk. The intermediate steps within a scoring process can sometimes employ quantitative risk estimation.

4.4 Risk Control

Risk control includes decision making to reduce and/or accept risks. The purpose of risk control is to reduce the risk to an acceptable level. The amount of effort used for risk control should be proportional to the significance of the risk. Decision makers might use different processes, including benefit-cost analysis, for understanding the optimal level of risk control.

Risk control might focus on the following questions:

- Is the risk above an acceptable level?

- What can be done to reduce or eliminate risks?

- What is the appropriate balance among benefits, risks and resources?

- Are new risks introduced as a result of the identified risks being controlled?

Risk reduction focuses on processes for mitigation or avoidance of quality risk when it exceeds a specified (acceptable) level (see Fig. 1). Risk reduction might include actions taken to mitigate the severity and probability of harm. Processes that improve the detectability of hazards and quality risks might also be used as part of a risk control strategy. The implementation of risk reduction measures can introduce new risks into the system or increase the significance of other existing risks. Hence, it might be appropriate to revisit the risk assessment to identify and evaluate any possible change in risk after implementing a risk reduction process.

Risk acceptance is a decision to accept risk. Risk acceptance can be a formal decision to accept the residual risk or it can be a passive decision in which residual risks are not specified. For some types of harms, even the best quality risk management practices might not entirely eliminate risk. In these circumstances, it might be agreed that an appropriate quality risk management strategy has been applied and that quality risk is reduced to a specified (acceptable) level. This (specified) acceptable level will depend on many parameters and should be decided on a case-by-case basis.

4.5 Risk Communication

Risk communication is the sharing of information about risk and risk management between the decision makers and others. Parties can communicate at any stage of the risk management process (see Fig. 1: dashed arrows). The output/result of the quality risk management process should be appropriately communicated and documented (see Fig. 1: solid arrows). Communications might include those among interested parties;

e.g., regulators and industry, industry and the patient, within a company, industry or regulatory authority, etc. The included information might relate to the existence, nature, form, probability, severity, acceptability, control, treatment, detectability or other aspects of risks to quality. Communication need not be carried out for each and every risk acceptance. Between the industry and regulatory authorities, communication concerning quality risk management decisions might be effected through existing channels as specified in regulations and guidances.

4.6 Risk Review

Risk management should be an ongoing part of the quality management process. A mechanism to review or monitor events should be implemented.

The output/results of the risk management process should be reviewed to take into account new knowledge and experience. Once a quality risk management process has been initiated, that process should continue to be utilized for events that might impact the original quality risk management decision, whether these events are planned (e.g. results of product review, inspections, audits, change control) or unplanned (e.g. root cause from failure investigations, recall). The frequency of any review should be based upon the level of risk. Risk review might include reconsideration of risk acceptance decisions (section 4.4).

5. *Risk Management Methodology*

Quality risk management supports a scientific and practical approach to decision-making. It provides documented, transparent and reproducible methods to accomplish steps of the quality risk management process based on current knowledge about assessing the probability, severity and sometimes detectability of the risk.

Traditionally, risks to quality have been assessed and managed in a variety of informal ways (empirical and/ or internal procedures) based on, for example, compilation of observations, trends and other information. Such approaches continue to provide useful information that might support topics such as handling of complaints, quality defects, deviations and allocation of resources.

Additionally, the pharmaceutical industry and regulators can assess and manage risk using recognized risk management tools and/ or internal procedures (e.g., standard operating procedures). Below is a non-exhaustive list of some of these tools (further details in Annex 1 and chapter 8):

- Basic risk management facilitation methods (flowcharts, check sheets etc.)

- Failure Mode Effects Analysis (FMEA)

- Failure Mode, Effects and Criticality Analysis (FMECA)

- Fault Tree Analysis (FTA)

- Hazard Analysis and Critical Control Points (HACCP)

- Hazard Operability Analysis (HAZOP)

- Preliminary Hazard Analysis (PHA)

- Risk ranking and filtering

- Supporting statistical tools

It might be appropriate to adapt these tools for use in specific areas pertaining to drug substance and drug (medicinal) product quality. Quality risk management methods and the supporting statistical tools can be used in combination (e.g. Probabilistic Risk Assessment). Combined use provides flexibility that can facilitate the application of quality risk management principles.

The degree of rigor and formality of quality risk management should reflect available knowledge and be commensurate with the complexity and/ or criticality of the issue to be addressed.

6. Integration of Quality Risk Management into Industry and Regulatory Operations

Quality risk management is a process that supports science-based and practical decisions when integrated into quality systems (see Annex II). As outlined in the introduction, appropriate use of quality risk management does not obviate industry's obligation to comply with regulatory requirements. However, effective quality risk management can facilitate better and more informed decisions, can provide regulators with greater assurance of a company's ability to deal with potential risks, and might affect the extent and level of direct regulatory oversight. In addition, quality risk management can facilitate better use of resources by all parties.

Training of both industry and regulatory personnel in quality risk management processes provides for greater understanding of decision-making processes and builds confidence in quality risk management outcomes.

Quality risk management should be integrated into existing operations and documented appropriately. Annex II provides examples of situations in which the use of the quality risk management process might provide information that could then be used in a variety of pharmaceutical operations. These examples are provided for illustrative purposes only and should not be considered a definitive or exhaustive list. These examples are not intended to create any new expectations beyond the requirements laid out in the current regulations.

Examples for industry and regulatory operations (see Annex II):

- Quality management

Examples for industry operations and activities (see Annex II):

- Development

- Facility, equipment and utilities

- Materials management

- Production

- Laboratory control and stability testing

- Packaging and labeling

- Inspection and assessment activities

Examples for regulatory operations (see Annex II):

- Inspection and assessment activities

While regulatory decisions will continue to be taken on a regional basis, a common understanding and application of quality risk management principles could facilitate mutual confidence and promote more consistent decisions among regulators on the basis of the same information. This collaboration could be important in the development of policies and guidelines that integrate and support quality risk management practices.

7. *Definitions*

Decision maker(s)
Person(s) with the competence and authority to make appropriate and timely quality risk management decisions

Detectability
the ability to discover or determine the existence, presence, or fact of a hazard

Harm
damage to health, including the damage that can occur from loss of product quality or availability

Hazard
the potential source of harm (ISO/IEC Guide 51)

Product Lifecycle
all phases in the life of the product from the initial development through marketing until the product's discontinuation

Quality
the degree to which a set of inherent properties of a product, system or process fulfills requirements (see ICH Q6a definition specifically for "quality" of drug substance and drug (medicinal) products.)

Quality risk management

a systematic process for the assessment, control, communication and review of risks to the quality of the drug (medicinal) product across the product lifecycle

Quality system

the sum of all aspects of a system that implements quality policy and ensures that quality objectives are met

Requirements

the explicit or implicit needs or expectations of the patients or their surrogates (e.g. health care professionals, regulators and legislators). In this document, "requirements" refers not only to statutory, legislative, or regulatory requirements, but also to such needs and expectations.

Risk

the combination of the probability of occurrence of harm and the severity of that harm (ISO/IEC Guide 51)

Risk acceptance

the decision to accept risk (ISO Guide 73)

Risk analysis

the estimation of the risk associated with the identified hazards

Risk assessment

a systematic process of organizing information to support a risk decision to be made within a risk management process. It consists of the identification of hazards and the analysis and evaluation of risks associated with exposure to those hazards.

Risk communication

the sharing of information about risk and risk management between the decision maker and other stakeholders

Risk control

actions implementing risk management decisions (ISO Guide 73)

Risk evaluation

the comparison of the estimated risk to given risk criteria using a quantitative or qualitative scale to determine the significance of the risk

Risk identification

the systematic use of information to identify potential sources of harm (hazards) referring to the risk question or problem description

Risk management

the systematic application of quality management policies, procedures, and practices to the tasks of assessing, controlling, communicating and reviewing risk

Risk reduction

actions taken to lessen the probability of occurrence of harm and the severity of that harm

Risk review

review or monitoring of output/results of the risk management process considering (if appropriate) new knowledge and experience about the risk

Severity

a measure of the possible consequences of a hazard

Stakeholder

any individual, group or organization that can affect, be affected by, or perceive itself to be affected by a risk. Decision makers might also be stakeholders. For the purposes of this guideline, the primary stakeholders are the patient, healthcare professional, regulatory authority, and industry

Trend

a statistical term referring to the direction or rate of change of a variable(s)

8. References

ICH Q8 Pharmaceutical development

ISO/IEC Guide 73:2002 - Risk Management - Vocabulary - Guidelines for use in Standards

ISO/IEC Guide 51:1999 - Safety Aspects - Guideline for their inclusion in standards

Process Mapping by the American Productivity & Quality Center 2002, ISBN 1928593739

IEC 61025 - Fault Tree Analysis (FTA)

IEC 60812 Analysis Techniques for system reliability—
Procedures for failure mode and effects analysis (FMEA)

Failure Mode and Effect Analysis, FMEA from Theory to
Execution, 2nd Edition 2003, D. H. Stamatis, ISBN
0873895983

Guidelines for Failure Modes and Effects Analysis (FMEA) for
Medical Devices, 2003 Dyadem Press ISBN 0849319102

The Basics of FMEA, Robin McDermott, Raymond J. Mikulak,
Michael R. Beauregard 1996 ISBN 0527763209

WHO Technical Report Series No 908, 2003 Annex 7
Application of Hazard Analysis and Critical Control Point
(HACCP) methodology to pharmaceuticals.

IEC 61882 - Hazard Operability Analysis (HAZOP)

ISO 14971:2000 - Application of Risk Management to Medical
Devices

ISO 7870:1993 - Control Charts

ISO 7871:1997 - Cumulative Sum Charts

ISO 7966:1993 - Acceptance Control Charts

ISO 8258:1991 - Shewhart Control Charts

What is Total Quality Control?; The Japanese Way, Kaoru
Ishikawa (Translated by David J. Liu, 1985, ISBN
0139524339

Annex I: Risk Management Methods and Tools

The purpose of this annex is to provide a general overview of and references for some of the primary tools that might be used in quality risk management by industry and regulators. The references are included as an aid to gain more knowledge and detail about the particular tool. This is not an exhaustive list. It is important to note that no one tool or set of tools is applicable to every situation in which a quality risk management procedure is used.

I.1 Basic Risk Management Facilitation Methods

Some of the simple techniques that are commonly used to structure risk management by organizing data and facilitating decision-making are:

- Flowcharts

- Check Sheets

- Process Mapping

- Cause and Effect Diagrams (also called an Ishikawa diagram or fish bone diagram)

I.2 Failure Mode Effects Analysis (FMEA)

FMEA (see IEC 60812) provides for an evaluation of potential failure modes for processes and their likely effect on outcomes and/or product performance. Once failure modes are established, risk reduction can be used to eliminate, contain, reduce or control the potential failures. FMEA relies on product and process understanding. FMEA methodically breaks down the analysis of complex processes into manageable steps. It is a powerful tool for summarizing the important modes of failure, factors causing these failures and the likely effects of these failures.

Potential Areas of Use(s)

FMEA can be used to prioritize risks and monitor the effectiveness of risk control activities.

FMEA can be applied to equipment and facilities and might be used to analyze a manufacturing operation and its effect on product or process. It identifies elements/operations within the system that render it vulnerable. The output/ results of FMEA can be used as a basis for design or further analysis or to guide resource deployment.

I.3 Failure Mode, Effects and Criticality Analysis (FMECA)

FMEA might be extended to incorporate an investigation of the degree of severity of the consequences, their respective probabilities of occurrence, and their detectability, thereby becoming a Failure Mode Effect and Criticality Analysis (FMECA; see IEC 60812). In order for such an analysis to be performed, the product or process specifications should be established. FMECA can identify places where additional preventive actions might be appropriate to minimize risks.

Potential Areas of Use(s)

FMECA application in the pharmaceutical industry should mostly be utilized for failures and risks associated with manufacturing processes; however, it is not limited to this application. The output of an FMECA is a relative risk "score" for each failure mode, which is used to rank the modes on a relative risk basis.

I.4 Fault Tree Analysis (FTA)

The FTA tool (see IEC 61025) is an approach that assumes failure of the functionality of a product or process. This tool evaluates system (or subsystem) failures one at a time but can combine multiple causes of failure by identifying causal chains. The results are represented pictorially in the form of a tree of fault modes. At each level in the tree, combinations of fault modes are described with logical operators (AND, OR, etc.). FTA relies on the experts' process understanding to identify causal factors.

Potential Areas of Use(s)

FTA can be used to establish the pathway to the root cause of the failure. FTA can be used to investigate complaints or deviations in order to fully understand their root cause and to ensure that intended improvements will fully resolve the issue and not lead to other issues (i.e. solve one problem yet cause a different problem). Fault Tree Analysis is an effective tool for evaluating how multiple factors affect a given issue. The output of an FTA includes a visual representation of failure modes. It is useful both for risk assessment and in developing monitoring programs.

I.5 Hazard Analysis and Critical Control Points (HACCP)

HACCP is a systematic, proactive, and preventive tool for assuring product quality, reliability, and safety (see WHO Technical Report Series No 908, 2003 Annex 7). It is a structured approach that applies technical and scientific principles to analyze, evaluate, prevent, and control the risk or adverse consequence(s) of hazard(s) due to the design, development, production, and use of products.

HACCP consists of the following seven steps:

(1) conduct a hazard analysis and identify preventive measures for each step of the process;

(2) determine the critical control points;

(3) establish critical limits;

(4) establish a system to monitor the critical control points;

(5) establish the corrective action to be taken when monitoring indicates that the critical control points are not in a state of control;

(6) establish system to verify that the HACCP system is working effectively;

(7) establish a record-keeping system.

Potential Areas of Use(s)

HACCP might be used to identify and manage risks associated with physical, chemical and biological hazards (including microbiological contamination). HACCP is most useful when product and process understanding is sufficiently comprehensive to support identification of critical control points. The output of a HACCP analysis is risk management information that facilitates monitoring of critical points not only in the manufacturing process but also in other life cycle phases.

I.6 Hazard Operability Analysis (HAZOP)

HAZOP (see IEC 61882) is based on a theory that assumes that risk events are caused by deviations from the design or operating intentions. It is a systematic brainstorming technique for identifying hazards using so-called "guide-words". "Guide-words" (e.g., No, More, Other Than, Part of, etc.) are applied to relevant parameters (e.g., contamination, temperature) to help identify potential deviations from normal use or design intentions. It often uses a team of people with expertise covering the design of the process or product and its application.

Potential Areas of Use(s)

HAZOP can be applied to manufacturing processes, including outsourced production and formulation as well as the upstream suppliers, equipment and facilities for drug substances and drug (medicinal) products. It has also been used primarily in the pharmaceutical industry for evaluating process safety hazards. As is the case with HACCP, the output of a HAZOP analysis is a list of critical operations for risk management. This facilitates regular monitoring of critical points in the manufacturing process.

I.7 Preliminary Hazard Analysis (PHA)

PHA is a tool of analysis based on applying prior experience or knowledge of a hazard or failure to identify future hazards, hazardous situations and events that might cause harm, as well as to estimate their probability of occurrence for a given activity, facility, product or system. The tool consists of: 1) the identification of the possibilities that the risk event happens, 2) the qualitative evaluation of the extent of possible injury or damage to health that could result and 3) a relative ranking of the hazard using a combination of severity and likelihood of occurrence, and 4) the identification of possible remedial measures

Potential Areas of Use(s)

PHA might be useful when analyzing existing systems or prioritizing hazards where circumstances prevent a more extensive technique from being used. It can be used for product, process and facility design as well as to evaluate the types of hazards for the general product type, then the product class, and finally the specific product. PHA is most commonly used early in the development of a project when there is little information on design details or operating procedures; thus, it will often be a precursor to further studies. Typically, hazards identified in the PHA are further assessed with other risk management tools such as those in this section.

I.8 Risk Ranking and Filtering

Risk ranking and filtering is a tool for comparing and ranking risks. Risk ranking of complex systems typically requires evaluation of multiple diverse quantitative and qualitative factors for each risk. The tool involves breaking down a basic risk question into as many components as needed to capture factors involved in the risk. These factors are combined into a single relative risk score that can then be used for ranking risks. "Filters," in the form of weighting factors or cut-offs for risk scores, can be used to scale or fit the risk ranking to management or policy objectives.

Potential Areas of Use(s)

Risk ranking and filtering can be used to prioritize manufacturing sites for inspection/audit by regulators or industry. Risk ranking methods are particularly helpful in situations in which the portfolio of risks and the underlying consequences to be managed are diverse and difficult to compare using a single tool. Risk ranking is useful when management needs to evaluate both quantitatively-assessed and qualitatively-assessed risks within the same organizational framework.

I.9 Supporting Statistical Tools

Statistical tools can support and facilitate quality risk management. They can enable effective data assessment, aid in determining the significance of the data set(s), and facilitate more reliable decision making. A listing of some of the principal statistical tools commonly used in the pharmaceutical industry is provided:

(i) Control Charts, for example:

- Acceptance Control Charts (see ISO 7966)

- Control Charts with Arithmetic Average and Warning Limits (see ISO 7873)

- Cumulative Sum Charts (see ISO 7871)

- Shewhart Control Charts (see ISO 8258)

- Weighted Moving Average

(ii) Design of Experiments (DOE)

(iii) Histograms

(iv)Pareto Charts

(v) Process Capability Analysis

Annex II: Potential Applications for Quality Risk Management

This Annex is intended to identify potential uses of quality risk management principles and tools by industry and regulators. However, the selection of particular risk management tools is completely dependent upon specific facts and circumstances.

These examples are provided for illustrative purposes and only suggest potential uses of quality risk management. This Annex is not intended to create any new expectations beyond the current regulatory requirements.

II.1 Quality Risk Management as Part of Integrated Quality Management

Documentation

To review current interpretations and application of regulatory expectations

To determine the desirability of and/or develop the content for SOPs, guidelines, etc.

Training and education

To determine the appropriateness of initial and/or ongoing training sessions based on education, experience and working habits of staff, as well as on a periodic assessment of previous training (e.g., its effectiveness)

To identify the training, experience, qualifications and physical abilities that allow personnel to perform an operation reliably and with no adverse impact on the quality of the product

Quality defects

To provide the basis for identifying, evaluating, and communicating the potential quality impact of a suspected quality defect, complaint, trend, deviation, investigation, out of specification result, etc.

To facilitate risk communications and determine appropriate action to address significant product defects, in conjunction with regulatory authorities (e.g., recall)

Auditing/Inspection

To define the frequency and scope of audits, both internal and external, taking into account factors such as:

- Existing legal requirements

- Overall compliance status and history of the company or facility

- Robustness of a company's quality risk management activities

- Complexity of the site

- Complexity of the manufacturing process

- Complexity of the product and its therapeutic significance

- Number and significance of quality defects (e.g, recall)

- Results of previous audits/inspections

- Major changes of building, equipment, processes, key personnel

- Experience with manufacturing of a product (e.g. frequency, volume, number of batches)

- Test results of official control laboratories

Periodic review

To select, evaluate and interpret trend results of data within the product quality review

To interpret monitoring data (e.g., to support an assessment of the appropriateness of revalidation or changes in sampling)

Change management / change control

To manage changes based on knowledge and information accumulated in pharmaceutical development and during manufacturing

To evaluate the impact of the changes on the availability of the final product

To evaluate the impact on product quality of changes to the facility, equipment, material, manufacturing process or technical transfers

To determine appropriate actions preceding the implementation of a change, e.g., additional testing, (re)qualification, (re)validation or communication with regulators

Continual improvement

To facilitate continual improvement in processes throughout the product lifecycle.

II.2 Quality Risk Management as Part of Regulatory Operations

Inspection and assessment activities

To assist with resource allocation including, for example, inspection planning and frequency, and inspection and assessment intensity (see "Auditing" section in Annex II.1)

To evaluate the significance of, for example, quality defects, potential recalls and inspectional findings

To determine the appropriateness and type of post-inspection regulatory follow-up

To evaluate information submitted by industry including pharmaceutical development information

To evaluate impact of proposed variations or changes

To identify risks which should be communicated between inspectors and assessors to facilitate better understanding of how risks can be or are controlled (e.g., parametric release, Process Analytical Technology (PAT)).

II.3 Quality Risk Management as Part of development

To design a quality product and its manufacturing process to consistently deliver the intended performance of the product (see ICH Q8)

To enhance knowledge of product performance over a wide range of material attributes (e.g. particle size distribution, moisture content, flow properties), processing options and process parameters

To assess the critical attributes of raw materials, solvents, Active Pharmaceutical Ingredient (API) starting materials, APIs, excipients, or packaging materials

To establish appropriate specifications, identify critical process parameters and establish manufacturing controls (e.g., using information from pharmaceutical development studies regarding the clinical significance of quality attributes and the ability to control them during processing)

To decrease variability of quality attributes:

- reduce product and material defects

- reduce manufacturing defects

To assess the need for additional studies (e.g., bioequivalence, stability) relating to scale up and technology transfer

To make use of the "design space" concept (see ICH Q8)

II.4 Quality Risk Management for Facilities, Equipment and Utilities

Design of facility / equipment
To determine appropriate zones when designing buildings and facilities, e.g.,

- flow of material and personnel

- minimize contamination

- pest control measures

- prevention of mix-ups • open versus closed equipment

- clean rooms versus isolator technologies

- dedicated or segregated facilities / equipment

To determine appropriate product contact materials for equipment and containers (e.g., selection of stainless steel grade, gaskets, lubricants)

To determine appropriate utilities (e.g., steam, gases, power source, compressed air, heating, ventilation and air conditioning (HVAC), water)

To determine appropriate preventive maintenance for associated equipment (e.g., inventory of necessary spare parts)

Hygiene aspects in facilities

To protect the product from environmental hazards, including chemical, microbiological, and physical hazards (e.g., determining appropriate clothing and gowning, hygiene concerns)

To protect the environment (e.g., personnel, potential for cross-contamination) from hazards related to the product being manufactured

Qualification of facility/equipment/utilities

To determine the scope and extent of qualification of facilities, buildings, and production equipment and/or laboratory instruments (including proper calibration methods)

Cleaning of equipment and environmental control

To differentiate efforts and decisions based on the intended use (e.g., multi- versus single-purpose, batch versus continuous production)

To determine acceptable (specified) cleaning validation limits

Calibration/preventive maintenance

To set appropriate calibration and maintenance schedules

Computer systems and computer controlled equipment

To select the design of computer hardware and software (e.g., modular, structured, fault tolerance)

To determine the extent of validation, e.g.,

- identification of critical performance parameters

- selection of the requirements and design

- code review

- the extent of testing and test methods

- reliability of electronic records and signatures

II.5 Quality Risk Management as Part of Materials Management

Assessment and evaluation of suppliers and contract manufacturers
To provide a comprehensive evaluation of suppliers and contract manufacturers (e.g., auditing, supplier quality agreements)

Starting material
To assess differences and possible quality risks associated with variability in starting materials (e.g., age, route of synthesis).

Use of materials
To determine whether it is appropriate to use material under quarantine (e.g., for further internal processing)

To determine appropriateness of reprocessing, reworking, use of returned goods

Storage, logistics and distribution conditions
To assess the adequacy of arrangements to ensure maintenance of appropriate storage and transport conditions (e.g., temperature, humidity, container design)

To determine the effect on product quality of discrepancies in storage or transport conditions (e.g. cold chain management) in conjunction with other ICH guidelines

To maintain infrastructure (e.g. capacity to ensure proper shipping conditions, interim storage, handling of hazardous materials and controlled substances, customs clearance)

To provide information for ensuring the availability of pharmaceuticals (e.g., ranking risks to the supply chain).

II.6 Quality Risk Management as Part of Production

Validation
To identify the scope and extent of verification, qualification and validation activities (e.g., analytical methods, processes, equipment and cleaning methods

To determine the extent for follow-up activities (e.g., sampling, monitoring and re-validation)

To distinguish between critical and non-critical process steps to facilitate design of a validation study

In-process sampling & testing

To evaluate the frequency and extent of in-process control testing (e.g., to justify reduced testing under conditions of proven control)

To evaluate and justify the use of process analytical technologies (PAT) in conjunction with parametric and real time release

Production planning

To determine appropriate production planning (e.g., dedicated, campaign and concurrent production process sequences).

II.7 Quality Risk Management as Part of Laboratory Control and Stability Studies

Out of specification results

To identify potential root causes and corrective actions during the investigation of out of specification results

Retest period / expiration date

To evaluate adequacy of storage and testing of intermediates, excipients and starting materials

II.8 Quality Risk Management as Part of Packaging and Labelling

Design of packages

To design the secondary package for the protection of primary packaged product (e.g., to ensure product authenticity, label legibility)

Selection of container closure system

To determine the critical parameters of the container closure system

Label controls

To design label control procedures based on the potential for mix-ups involving different product labels, including different versions of the same label

Annex 20

Glossary

Glossary

Definitions given below apply to the words as used in this guide. They may have different meanings in other contexts.

Air-Lock

An enclosed space with two or more doors, and which is interposed between two or more rooms, e.g. of differing class of cleanliness, for the purpose of controlling the air-flow between those rooms when they need to be entered. An air-lock is designed for and used by either people or goods.

Batch (or Lot)

A defined quantity of starting material, packaging material or product processed in one process or series of processes so that it could be expected to be homogeneous.

Note: To complete certain stages of manufacture, it may be necessary to divide a batch into a number of sub batches, which are later brought together to form a final homogeneous batch. In the case of continuous manufacture, the batch must correspond to a defined fraction of the production, characterised by its intended homogeneity.

For control of the finished product, the following definition has been given in Annex 1 of Directive 2001/83/EC as amended by Directive 2003/63/EC: 'For the control of the finished product, a batch of a proprietary medicinal product comprises all the units of a pharmaceutical form which are made from the same initial mass of material and have undergone a single series of manufacturing operations or a single sterilisation operation or, in the case of a continuous production process, all the units manufactured in a given period of time'.

Batch Number (or Lot Number)

A distinctive combination of numbers and/or letters which specifically identifies a batch.

Biogenerator

A contained system, such as a fermenter, into which biological agents are introduced along with other materials so as to effect their multiplication or their production of other substances by reaction with the other materials. Biogenerators are generally fitted with devices for regulation, control, connection, material addition and material withdrawal.

Biological Agents

Micro-organisms, including genetically engineered micro-organisms, cell cultures and endoparasites, whether pathogenic or not.

Bulk Product

Any product which has completed all processing stages up to, but not including, final packaging.

Calibration

The set of operations which establish, under specified conditions, the relationship between values indicated by a measuring instrument or measuring system, or values represented by a material measure, and the corresponding known values of a reference standard.

Cell Bank

Cell bank system: A cell bank system is a system whereby successive batches of a product are manufactured by culture in cells derived from the same master cell bank. A number of containers from the master cell bank are used to prepare a working cell bank. The cell bank system is validated for a passage level or number of population doublings beyond that achieved during routine production.

Master cell bank: A culture of [fully characterised] cells distributed into containers in a single operation, processed together in such a manner as to ensure uniformity and stored in such a manner as to ensure stability. A master cell bank is usually stored at - 70°C or lower.

Working cell bank: A culture of cells derived from the master cell bank and intended for use in the preparation of production cell cultures. The working cell bank is usually stored at - 70°C or lower.

Cell Culture

The result from the in-vitro growth of cells isolated from multicellular organisms.

Clean Area

An area with defined environmental control of particulate and microbial contamination, constructed and used in such a way as to reduce the introduction, generation and retention of contaminants within the area.

Note: The different degrees of environmental control are defined in the Supplementary Guidelines for the Manufacture of sterile medicinal products.

Clean/Contained Area

An area constructed and operated in such a manner that will achieve the aims of both a clean area and a contained area at the same time.

Containment

The action of confining a biological agent or other entity within a defined space.

Primary containment: A system of containment which prevents the escape of a biological agent into the immediate working environment. It involves the use of closed containers or safety biological cabinets along with secure operating procedures.

Secondary containment: A system of containment which prevents the escape of a biological agent into the external environment or into other working areas. It involves the use of rooms with specially designed air handling, the existence of airlocks and/or sterilisers for the exit of materials and secure operating procedures. In many cases it may add to the effectiveness of primary containment.

Contained Area

An area constructed and operated in such a manner (and equipped with appropriate air handling and filtration) so as to prevent contamination of the external environment by biological agents from within the area.

Controlled Area

An area constructed and operated in such a manner that some attempt is made to control the introduction of potential contamination (an air supply approximating to grade D may be appropriate), and the consequences of accidental release of living organisms. The level of control exercised should reflect the nature of the organism employed in the process. At a minimum, the area should be maintained at a pressure negative to the immediate external environment and allow for the efficient removal of small quantities of airborne contaminants.

Computerised System
A system including the input of data, electronic processing and the output of information to be used either for reporting or automatic control.

Cross Contamination
Contamination of a material or of a product with another material or product.

Crude Plant (Vegetable Drug)
Fresh or dried medicinal plant or parts thereof.

Cryogenic Vessel
A container designed to contain liquefied gas at extremely low temperature.

Cylinder
A container designed to contain gas at a high pressure.

Exotic Organism
A biological agent where either the corresponding disease does not exist in a given country or geographical area, or where the disease is the subject of prophylactic measures or an eradication programme undertaken in the given country or geographical area.

Finished Product
A medicinal product which has undergone all stages of production, including packaging in its final container.

Herbal Medicinal Product
Medicinal product containing, as active ingredients, exclusively plant material and/or vegetable drug preparations.

Infected
Contaminated with extraneous biological agents and therefore capable of spreading infection.

In-Process Control

Checks performed during production in order to monitor and if necessary to adjust the process to ensure that the product conforms its specification. The control of the environment or equipment may also be regarded as a part of in-process control.

Intermediate Product

Partly processed material which must undergo further manufacturing steps before it becomes a bulk product.

Liquifiable Gases

Those which, at the normal filling temperature and pressure, remain as a liquid in the cylinder.

Manifold

Equipment or apparatus designed to enable one or more gas containers to be filled simultaneously from the same source.

Manufacture

All operations of purchase of materials and products, Production, Quality Control, release, storage, distribution of medicinal products and the related controls.

Manufacturer

Holder of a Manufacturing Authorisation as described in Article 40 of Directive 2001/83/EC[40].

Medicinal Plant

Plant the whole or part of which is used for medicinal purpose.

Medicinal Product

Any substance or combination of substances presented for treating or preventing disease in human beings or animals.

Any substance or combination of substances which may be administered to human beings or animals with a view to making a medical diagnosis or to restoring, correcting or modifying physiological functions in human beings or in animals is likewise considered a medicinal product.

---

[40] Article 44 of Directive 2001/82/EC

Packaging

All operations, including filling and labelling, which a bulk product has to undergo in order to become a finished product.

Note: Sterile filling would not normally be regarded as part of packaging, the bulk product being the filled, but not finally packaged, primary containers.

Packaging Material

Any material employed in the packaging of a medicinal product, excluding any outer packaging used for transportation or shipment. Packaging materials are referred to as primary or secondary according to whether or not they are intended to be in direct contact with the product.

Procedures

Description of the operations to be carried out, the precautions to be taken and measures to be applied directly or indirectly related to the manufacture of a medicinal product.

Production

All operations involved in the preparation of a medicinal product, from receipt of materials, through processing and packaging, to its completion as a finished product.

Qualification

Action of proving that any equipment works correctly and actually leads to the expected results. The word validation is sometimes widened to incorporate the concept of qualification.

Quality Control

See Chapter 1.

Quarantine

The status of starting or packaging materials, intermediate, bulk or finished products isolated physically or by other effective means whilst awaiting a decision on their release or refusal.

Radiopharmaceutical

"Radiopharmaceutical" shall mean any medicinal product which, when ready for use, contains one or more radionuclides (radioactive isotopes) included for a medicinal purpose (Article 1(6) of Directive 2001/83/EC.

Reconciliation

A comparison, making due allowance for normal variation, between the amount of product or materials theoretically and actually produced or used.

Record

See Chapter 4.

Recovery

The introduction of all or part of previous batches of the required quality into another batch at a defined stage of manufacture.

Reprocessing

The reworking of all or part of a batch of product of an unacceptable quality from a defined stage of production so that its quality may be rendered acceptable by one or more additional operations.

Return

Sending back to the manufacturer or distributor of a medicinal product which may or may not present a quality defect.

Seed Lot

Seed lot system: A seed lot system is a system according to which successive batches of a product are derived from the same master seed lot at a given passage level. For routine production, a working seed lot is prepared from the master seed lot. The final product is derived from the working seed lot and has not undergone more passages from the master seed lot than the vaccine shown in clinical studies to be satisfactory with respect to safety and efficacy. The origin and the passage history of the master seed lot and the working seed lot are recorded.

Master seed lot: A culture of a micro-organism distributed from a single bulk into containers in a single operation in such a manner as to ensure uniformity, to prevent contamination and to ensure stability. A master seed lot in liquid form is usually stored at or below - 70°C. A freeze-dried master seed lot is stored at a temperature known to ensure stability.

Working seed lot: A culture of a micro-organism derived from the master seed lot and intended for use in production. Working seed lots are distributed into containers and stored as described above for master seed lots.

Specification

See Chapter 4.

Starting Material

Any substance used in the production of a medicinal product, but excluding packaging materials.

Sterility

Sterility is the absence of living organisms. The conditions of the sterility test are given in the European Pharmacopoeia.

System

Is used in the sense of a regulated pattern of interacting activities and techniques which are united to form an organised whole.

Validation

Action of proving, in accordance with the principles of Good Manufacturing Practice, that any procedure, process, equipment, material, activity or system actually leads to the expected results (see also qualification).

Other Documents Related to GMP

Inspections - Good Manufacturing Practice

Compilation of Community Procedures on Inspections and Exchange of Information

The EMEA is responsible for maintaining and publishing the Compilation of Procedures on behalf of the European Commission. The Compilation of Procedures[41] is a collection of GMP inspection- related procedures and forms agreed by the GMP inspectorates of all the Member States and designed to facilitate administrative collaboration, harmonisation of inspections and exchange of inspection-related information. Article 3 of the GMP Directive, 2003/94/EC, requires Member States to take account of these procedures, and they are used as the basis for standard operating procedures of the quality systems established within the inspectorates themselves.

London, 2 August 2008

EMEA/INS/GMP/313483/2006 Rev. 9

Published In Agreement With the European Commission by EMEA (European Medicines Agency)

Note: This document forms part of the Compilation of Community Procedures on Inspections and Exchange of Information. Please check for updates on the EMEA website (Inspections pages).

---

[41] Available for download from the EMEA website at http://www.emea.europa.eu/Inspections/GMPCompproc.html

Table of Contents

#	Document Title	Date
1	Introduction	27/03/2007
2	Quality Systems Framework for GMP Inspectorates	April 2008
3	Procedures related to Rapid Alerts:	
3.1	Handling of reports of suspected quality defects in medicinal products	20/09/2006
3.2	Procedure for Handling Rapid Alerts and Recalls Arising from Quality Defects	20/09/2006
3.3	Rapid Alert Notification form	2006
3.4	Rapid Alert Follow up form	2006
4	Procedures related to GMP Inspections:	
4.1	Conduct of Inspections of Pharmaceutical Manufacturers	20/09/2006
4.2	Outline of a Procedure for Co-ordinating the Verification of the GMP status of Manufacturers in Third Countries	20/09/2006
4.3	Guideline on Training and Qualifications of GMP Inspectors	2/08/2008
4.4	Exchange of Information on Manufacturers and Manufacturing or Wholesale Distribution Authorisations between Competent Authorities in the European Economic Area	20/09/2006
4.5	Guidance on the occasions when it is appropriate for Competent Authorities to conduct inspections at the premises of Manufacturers of Active Substances used as starting materials	20/09/2006
4.6	The issue and update of GMP certificates	07/12/2006
4.7	Risk based inspection planning	April 2008
5	Forms used by Regulators:	
5.1	GMP Inspection report – Community format	20/09/2006
5.2	Community Basic Format for Manufacturers Authorisation	20/09/2006
5.3	GMP Certificate	11/09/2007
6	Procedures related to Centralised Procedures:	
6.1	Procedure for Co-ordinating Foreign and Community Pre-Authorisation Inspections during the Assessment of Applications	20/09/2006

6.2	Guideline on the Preparation of Reports on GMP Inspections Requested by either the CHMP or CVMP in connection with Applications for Marketing Authorisations and with Products Authorised under the Centralised System	20/09/2006
6.3	Delegation of Responsibilities for GMP Inspections for Products covered under the Centralised Procedure	03/10/2006
7	Compilation History:	
7.1	History of changes to Compilation of Procedures	02/08/2008

Introduction to the Compilation of Procedures on Inspections and Exchange of Information

The Compilation of Community Procedures on Inspections and Exchange of Information, formerly known as the Compilation of Community Procedures on Administrative Collaboration and Harmonisation of Inspections, is a tool for facilitating co-operation between the GMP inspectorates of the Member States and a means of achieving harmonisation. The procedures within it provide the basis for national procedures that form part of the national GMP inspectorates' quality systems. These quality systems are based on a framework laid down in one of the documents of the Compilation.

The contents of the Compilation of Procedures are constantly updated developed and agreed, under the co-ordination of the European Medicines Agency, by representatives of the GMP Inspectorates of each member state, including those supervising the manufacture and import of veterinary medicinal products only. Once agreed, they are adopted by the European Commission and then published on its behalf by the European Medicines Agency.

The Heads of Medicines Agencies have agreed to the setting up of a joint audit programme of GMP inspectorates to maintain mutual confidence in the GMP inspection systems of each member state by the other member states, and the Compilation provides criteria on which the audits are based.

Member states are obliged to take account of the Compilation of Procedures by virtue of Art. 3(1) of Directive 2003/94/EC. Until such time as the corresponding GMP directive for veterinary medicinal products, Directive 91/412/EEC, is amended accordingly, GMP Inspectorates dealing exclusively with veterinary medicinal products have voluntarily agreed to abide by it, although it is recognised that the formats for inspection reports, manufacturing authorisations and GMP certificates are of a binding nature by virtue of Art. 51 of Directive 2001/82/EC, as amended.

Quality Systems Framework for GMP Inspectorates

London, 2 August 2007

EMEA/INS/GMP/313500/2006 Rev1

Note: *This document forms part of the Compilation of Community Procedures on Inspections and Exchange of Information. Please check for updates on the EMEA website (Inspections pages).*

Title: *Quality Systems Framework for GMP Inspectorates*

Date of adoption: *November 2007*

Date of entry into force: *April 2008*

Supersedes: *Version in force from March 2004*

Reason for revision: *Following the implementation of ICH Q9 guideline the text was amended to introduce a quality risk management approach including minor editorial changes.*

1. Introduction

1.1 One of the main purposes of the GMP/GDP Inspectors Working Group is to establish and maintain a system for mutual recognition of national inspections in respect of the manufacture and, where relevant, wholesale distribution of medicinal products and for the administrative collaboration between Member States (MS) of the European Economic

Area (EEA). The general requirements for national pharmaceutical inspectorates are to fulfil the requirements of national legislation and of the relevant European Directives for EEA countries. Specific obligations of inspections as contained in national law and if any European Directives must be included in the national Inspectorate's quality systems.

1.2 This document outlines the quality system requirements for GMP pharmaceutical inspectorates. It is intended that each GMP pharmaceutical inspectorate uses the document as the basis for developing and implementing its quality system and for preparing the quality manual. In addition to providing a basis for self-assessment and a reference document for use by external assessors, establishing and maintaining an effective quality system will generate confidence within and between GMP national pharmaceutical inspectorates in the assessment of compliance with good manufacturing practice and/or good wholesale distribution practice.

1.3 National GMP pharmaceutical inspectorates, the European Commission (EC), the European Medicines Agency (EMEA) and the pharmaceutical Inspection Cooperation Scheme – (PIC/S) should co-operate with one another in exchanging experiences in the maintenance and operation of quality systems and in the further development of this document.

1.4 Only on voluntary basis, this document could be useful for (other) inspectorates assessing compliance with GXP or for the inspection of pharmacies.

1.5 In preparing this text, the working group was advised by:

EN ISO/IEC 17020:2005
General criteria for the operation of various types of bodies performing inspections;

EN ISO/IEC 17023:2006
General requirements for bodies operating assessment and certification/ registration of quality system;

ISO 9001-2000
Quality management systems-Requirements;

ISO 9004-2000
Quality management systems: guidelines for performance improvements;

ISO 19011 : 2002
> Guidelines for quality and/or environmental managerial systems auditing;

PI 002-1 : 2000
> Recommendations on quality system requirements for pharmaceutical inspectorates;

May 2001
> Revised Compilation of Community procedures on administrative collaboration and harmonisation of inspections;

1998
> Proceedings of the PIC-PIC/S seminar on quality systems for pharmaceutical inspectorates.

2. Purpose

2.1 The primary purpose of a quality system is to ensure that adequate quality standards are maintained. The purpose of adopting a common standard for quality system requirements is to achieve consistency in inspection standards between GMP national pharmaceutical inspectorates and thus to facilitate mutual recognition of those inspectorates. This standard should facilitate implementation of the European Joint Audit Programme and PIC/S Joint Re-assessment Programme.

2.2 Each GMP national inspection service should use this document as the basis for developing its own quality system, so that inspection activities within each inspection service are carried out in accordance with a system compatible with those of the other member states.

3. Scope

3.1 This document specifies the quality system requirements for national pharmaceutical inspection services concerned with good manufacturing practice.

3.2 Where wholesale inspections are required by national legislation to be carried out by GMP national pharmaceutical inspection service, this document specifies the quality system requirements for national pharmaceutical inspection services concerned with good wholesale distribution practice of medicinal products.

3.3 The quality system should include all activities involved in the inspection process.

4. Definitions

4.1 *Quality system:* The sum of all that is necessary to implement an organisation's quality policy and meet quality objectives. It includes organisation structure, responsibilities, procedures, systems, processes and resources. Typically these features will be addressed in different kinds of documents as the quality manual and documented   procedures, modus operandi

4.2 *Quality:* The totality of characteristics of an entity that bear on its ability to satisfy stated and implied needs

4.3 *Pharmaceutical Inspectorate:* The national body responsible for co-ordinating and carrying out GMP inspections, including inspections of pharmaceutical manufacturers and/or wholesale distributors. If relevant, this could include making decisions concerning the issue or withdrawal of establishment licences or authorisations for their activities, the issue or withdrawal of GMP certificates, providing advice and handling suspected quality defects.

4.4 *Licence:* For the purposes of this document, a licence is defined as an authorisation to manufacture or distribute medicinal products.

5. Quality Manual

5.1 The pharmaceutical inspectorate shall prepare and maintain a quality manual covering the elements described in this document. It is for each pharmaceutical inspectorate to decide on the format and style of their quality manual, but it must include, or make reference to, the quality system procedures which define the activities of the Inspectorate and the arrangements for maintaining the quality system. The reference used to complete it (as ISO or EN norms) must be quoted too.

6. Administrative Structure

6.1 The structure, membership and operation of the GMP pharmaceutical inspectorate shall be such as to enable it to meet the objectives of quality management and to ensure that impartiality is safeguarded.

6.2 The personnel of the inspection service, including sub-contracted personnel and experts, shall be free from any commercial, financial and other pressures which might affect their judgement and freedom to act. The pharmaceutical inspectorate shall ensure that persons or organisations external to the inspection organisation cannot influence the result of inspections. The system for obtaining fees should not improperly influence the inspection procedure. Rules for deontology, ethic and conflict of interests should be clearly defined.

6.3 The relationship of the pharmaceutical inspectorate to other agencies and to other organisations within and outside the Inspectorate shall be described where relevant.

6.4 The pharmaceutical inspectorate shall implement a policy which distinguishes between the process of inspection and that of issuing a GMP manufacturing authorisation.

6.5 Where relevant, the pharmaceutical inspectorate shall implement a policy which distinguishes between the process of inspection and that of providing an advisory service to clients. This service should be of benefit to all of industry and not solely to individual organisations.

7. *Organisation and Management*

7.1 Senior management of the pharmaceutical inspectorate shall make a formal commitment to the recommended principles embodied in this document by ensuring that the quality policy of the Inspectorate is documented, that it is relevant to the objectives of that organisation and that it is implemented.

7.2 The responsibility, authority and reporting structure of the pharmaceutical inspectorate shall be clearly defined and documented. The structure shall be defined in organisation charts and shall be supported by written job descriptions for each member of staff.

7.3 There shall be nominated an appropriately qualified and experienced person or persons with responsibility to carry out the quality assurance function, including implementing and maintaining the quality system. This person shall have direct access to senior management.

7.4 Senior management of the competent authority shall ensure that the pharmaceutical inspectorate has sufficient resources at all levels to enable it to meet its objectives effectively and efficiently. The senior management of the pharmaceutical inspectorate shall ensure that all personnel are competent and qualified to carry out their assigned duties and that they receive appropriate training. Such training shall be documented and its effectiveness assessed.

7.5 There shall be a system for periodic management review of the quality system. Such reviews shall be documented and records shall be retained for a defined period.

8. Documentation and Change Control

8.1 The pharmaceutical inspectorate shall establish and maintain a system for the control of all documentation relating to the inspection system. This shall include policies, procedures, guidelines and any documents of external origin such as regulations and directives which may direct the activities of the Inspectorate or influence the quality of its operations.

8.2 The document control system shall ensure that documents are authorised by appropriate persons prior to issue and that only current versions are held by nominated individuals. A record of all relevant documents and document holders shall be maintained. The system shall ensure that superseded documents are withdrawn from use. Superseded documents shall be retained for an appropriate and defined period.

8.3 The documentation system shall ensure that any changes to documents are made in a controlled manner and are properly authorised. There shall be a means of identifying changes in individual documents.

9. Records

9.1 The pharmaceutical inspectorate shall establish and maintain a system of records relating to its activities which complies with any existing regulations. If relevant, the system shall include documents received from licence applicants and licence holders as appropriate.

9.2 Records shall provide detailed information about the planning of inspections, the way in which each inspection was applied, a description of the inspection process, follow-up activities and recommendations to the body responsible for issuing licences.

9.3 All records shall be handled in such a way as to prevent their damage or loss and shall be retained for an adequate period consistent with any legal requirements. All records shall be maintained in confidence to the inspected party unless otherwise required under freedom of information legislation, or unless required under exchange of information procedures and arrangements between national pharmaceutical inspectorates, the EU/EEA, the EMEA and Mutual Recognition Agreement (MRA) or PECA partners.

10. *Inspection Procedures*

10.1   The pharmaceutical inspectorate shall conduct repeated inspections of manufacturers and/ or wholesale distributors and shall issue inspection reports in accordance with national or European Community requirements as appropriate.

10.2   The pharmaceutical inspectorate shall have the documented procedures and resources to enable inspection of manufacturing and wholesale distribution operations to be carried out in accordance with the official guidelines and national legislation and in accordance with a formal inspection plan. All instructions, standards or written procedures, worksheets, check lists and reference data relevant to the work of the pharmaceutical inspectorate shall be maintained up-to-date and be readily available to staff.

10.3   When more than one inspector is involved in an inspection, a lead inspector shall be appointed to co-ordinate inspection activities. The inspection report shall normally be prepared by the lead inspector and shall be agreed by all participating inspectors.

10.4   The inspection report format should be in compliance with the European model.

10.5   The report should be sent to the responsible person of the inspected structure (preferably the qualified person).

The lead inspector and all concerned inspectors should participate in assessing the reply.

10.6   Observations and/or data obtained in the course of inspections shall be recorded in a timely manner to prevent loss of relevant information.

10.7   Completed inspections shall be reviewed to ensure that requirements are met.

11. Inspection Resources

11.1   Personnel

11.1.1   The pharmaceutical inspectorate shall possess the required personnel, expertise and other resources to perform inspections of manufacturers and/ or wholesale distributors to determine their compliance with the principles and guidelines of current good practices and with the relevant legislation.

11.1.2   The staff responsible for inspections shall have appropriate qualifications, training, experience and knowledge of the inspection process. They shall have the ability to make professional judgements as to the conformance of the inspected party with the requirements of good practices and the relevant legislation and be able to apply an appropriate degree of risk assessment. They shall have knowledge of current technology, including computerised systems and information technology.

11.1.3   The pharmaceutical inspectorate shall establish a documented system for recruiting and training its personnel and shall carry out a regular review of the training received and the training needs for each member of staff. Individual training and qualification records shall be maintained.

11.2   Resources and equipment

11.2.1   The pharmaceutical inspectorate shall have available the necessary resources and equipment to enable it to carry out its obligations effectively and efficiently.

11.3 Risk management

11.3.1 The pharmaceutical inspectorate should implement risk management for assigning resources and prioritizing tasks and activities to carry out its obligations.(e.g. planning of inspections).

11.3.2 The pharmaceutical inspectorate should also implement risk approach in the conducting of inspection.

12. Internal Audit

12.1   The pharmaceutical inspectorate shall carry out and document periodic internal audits of its operations to assess compliance with the requirements of the quality system. Results of internal audits and associated corrective actions shall be reviewed as part of the management review process.

12.2   Internal audit processes and documents, auditors qualifications should be clearly defined (e.g. reference to ISO 19011 : 2002).

12.3   Internal audit records shall be retained for a defined period.

13. Quality Improvement and Corrective/Preventive Action

13.1   Quality indicators:

13.1.1   The pharmaceutical inspectorate should establish and maintain quality indicators related to its activities notably in the area of timeframe mentioned in existing EU or national regulations (e.g. licensing system for manufacturing or marketing authorizations) and/ or documentation (e.g. writing reports).

13.1.2   Quality indicators should be reviewed as part of the management review process.

13.2   Corrective/ preventive action:

13.2.1   The pharmaceutical inspectorate shall establish and maintain a procedure for the investigation of non-compliances with the quality system which are identified through internal or external audit of its activities. The procedure shall include the prescribing, implementation and verification of corrective action. The procedure shall cover also corrective actions arising from the investigation of complaints and other observations relating to the activities of the Inspectorate.

13.2.2   The system shall include a description of the steps to be taken in assessing the need for quality improvement and preventive action.

13.2.3   Corrective and preventive actions shall be documented and records shall be retained for a defined period.

14. Complaints

14.1   The pharmaceutical inspectorate shall establish and maintain a procedure for dealing with complaints relating to its activities, or those of its personnel, and any contracted persons or organisations. The procedure shall describe the application and verification of corrective action arising from the investigation of complaints.

14.2   Records shall be maintained of all complaints received and actions taken and shall be retained for a defined period.

15. Issue and Withdrawal of Licences and GMP Certificates

Manufacturing/ Importing licences and GMP certificates

15.1   The pharmaceutical inspectorate shall establish and maintain a system for the issue and withdrawal of licences and GMP certificates, or for advising about the issue and withdrawal of licences and GMP certificates, as appropriate.

15.2   Licence and GMP certificate applications shall be assessed and determined in a timely manner and within any time limits imposed by national or European Community requirements. Where time limits are imposed, inspection activities shall be included in the total time taken to determine the application.

15.3   There shall be a documented system for taking appropriate action against a licence and/ or a GMP certificate notably in the event of an adverse inspection report and for notifying other Member States. The system shall be based on QRM and include descriptions of the actions available to the Inspectorate; such actions may include suspension, variation or revocation of the licence and/ or the GMP certificate(s). There shall be a system for assessing compliance of an organisation with the imposed licensing action.

15.4   The system shall include a description of the appeals procedure available to licence holders.

15.5   If the licensing system is not part of the pharmaceutical inspectorate, the latter should establish and maintain a defined liaison with it to obtain and guarantee the objectives mentioned above.

Marketing authorisation

15.6   The pharmaceutical inspectorate should establish and maintain a defined liaison with units responsible for marketing authorisation in order to facilitate actions against marketing authorisation following an inspection, if appropriate.

15.7   Other Member states should be informed with such actions, if appropriate.

16. Handling Suspected Quality Defects and Rapid Alert System

16.1   The pharmaceutical inspectorate shall establish and maintain a system for handling of reports of suspected quality defects in medicinal products as defined in the related Community procedure. This system shall be based on QRM.

16.2   The pharmaceutical inspectorate shall establish and maintain a system for issuing Rapid Alerts as defined in the related Community procedure.

16.3   The pharmaceutical inspectorate shall establish and maintain an updated list of all performed recalls.

16.4   If the organization in charge of handling suspected quality defects and the rapid alert system is not part of the pharmaceutical inspectorate, the latter should establish and maintain a defined liaison with it to obtain and guarantee the objectives mentioned above.

17. Liaison with the Official Medicines Control Laboratory (OMCL)

17.1   The pharmaceutical inspectorate should establish and maintain a defined liaison with the OMCL(s) of its own MS in order to exchange information concerning the quality of medicines on the national market. In particular, a validated SOP shall define sampling processes for starting materials and medicinal products.

18. Sub-Contracting and Assessing

18.1   The pharmaceutical inspectorate shall normally carry out the inspections for which it is responsible and whilst it may sub-contract some of its work it cannot sub-contract any of its responsibility. Sub-contracted personnel or experts may be employed as part of an inspection team to assist or advise in a technical capacity, but that team shall normally be led by a GMP lead inspector. Sub-contracted personnel shall be bound by the requirements of the quality system and there shall be a written contractual agreement between the parties.

18.2   Persons or organisations to whom inspection activities are contracted out and experts shall be free from any commercial or financial pressures which might affect their freedom to act. They should follow defined rules to avoid conflict of interests and regarding ethic and deontology. Senior management of the pharmaceutical inspectorate shall ensure that these persons are appropriately qualified and experienced and that they are independent of any organisations which they might be asked to inspect.

19. Publications

19.1   The pharmaceutical inspectorate should have at its disposal an updated list of licensed manufacturers and/or wholesale distributors. The list shall be made available on demand made by authorised bodies.

Procedures Related to Rapid Alerts

Handling of Reports of Suspected Quality Defects in Medicinal Products

London, 20 September 2006

EMEA/INS/GMP/313507/2006

**Published on Behalf of the European Commission By
EMEA (European Medicines Agency)**

Note: *This document forms part of the Compilation of Community
Procedures on Inspections and Exchange of Information.
Please check for updates on the EMEA website (Inspections
pages).*

Guideline Title: *Handling of Reports of Suspected Quality
Defects in Medicinal Products*

Adopted: *April 2003*

Date of entry into force: *1 September 2003*

Supercedes: *Not applicable, 1st version*

Reason for Revision: *Not applicable*

1. Scope

This guidance covers the handling of reports of suspected quality defects in medicinal products for humans and animals made to a Competent Authority before, if necessary, a Rapid Alert is transmitted. It recommends the elements of a procedure for receiving, assessing and categorising reports of suspected defective products that necessarily precedes a Rapid Alert.

2. Introduction

2.1. Discussion at the Inspectors' WP and elsewhere has indicated the need to harmonise the handling of reports of suspected quality defects in medicinal products and confirm mutual confidence in member states' procedures for assessing the need to transmit a Rapid Alert of a quality defect.

2.2. Holders of an authorisation under Article 40 of Directive 2001/83/EC and under Article 44 of Directive 2001/82/EC (i.e. manufacturers and importers of medicinal products) are obliged under Article 13 of Directive 91/356/EEC and Article 13 of Directive 91/412/EEC and GMP Guide 8.8 to report to their Competent Authority any defect in a medicinal product handled under their authorisation that could result in a recall or abnormal restriction in supply. It is normally the Qualified Person who has this responsibility.

Reports of suspected defects may also be sent to the authorities by health professionals, wholesale dealers and members of the general public. In addition, a report of an adverse drug reaction may in fact be due to a defect in the quality of the product concerned.

2.3. Member States are obliged to take all appropriate measures to ensure that a medicinal products is withdrawn from the market if it proves to be harmful under normal conditions of use, if its composition is not as declared or if the controls on the finished product or during the manufacturing process or other requirement of the manufacturing authorisation has not been fulfilled [Article 117 of Directive 2001/83/EC and Article 83 of Directive 2001/82/EC].

2.4. It is normally the responsibility of the company to recall a batch and to notify customers accordingly. It is normally the responsibility of the Competent Authority to notify other authorities of the recall. Responsibilities for notifying health professionals, media and the general public may vary between member states.

3. Definitions

Suspected defective product.
A medicinal product about which a report has been received suggesting that it is not of the correct quality, as defined by its Marketing Authorisation.

Batch recall.
The action of withdrawing a batch from the distribution chain and users. A batch recall may be partial, in that the batch is only withdrawn from selected distributors or users.

Rapid Alert.
An urgent notification from one competent authority to other authorities that a batch recall has been instituted in the country originating the rapid alert. The procedure for issuing rapid alerts is defined in the Compilation of Community Procedures, May 2001[42].

4. Handling Process

4.1 Aim

To record and assess, during and outside office hours, reports of suspected defective products and to implement action with appropriate urgency.

4.2 Process Steps

4.2.1. Contact details for reporting suspected defective medicinal products to the Competent Authority should be made widely known and readily available to those likely to need to make a report. This would include manufacturers and MA holders and may also include wholesalers, hospitals, pharmacists, veterinary practitioners and local health authorities.

---

[42] 'Compilation of Community Procedures on Inspections and Exchange of Information' October 2003.

A dedicated, continuously manned telephone line is preferred. Arrangements should be made to divert calls if necessary during out-of-office hours. If other means such as fax or e-mail are used they should be monitored frequently, including during out-ofoffice hours.

4.2.2. Every contact should be recorded, using a standard format for recording information. The first informant is unlikely to have all the required information so it is most important that a contact is agreed from whom further information may be obtained. A registered file should be established for each suspected defect to collect information as it becomes available.

4.2.3. The report should be referred with minimum delay to a person(s) able to make an initial professional assessment of the nature, extent and urgency of possible public health risk. A target time should be set for reports to be referred to this person, normally less than one hour. It may be possible to give guidance to the person receiving out-of-hours reports on the nature of reports which must be relayed to the professional assessor before the next routine working day.

4.2.4. The initial professional assessment should include the following considerations: -risk to health of an individual (human or animal) if the suspected defect is real (consider risk to vulnerable patients as well as normal individuals, risk of not receiving the correct medication, risk from incorrect dosage (consider the therapeutic index), long-term risk as well as immediate risk (e.g. if a complete dispensed container is faulty the impact on the individual will be cumulative, risk to persons administrating a defective veterinary medicinal product, risk to the consumer of animal foodstuff in view of possible residues in the foodstuff): -probability that the defect is real and occurs in the medicine supplied by the manufacturer (e.g. not a clinical effect with a different cause, not a defect introduced at the time of dispensing). -in the case of suspicion of defective vaccines (cross contamination with a virus), risk of distorting the analysis in national programmes against certain viral diseases.

4.2.5. At this stage it will be decided whether the potential hazard to health is such that extraordinary measures must be taken (including the convening of an emergency action group out-of-office hours) or whether further consideration may be left for normal office hours.

4.2.6. Further professional assessment of the risk from the product should involve discussion with the manufacturer and include consideration of: -any other reports which may be related; -the distribution of the batch (e.g. restricted to known hospitals, widespread through wholesalers); -date of first distribution and last distribution;

- any remaining stock with the manufacturer;

- probability that other batches are affected in the same way, and their distribution.

4.2.7. If a recall is being considered extremely important issues to consider include:

- possibility of an out-of stock situation;

- availability of alternative products;

- clinical effect of a disruption in supply.

Note: No supply of a product may be worse than use of product with a suspected deficiency.

4.2.8. Direct personal contacts are important, especially with the person making the report, the person co-ordinating action for the company (usually the QP), the inspector familiar with the manufacturer and persons responsible for vigilance within the Competent Authority.

It is often helpful in detailed discussions if communications are between professional equivalents, e.g. medical assessor with medical staff of the company, inspectors with QPs or production staff, analytical assessors with QC staff, etc.

All information obtained verbally should be confirmed in writing.

4.3 Samples

Wherever possible the sample involved in the defect report should be obtained by the Competent Authority. It should normally be examined by an Official Medicines Control Laboratory as agreed by the Competent Authority. In certain cases samples should be provided to the company for examination under full supervision of the Competent Authority. Results should always be made available to the company.

Note: *A company should have instructions for release of retained samples in order not to have all of them used up during an emergency situation other than with consent from the Competent Authority.*

4.4 Inspection

The inspector normally associated with the manufacturing site should be made aware of the report and may comment on general GMP compliance and what related products made.

On-site inspection may be required to assess batch records of the product concerned, plant records and records of other batches or products which could also be affected.

Samples may be taken of the batch concerned, related batches and related starting materials. When considering taking material from the company's retained samples, consideration must be given to the quantity available and all tests which may be required for further investigations. These may be prescribed by the MA and/or national requirements. This could also be applied to the European Agency.

4.5 Preparing a Decision

4.5.1. Having considered all the available information, including the need to make a decision without waiting for full information to be available because of the potential risk to public health, a decision will be taken on appropriate action, which may be one or more of the following according to national procedures:

- filing without follow-up (no further action);

- further investigation;

- quarantine of remaining stock at manufacturer and quarantine or recall at wholesalers either While further investigation occurs or to prevent further distribution even if a full recall is not required;

- GMP measures to avoid a recurrence;

- distribution of a 'caution in use' notice to concerned health professionals;

- notification of the batch recall to selected health professionals (e.g. particular hospitals, clinics, dentists);

- notification of the batch recall to all health professionals (e.g. including all hospitals, doctors, community pharmacies, veterinary practitioners etc.);

- notification of the batch recall through the media;

- publication on the competent authority website, newsletter or similar.

- an assessment should be made if other batches of the same products or other products could be affected the same GMP deficiency.

The exact wording of any notification should be checked and if possible agreed with the company. Particular attention should be paid to check the batch number(s), expiry dates and product name and strength. Advice should be given on where further information may be obtained (normally from the company).

The distribution of the notification to interested parties within the authorities should be agreed. This may include national Ministers and other government departments, government press officers and, by means of a Rapid Alert[43], authorities and organisations in other countries (EU/EEA, MRA Partners, PIC/S, WHO, others).

As far as possible standard formats, wording and distribution lists should be used for the notifications with the aim of ease of understanding by the recipient and lack of ambiguity.

---

[43] 'Compilation of Community Procedures on Inspections and Exchange of Information' October 2003.

4.6 Validating the Decision

According to the national Competent Authority procedures, approval should be obtained for the proposed action.

4.7 Implementing the Decision

Refer to national procedures and the EU Rapid Alert Procedure[44].

4.8 Follow-Up

4.8.1. There should be consideration of what if any action to take concerning the Marketing or Manufacturing Authorisations and their holders.

4.8.2. The Inspectorate should asses the follow-up actions by the company, including the reconciliation of issued, returned and remaining stocks, the investigation into the cause of the defect and actions to prevent a repetition.

4.8.3. Completion of any follow-up actions should be checked, for example completing and organising records and archiving according to national procedures.

5. *Quality Assurance*

5.1. All procedures should be documented and maintained up to date.

5.2. Contact lists for officials and companies should be maintained up-to-date and should be verified at intervals (e.g. a rolling programme of annual checks of company contacts, possibly as part of GMP inspections).

5.3. All staff who could be involved in receiving a report of a suspected defective product or handling a Rapid Alert should be trained in the relevant procedures and have access to a copy of the SOPs and report forms wherever they may be required to act (including at home if they are on call outside-office hours).

5.4. It is particularly important that those procedures which may need to be followed by staff not routinely involved

---

[44] 'Compilation of Community Procedures on Inspections and Exchange of Information' October 2003.

(e.g. called upon as a reserve) and/or required to be involved when away from their office should be detailed and easy to follow.

Reference

1. 'Compilation of Community Procedures on Inspections and Exchange of Information' October 2003.

Procedure for Handling Rapid Alerts and Recalls Arising from Quality Defects

London, 20 September 2006

EMEA/INS/GMP/313510/2006 corr

Published on Behalf of the European Commission by EMEA (European Medicines Agency)

Note: This document forms part of the Compilation of Community Procedures on Inspections and Exchange of Information. Please check for updates on the EMEA website (Inspections pages).

Guideline Title: Procedure for Handling Rapid Alerts and Recalls Arising from Quality Defects

Adopted: 7 July 2004 minor modification agreed September 2005.

Date of entry into force: 1 September 2004. (The minor modification is immediately applicable following agreement)

Supercedes: Version in force from 28 July 2003.

Reason for Revision: Minor amendment to section 4.1.2, as a result of experience gained, introducing some flexibility on which Competent Authority should take responsibilty for issuing a rapid alert.

Notes: Pharmacovigilance alerts are not included within the scope of this procedure. For information on procedures for pharmacovigilance rapid alerts, reference should be made to document reference CPMP/PhVWP/005/96, rev. 1 Rapid Alert System (RAS) and Non-Urgent Information System (NUIS) in human pharmacovigilance or subsequent updates.

1. Scope

This procedure covers the transmission of information by means of a rapid alert between the Competent Authorities of EU and EEA countries (the "Member States"), CADREAC, PIC/S, EDQM and MRA partners relating to the recall of medicinal products which have quality defects, including counterfeit or tampered products, when urgent action is required to protect public health and animal health. The procedure may be used also for transmission of other information such as cautions-in-use, product withdrawals for safety reasons or for follow-up messages to any of the above listed categories. This procedure covers both human and veterinary medicinal products and operates within the scope of the relevant Two Way Alert programmes established between Member States and MRA partners. Pharmacovigilance or Medical Device alerts are not included within the scope of this procedure.

2. Introduction

2.1. In order to protect public health and animal health, it may become necessary to implement urgent measures such as the recall of one or more defective batch (es) of a medicinal product during its marketing period.

2.2. Each holder of an authorisation referred to in Article 40 of Directive 2001/83/EEC or Article 44 of Directive 2001/82/EC (for veterinary products) is required by Article 13 of Directive 2003/94/EC or Article 13 of Directive 91/412/EEC (for veterinary products) to implement an effective procedure for the recall of defective products. The authorisation holder is required to notify the relevant Competent Authority of any defect that could result in a recall and indicate, as far as possible, the countries of destination of the defective product.

2.3. In addition, for centrally authorised products Council Regulation (EEC) 2309/93, Art. 15(2) or Article 37(2) of Regulation 2309/93 (for veterinary products) the MAH is obliged to keep the EMEA informed of certain new information (e.g. suspension of the manufacturing authorisation, FDA Warning Letters, etc)

2.4. Each Competent Authority should have a written procedure that covers the receipt and handling of notifications of suspected defective products and batch recalls from companies or health professionals both during and outside normal working hours.

2.5. The Competent Authority of each Member State should assist the authorisation holder in the recall process, as appropriate, and monitor its effectiveness. The Competent Authority should ensure that information concerning the recall of medicinal products is notified rapidly to other Member States, if the nature of the defect presents a serious risk to public health. This information should be transmitted by means of the "Rapid Alert System".

2.6. Each Competent Authority should have a written procedure that covers the issue of rapid alerts both during and outside normal working hours (if the urgency of the situation warrants such action).

3. *Criteria for Issuing a Rapid Alert*

3.1. The aim of the Rapid Alert System is to transmit only those alerts whose urgency and seriousness cannot permit any delay in transmission. To ensure its effectiveness, the system must not be saturated by the transmission of less urgent information. In each case a professional assessment must be made of the seriousness of the defect, its potential for causing harm to the patient or (in the case of a veterinary product) harm to animals, consumers, operators and the environment, and the likely distribution of the affected batch(es). Appendix 1 provides guidance on the classification of the urgency of the recall of defective medicinal products.

3.2. Class I defects are potentially life threatening. A rapid alert notification must be sent to all Member States, CADREAC countries, PIC/S, EDQM and MRA partners, irrespective of whether or not the batch was exported to that country.

3.3. Class II defects could cause illness or mistreatment, but are not Class I. A rapid alert notification should be sent only to those Member States, CADREAC countries, PIC/S, EDQM and MRA partners to which it is known, or believed, that the batch has been distributed. In identifying those countries, due consideration should be given to parallel distribution and import arrangements and the free trade between wholesale distributors within the EEA. In the case of parallel imports where there is difficulty in establishing the traceability of batches, consideration should be given to notifying all Member States through the Rapid Alert System.

3.4. Class III defects may not pose a significant hazard to health, but withdrawal may be initiated for other reasons. These are not notified through the Rapid Alert System.

3.5. Where appropriate, the rapid alert system may be used for notification to Member States or MRA partners of the recall of products or an embargo on the distribution of products following suspension or withdrawal of a manufacturing authorisation.

4. Issue of a Rapid Alert Notification

Responsibility

4.1. For a batch manufactured in a Member State, or a batch manufactured in a third country and imported into the EEA, which is the subject of a national or mutually recognised (decentralised) marketing authorisation, the Competent Authority of the Member State in which the defect was first identified should investigate the defect and issue the rapid alert. MRA partners identified by the manufacturer or importer as countries to which the defective batch was distributed should also be notified through the rapid alert system.

4.2. In the case of a centrally authorised product, and in the exceptional case of a product that has both a centralised and a national authorisation, the Competent Authority of the Member State in which the defect was first identified should lead the investigation of the defect and issue a rapid alert (the issuing authority). The alert should include a recommendation on proposed action for all affected authorities.

When time allows, the issuing authority should, as part of the investigation, come to an agreement on the content of the proposed action with the supervisory authority, the EMEA and the CxMP rapporteur. In some circumstances and especially when the Supervisory Authority has conducted all the investigations, the Member State in which the defect was first identified may delegate to the Supervisory Authority the issuing of the Rapid Alert.

When, due to the urgency of the defect there is not sufficient time to develop a harmonized proposed action this section of the Rapid alert notification should inform all recipients that EMEA will co-ordinate further action in co-operation with the relevant Supervisory Authority, in accordance with EMEA's Crisis Management Procedures and that harmonised follow-up actions will be transmitted through the rapid alert channel when ready

4.3.　In the case of parallel distribution of a centrally authorised product and where no repackaging is carried out, the procedure described under 4.2 applies. This procedure also applies if the defect resulted from a repackaging operation. Where repackaging is carried out but the defect results from the original manufacturing process, the procedure described under 4.2 still applies, but the rapid alert should include descriptions of the different packaging in which the product might appear (for example different language versions and pack sizes) where this information is available from EMEA.

4.4.　In the case of a parallel import, the Competent Authority of the Member State in which the defect was first identified should issue the rapid alert, notifying MRA partners as appropriate. The Competent Authority should also notify the Supervisory Authority of the Member State in which the batch was manufactured or repackaged depending on the nature of the defect.

Format of the rapid alert and its transmission

4.5.　A suitable format for the notification of quality defects by the Rapid Alert System is given in Appendix 2. The form should be completed clearly and (preferably) in English. It should be attached to a distribution list and the documents sent by fax or electronic mail where relevant, to the persons nominated in the EMEA rapid alert list, which includes working hours and out-of-hours contact names and numbers. Changes to contact names and/or numbers must be notified to EMEA so that the list can be updated as necessary.

The rapid alert should be given a reference number with the following format: Country code (country where the original alert was issued)/Region or Authority code (where applicable)/classification/sequential number/correspondence number. (For example ES//II/05/02 would indicate a class II rapid alert initiated by Spain, being the 5th rapid alert initiated by Spain and that it is the second correspondence regarding this rapid alert.) In the case of a Class I defect which must be notified out of hours, it may be necessary to use the out-of-hours contact telephone numbers in addition to the rapid alert fax.

4.6.   Transmission of a Class I rapid alert must be concurrent with the national action. Whenever feasible, transmission of a Class II rapid alert should be concurrent with the national action but in all cases should be within 24 hours of the national notification.

When an authority issues a further rapid alert for a batch, the field 18 in the form in Appendix 2 "Detail of Defect/Reason for recall" should begin with the text: "Rapid Alert following original rapid alert #ref.no.#".

Action on receiving a notification under the Rapid Alert System:

4.7.   Each Competent Authority should have a written procedure for the receipt and handling of rapid alerts from other authorities during and outside working hours. Unless it can be established unequivocally that the defective batch in question has not been distributed in the Member State (including parallel imports) the Competent Authority should apply its national procedure for ensuring recipients of the batch are alerted. The class and urgency of the alert should correspond to those of the initial rapid alert.

5. *Fraud and Counterfeit Products*

The Rapid Alert System should be used to notify EEA Member States and MRA partners of the possible presence in the distribution network of counterfeit products or those resulting from fraud in manufacture, packaging, distribution or promotion and products containing counterfeit starting materials.

The Competent Authority of the Member State or MRA partner in which the fraud or counterfeit was first detected should issue the notification. The format for a rapid alert notification may be used, but the heading on the document should make clear that the notification relates to fraud or to a counterfeit product and sufficient information should be provided under "details of defect" to enable it to be identified. Notification should be sent to the parties as indicated in section 3.2 for a class 1 defect and concurrently to EMEA.

6. Follow-Up Action

Each Competent Authority should have a written procedure to describe follow-up action to a rapid alert notification. The Competent Authority of each Member State and MRA partner to which a recalled product was exported should monitor the conduct and effectiveness of any national recall that it initiates as a result of the rapid alert notification.

The relevant Supervisory Authority should investigate the circumstances that led to the distribution of the defective product and ensure that any necessary corrective action is taken by the manufacturer and marketing authorisation holder as appropriate.

EMEA should co-ordinate follow-up action for recalls of centrally authorised products.

All follow-up actions transmitted through the Rapid Alert System should use the form for Follow-up and non-urgent messages for Quality Defects detailed in Appendix 3 to separate it from Rapid Alerts. It should have a reference number linking it to the original Rapid alert following the same format as described above.

7. Appendices

7.1.   Appendix 1: Classification of Rapid Alerts

7.2.   Appendix 2: Format for Rapid Alert Notification of a Quality Defect

7.3.   Appendix 3: Format for Follow-up and non-urgent information for Quality Defects.

Appendix 1

Rapid Alert System : Classification of Urgency of Defective Medicinal Product Alerts

Class I

Class I defects are potentially life threatening or could cause a serious risk to health. These must be notified through the Rapid Alert System in all cases.

Examples:

- Wrong product (label and contents are different products)

- Correct product but wrong strength, with serious medical consequences

- Microbial contamination of sterile injectable or ophthalmic product

- Chemical contamination with serious medical consequences

- Mix-up of some products (rogues) with more than one container involved

- Wrong active ingredient in a multi-component product, with serious medical consequences.

Class II

Class II defects could cause illness or mistreatment, but are not Class I. These should be notified through the Rapid Alert System only to Member States and MRA partners to which it is likely or known that the batch has been distributed (including parallel import/distribution).

Examples:

- Mislabelling, e.g. wrong or missing text or figures

- Missing or incorrect information (leaflets or inserts)

- Microbial contamination of non-injectable, non-ophthalmic sterile product with medical consequences

- Chemical/physical contamination (significant impurities, cross-contamination, particulates)

- Mix up of products in containers (rogues)

- Non-compliance with specification (e.g. assay, stability, fill/weight)

- Insecure closure with serious medical consequences (e.g. cytotoxics, child- resistant containers, potent products).

Class III

Class III defects may not pose a significant hazard to health, but withdrawal may have been initiated for other reasons.

Examples:

- Faulty packaging, e.g. wrong or missing batch number or expiry date
- Faulty closure
- Contamination, e.g. microbial spoilage, dirt or detritus, particulate matter

Appendix 2

IMPORTANT - DELIVER IMMEDIATELY
Rapid Alert Notification of a Quality Defect / Recall

[add title in national language if necessary] [add letter head of sender] [turn into bilingual model as required].	
1. To: (see list attached, if more than one)	
2. Product Recall Class of Defect: I II (circle one)	3. Counterfeit / Fraud (specify)*
4. Product:	5. Marketing Authorisation Number: * For use in humans/animals (delete as required)
6. Brand/Trade Name:	7. INN or Generic Name:
8. Dosage Form:	9. Strength:
10. Batch/Lot Number:	11. Expiry Date:
12. Pack size and Presentation:	13. Date Manufactured: *
14. Marketing Authorisation Holder: *	
15. Manufacturer†: Contact Person: Telephone:	16. Recalling Firm (if different): Contact Person: Telephone:
17. Recall Number Assigned (if available):-	
18. Details of Defect/Reason for Recall:	
19. Information on distribution including exports (type of customer, e.g. hospitals): *	
20. Action taken by Issuing Authority:	
21. Proposed Action:	
22. From (Issuing Authority):	23. Contact Person: Telephone:
24. Signed:	25. Date: 26. Time: *

* Information not required, when notified from outside EU.

† The holder of an authorisation referred to under Article 40 of Directive 2001/83/EC or Article 44 of Directive 2001/82/EC and the holder of the authorisation on behalf of whom the Qualified Person has certified the batch for release in accordance with Article 51 of Directive 2001/83/EC or Article 55 of Directive 2001/82/EC if different.

This is intended only for the use of the party to whom it is addressed and may contain information that is privileged, confidential, and protected from disclosure under applicable law. If you are not the addressee, or a person authorized to deliver the document to the addressee, you are hereby notified that any review, disclosure, dissemination, copying, or other action based on the content of this communication is not authorized. If you have received this document in error, please notify us by telephone immediately and return it to us at the above address by mail. Thank you

****

Note: This form and all others are available for download on the EMEA website at http://www.emea.europa.eu/Inspections/GMPCompproc.html

Appendix 3

Follow-up and non-urgent Information for Quality Defects

[add title in national language if necessary] [add letter head of sender] [turn into bilingual model as required].			
1	To: (see list attached, if more than one)		
2	Recall Number Assigned:	2a National reference number (When applicable)	
4	Product:	5 Marketing Authorisation number:	
6	Brand/Trade name:	7 INN or Generic Name:	
8	Dosage form:	9 Strength:	
10	Batch number:		
14	Marketing Authorisation holder:		
15	Manufacturer[1]:	16 Contact Person:	
17	Subject title *Add bulk message here*		
22	From (issuing Authority):	23 Contact person:	
24	Signed:	25 Date:	26 Time:

---

[1] The holder of an authorisation to under Article 40 of Directive 2001/83/EC and Article 44 of Directive 2001/82/EC and the holder of the authorisation on behalf of whom the Qualified Person has certified the batch for release in accordance with Article 51 of Directive 2001/83/EC or Article 55 of Directive 2001/82/EC, if different

Procedure for Handling Rapid Alerts and Recalls Arising from Quality Defects [Pending Adoption]

London, 18 May 2009

EMEA/INS/GMP/313510/2006 Rev 1

[PENDING ADOPTION]

Note: *This document forms part of the Compilation of Community Procedures on Inspections and Exchange of Information. Please check for updates on the EMEA website (Inspections pages).*

Guideline Title: *Procedure for Handling Rapid Alerts and Recalls Arising from Quality Defects [Pending Adoption]*

Adopted: *[Pending Adoption]*

Date of entry into force: *1 September 2009*

Supercedes: *Version in force 20 September 2006.*

Reason for Revision: *Transmission of notifications changed from fax to email, Class I and II defects to be circulated to all contacts on notification list. The scope was extended to include APIs and IMPs.*

Notes: *Pharmacovigilance or medical device alerts are not included within the scope of this procedure.*

1. Scope

This procedure covers the transmission of information by means of a rapid alert between Competent Authorities in the European Economic Area (EEA) (the "Member States"), EU accession countries, PIC/S participating authorities, MRA partner authorities and international organisations (Council of Europe/EDQM, WHO, European Commission) relating to the recall of medicinal products which have quality defects, including counterfeit or tampered products, when urgent action is required to protect public health and animal health. The procedure may be used also for transmission of other information such as cautions-in-use, product withdrawals for safety reasons or for follow-up messages to any of the above listed categories. This procedure covers both human and veterinary medicinal products and operates within the scope of the relevant Two Way Alert programmes established between the Community and MRA partners.

The procedure may also be used to notify quality defects, counterfeit or fraud in active pharmaceutical ingredients or investigational medicinal products when deemed relevant by the issuing authority.

Pharmacovigilance or Medical Device alerts are not included within the scope of this procedure.

2. Introduction

2.1.   In order to protect public health and animal health, it may become necessary to implement urgent measures such as the recall of one or more defective batch(es) of a medicinal product during its marketing period or an investigational product during clinical trials.

2.2.   Each holder of an authorisation referred to in Article 40 of Directive 2001/83/EC or Article 44 of Directive 2001/82/EC (for veterinary products) is required by Article 13 of Directive 2003/94/EC or Article 13 of Directive 91/412/EEC (for veterinary products) to implement an effective procedure for the recall of defective products. The authorisation holder is required to notify the relevant Competent Authority of any defect that could result in a recall and indicate, as far as possible, the countries of destination of the defective product.

2.3.   In addition, for centrally authorised products Council Regulation EC/726/2004, Art. 16(2) or Article 41(4) (for veterinary products) the marketing authorisation holder is obliged to keep the EMEA informed of certain new information (e.g. restrictions of supply).

2.4.   Each Competent Authority should have a written procedure for the issue, receipt and handling of notifications of defective products, batch recalls and other rapid alerts during and outside normal working hours.

2.5.   The Competent Authority of each Member State should assist the authorisation holder in the recall process, as appropriate, and monitor its effectiveness. The Competent Authority should ensure that information concerning the recall of medicinal products is notified rapidly to other Member States, if the nature of the defect presents a serious risk to public health. This information should be transmitted by means of the "Rapid Alert System".

3. Criteria for Issuing a Rapid Alert

3.1.   The aim of the Rapid Alert System is to transmit only those alerts whose urgency and seriousness cannot permit any delay in transmission. To ensure its effectiveness, the system must not be saturated by the transmission of less urgent information. In each case a professional assessment must be made of the seriousness of the defect, its potential for causing harm to the patient or (in the case of a veterinary product) harm to animals, consumers, operators and the environment, and the likely distribution of the affected batch(es). Appendix 1 provides guidance on the classification of the urgency of the recall of defective medicinal products.

3.2.   Class I defects are potentially life threatening. A rapid alert notification must be sent to all contacts of the rapid alert notification list irrespective of whether or not the batch was exported to that country.

3.3.   Class II defects could cause illness or mistreatment, but are not Class I. A rapid alert notification should be sent to all contacts of the rapid alert notification list as it might be difficult to know where a batch has been distributed. If the product distribution is known, the notification should be only sent to the contacts concerned.

3.4.   Class III defects may not pose a significant hazard to health, but withdrawal may be initiated for other reasons. These are not normally notified through the Rapid Alert System.

3.5.   Where appropriate, the rapid alert system may be used for notification to Member States or MRA partners of the recall of products or an embargo on the distribution of products following suspension or withdrawal of a manufacturing / wholesale authorisation.

4. Issue of a Rapid Alert Notification

Responsibility

4.1.   For a batch manufactured in a Member State, or a batch manufactured in a third country and imported into the EEA, which is the subject of a national or mutually recognised (decentralised) marketing authorisation, the Competent Authority of the Member State in which the defect was first identified should investigate the defect and issue the rapid alert.

4.2.   In the case of a centrally authorised product, and in the exceptional case of a product that has both a centralised and a national authorisation, the Competent Authority of the Member State in which the defect was first identified should lead the investigation of the defect and issue the rapid alert (the issuing authority). The alert should include a recommendation on proposed action for all affected authorities.

When time allows, the content of the proposed action should be agreed with the supervisory authority, the EMEA and the CxMP rapporteur. In some circumstances and especially when the Supervisory Authority has conducted all the investigations, the Member State in which the defect was first identified may delegate to the Supervisory Authority the issuing of the Rapid Alert.

When, due to the urgency of the defect there is not sufficient time to develop a harmonised proposed action this section of the Rapid alert notification should inform all recipients that EMEA will co-ordinate further action in co-operation with the relevant Supervisory Authority, in accordance with EMEA's Crisis Management Procedures and that harmonised follow-up actions will be transmitted when ready.

4.3.   In the case of parallel distribution of a centrally authorised product and where no repackaging is carried out, the procedure described under 4.2 applies. This procedure also applies if the defect resulted from a repackaging operation. Where repackaging is carried out but the defect results from the original manufacturing process, the procedure described under 4.2 still applies, but the rapid alert should include descriptions of the different packaging in which the product might appear (for example different language versions and pack sizes) where this information is available from EMEA.

4.4.   In the case of a parallel import, the Competent Authority of the Member State in which the defect was first identified should issue the rapid alert.

Format of the rapid alert and its transmission

4.5.   A suitable format for the notification of quality defects by the Rapid Alert System is given in Appendix 2. The form should be completed clearly in English. The notification and relevant documents should be send to the rapid alert contact list by electronic mail. The contact list and any relevant documents should be attached to the notification.

The electronic mail message should use a unique subject line to identify the rapid alert and any follow-up messages. The subject line should consist of the following: RapidAlert; [QDefect / Counterfeit / Fraud], Class [I / II]; Product [Name / INN], Action [Recall / No Recall / Follow-up], Rapid alert reference number. (For example RapidAlert; QDefect; I, ProductX; Follow-up, CH/I/07/01).

The rapid alert should be given a unique reference number with the following format: Country code (country where the original alert was issued)/Region or Authority code (where applicable)/classification/sequential number/correspondence number. (For example ES/II/05/02 would indicate a class II rapid alert initiated by Spain, being the 5th rapid alert initiated by Spain and that it is the second correspondence regarding this rapid alert.)

4.6. Transmission of a Class I rapid alert must be concurrent with the national action. Whenever feasible, transmission of a Class II rapid alert should be concurrent with the national action but in all cases should be within 24 hours of the national notification.

In the case of a Class I notification, it may be necessary to alert authorities in different time zones in addition by telephone.

When an authority issues a further rapid alert for a batch, the field 18 in the form in Appendix 2 "Detail of Defect/Reason for recall" should begin with the text: "Rapid Alert following original rapid alert #ref. no.#".

Rapid alert contact list

4.7. EMEA maintains the contact list for the rapid alert notifications. Members of the list are human and veterinary authorities of EEA including acceding countries, MRA, PIC/S and international organisations (European Commission, EDQM, WHO). There is normally one contact per authority nominated by each member state. Changes to contact names or details must be notified to EMEA (qdefect@emea.europa.eu) and are circulated immediately to the entire list by electronic mail. Contact details include telephone and fax numbers, electronic mail address, which should be monitored at all times.

5. Fraud and Counterfeit Products

The Rapid Alert System should be used to notify competent authorities of the possible presence in the legal distribution network of counterfeit products or those resulting from fraud in manufacture, packaging, distribution or promotion and products containing counterfeit starting materials.

The Competent Authority of the Member State or MRA partner in which the fraud or counterfeit was first detected should issue the notification. The format for the rapid alert notification in Appendix 2 may be used, but the heading on the document should make clear that the notification relates to fraud or to a counterfeit product and sufficient information should be provided under "details of defect" to enable it to be identified. Notification should be sent to the entire contact list.

6. Follow-Up Action

Each Competent Authority should have a written procedure to describe follow-up action to a rapid alert notification. The Competent Authority of each Member State and MRA partner to which a recalled product was exported should monitor the conduct and effectiveness of any national recall that it initiates as a result of the rapid alert notification.

The relevant Supervisory Authority should investigate the circumstances that led to the distribution of the defective product and ensure that any necessary corrective action is taken by the manufacturer and marketing authorisation holder as appropriate.

EMEA should co-ordinate follow-up action for recalls of centrally authorised products.

All follow-up actions transmitted through the Rapid Alert System should use the form for Follow-up and non-urgent messages for Quality Defects detailed in Appendix 3 to separate it from Rapid Alerts. It should have a reference number linking it to the original Rapid alert following the same format as described above.

7. Further use of Rapid Alert contact list

Although the contact list for rapid alert notifications shall be only used for the transmission of notification falling in the scope of this procedure and the GMP non-compliance procedure, in exceptional cases, if deemed relevant by the competent authority, the list may be used for the communication of other important and urgent information related to pharmaceutical products. These messages should clearly identify the subject and whether they are for information or action. For example, EMEA disseminates urgent information from its scientific committees in this way.

8. Appendices

8.1.   Appendix 1: Classification of Rapid Alerts

8.2.   Appendix 2: Format for Rapid Alert Notification of a Quality Defect

---

8.3.   Appendix 3: Format for Follow-up and non-urgent information for Quality Defects.

Appendix 1

Rapid Alert System: Classification of Urgency of Defective Medicinal Product Alerts

Class I

Class I defects are potentially life threatening or could cause a serious risk to health. These must be notified through the Rapid Alert System in all cases.

Examples:

- Wrong product (label and contents are different products)

- Correct product but wrong strength, with serious medical consequences

- Microbial contamination of sterile injectable or ophthalmic product

- Chemical contamination with serious medical consequences

- Mix-up of some products (rogues) with more than one container involved

- Wrong active ingredient in a multi-component product, with serious medical consequences.

Class II

Class II defects could cause illness or mistreatment, but are not Class I. A rapid alert notification should be sent to all contacts of the rapid alert notification list as it might be difficult to know where a batch has been distributed. If the product distribution is known, the notification should be only sent to the contacts concerned.

Examples:

- Mislabelling, e.g. wrong or missing text or figures

- Missing or incorrect information (leaflets or inserts)

- Microbial contamination of non-injectable, non-ophthalmic sterile product with medical consequences

- Chemical/physical contamination (significant impurities, cross-contamination, particulates)

- Mix up of products in containers (rogues)

- Non-compliance with specification (e.g. assay, stability, fill/weight)

- Insecure closure with serious medical consequences (e.g. cytotoxics, child- resistant containers, potent products).

Class III

Class III defects may not pose a significant hazard to health, but withdrawal may have been initiated for other reasons. If deemed relevant by the issuing authority, the rapid alert system may be used.

Examples:

- Faulty packaging, e.g. wrong or missing batch number or expiry date

- Faulty closure

- Contamination, e.g. microbial spoilage, dirt or detritus, particulate matter

Appendix 2

IMPORTANT - DELIVER IMMEDIATELY

Rapid Alert Notification of a Quality Defect / Recall

	Reference Number

[add letter head of sender]				
1. To: (see list attached, if more than one)				
2. Product Recall Class of Defect: (circle one)	I	II	3. Counterfeit / Fraud (specify)*	
4. Product:	5. Marketing Authorisation Number: * For use in humans/animals (delete as required)			
6. Brand/Trade Name:	7. INN or Generic Name:			
8. Dosage Form:	9. Strength:			
10. Batch number (and bulk, if different):	11. Expiry Date:			
12. Pack size and Presentation:	13. Date Manufactured: *			
14. Marketing Authorisation Holder: *				
15. Manufacturer†: Contact Person: Telephone:	16. Recalling Firm (if different): Contact Person: Telephone:			
17. Recall Number Assigned (if available):-				
18. Details of Defect/Reason for Recall:				
19. Information on distribution including exports (type of customer, e.g. hospitals): *				
20. Action taken by Issuing Authority:				
21. Proposed Action:				
22. From (Issuing Authority):	23. Contact Person: Telephone:			
24. Signed:	25. Date:	26. Time: *		

* Information not required, when notified from outside EU.

* Form Download:
   www.emea.europa.eu/Inspections/GMPCompproc.html

† The holder of an authorisation referred to under Article 40 of Directive 2001/83/EC or Article 44 of Directive

2001/82/EC and the holder of the authorisation on behalf of whom the Qualified Person has certified the batch for release in accordance with Article 51 of Directive 2001/83/EC or Article 55 of Directive 2001/82/EC if different.

This is intended only for the use of the party to whom it is addressed and may contain information that is privileged, confidential, and protected from disclosure under applicable law. If you are not the addressee, or a person authorized to deliver the document to the addressee, you are hereby notified that any review, disclosure, dissemination, copying, or other action based on the content of this communication is not authorized. If you have received this document in error, please notify us by telephone immediately and return it to us at the above address by mail. Thank you

****

Appendix 3

Follow-up and non-urgent Information for Quality Defects

	[add letter head of sender]		
1	To: (see list attached, if more than one)		
2	Recall Number Assigned:	2a	National reference number (When applicable)
4	Product:	5	Marketing Authorisation number:
6	Brand/Trade name:	7	INN or Generic Name:
8	Dosage form:	9	Strength:
10	Batch number (and bulk, if different):		
14	Marketing Authorisation holder:		
15	Manufacturer[1]:	16	Contact Person:
17	Subject title *Add bulk message here*		
22	From (issuing Authority):	23	Contact person:
24	Signed:	25 Date:	26 Time:

[1] The holder of an authorisation to under Article 40 of Directive 2001/83/EC and Article 44 of Directive 2001/82/EC and the holder of the authorisation on behalf of whom the Qualified Person has certified the batch for release in accordance with Article 51 of Directive 2001/83/EC or Article 55 of Directive 2001/82/EC, if different

* Form Download:
   www.emea.europa.eu/Inspections/GMPCompproc.html

Procedures Related to
GMP Inspections

Procedure for Dealing with Serious GMP Noncompliance or Voiding/Suspension of CEPs thus Requiring Co-ordinated Administrative Action

London, 9 December 2008 Doc. Ref.

EMEA/INS/GMP/23567/2009

Published in Agreement with the European Commission by EMEA (European Medicines Agency)

Note: This document forms part of the Compilation of Community Procedures on Inspections and Exchange of Information. Please check for updates on the EMEA website (Inspections pages).

Procedure for Dealing with
Serious GMP Noncompliance or Voiding/Suspension of CEPs thus Requiring
Co-ordinated Administrative Action

Guideline Title:	*Procedure for Dealing with Serious GMP non-compliance or Voiding/Suspension of CEPs thus requiring co-ordinated administrative Action*
Adopted:	*[pending adoption]*
Date of entry into force:	*Immediately*
Supercedes:	*n/a*
Reason for Revision:	*n/a*

1. Summary

A consolidated procedure for dealing with all circumstances of serious GMP non-compliance, whether found at a manufacturing authorisation holder, third country manufacturer or active substance manufacturer is necessary to ensure a coordinated approach to potential risks to public/animal health.

This document replaces Appendix 3 of the Community procedure for the exchange of Information on Manufacturers and Manufacturing or Wholesale Distribution Authorisations between Competent Authorities in the European Economic Area. The appendix of which deals with serious GMP noncompliance found at a third country manufacturing site where co-ordinated administrative action is necessary.

Suspension or voiding of a Certificate of the European Pharmacopoeia (CEP) may be a recommended action following an inspection of an active substance manufacturer but this procedure additionally addresses action to be taken in the event of notification by EDQM that a CEP has been voided or suspended for reasons other than serious GMP non-compliance as the actions and consequences are similar.

The reporting inspectorate should enter the information on serious GMP non-compliance in EudraGMP, as referred in Article 111(6) (80(7)) of Directive 2001/83(2)/EC.

The procedure requires the inspectorate discovering serious GMP non-compliance to recommend appropriate action, involving other authorities that share supervisory responsibility in developing those recommendations, and to communicate the recommendations to all other authorities in the Community.

Communication with MRA partner authorities may also be necessary.

Provision is made in the procedure for a teleconference to give authorities receiving notification of serious GMP non compliance an opportunity to seek clarifications and to confirm the appropriateness of the recommended actions before they are implemented at Community level.

National competent authorities must take into account the information on serious GMP noncompliance received and should follow the actions recommended, where the procedure requires it to do so, unless it can justify alternative action based on specific national considerations and where those alternative actions have no impact on other Member States.

With regard to actions, directly or consequential, against marketing authorisations, the Reference Member State takes the initiative for mutual recognition/de-centralised products. EMEA co-ordinates action for centrally authorised products. Each national competent authority takes responsibility for marketing authorisations that exist purely at national level.

2. Definitions

2.1   For the purposes of this procedure, serious GMP non-compliance is non-compliance with GMP that in the opinion of the reporting inspectorate is of such a nature that administrative action is necessary to remove a potential risk to public/animal health.

2.2   For the purposes of this procedure, administrative action is one of the actions described in section 6.

3. Principles

3.1   A GMP inspection report should make a clear conclusion as to whether a manufacturer generally complies with the principles and guidelines of GMP as defined in Directive 93/2004/EC and/or 91/412/EEC or not. It is understood that a company can be considered to be in general compliance even if there is degree of non-compliance, which the inspector is satisfied can be resolved without administrative action being taken.

3.2   Action following the discovery of any non-compliance should be commensurate with the level of risk posed by

Procedure for Dealing with
Serious GMP Noncompliance or Voiding/Suspension of CEPs thus Requiring
Co-ordinated Administrative Action

the non-compliance. Serious non-compliance by definition requires administrative action to be taken.

3.3 All inspections carried out by the inspection services of any Member States are performed on behalf of the entire Community[45]. The discovery of serious GMP non-compliance may have implications not only for the Member State carrying out the inspection but also other, possibly all, Member States. Therefore a mechanism that ensures consistent, co-ordinated action throughout the Community is required.

3.4 Although Member States may make a reasoned request to another Member State to receive an inspection report, the authority that carries out the inspection, with first-hand information is best placed to assess the potential impact of, and to manage the risk posed by, the level of GMP noncompliance discovered.

3.5 Exceptionally, where, following proper assessment, specific national factors alter the risk such that the agreed Community action in connection with a marketing authorisation, or a rapid alert is not considered, on balance, to be in the interest of public/animal health in any particular Member State, that Member State may, in accordance with Community legislation, decide to take alternative action to that proposed by the Member State revealing the serious GMP non-compliance.

3.6 With regard to actions, directly or consequential, against marketing authorisations, the Reference Member State takes the initiative for mutual recognition/de-centralised products. EMEA co-ordinates action for centrally authorised products. Each national competent authority takes responsibility for marketing authorisations that exist purely at national level.

3.8. Unnecessary communication of non-compliance should be avoided in order to make efficient use of the Community alert mechanisms.

---

[45] This includes inspections requested by the European Commission, EMEA and EDQM but excludes those performed under contract to WHO. Until further notice serious non-compliance discovered during an inspection on behalf of WHO is not subject to this procedure.

---

4. Scope

4.1 Most GMP inspections reveal a degree of non-compliance and even if failures to comply are cited as being "major", or occasionally, "critical", matters can usually reach a satisfactory conclusion, sometimes involving follow-up inspections, without administrative action being taken. This procedure applies only when the level of non-compliance is such that the inspector concerned recommends that administrative action is taken to remove a potential risk to public/animal health and that recommendation is ratified in accordance with internal national procedures. Procedures should require the adherence to timelines that ensure that serious non-compliance is dealt with in a timely manner.

4.2 This procedure applies to all GMP inspections where serious GMP non-compliance is discovered whether in the territory of the Supervisory Authority or, in third countries, including inspections requested by the manufacturer, European Commission, EMEA or EDQM. It applies to inspections of active substance manufacturers, manufacturers of medicinal products, manufacturers of investigational medicinal products as well as quality control laboratories. It applies to inspections in third countries covered under the distant assessment procedure.

4.3 In order to avoid unnecessary use of Community alert mechanisms, communication of serious GMP non-compliance in accordance with this procedure should not be initiated when the information and action is of no interest to any other Member State. Examples are given in 6.1.2

4.4 All serious GMP non-compliance relating to active substance manufacturers and all types of manufacturers located in third countries must be communicated even if it is known that no other Member State has an interest at the time as it may be important for all Member States to have the information available in the future.

4.5 The discovery of serious GMP non-compliance at an active substance manufacturer associated with a CEP and inspected at the request of EDQM may lead to action by EDQM in connection with the CEP, such as suspension or voiding, this procedure must nevertheless

Procedure for Dealing with
Serious GMP Noncompliance or Voiding/Suspension of CEPs thus Requiring
Co-ordinated Administrative Action

still be invoked in order to ensure coordinated, harmonised action regarding the serious GMP non-compliance itself.

4.6   The procedure also deals with cases where a CEP is declared void by EDQM for reasons unrelated to an inspection outcome as consequential action may be needed, which must be properly implemented and coordinated.

5. Responsibilities

5.1   Following a GMP inspection, the inspection report must conclude whether the inspected company complies with the principles and guidelines of GMP or not. If the conclusion is that the inspected company does not comply, then the inspector concerned should recommend what risk-mitigating action is necessary such as administrative action, including whether a rapid alert is necessary for products/batches released onto the market and/or whether a prohibition of supply should be enforced.

5.2   With regard to inspections relating to medicinal products and investigational medicinal products, if the authority performing the inspection is not the Supervisory Authority it should involve the Supervisory Authority before issuing any non-compliance report so that any proposed regulatory action can be initially agreed.

5.3   Each national competent authority should have an internal national procedure to review inspection reports from its own inspectors which recommend administrative action in order to decide whether to support the inspectors recommended action or whether alternative action is more appropriate. This decision should be reached, and if administrative action is supported, communicated to other competent authorities in accordance with this procedure, within a timeframe appropriate to the potential threat to public health.

5.4   The Supervisory Authority is responsible for taking action against manufacturing authorisation holders under its supervision and/or disciplinary action against QPs connected with manufacturing authorisations under its supervision.

5.5   With regard to marketing authorisations, any recommendations made by the authority reporting the serious GMP non-compliance must take account of the interests of the Community as a whole, regardless as to any specific national considerations as referred to in the principle 3.5 above.

5.6   With regard to actions, directly or consequential, against marketing authorisations, the Reference Member State takes the initiative for mutual recognition/de-centralised products. EMEA co-ordinates action for centrally authorised products. Each national competent authority takes responsibility for marketing authorisations that exist purely at national level.

5.7   Prohibition of supply as a result of GMP non-compliance is action in connection with the marketing authorisation and responsibility should be taken as described in 5.6.

5.8   MRA partners are obliged to notify recipients of GMP certificates exchanged in the context of the MRA when those certificates are withdrawn due to GMP non-compliance. Since manufacturers themselves may also request GMP certificates to provide to MRA partner authorities Member States inspectorates should notify all MRA partners when serious GMP non-compliance has been discovered.

5.9   Where an inspection of an active substance manufacturer has been carried out at the request of the EDQM in connection with the CEP scheme and serious GMP non-compliance is revealed the inspectors involved should bear in mind that they have a dual responsibility. They should follow the procedures established by EDQM to determine the consequences for the CEP(s) in question, and they have an obligation to the Community to follow this procedure for notifying the serious GMP noncompliance. Every effort should be made to issue the non-compliance statement at the same time as the notification from EDQM concerning affected CEPs.

5.10 In cases where a CEP has been voided for non-GMP reasons EDQM notifies all national competent authorities using the agreed contact points. In its notification EDQM should indicate the reasons for voiding in order that authorities receiving the information can decide whether the quality, safety or efficacy of medicinal products

Procedure for Dealing with
Serious GMP Noncompliance or Voiding/Suspension of CEPs thus Requiring
Co-ordinated Administrative Action

already on the market is adversely affected and whether therefore a rapid alert is needed.

5.11 If the authority reporting the serious GMP non-compliance considers it necessary to remove products or certain batches from the market, it is responsible for issuing the Rapid Alert.

5.12 In the event that a rapid alert is necessary in response to CEP voiding or suspension in the circumstances mentioned in 5.9, 5.10 and 7.2, responsibility for issuing the rapid alert is as follows:

- For affected products subject to the Decentralised or Mutual Recognition procedures the Reference Member State,

- For centrally authorised products, EMEA will co-ordinate in the same way as a quality defect.

- For products subject to national marketing authorisations only, a national recall may suffice. No rapid alert is necessary unless under the specific circumstances it is concluded that a class 1 defect is being handled, or, it is likely that the batches in question are on the market in other Member States.

5.13 Where the agreed action is suspension of a clinical trial each National Competent Authority authorising the trial in question should make appropriate entry into the EudraCT database.

6. Types and consequences of administrative action

Some actions may lead to consequential actions. For example if a manufacturing authorisation is revoked or suspended or a CEP is voided or suspended it will have an impact on one or more marketing authorisations. Serious GMP non-compliance found at an active substance manufacturer means that manufacturing authorisation holders using the active substance in question as a starting material have failed to fulfil their legal obligations and therefore action may be taken against the manufacturing authorisation or QPs connected with it.

One or more of the following actions is/are possible. It is stressed that these are options and the Member States should take measures that are the most appropriate to the specific circumstances:

6.1 A Community notification of GMP non-compliance

6.1.1 Subject to the exceptions outlined in 6.1.2 an entry of non-compliance must be made into the EudraGMP database.

6.1.2 Community notification of serious GMP non-compliance is not necessary where the action to be taken is of no interest to any other Member State. Examples include:

- Action restricted to disciplining a QP

- Action restricted to refusal to grant a manufacturing authorisation or application to vary a manufacturing authorisation

- For manufacturers located in the Community, action limited to the issue of a restricted GMP certificate without corresponding action being deemed necessary, at the time, with regard to the relevant manufacturing authorisation.

Note: *Such action would allow continued manufacture but would put pressure on the manufacturing authorisation holder concerned to take corrective action before steps against the manufacturing authorisation are taken, and the remainder of this procedure invoked. This approach is not suitable for manufacturers located in third countries since the close level of supervision implied is not feasible. Furthermore the GMP certificate for a third country manufacturer carries more weight within the Community regulatory system than it does for manufacturers subject to a Community manufacturing authorisation, where the manufacturing authorisation is the primary means of confirming GMP compliance.*

6.2 Withdrawal of GMP certificate or Issue of GMP certificate with restricted scope

6.2.1 Existing valid GMP certificates with conflicting information will be superseded and should therefore be withdrawn in accordance with the Community procedure for the issue and update of GMP certificates. In some cases if the non-compliance is partial e.g. involving a limited category of dosage forms a new GMP certificate might also be issued, but restricted as appropriate.

Procedure for Dealing with
Serious GMP Noncompliance or Voiding/Suspension of CEPs thus Requiring
Co-ordinated Administrative Action

6.2.2 A GMP certificate may be restricted for reasons other than serious GMP non-compliance, for example where a third country manufacturer is only partly inspected. However if a certificate is restricted because of serious non-compliance then this procedure must be followed and a notification of non-compliance entered into EudraGMP, unless section 6.1.2 applies

6.3 Action against a manufacturing authorisation (including importers)

6.3.1 Except in the specific circumstances described in section 6.1.2, consequential administrative action will be required for any directly affected manufacturing authorisation; otherwise there will be an unintentional inconsistency in the information available in the EudraGMP database.

6.3.2 The actions against a manufacturing authorisation (including importers) may involve the following:

6.3.2.a. Refusal to grant a manufacturing authorisation or an application to vary a manufacturing authorisation

6.3.2.b. Total or partial suspension or revocation of manufacturing authorisation.

6.4 Voiding or suspension of CEP

6.4.1 EDQM is responsible for actions directly involving CEPs. However, if a CEP is voided, marketing authorisations depending solely on the CEP are invalid and should be suspended until the dossier is supplemented through variation with new information on the active substance. If the grounds for voiding the CEP are related to GMP non-compliance then an alternative active substance manufacturer would need to be added through a variation unless an alternative active substance manufacturer is already authorised, in which case the non-compliant active substance manufacturer should be removed through a variation.

6.4.2. CEPs may be voided for reasons unrelated to inspections, for example failure to fulfil critical commitments. Upon such notification by EDQM, each Competent Authority should establish whether they have issued national marketing authorisations that depend on the CEP(s) in question, and, where relevant, whether it is a Reference Member State. EMEA will assess any impact on centrally authorised products.

6.4.3 Marketing authorisations depending on the CEP are invalid and should be suspended until the dossier is supplemented through variation with new information on the active substance and should therefore be suspended, unless an alternative source of active substance is authorised which is unaffected by the voided CEP. The Reference Member State should take the initiative in taking action on marketing authorisations subject to the mutual recognition or de-centralised procedures. EMEA will co-ordinate action relating to centralised products. Individual national competent authorities take action against the marketing authorisation in the case of products authorised solely on a national basis.

6.5 Action in connection with marketing authorisations

6.5.1 Actions that can be taken include refusal to grant a marketing authorisation or application for variation, suspension or revocation. A marketing authorisation holder may also decide to withdraw a marketing authorisation voluntarily.

6.5.2 In the context of this procedure actions against marketing authorisations may be a consequence of action against the manufacturing authorisation or as a result of suspension or voiding of a CEP. It is possible however that the most appropriate course of action is against the marketing authorisation(s) alone. For example, a marketing authorisation listing a seriously non-compliant third country manufacturing site may need to be suspended or revoked unless an alternative manufacturing site is already authorised. A seriously non-compliant third country manufacturing site may need to be removed from a marketing authorisation through a variation.

6.5.3. Automatically suspending marketing authorisations associated with a non-compliant manufacturing site, where no alternative manufacturing site is authorised may not always be the most appropriate approach since if the manufacturing activity is suspended then this alone should serve to protect public/animal health. If the suspension or revocation of the manufacturing

Procedure for Dealing with
Serious GMP Noncompliance or Voiding/Suspension of CEPs thus Requiring
Co-ordinated Administrative Action

authorisation is partial then not all marketing
authorisations listing the site will be affected.

6.5.4 In this case the Reference Member State, for products
subject to de-centralised or mutual recognition
procedures, EMEA in the case of centralised products, or
the individual National Competent Authority in the case of
products authorised on a national basis only takes action
against the marketing authorisation.

6.6 Impact on clinical trials

6.6.1. If serious GMP non-compliance is discovered at the
manufacturer of investigational medicinal products the
impact on any completed or ongoing clinical trials will
need to be taken into account in the recommendations of
the reporting inspectorate. Trials may need to be
suspended. Furthermore in some cases the results of
completed trials may be thrown into question.
Interruption, suspension or prohibition of trial must be
entered into EudraCT.

6.6.2 The authority that carried out the inspection should
involve the sponsor as well as the manufacturer in order
to identify all affected trials. If trials are prematurely
terminated appropriate entries in EudraCT must be
made.

6.7 Rapid Alert

6.7.1 Based on the information in the inspection report the
authority reporting the serious GMP non-compliance
should decide, in addition to any other action, whether or
not it is necessary to take action with respect to batches
of affected product(s) already on the market or being
used in clinical trials.

6.7.2 For CEP voiding by EDQM that is unrelated to the
outcome of an inspection, the Reference Member State
(or EMEA in the exceptional case that centralised
products are affected) should recommend whether any
batches should be recalled and invoke any Rapid Alert
based on the information provided by EDQM on the
reasons for voiding or suspension in its notice of
voiding/suspension or, if necessary, following discussion
with EDQM.

6.7.3 In the context of this procedure responsibility for issuing a rapid alert is outlined in section 5.12.

6.8 Prohibition on supply

6.8.1 Based on the information in the inspection report the authority reporting the serious GMP non-compliance should decide, in addition to any other action, whether or not to recommend a prohibition on supply to prevent products or batches from being released to the market or for use in clinical trials.

6.9 Disciplinary measures against the Qualified Person(s)

6.9.1. This action can be taken by the Supervisory authority if deemed appropriate. In some cases it may be the only action considered necessary. If this is the only action taken there is no impact on other Member States (see 6.1.2).

7. *Communication*

7.1 Serious GMP non-compliance

7.1.1 Notification of serious GMP non-compliance should take place after national procedures for dealing with adverse inspection reports have been followed and the action recommended by the inspector ratified or alternative action decided upon.

7.1.2 In principle unilateral action by one Member State should be avoided, unless justified. In order to facilitate co-ordinated action at Community level, notification of serious GMP noncompliance should be made prior to the execution of any action. In so far as is possible, the authority that carried out the inspection revealing the non-compliance should establish the following as appropriate:

- the identity of Member States with products directly affected by the inspection findings
- where relevant, the Reference Member State(s)
- whether centrally authorised products are involved

Procedure for Dealing with
Serious GMP Noncompliance or Voiding/Suspension of CEPs thus Requiring
Co-ordinated Administrative Action

- the identity of other Supervisory Authorities in the case of medicinal or investigational medicinal products

- For investigational medicinal products the EudraCT trial reference numbers should be identified

- In the case of active substance manufacturer whether CEPs are affected in addition to marketing authorisations directly affected.

  The authority that discovers the non-compliance should involve the manufacturer concerned, the importer and trial sponsor as appropriate to gather this information. It may be necessary to issue the notice of non-compliance without complete information if the risk to patient health is considered particularly severe.

7.1.3 Where there is more than one Supervisory Authority they should all be consulted by the reporting authority on proposed actions before wider transmission of the non-compliance information.

7.1.4 The agreed Community GMP non-compliance format should be used to report the noncompliance information to the EudraGMP database. The rapid alert distribution list should be used for this purpose.

7.1.5 The GMP non-compliance notification should explain the nature of any proposed action, or where justified, action already taken.

7.1.6 Any further communication with the issuing authority requesting clarification the noncompliance or providing relevant data, should be made via EudraGMP. All these questions and answers will then be available to all NCAs.

7.1.7 Where relevant, a contact telephone number should be given in the notification form together with a proposed time and date for a teleconference in which all affected member states can join, and in which co-ordinated action can be ratified. EDQM should be invited to join the teleconference if a CEP is affected.

7.1.8 The outcome of the teleconference, if held, should be communicated in a follow up message to confirm that the recommended action in the initial notification was agreed or to communicate any other agreed Community action. EudraGMP will be used for this once this module is operational.

7.1.9 If an inspection of an active substance manufacturer has been carried out other than at the request of EDQM and serious non-compliance is found, EDQM should be included in the communication of the serious non-compliance, unless it is clear that no CEPs are affected.

7.1.10   MRA partners are obliged to notify recipients of GMP certificates issued in the context of the MRA withdrawing those certificates if serious non-compliance is discovered. MRA partners given access to EudraGMP will be notified automatically of GMP non-compliance statements placed into the database.

7.1.11.   The issuing authority may be modified the non-compliance information entered in EudraGMP, if necessary. Any new modification of the non-compliance information should be distributed to the rapid alert distribution list.

7.2 Voiding of CEPs for non-GMP reasons

7.2.1. In cases where a CEP has been voided for non-GMP reasons EDQM notifies all national competent authorities using the agreed contact points. In its notification EDQM should indicate the reasons for voiding in order that authorities receiving the information can decide whether the quality, safety or efficacy of medicinal products already on the market is adversely affected and whether therefore a rapid alert is needed. Responsibilities are defined in 5.12.

8. Procedure post-communication: Serious GMP Non-compliance

8.1   On receipt of a form notifying serious GMP non-compliance, either by fax or through EudraGMP, authorities should check whether nationally authorised products on their own territories are affected, and whether they are the Reference Member State for any affected products, seeking assistance from the inspectorate carrying out the inspection, if different, and the manufacturer(s) concerned as needed. If either applies, they should join the teleconference if there is to

Procedure for Dealing with
Serious GMP Noncompliance or Voiding/Suspension of CEPs thus Requiring
Co-ordinated Administrative Action

be one. If no teleconference is proposed, receiving authorities should, where appropriate, take the actions on its own territory that correspond with the actions proposed or already executed by the authority reporting the non-compliance. In the case of action against marketing authorisations subject to the decentralised/mutual recognition procedures, the Reference Member State should take the initiative in following the recommendations of the Authority reporting the non-compliance. EMEA will coordinate action relating to centralised products.

8.2 Disagreement with the actions proposed, if not resolved at the teleconference, should be dealt with through procedures established in accordance with Art. 122(90) of Directive 2001/83(2)/EC.

8.3 In the case of actions proposed for marketing authorisations subject to the De-centralised or Mutual Recognition procedures, CMD (h) or CMD (v) may decide to discuss the coordination of actions at a meeting of the relevant group before implementation.

8.4 Exceptionally, where, following proper assessment, specific national factors alter the risk such that the agreed Community action in connection with a marketing authorisation, or a rapid alert is not considered, on balance, to be in the interest of public health in any particular Member State, that Member State may decide to take alternative action to that proposed by the Member State initiating this procedure so long as this does not affect any other Member State. In such cases Art. 122(90) of Directive 2001/83(2)/EC obliges the Member State in question to notify the EMEA and the Commission. The Supervisory Authority or Reference Member State may find itself in this position but should nevertheless fulfil its responsibilities under section 5.

9. Legal References

Directive 2001/83(2)/EC Title XI (VIII) Supervision and Sanctions.

Directive 2001/83(2)/EC Title XIII (X) General Provisions.

Regulation (EC) No. 726/2004 Title II Chapter 2 Supervision and Penalties, Title III Chapter 2 Supervision and Sanctions.

The Compilation of Community Procedures for Inspections and the Exchange of Information. (Art. 3.3 Directive 2003/94/EC).

Annex 1 - Action by Authority Discovering GMP Non-Compliance

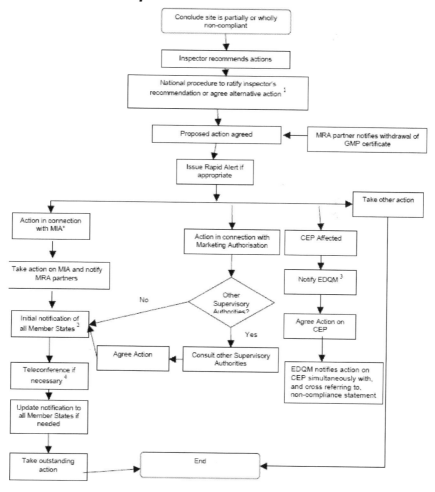

*MIA = Manufacturing Authorisation

Procedure for Dealing with
Serious GMP Noncompliance or Voiding/Suspension of CEPs thus Requiring
Co-ordinated Administrative Action

[1] If action against marketing authorisations is under consideration, the action ratified is that regarded as appropriate for the Community. If the reporting authority is not the Supervisory Authority the Supervisory Authority must be involved in the decision process.

[2] Via EudraGMP

[3] This is the starting point for CEPs voided for reasons unrelated to a GMP inspection.

[4] If a CEP is involved EDQM is invited to join. If desired coordination of action in respect of marketing authorisations subject to the mutual recognition or de-centralised procedures may be discussed at the next meeting of CMD(h) or CMD(v).

Annex 2 - Action by Authorities following receipt of information of GMP non-compliance

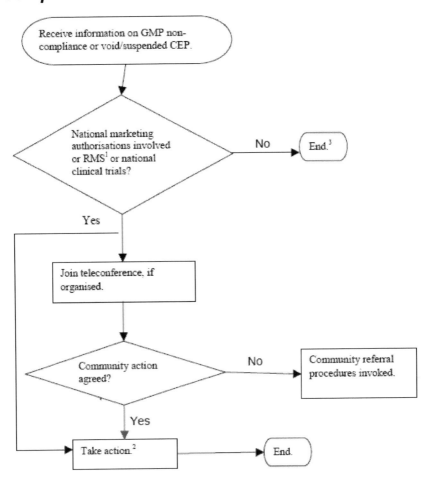

[1]For centralised products EMEA co-ordinates action.

[2]Reference Member States should take the agreed action at Community level.

[3]Nothwithstanding appropriate responses to consequential rapid alerts or other consequential actions agreed at Community level.

STATEMENT OF NON-COMPLIANCE WITH GMP

Exchange of information between National Competent Authorities (NCAs) of the EEA following the discovery of serious GMP non-compliance at a manufacturer[1]

Part 1

Issued following an inspection in accordance with Art. 111(7) of Directive 2001/83/EC, Art. 80(7) of Directive 2001/82/EC or Art. 15 of Directive 2001/20/EC.*

The competent authority of...*[Member State]* confirms the following:
The manufacturer...
Site address...
....

From the knowledge gained during inspection of this manufacturer, the latest of which was conducted on ...../....../...... *[date]*, it is considered that **it does not comply with the Good Manufacturing Practice** requirements referred to in the principles and guidelines of Good Manufacturing Practice laid down in Directive 2003/94/EC/Directive 91/412/EEC/the principles of GMP for active substances referred to in Article 47 of Directive 2001/83/EC / Article 51 of Directive 2001/82/EC.*

[1] The statement of non-compliance referred to in paragraph 111(7) of Directive 2001/83/EC and 80(7) of Directive 2001/82/EC, as amended, shall also be required for imports coming from third countries into a Member State.

Procedure for Dealing with
Serious GMP Noncompliance or Voiding/Suspension of CEPs thus Requiring
Co-ordinated Administrative Action

Part 2

☐ Human Medicinal Products*

☐ Veterinary Medicinal Products*

☐ Human Investigational Medicinal Products*

1 NON-COMPLIANT MANUFACTURING OPERATIONS ·	
Include total and partial manufacturing (including various processes of dividing up, packaging or presentation), batch release and certification, storage, importation and distribution of specified dosage forms unless informed to the contrary;	
1.1	**Sterile Products**
	1.1.1 Aseptically prepared (list of dosage forms) 1.1.1.1 Large volume liquids 1.1.1.2 Lyophilisates 1.1.1.3 Semi-solids 1.1.1.4 Small volume liquids 1.1.1.5 Solids and implants 1.1.1.6 Other aseptically prepared products <free text>
	1.1.2 Terminally sterilised (list of dosage forms) 1.1.2.1 Large volume liquids 1.1.2.2 Semi-solids 1.1.2.3 Small volume liquids 1.1.2.4 Solids and implants 1.1.2.5 Other terminally sterilised prepared products <free text>
	1.1.3 Batch certification only
1.2	**Non-sterile products**
	1.2.1 Non-sterile products (list of dosage forms) 1.2.1.1 Capsules, hard shell 1.2.1.2 Capsules, soft shell 1.2.1.3 Chewing gums 1.2.1.4 Impregnated matrices 1.2.1.5 Liquids for external use 1.2.1.6 Liquids for internal use 1.2.1.7 Medicinal gases 1.2.1.8 Other solid dosage forms 1.2.1.9 Pressurised preparations 1.2.1.10 Radionuclide generators 1.2.1.11 Semi-solids 1.2.1.12 Suppositories 1.2.1.13 Tablets 1.2.1.14 Transdermal patches 1.2.1.15 Intraruminal devices 1.2.1.16 Veterinary premixes 1.2.1.17 Other non-sterile medicinal product <free text>

	1.2.2 Batch certification only
1.3	**Biological medicinal products**
	1.3.1 Biological medicinal products 1.3.1.1 Blood products 1.3.1.2 Immunological products 1.3.1.3 Cell therapy products 1.3.1.4 Gene therapy products 1.3.1.5 Biotechnology products 1.3.1.6 Human or animal extracted products 1.3.1.7 Other biological medicinal products <free text >
	1.3.2 Batch certification only (list of product types) 1.3.2.1 Blood products 1.3.2.2 Immunological products 1.3.2.3 Cell therapy products 1.3.2.4 Gene therapy products 1.3.2.5 Biotechnology products 1.3.2.6 Human or animal extracted products 1.3.2.7 Other biological medicinal products <free text >
1.4	**Other products or manufacturing activity** (any other relevant non-compliant manufacturing activity/product type that is not covered above e.g. sterilisation of active substances, manufacture of biological active starting materials, herbal or homeopathic products, bulk or total manufacturing, etc).
	1.4.1 Manufacture of: 1.4.1.1 Herbal products 1.4.1.2 Homoeopathic products 1.4.1.3 Biological active starting materials 1.4.1.4 Other <free text > *1.4.2 Sterilisation of active substances/excipients/finished product:* 1.4.2.1 Filtration 1.4.2.2 Dry heat 1.4.2.3 Moist heat 1.4.2.4 Chemical 1.4.2.5 Gamma irradiation 1.4.2.6 Electron beam *1.4.3 Others <free text>*

Procedure for Dealing with
Serious GMP Noncompliance or Voiding/Suspension of CEPs thus Requiring
Co-ordinated Administrative Action

1.5	Packaging only
	1.5.1 Primary packing
	1.5.1.1 Capsules, hard shell
	1.5.1.2 Capsules, soft shell
	1.5.1.3 Chewing gums
	1.5.1.4 Impregnated matrices
	1.5.1.5 Liquids for external use
	1.5.1.6 Liquids for internal use
	1.5.1.7 Medicinal gases
	1.5.1.8 Other solid dosage forms
	1.5.1.9 Pressurised preparations
	1.5.1.10 Radionuclide generators
	1.5.1.11 Semi-solids
	1.5.1.12 Suppositories
	1.5.1.13 Tablets
	1.5.1.14 Transdermal patches
	1.5.1.15 Intraruminal devices
	1.5.1.16 Veterinary premixes
	1.5.1.17 Other non-sterile medicinal products < free text >
	1.5.2 Secondary packing
1.6	**Quality control testing**
	1.6.1 Microbiological: sterility
	1.6.2 Microbiological: non-sterility
	1.6.3 Chemical/Physical
	1.6.4 Biological

2 NON-COMPLIANT IMPORTATION OPERATIONS*	
- importation activities without manufacturing activity	
- importation activities include storage and distribution unless informed to the contrary	
2.1	**Quality control testing of imported medicinal products**
	2.1.1 Microbiological: sterility
	2.1.2 Microbiological: non-sterility
	2.1.3 Chemical/Physical
	2.1.4 Biological
2.2	**Batch certification of imported medicinal products**
	2.2.1 Sterile Products
	2.2.1.1 Aseptically prepared
	2.2.1.2 Terminally sterilised
	2.2.2 Non-sterile products
	2.2.3 Biological medicinal products
	2.2.3.1 Blood products
	2.2.3.2 Immunological products
	2.2.3.3 Cell therapy products
	2.2.3.4 Gene therapy products
	2.2.3.5 Biotechnology products
	2.2.3.6 Human or animal extracted products
	2.2.3.7 Other biological medicinal products < free text >
	2.2.4 Other importation activities (any other relevant importation non-compliant activity that is not covered above e.g. importation of radiopharmaceuticals, medicinal gases, herbal or homeopathic products, etc.)
	2.2.4.1 Radiopharmaceuticals/Radionuclide generators
	2.2.4.2 Medicinal gases
	2.2.4.3 Herbal products
	2.2.4.4 Homoeopathic products
	2.2.4.5 Biological active starting materials
	2.2.4.6 Other < free text >

Manufacture of active substance. Names of substances subject to non-compliance *:
....
....

Any restrictions or clarifying remarks related to the scope of this statement*:
....
....

Procedure for Dealing with
Serious GMP Noncompliance or Voiding/Suspension of CEPs thus Requiring
Co-ordinated Administrative Action

Part 3

---

1. Nature of non-compliance (check all relevant boxes)

<free text >..

....

---

2. Action taken/proposed by the NCA

☐ Suspension/variation/revocation* of the manufacturing authorisation No. .... in full/in part*

<free text >...

☐ Restriction of current valid GMP certificate No. ....

<free text >...

☐ Suspension/revocation/requested variation/ refusal to grant * of Marketing Authorisation(s)

<free text >...

☐ Recall of batches already released (separate Rapid Alert to follow)

<free text >...

☐ Prohibition of supply

<free text >...

☐ Suspension or voiding of CEP (action to be taken by EDQM)

<free text >...

☐ Suspension of clinical trials

<free text >...

☐ Others <free text >

<free text >...

---

3. Additional comments

<free text >...

....

Annex 2 - Action by Authorities following receipt of information of GMP non-compliance

Teleconference Date		Teleconference Time (CET)		Dial in no.	
Products manufactured at site, if known	Product	Dosage Form	Reference Member State, National or EMEA		
Human medicinal product(s)					
Veterinary medicinal product(s)					
Investigational medicinal product(s)	EudraCT nos.				

...../......./........ [date]

Name and signature of the authorised person of the Competent Authority of [country][*]

....
[Name, title, national authority, phone & fax numbers in case of enquiries]

(*): delete that which does not apply.

[1] The signature, date and contact details should appear on each page of the non-compliance document.

Conduct of Inspections of Pharmaceutical Manufacturers

London, 20 September 2006

EMEA/INS/GMP/313513/2006

Published on Behalf of the European Commission by EMEA (European Medicines Agency)

Note: *This document forms part of the Compilation of Community Procedures on Inspections and Exchange of Information. Please check for updates on the EMEA website (Inspections pages).*

Guideline Title: *Conduct of Inspections of Pharmaceutical Manufacturers*

Adopted: *2-3 December 1996. Annex on Investigational Medicinal Products adopted October 2002.*

Date of entry into force: *Immediate. Annex on Investigational Medicinal Products applies from May 2004.*

Supercedes: *Not applicable.*

Reason for Revision: *New annex added.*

1. Introduction

The purpose of this document is to provide guidance on the conduct of inspection of a manufacturer of medicinal products holding or seeking an authorization referred to in Article 40 of Directive 2001/83/EC and Article 44 of Directive 2001/82/EC in order to harmonize inspection procedures, frequency of inspections and follow-up procedures thus ensuring a consistent approach to assessment and decision-making by Competent Authorities.

2. Glossary of Terms

The definition of terms in the detailed guidelines published in Good Manufacturing Practice for Medicinal Products in the European Community, Volume IV are applicable to this document. In addition, the following apply:

3. Inspection:

On-Site assessment of the compliance with the Community GMP principles performed by officials of Community Competent Authorities.

A general GMP Inspection covering general GMP aspects should be carried out before the authorization referred to in Article 40 of Directive 2001/83/EC and Article 44 of Directive 2001/82/EC respectively, is granted and periodically afterwards as required.

An inspection may be more product-or process-related when it focuses on the adherence by the manufacturer to the marketing authorization of a medicinal product and on the manufacture and documentation related to the product or to a specific manufacturing process.

4. QC Laboratory Inspections:

On-Site assessment of the adherence to Good Quality Control Laboratory Practice is normally part of the GMP Inspection.

Contract QC Laboratories authorized according to Article 20(b) of Directive 2001/83/EC or Article 24(b) of Directive 2001/82/EC are also subject to these inspections.

Laboratory Inspection for compliance with GLP Principles is performed in accordance with guidelines given in the annexes to the Directive 88/320/EEC and is not part of this document.

5. Inspection Report:

Report prepared by the official representing the Competent Authority stating whether the company inspected in general complies with the Community GMP principles.

6. General Considerations on Inspections

Report prepared by the official representing the Competent Authority stating whether the company inspected in general complies with the Community GMP principles.

6.1 The primary role of the inspector is the protection of public health in accordance with Community provisions.

6.2 The function of the inspector is to ensure adherence by manufacturers to GMP principles and guidelines including licensing provisions.

6.3 The primary goal for the inspector should be to determine whether the various elements within the quality assurance system are effective and suitable for achieving compliance with GMP principles. In addition to that, determining whether the medicinal product complies with the master formula approved by the licensing authority and thus with the licensing provisions for the standard product should be considered as one of the inspectors responsibilities.

6.4 Inspectors should strive to create a positive atmosphere during the inspection.

6.5 An inspector should be aware of his influence in decision making processes. The inspector should answer questions but avoid entering the role of a consultant.

6.6 The task of an inspector is not limited to the disclosure of faults, deficiencies and discrepancies. The inspector should connect an observation with assistance in making the necessary improvements. An inspection should normally include educational and motivating elements.

6.7 Different types of inspection may be carried out according to the activities of the company.

Conduct of inspections may vary according to their objectives and may focus for example on the general level of GMP, or on the manufacture of a specific medicinal product or on a specific manufacturing process.

General GMP inspections (also termed regular, periodic, planned or routine) should be carried out before a manufacturing authorization is granted. This kind of inspection may also be necessary for a significant variation of the manufacturing authorization and if there is a history of non-compliance.

Re-inspections (also termed follow-up or reassessment) may be indicated to monitor the corrective actions required during the previous inspection.

Product-or process-related inspections (also termed special or problem oriented) may be indicated to assess the adherence of the manufacturer to the marketing authorization dossier and the way the batch documentation is kept. It is also indicated when complaints and recalls may concern one product or group of products or processing procedures (e.g.sterilization, labelling, etc).

6.8 The wide diversity of facilities (both in terms of physical lay-out and management structure) together with the variety of products and production processes as well as analytical methods means that judgement by inspectors on-site of the degree of compliance with GMP is essential.

6.9 A consistent approach to evaluation of the GMP standard of companies is essential.

6.10 Inspections may disturb the normal work patterns within a company. Therefore, inspectors should take care not to put the product at risk, and should carry out their work in a careful and planned way.

6.11 Inspectors will, while conducting the inspection, have access to confidential information and should handle it with integrity and great care.

7. *Inspection Procedures*

7.1 Planning of inspections: the Competent Authority should plan the succession of inspections in advance and elaborate a programme. This programme should ensure that the frequency of inspection of individual manufacturers can be adhered to as planned. Sufficient resources must be determined and made available to ensure that the designated programme of inspections can be carried out in an appropriate manner.

7.2 Preparation of inspections: prior to conducting an inspection the inspector(s) should familiarise themselves with the company to be inspected.

This may include:

– examination of a site master file (if available) -a review of the products manufactured by the company

– a review of the reports from previous inspections

– a review of the follow-up actions (if any) arising from previous inspections

– familiarisation with the relevant aspects of the manufacturing authorization

– a review of product recalls initiated since the previous inspection

– an examination of relevant product defects notified since the previous inspection

– a review of the analysis of any samples analyzed by the Competent Authority since the previous inspection

– a review of any special standards or guidelines associated with the site to be inspected

– a review of relevant parts of the registration file of one or more selected products to be examined during the inspection

An aide-memoire may be prepared specifically for the inspection to be performed. The aide memoire helps to avoid missing important aspects of GMP.

It is recommended that inspectors prepare an inspection plan which may include:

–   the objectives and the scope of the inspection, in the light of previous inspections

–   identification of the people who are directly responsible for production and quality control / quality assurance. In cases where particular products and/or processes are to be inspected, the people directly responsible for these products and/or processes

–   identification of the inspection team members and their respective roles, if more than one inspector is going to conduct the inspection -the date and place, where the inspection is to be conducted

–   identification of the organizational units to be inspected

–   the expected time and duration for each major inspection activity (premises, processes etc.)

–   samples (if any) to be taken

–   the schedule for the final meeting

–   the approximate schedule for the transmission of the inspection report

7.3   Announcement of inspection: Competent Authorities have the right to inspect at any time (including during shift work). Prior announcement of inspection may be given. By informing in advance the day/days for the inspection to take place and the length of time the inspector expects to be at the premises, the objectives of the inspection will be known to the company and the relevant personnel and documentation can more easily be made available.

7.4   Opening Meeting: The inspector should normally meet the management and the key personnel of the company to introduce himself and any accompanying official(s) or specialist(s) and to discuss his inspection plan (of course subject to unannounced modifications).

During the opening meeting the inspector should:

– outline the purpose and scope of the inspection - review the management structure of the company (organization chart)

– identify some of the documentation which may be required during the inspection

During the opening meeting the company should:

– describe the Quality Management System

– explain the company's quality policy

– explain significant changes in facilities, equipment, products and personnel since the last inspection

– explain how deficiencies have been resolved if this information has not already been forwarded to the competent authority

– designate the people to accompany the inspector during the inspection

– allocate a room for the inspector if needed

Immediate inspection after arrival on site may be of value in some cases.

7.5 Inspection of the plant facilities: a rapid plant tour is often useful for familiarisation with the site and any major changes. This is followed by a detailed plant tour to determine whether the facilities and equipment are of suitable lay-out and design and whether the way in which they are used suits the intended operations. Normally, the inspector follows the logical flow of the starting materials, goods inwards warehouse, through the production areas, quality control areas to the warehouse for released finished goods, taking into account the detailed guidelines of GMP.

Sometimes it is appropriate to concentrate effort in one department of the company if there are special problems or requirements, e.g. a department only producing sterile dosage forms or non sterile dosage forms. Relevant service areas should be included, e.g. water, steam and ventilation/dust extraction systems and engineering support.

During the plant tour the inspector should always discuss observations as they arise with the key personnel, supervisors and operators in order to establish facts, indicate areas of concern and to assess the knowledge and competence of these personnel.

7.6 Review of documentation: the whole system of documentation, based on specifications, manufacturing formulae and processing and packaging instructions, procedures and records covering the different production, QC and distribution operations should be checked by examining particular examples both during use and after compilation into complete batch records.

A general GMP-orientated inspection will normally, in order to assess compliance with the terms and conditions of the manufacturing authorization, include examination of the documentation relating to:

- job descriptions -standard operating procedures (SOP's)

- validation reports

- manufacturing formulae, records and instructions

- specifications

- batch release procedure and the role of the QP(s)

A product-related inspection will normally, in order to assess compliance with the terms and conditions of the marketing authorization, include examination of the specific documentation relating to one or several completed batches of a specified product including:

- standard operating procedures (SOP's)

- manufacturing formulae, records and instructions

- specifications, sampling and methods of analysis of components, starting materials, intermediates and finished products

7.7 Contract manufacture and analysis: operations contracted out and the responsibilities of the different parties should be clearly identified. The contract between the contract giver and the contract acceptor should be examined for compliance with the detailed guidelines of GMP.

7.8 Complaints and product recall: the system for recording and reviewing complaints as well as the system for recalling batches of medicinal products from within and outside the Member States should be examined during the inspection.

The complaints file should be examined. Defect reports and recalls should be discussed.

7.9 Self-Inspection: the system for performing self-inspections in the company should be examined, although the reports themselves should not normally be read by the inspector.

8. Final Meeting

8.1 When the inspection has been completed, the inspector should summarize the findings in the final meeting with representatives of the company, normally the technical management including the key personnel and preferably some or all of the senior management, if these are different from the key personnel.

8.2 The final meeting is a significant part of the inspection. The deficiencies observed during the inspection should be discussed. Their importance should also be discussed so that deadlines for remedial actions may be fixed.

8.3 Facts and objective evidence supporting the observations should preferably be agreed by the company. The company may if they so wish discuss initial proposals for remedial action.

8.4 As far as possible all relevant observations should be reported at this meeting so that the company can initiate the necessary corrective actions at the earliest possible date.

8.5 In case of serious deficiencies leading to possible serious risk for the patients, immediate action should be taken by the inspector.

9. Notes

Inspection reports should be based on notes taken during the inspection. These notes should be clear and legible.

10. Inspection Report

10.1 An inspection report should describe the scope of the inspection and cover the observations arising from the inspection. Deficiencies should be mentioned in the conclusion.

10.2 The report should contain the general information on the company, a description of the inspection itself and the inspector's observations and conclusions.

10.3 The conclusions should clearly identify the critical deficiencies and contain a clear statement by the inspector whether or not the manufacturer complies with the Community GMP principles. It is recommended that a date be agreed by which the manufacturer should submit proposals and a time schedule for rectifying the deficiencies outlined in the report.

10.4 The action taken by the Competent Authority will depend upon the nature and the extent of non-compliance.

10.5 A report prepared for communication to another Member State or a community body

(e.g. CPMP) should include the general information of the company which may be based on the information contained in an up-to-date Site Master File prepared by the company and agreed by the inspector.

10.6 The need for an early re-inspection to ensure that required changes have been carried out should be considered.

11. Inspection Frequency

11.1 Inspections should be carried out at least every two years. Large companies may be inspected department by department, a full general GMP inspection being completed at least every five years. The interval between inspections should never exceed 3 years as lack of continuity may give rise to lower awareness of current GMP or allow significant deficiencies to develop.

11.2 It should be stressed that the activities of the individual company (products and dosage forms manufactured, units and substances handled and personnel, premises and equipment involved in the manufacture) and its past record of GMP compliance should be taken into consideration when planning the frequency, and duration of inspection.

12. Quality Management of the Inspector's Activity

12.1 Most inspectors work alone or, at most, in pairs. The possibility of a specialist participating in the inspection should be taken into consideration. There should be a system to monitor and control the inspector's performance in order to ensure a correct and consistent approach on different occasions and between different inspectors. Monitoring should be planned to assess at least:

  – the extent and depth of the inspection -the ability to recognise deficiencies -the assessment of the seriousness of deficiencies -the action recommended -the effectiveness with which the determined action is carried out

12.2 This quality system should include periodic joint visits with senior or specialist inspectors, and follow-up of recommendations and subsequent action.

13. Annexes

13.1 Annex 1 on: Conduct of Product Related Inspections

13.2 Annex 2 on: Conduct of Inspections For Investigational Medicinal Products For Human Use

Annex on Conduct of Product Related Inspections

Introduction

The purpose of this annex is to outline the extent to which the inspector may become involved in:

(a) the pre-marketing assessment of an application for a marketing authorisation and

(b) the assessment of compliance with the terms and conditions of a marketing authorisation granted in the European Community.

An application for a marketing authorisation is made in the format set out in Volume II of the *Rules Governing Medicinal Products in the European Community.*

Information concerning the quality of a medicinal product is largely to be found in "Part II : Chemical, Pharmaceutical and Biological Documentation"

The role of inspectors in the pre-marketing assessment of an application for a marketing authorisation

Verification of authorisations:

There should be a systematic procedure whereby the person responsible for assessment of an application consults the inspectorate. The extent of such consultation will depend upon the nature of the product, the manufacturing and control operations involved and on the quality of the application.

Consultation should include the following:

1. Verification that the proposed manufacturer holds the appropriate manufacturing authorisations for the product concerned (Article 40 of Directive 2001/83/EC and Article 44 of Directive 2001/82/EC).

2. Verification that the appropriate authorisation is held where third country importation is proposed (Article 40 of Directive 2001/83/EC and Article 44 of Directive 2001/82/EC).

3. Verification that any contract Quality Control laboratory has been inspected and approved (Article 20(b) of Directive 2001/83/EC or Article 24(b) of Directive 2001/82/EC).

The role of inspectors in assessing compliance with marketing authorisations

The inspector carries out an inspection of a manufacturer in order to assess the latter's compliance with GMP. GMP includes ensuring that all manufacturing operations are in accordance with the relevant marketing authorisation (Articles 5 of Directive 2003/94/EC and 91/412/EEC). The inspector is also in a position to verify that the details relating to the manufacture and control of a product which were provided in the marketing authorisation application for that product, as modified and/or agreed during the assessment, are being adhered to in the manufacture of batches of that product for sale.

In certain circumstances, for example in relation to biological, biotechnological and other high technology products, it may be appropriate for the inspector to be accompanied by a relevant assessor. Alternatively, the inspector can be accompanied by the competent authority's expert on the particular type of product or by an independent expert nominated by the competent authority.

The inspector should have all relevant sections from the marketing authorisation application to hand during the inspection for ready reference. This would be considerably facilitated by having an up to date summary of these sections readily available to the inspector.

Carrying out the inspection

Adherence to chemistry and pharmacy data supplied and approved in the marketing authorisation application.

The inspection should seek to verify, by means of examination of all relevant facilities, equipment and documents, that the information provided in the marketing authorisation application is being strictly adhered to. This examination might include:

(a) composition of the medicinal product

(b) container

(c) manufacturing formula

(d) manufacturing process including in-process controls

(e) source and nature of active ingredients

(f) other ingredients

(g) packaging materials

(h) control tests on intermediate products

(i) control tests on the finished product

(j) labelling

(k) any other data requested by assessors, including ongoing stability investigations. In addition to this verification the following specific points should also be borne in mind:

Samples

Consideration should be given to taking the following samples:

(a) active ingredient (if material from more than one source is available, take a sample of each).

(b) excipients (samples may be taken of non-pharmacopoeial and unusual materials).

(c) finished product (sufficient to carry out full duplicate analysis and to meet the legal provisions of the Member State).

(d) label

(e) printed carton

(f) data sheet

If finished product samples are to be taken directly from the market, the company should deliver relevant samples of

(a) active ingredients, and

(b) excipients to the competent authority upon request.

(c) any other samples requested by assessors.

All samples should be submitted for testing/review and, if indicated by the results, necessary follow up action should be taken.

Copies of documents

If necessary, copies of the finished product specification and method of analysis should be taken relating to the samples taken (if any) during the inspection.

If necessary, copies of the batch manufacturing document and of the finished product specification and method of analysis should be delivered to the competent authority upon request.

Complaints

Review any complaints relating to the product.

Amendments and variations

Following the granting of a marketing authorisation, the holder of a marketing authorisation may subsequently apply for amendments and variations to the original information to be approved by the competent authority.

Where such amendments and variations have been approved by the competent authority, the inspector should check that any master document to which an amendment or variation related, was altered to include the amendment or variation shortly after this was approved by the competent authority.

Review of documentation relating to the product

This should be carried out as set out in Section 12 of the main guideline. Documentation for a number of batches should be reviewed.

Section 6.9. of the Rules Governing Medicinal Products in the European Community, Volume IV, recommends that trend evaluation of analytical test results be carried out. If this has been done the evaluation should be reviewed.

****

Annex on Conduct of Inspections for Investigational Medicinal Products for Human Use

Introduction

The purpose of this document is to fulfil the requirements of Article 15.5 of Directive 2001/20/EC to provide guidance on the conduct of inspection of manufacturers (or importers) of investigational medicinal products holding or seeking the authorisation referred to in Article 13.1 of Directive 2001/20/EC, in order to harmonise inspection procedures, frequency of inspections and follow-up thus ensuring a consistent approach to assessment and decision-making by Competent Authorities.

Scope

This guideline applies to the inspection of manufacturers, importers or analytical laboratories authorised in accordance with Article 13.1 of Directive 2001/20/EC by the competent authority of the Member State concerned. It also applies to inspections of manufacturers based in third countries where these are inspected in accordance with Article 15.4 of Directive 2001/20/EC. In both cases the inspection is carried out on behalf of the European Community and the outcome is recognised by all Member States.

Article 15.1 of Directive 2001/20/EC additionally refers to inspections carried out at other locations connected with any clinical trial and in some cases there will be overlap between Good Manufacturing and Good Clinical Practice. Examples include: release of investigational medicinal products, the generation of emergency code break systems in blinded clinical trials, preparation of investigational products at investigational sites including labelling, complaints, adverse events and recalls. Member States, particularly those that maintain separate inspectorates for these Good Practices, should ensure that overlap areas are identified, responsibilities understood and inspections performed by Inspectors with appropriate qualifications and training.

THIS ANNEX SHOULD BE READ IN CONJUNCTION WITH THE MAIN PROCEDURE. THE ANNEX PROVIDES ADDITIONAL INFORMATION ONLY

Glossary of Terms

The definition of terms in the detailed guidelines published in Good Manufacturing Practice for Medicinal Products in the European Community, Volume IV are applicable to this document, in particular those given in Annex 13. In addition, the following apply:

Inspection:

On-Site assessment of the compliance with the Community GMP principles performed by officials of Community Competent Authorities.

A general GMP Inspection covering general GMP aspects should be carried out before the authorisation referred to in Article 13.1 of Directive 2001/20/EC, is granted and periodically afterwards as required.

An inspection may be more product-or process-related when it focuses on the adherence by the manufacturer to the dossier of an investigational medicinal product submitted to the Competent Authority in order to obtain authorisation to conduct a clinical trial pursuant to Article 9.2 of Directive 2001/20/EC and on the manufacture and documentation related to the product or to a specific manufacturing process.

QC Laboratory Inspection:

On-Site assessment of the adherence to Good Quality Control Laboratory Practice is normally part of a GMP Inspection.

Contract QC Laboratories authorised according to Article 13.1 of Directive 2001/20/EC are also subject to these inspections.

Laboratory inspection for compliance with GLP Principles is performed in accordance with guidelines given in the annexes to Directive 90/18/EEC and is not part of this document. Inspections performed in laboratories analysing samples taken from trial subjects are likewise not included.

General Obligations

Member States.

Member States should establish the legal and administrative framework within which Inspections relating to clinical trials including Good Manufacturing Practice (GMP) inspections as applied to investigational medicinal products operate.

Inspectors should be issued with an official means of identification, which includes reference to powers of entry, access to data and the collection of samples and documents for the purpose of inspection.

Member States should ensure that there are sufficient resources at all levels to effectively verify compliance with GMP for investigational medicinal products and that inspectors are competent and trained in order to carry out their tasks as referred to in the detailed guidelines for qualifications of GMP inspectors engaged in verifying GMP Compliance for Investigational Medicinal Products.

Inspectorates should adopt quality systems to ensure consistency of approach to inspection and evaluation of findings. Within the quality system inspectorates should develop detailed procedures in line with this guideline to suit national requirements and practices but consistent with procedures agreed at Community level such as report formats for the exchange of information.

EMEA and Commission

The EMEA should establish a GMP inspection program for investigational medicinal products falling within the remit of Regulation (EEC)2309/93 and agree with Member States the processes for contracting the conduct of these inspections, maintain records of the inspections requested, the reports and their follow-up.

The EMEA or Commission should establish a process for arranging inspections in third countries.

The Commission should establish a process for requesting re-inspections as referred to in Article 15.3 of the Directive should verification of compliance with Directive 2001/20/EC reveal differences between Member States.

General Considerations on Inspections of Investigational Medicinal Products

The primary goal for the inspector should be to determine whether the various elements within the quality assurance system are effective and suitable for achieving compliance with GMP principles. In addition, determining whether the investigational medicinal products comply with the dossiers submitted to the Competent Authority in order to obtain authorisation to conduct a clinical trial pursuant to Article 9.2 of Directive 2001/20/EC.

Product-or process-related inspections (also termed special or problem oriented) may be indicated to assess the adherence of the manufacturer to the investigational medicinal product dossier and the way the batch documentation is kept. It is also indicated when complaints, recalls or adverse event patterns may concern one product or group of products or processing procedures (e.g.sterilisation, labelling, etc). These inspections may be triggered by an Assessor raising questions during the evaluation of an application for authorisation to conduct a clinical trial or marketing authorisation. They may also arise from questions raised during a GCP inspection.

Inspection Procedures

Preparation of inspections: prior to conducting an inspection the inspector(s) should familiarise themselves with the organisation to be inspected.

This may include:

- Review of relevant parts of the investigational medicinal product dossier of one or more selected products to be examined during the inspection, including the History file

- For triggered inspections, a review of the questions raised by the Assessor or GCP Inspector (arising from a GCP inspection).

Review of documentation:

The system of documentation, based on the Product Specification Files, procedures and records covering the different production, QC and distribution operations should be checked by examining particular examples both during use and after compilation into complete batch records. Change control and the traceability of changes should be examined.

A general GMP-orientated inspection will normally, in order to assess compliance with the terms and conditions of the manufacturing authorisation, include examination of the documentation relating to:

- Product Specification Files

- Two-step batch release procedure and the role of the QP(s) including the assessment of products imported from third countries.

A product-related inspection will normally, in order to assess compliance with the terms and conditions of the investigational medicinal product dossier, include examination of the specific documentation relating to one or several completed batches of a specified product including:

- standard operating procedures (SOP's)

- the Product Specification File

Complaints and product recall

The system for recording and reviewing complaints, interactions with the clinical research personnel as well as the system for recalling batches of investigational medicinal products from within and outside the Member States should be examined during the inspection. The system for retrieving recall information on comparator products should also be included.

The complaints file should be examined. Defect Reports and recalls should be discussed.

Final Meeting

In case of serious deficiencies leading to possible serious risk for trial subjects, the inspector should take immediate action.

Outline of a Procedure for Co-ordinating the Verification of the GMP Status of Manufacturers in Third Countries

London, 20 September 2006

EMEA/INS/GMP/313523/2006

Published on Behalf of the European Commission by EMEA (European Medicines Agency)

Note: *This document forms part of the Compilation of Community Procedures on Inspections and Exchange of Information. Please check for updates on the EMEA website (Inspections pages).*

Guideline Title:	*Outline of a Procedure for Co-ordinating the Verification of the GMP Status of Manufacturers in Third Countries*
History:	*Replaces the document of the same title published 8 December 1997 reinforcing responsibilities for inspection and includes reference to investigational medicinal products. Provision is made for "Distant Assessment" in exceptional circumstances.*
Date of Adoption:	*December 2004.*
Date of entry into force:	*1 July 2005.*

1. Verification of the GMP Compliance Status of Third Country Manufacturers of Medicinal and Investigational Medicinal Products.

1.1. The Supervisory Member State for the manufacturing authorisation holder who is responsible for importation of a product should verify the GMP compliance status of any third country manufacturer(s) mentioned in an application in accordance with their own policies and procedures. This may be based on the following:

1.1.1. A report of an inspection for the product or product category concerned carried out by the Supervisory Member State, or

1.1.2. Information supplied by another EEA Competent Authority in accordance with the exchange of information procedure contained in the Compilation of Community Procedures,

Or

1.1.3. A report of an inspection for the product or product category concerned carried out by another EEA competent authority,

Or

1.1.4. Either an inspection report or a statement of GMP compliance obtained under an operational Mutual Recognition Agreement between the European

Community and the Competent Authorities of the third country in which the manufacturer is located.

1.2. Where the Supervisory Member State is unable to verify the GMP status of any third country manufacturer(s) on the above basis it may request another EEA Competent Authority to carry out an inspection and to provide confirmation of the manufacturer's GMP compliance status. For centralised products this arrangement should be subject to obtaining the written consent of any other Supervisory Member States involved.

1.3. The means of verification will normally be through inspection-based information as described above, however other information may be used as part of, or in exceptional cases, as the primary means for verification. For example:

1.3.1. Under the provisions of the existing MRAs, information from MRA partners is only accepted in connection with inspections performed in their own territories, however, the use of other information from MRA partners, PIC/S participating authorities and/or other authorities may nevertheless provide supporting evidence in the verification of the GMP status of a manufacturing site. The Supervisory Authority should perform a risk assessment on each occasion to determine an appropriate degree of evidence that a 3rd country manufacturer operates to an equivalent level of GMP.

1.3.2. Where an inspection has been performed by a Member State or MRA partner but does not cover the dosage form in question. Compliance conclusions from inspection reports relating to a different dosage form may, with justification, be extended to other dose forms, if necessary requesting the report if it belongs to another Member State authority. In addition the elements below should be considered, together with, if considered necessary, elements of the distant assessment approach described in section (c). Reports concerning non-sterile dosage forms alone do not provide sufficient evidence to extend any GMP conclusions to sterile products.

– Inspection reports of the importer. If necessary a special inspection may be needed of the importer to assess measures undertaken by the importer to verify GMP compliance at the exporting site for the dosage form in question, such as audit reports from the QP.

— A site master file for the manufacturing site. If necessary written questions arising from a review of this may need to be raised and the responses reviewed.

— The inspection history of the manufacturing site performed by other authorities. The existence of warning letters or other regulatory action by third country authorities should be ascertained.

— The history of reported defects for batches of all products originating at the manufacturing site.

Subject to the information reviewed, it may be concluded not to conduct a pre-authorisation inspection but verification in accordance with point 1.1 above should be sought within 3 years.

1.3.3. A similar approach can be taken where inspections cannot be carried out because of unacceptable risks to EEA inspectors. The procedure for "distant assessment" is limited to inspections in 3rd countries that present an enhanced physical threat to the inspector (for political reasons, health reasons or others) and where the enhanced level of instability is expected to be transient. The procedure should not be used where the reporting authority has reason to believe that the instability could directly affect the quality of the product(s) under consideration.

A distant assessment may be performed based on a documented interview with the manufacturer that should be deep enough to evaluate the GMP compliance of the relevant manufacturing site.

This documented interview (taking place in the inspecting authority's country) should be carried out with nominated staff possessing an appropriately high level of knowledge of the process and facilities.

The table in the annex provides for two levels of assessment. A full assessment where the site which has been inspected more than 5 years ago by an EEA authority, and a reduced one for a site which has been inspected within 3 and 5 years ago by the same EEA Authority. If the last inspection was performed by another authority, the full assessment should be applied.

A distant assessment should not be carried out where the manufacturing site has never been inspected, by an EEA inspectorate, nor for a sterile manufacturing process or any unusually complex non-sterile process, nor should it replace inspection more than once.

1.4.   Investigational Medicinal Products

For investigational medicinal products, inspections should be reserved for higher risk situations rather than being routinely employed. The risk assessments should take the elements described in 1.above into account along with the following:

- the dosage form,

- type of product (e.g. placebo, marketed comparator, new technology),

- numbers of subjects involved and their clinical disposition,

- duration of treatment,

- number of clinical trials sourcing from the same site

- whether the manufacturer is in possession of the equivalent of a valid manufacturing authorisation issued by its local regulatory authority and is subject to inspections,

- whether the analytical testing performed in the third country is subject to appropriate authorisation.

2. Exchange of Information on Third Country Manufacturers.

2.1.   When exchanging information on third country manufacturing sites, the reporting authority should indicate whether the conclusions reached are derived from an inspection by an EEA inspectorate or MRA partner under the terms of an MRA, or whether alternative means were used such as those described in section 1.3.

2.2. On the basis of a "reasoned request" from the competent authorities of another Member State or from the EMEA the Supervisory Member State should provide a report of the most recent verification of the GMP status of a third country manufacturer for a particular product or product category.

2.3. Where the Member State requested to supply the information is unable to do so the requesting authorities may carry out a GMP inspection of the third country manufacturer, in which case they will provide the other authorities with shared supervisory responsibility with a copy of their inspection report or a statement of GMP compliance.

3. Organisation and Records of Inspections and Composition of Inspection Teams.

3.1. The EMEA will maintain a plan of third country inspections connected with centralised products and will make this available on a regular basis.

3.2. Through the database on GMP certificates to be established in accordance with Article 111.6 of Directive 2004/27 (Art. 80.6 of Directive 2004/28), the EMEA will maintain a record of all inspections that have been carried out by the competent authorities of the EU/EEA, which will be available to all member states.

3.3. The competent authorities planning inspections of manufacturers in third countries may invite the participation of the other Member States who have shared "Supervisory" responsibilities for the product(s). This should take into account planned applications for marketing authorisations, problems encountered with the products from the manufacturer, their workloads, their experience in the type of inspections required, language capability for the inspection and overall economics of travel etc.

4. Communication between the "Supervisory Authority" and Industry

Member States should encourage potential applicants to make early contact with the inspectorate of the supervisory authority when planning a marketing authorisation submission or variation which includes a third country manufacturing site, in order to discuss the applicant's knowledge of the GMP status of the site, its inspection history and inspection-readiness. Ideally this should be at least 3 months before submission and is particularly important for investigational medicinal products given the short timelines available to authorise trials.

5. The "Supervisory Authorities"

5.1. The "Supervisory Authorities" for a medicinal product and their responsibilities are defined for products for human use in Article 18 and 19 of Council Regulation (EC) No 726/2004 and for products for veterinary use in Articles 43 and 44 of the same Regulation. They are the Competent Authorities which have granted the manufacturing authorisation either for the manufacturing site if it is in the EU or for the importer if the product is manufactured in a third country.

6. Re-inspection Frequency

6.1. In general authorities with supervisory responsibility for a third country manufacturing site should ensure that it is re-inspected by an EEA authority or MRA partner authority, under the terms of an MRA, between every two to three years.

6.2. Where inspection reports and information exchange based on inspections conducted more than three years ago are available, as there is evidence of acceptable GMP standards, it should not be necessary to withhold any application or variation pending the results of a new inspection unless information is available from other sources suggesting that this status may have changed. Steps should nevertheless be taken to obtain an updated report.

6.3. Inspection reports, and information exchange based on inspections or distant assessments conducted more than five years ago, from whatever source, should not normally be taken into consideration.

7. Disagreement between Member States on acceptability of Inspection Reports

7.1. Where the Supervisory Member State and the competent authorities of another Member State are unable to agree on the acceptability of an inspection report for a manufacturer in a third country they should utilise the arrangements described for human products in Article 19 of Regulation (EC) 726/2004 or where appropriate the arbitration procedure provided by Article 29 of Directive 2001/83/EC and for veterinary products Article 44 of Regulation (EC) 726/2004 or where appropriate the arbitration procedure provided by Article 33 of Directive 2001/82/EC.

****

Annex Scheme For Distant Assessment Of Manufacturing Sites

REQUIREMENT S / RATIONALE	Last EEA inspection more than 5 years ago	Last EEA inspection carried out between 3 and 5 years ago
Presentation of GMP and Regulatory Enforcement system for the country	Complete presentation of the regulatory system and full copy of the local GMP guide	Brief presentation of changes being effected since the last inspection
Copy of the manufacturing authorisation granted by local authorities together with a certified translation	Complete set of copies of all original/modified manufacturing authorization	Copy of any new/modified manufacturing authorization granted since the last inspection
SMF (site master file) documentation similar to the PIC/S guideline	SMF completed/ updated within 6 month from the assessment date And forecasted modifications	SMF updated with one year from the assessment date And forecasted modifications
Plans attached to SMF PI&D attached to SMF	Coloured printouts of Water treatment, Air Handling PI & Ds in A3 or A2 format	Coloured updated printouts may be acceptable in A3 or A2 format
List of all the products (medicinal or either) manufactured on site	The list should include proprietary names and INN	The list may include proprietary names and INN
Copy of the last inspection report with a certified translated copy if relevant *GMP certificates coming from these inspections*	Local authority report aged less than two years and, if available, copy of PIC/S or WHO or FDA report(s)	Last local authority report and last EU full report. PIC/S and WHO or FDA report(s) if aged less than 5 years
Photographic presentation of manufacturing site and utilities (outdoor/indoor)	External general view (aerial) Detailed rooms views of any step carried out (sample, weighing....)	Photographic presentation of any new room(s) of equipment not used at the time of inspection

REQUIREMENT S / RATIONALE	Last EEA inspection more than 5 years ago	Last EEA inspection carried out between 3 and 5 years ago
Qualification Master Plan (premises & equipment)	List of premises, equipment and utilities used in the manufacturing with their qualification status	List of all re-qualifications exercises carried out since the last inspection
Validation Master Plan (Manufacturing processes, cleaning, quality control)	List of processes used for the manufacturing / control of the product and their Val. status	List of all re-validations runs carried out since the last inspection
Full audit report of corporate / external audit dedicated to the product(s)	The report should include the product flow chart and should be one year old as a maximum	The report may be aged less than 5 years and accompanied with a recent follow-up internal report
Batch record(s) of the product(s) of interest	Last filled in batch record together the master batch record including the analytical part	Last filled in batch record including the analytical part
Complaints handling	Updated list of complaints for all products manufactured on site	Updated list of complaints of the concerned products
Others *	Number of rejected batches for all products Number of rejected batches for the concerned product	Number of rejected batches for all products Number of rejected batches for the concerned product
Others (concerning the concerned product / dosage form)	Out of specification procedures On going stability studies All 00s results and investigations* All process deviation reports (including reworked and reprocessed batches)* All quality deviation reports*	Out of specification procedures On going stability studies All 00s results and investigations* All process deviation reports (including reworked and reprocessed batches)* All quality deviation reports*

REQUIREMENT S / RATIONALE	Last EEA inspection more than 5 years ago	Last EEA inspection carried out between 3 and 5 years ago
Others	Q.P certification that site has been fully audited against EU GMP in the last 2 years and all deficiencies have been rectified	Q.P certification that site has been fully audited against EU GMP in the last 2 years and all deficiencies have been rectified
Others	All Q.C results for batches imported and tested in the member state.	All Q.C results for batches imported and tested in the member state.
According to EU draft	Product Quality Review	Product Quality Review
Manufacturing Contract between manufacturing site and European applicant	Original contract and revision if applicable	Original contract and revision if applicable

*data to be provided over a period of the last 3 years

Guideline on Training and Qualifications of GMP Inspectors

London, 2 August 2007

EMEA/INS/GMP/313525/2006 Rev1

Note: *This document forms part of the Compilation of Community Procedures on Inspections and Exchange of Information. Please check for updates on the EMEA website (Inspections pages).*

Guideline Title: *Outline of a Procedure for Co-ordinating the Verification of the GMP Status of Manufacturers in Third Countries*

Publisher: *European Medicines Agency on behalf of the European Commission*

Date of Publishing: *1995. Updated February 2004*

Responsible Authority: *GMP/GDP Inspectors Working Group*

Date of Adoption: *December 1996. Updated October 2002. Updated September 2007*

Date of entry into force: *May 2004*

1. Introduction

Taking into account its importance for the management of inspection services, this guideline establishes requirements concerning experience, training and qualifications of GMP inspectors.

Objectivity, professional integrity, competence in technical matters and inspection skills should be the main features of inspectors.

Inspectors should be very well trained in all the relevant topics concerning Quality Assurance management, manufacturing processes, control and distribution of medicinal products (including investigational medicinal product in the light of requirements of directive 2001/20/EC) and in the way of conducting an inspection (inspection methodology).

The guideline provides information on minimal requirements. Member States may decide to add supplementary national requirements.

2. Scope

This guideline applies to the training and qualifications required for an inspector who shall conduct an inspection to verify compliance with GMP for the competent authority of the Member State concerned. Inspections are carried out on behalf of the Community and the results shall be recognised by all the other Member States.

3. Background

3.1 General aspects

Member States should appoint inspectors to inspect the manufacturing sites according to Directive 2001/83/EC, Directive 2001/82/EC and Directive 2001/20/EC. There should be sufficient resources at all levels to meet, effectively and efficiently, the EU requirements of verifying compliance with GMP of medicinal products.

The inspectors shall be officials of, or appointed by, the competent authorities of the Member States in accordance with national regulations and follow the provisions for the national competent authority.

All inspectors should be competent to carry out their assigned duties and receive appropriate training. When needed, teams of inspectors may be nominated comprising inspectors with appropriate qualifications and experience to collectively fulfil the requirements necessary for conducting the inspection.

The inspectors should be made aware, of and maintain confidentiality whenever they gain access to confidential information as a result of GMP inspections according to applicable national laws, European requirements or international agreements.

There should be sufficient resource to ensure availability of competent inspectors to work according to contracts between EMEA and the competent authority in the case of inspections requested by the CHMP or CVMP.

The training needs of inspectors should regularly be assessed within the requirements of the applicable quality system of the Competent Authority/Inspectorate and appropriate actions taken by the competent authority to maintain and improve inspection skills.

Information on the relevant experience, training and qualifications of the individual inspector must be documented and maintained by the competent authority. These records should be kept up-todate.

3.2 Personal qualities

The inter-personal skills of an inspector are important in helping to achieve the objectives of inspections.

During an inspection the inspector should help in creating an open atmosphere. Inspectors need to remain objective during the inspection and in this context should answer questions or provide clarification but avoid entering into the role of a consultant.

The inspector should have a high level of personal integrity, maturity, be open-minded, understanding of complexity, possess sound judgement, assertiveness, analytical skills and tenacity and have the ability to perceive situations in a realistic way.

The inspector should have demonstrated competence in clearly and fluently expressing concepts and ideas orally and in writing in their officially recognised language.

4. Qualification and training

4.1 Qualification

Inspectors should preferably have the same level of qualification as the "Qualified Person" as defined in art. 48 of

Directive 2001/83/EC, in art. 52 of the Directive 2001/82/EC and therefore be eligible as a Qualified Person.

The inspector should have knowledge of the national legislation as well as systems, both at national and at Community level, for applications for marketing and control of medicinal products.

4.2 Training

The inspectors should have undergone training to the extent necessary to ensure their competence in the skills required for planning, carrying out and reporting inspections.

The training and experience should be documented individually and evaluated within the requirements of the applicable quality system of the Competent Authority/ Inspectorate.

4.2.1 Basic training

Moreover, in order to be appointed as GMP inspectors, the candidates should demonstrate their knowledge of the relevant matters in the pharmaceutical field, including:

- Community and national pharmaceutical legislation;

- Good Manufacturing Practice and Good Distribution Practice

- Principles of quality assurance and quality management systems (ISO 9000:2000);

- Technical aspects of pharmaceutical and API manufacturing (e.g. pharmaceutical technology, process and ventilation engineering, validation, computerized systems, analytical instrumentation, microbiology);

- Organization and quality systems of the Competent Authority/Inspectorate and training in working according to relevant national and Community SOPs and procedures related to inspections;

- Marketing and manufacturing authorisation systems and their relationship;

- Interrelation of licensing, inspection, sampling and analysis;

- Knowledge of MRA and other relevant Community arrangements;

- Structure and principles of operation of commercial organizations

- Inspection technique, acquired by attending relevant course(s) and or/by accompanying and/or guided by qualified GMP inspectors during inspection;

- Administration procedures required for managing an inspection, such as planning, organizing, communicating or providing feedback to the inspectee;

- Evaluation of findings and reporting;

- Pharmaceutical Development, Quality Risk Management and Pharmaceutical Quality System (incl. ICH Q8, Q9, Q10 as implemented in the relevant EU guidelines)

- International organisations their activities and documents (EDQM, ICH, PIC/S, WHO);

It is recognised that there are acceptable methods, other than those described in the Guide, which are capable of achieving the Quality Assurance principles of Good Manufacturing Practice. An inspector should be open and able to assess whether alternative methods and procedures meet these principles taking into account the principles of Quality Risk Management.

4.2.2 Further training

After recruitment and in addition to their basic training, new inspectors should be trained by senior inspectors. The theory of inspection should be explained and the practice should be shown in the field, so that concrete examples of the meaning and of the goals of inspections are given and can be discussed. New inspectors should participate, but only as observers, in on the spot inspections carried out during their initial training.

Beside this and where needed, training courses in inspection techniques and communication, reporting, languages, legal matters and management should be organised by national inspectorates.

To be able to act as lead inspector in inspections requested by CHMP or CVMP and coordinated by EMEA and to participate in the ongoing co-operation and harmonisation of procedures within EU, the inspector should also be able to write and speak in English.

For participating to activities as such as Joint Audit Programme, Joint Reassessment Programme, European Benchmarking, adequate training should be organized at EU or international level as appropriate.

4.2.3. Continuous training

Considering the rapid implementation of new manufacturing technologies, the ever more frequent utilization of automatic and computerized systems both in production and quality control of medicinal products, inspectors should also receive continuous training.

This could be achieved through their participation in courses, seminars, scientific meetings and conferences organized either by the national inspectorates or by national or international scientific organizations.

When appropriate, joint inspections or training visits with other inspectors of the same Member State or of other Member States may be a useful training method.

Prior to assuming responsibility for performing GMP inspections the new inspector should have gained experience by participation as team member in inspections led by senior inspectors. Preferably, the inspector should start with national GMP inspections as a member of a team and then deal progressively with more complex GMP inspections to be able to act as a team leader and/or reporting inspector in international inspections. This should be recorded within the requirements of the applicable quality system of the Competent Authority/ Inspectorate.

Ten days of training (e.g. courses, symposia, conferences, etc.) per year should be considered as a reasonable average.

4.3 Management capabilities

The inspectors should through suitable means demonstrate their knowledge and capability of using the necessary management skills required in the conduct of an inspection, i.e. planning, announcing, conducting and reporting an inspection.

4.4 Report writing

The inspector's capacity to write inspection reports according to national and Community requirements should demonstrated and documented.

5. *Maintenance of competence*

Inspectors should have their performance and qualifications periodically reviewed within the requirements of the applicable quality system of the Competent Authority/ Inspectorate. Their competence should be maintained and updated by practical experience and by participating in courses, seminars, scientific meetings, conferences and through review of relevant publications. This should be documented and its effectiveness assessed to ensure that:

- Knowledge of GMP, quality systems standards and requirements is current,

- Knowledge of inspection procedures and methods is current,

- Knowledge of quality assurance activities within the requirements of the applicable quality system of the Competent Authority/ Inspectorate is current.

6. *Harmonisation within EU*

In order to promote international harmonisation in the interpretation of the principles of GMP and compliance, the Inspectorate's management should facilitate training activities, including on the job training, at national and international levels.

Consultations with the staff of other GMP inspectorates and joint inspections or training visits is useful in this context and should be encouraged.

The management should also facilitate the exchange of information and practical experience gained by inspectors in the field of GMP, with inspectorates in other disciplines especially in those areas that are closely related e.g. laboratory facilities, computerised data recording and analyses and requirements in relation to medicinal products for investigational use.

Exchange of Information on Manufacturers and Manufacturing or Wholesale Distribution Authorisations between Competent Authorities in the European Economic Area

London, 20 September 2006

EMEA/INS/GMP/313535/2006

Note: This document forms part of the Compilation of Community
        Procedures on Inspections and Exchange of Information.
        Please check for updates on the EMEA website (Inspections
        pages).

Guideline Title: Exchange of information on manufacturers
                              and manufacturing or wholesale distribution
                              authorisations between Competent Authorities
                              in the European Economic Area

History: Replaces "Exchange of information on
                              manufacturers and manufacturing or
                              wholesale distribution authorisations between
                              Competent Authorities in the European
                              Economic Area", dated 1995.

Date of Adoption: 6 August 2004

Date of entry into force: 1 September 2004

1. Introduction

Effective control of medicinal products circulating within the Community requires a high level of administrative collaboration and consequently a good system of exchange of information between competent authorities.

Either within the context of a normal routine check or sampling programme of medicinal products distributed in a Member State, or in the event of suspicion concerning the origin of a medicinal product coming from another Member State, as for example in case of suspected counterfeited product, it may be necessary for a competent authority to seek confirmation of the manufacturer's authorisation from another competent authority.

In most cases, the transmission of inspection reports as provided for in article 122 of Directive 2001/83/EC, for medicinal products for use in man, or Article 15 of Directive 2001/20/EC, and in Directive 2001/82/EC, Article 90, for veterinary medicinal products would not be justified and would create a needless administrative workload. In addition, should exchange of information on individual authorisations concerning wholesale distributors as provided for in article 77 of Directive 2001/83/EC on the wholesale distribution of medicinal products for human use be needed, generally a simple confirmation of the existence of an appropriate authorisation would suffice.

Therefore, following data could be exchanged:

- a reference to the legal basis of the authorisation (Community and national provisions);

- reference number, if any, of the current valid authorisation;

- legally registered address of the holder of the authorisation;

- address(es) of the manufacturing and/or wholesale distribution site(s) covered by the authorisation, including contract Quality Control laboratories;

- scope of the authorisation:

  1. manufacture of medicinal products/investigational medicinal products for use in man or animals

  2. import from third countries;

3. manufacturing operations which are authorised: total or partial manufacture and for what dosage forms (pharmaceutical form).

4. wholesale distribution of medicinal products for use in man or animals.

The request form (appendix 1) should be used by competent authorities looking for confirmation of a manufacturer's or wholesaler's legal status. The reply form (appendices 2, and 2A where appropriate) should be used by competent authorities replying to a request. Appendix 2A allows the reporting authority to distinguish between authorisation for partial manufacture, full manufacture or importation. Further clarifying remarks can also be added if considered necessary.

2. Other reasons for exchange of information concerning manufacturers.

It may also be necessary for a competent authority to request information from the inspectorate of another competent authority on particular aspects of manufacture such as process validation (section 3) or concerning a site in a third country (section 4). Furthermore there is a need for the rapid

exchange of information to member states in the event of a third country inspection revealing serious non-compliance with GMP resulting in the possible need for co-ordinated administrative action. (section 5)

3. Other reasons for exchange of information concerning manufacturers.

Background.

The Note for Guidance to Applicants on Process Validation [CPMP/QWP/848/96, EMEA/CVMP/598/99, adopted February 2001, and implemented in September 2001] recognises that at the time of submission of an application for a marketing authorisation the manufacturer may not have completed formal validation studies on production scale batches. In this situation the applicant should outline the formal studies planned for production scale batches (normally three) before the product is placed on the market. The results of these studies should be available for verification by the supervisory authorities according to national procedures. When the validation plan is completed the MA holder is required to report according to

---

national procedures. Where the results show significant deviations from those expected, the MA holder is obliged to inform the regulatory authorities immediately.

GMP

Process validation is a standard requirement of GMP [Guide to GMP section 5.21 to 5. 24, and GMP annexes]. A manufacturer's procedure for validation should be checked routinely as part of repeated GMP inspections. It is not the intention of the CHMP/CVMP that the validation of every individual product should be verified routinely. However there may be exceptional occasions when the assessor will direct the attention of the inspector to verify a particular undertaking to validate a process.

Request for Verification.

When the manufacturer and the assessor are in the same member state this requires no Community procedure. When the manufacturer and the assessor are in different member states the following procedure should be followed:

-the assessor of the competent authority for the MA holder requests verification of process validation from the inspectorate in the same member state, according to the national procedure;

-the inspectorate requests the information from the inspectorate of the supervisory member state, using the request form (appendix 1). The reply form (appendix 2) should be used by the competent authority responding to the request.

The response should normally be either that the validation has been completed successfully and in accordance with the plan, or if it has not been completed this should be stated and some explanation attached.

4. Inspection Information Regarding Third Country Manufacturing Sites

During the assessment of a marketing authorisation application where a manufacturing site in a third country is listed, the applicant may indicate that an EEA inspectorate has inspected the site. The assessor should request verification of the GMP status of such manufacturing sites from the inspectorate within his own member state. If the inspectorate that carried out the inspection is from another member state then the inspectorate will request information from the inspecting member state's inspectorate using this exchange of information procedure. The requesting authority should complete the request form (appendix 1) and the responding authority should complete the reply forms (appendices 2 and 2A). Appendix 2A allows the reporting authority to clarify whether the information exchange covers partial manufacture or full manufacture depending on the scope of the inspections on which the exchange of information is based. Further clarifying remarks can also be added if considered necessary.

5. Adverse Outcome of Third Country Inspection

The form given in appendix 3 (with appendix 2A if necessary) should be completed and transmitted to all EEA GMP inspectorates (human and/or veterinary as appropriate) and EMEA when an inspection has been performed in a third country by the reporting inspectorate that reveals serious non-compliance with GMP and where action is deemed necessary such as recall, suspension of marketing authorisations etc. With a view to taking co-ordinated action at EU level, the form should be distributed prior to the execution of any action by the reporting authority, if time permits. In so far as is possible, the reporting authority will identify any other member states with national products directly affected by the inspection findings and whether centralised products are involved. The form should explain the nature of any proposed action taken by the reporting authority in its own territory. If the reporting authority considers it necessary, a contact telephone number is given with and a proposed time for a teleconference involving all concerned member states in which co-ordinated action can be agreed. The reporting authority will host the teleconference. The receiving authorities should check whether national products on their own territories are affected, seeking assistance from the reporting inspectorate as needed, and if so should join any teleconference. In cases where the reporting authority has performed the inspection on behalf of another authority, both authorities should have already discussed the inspection findings before transmission of the form. EMEA will co-ordinate actions involving centralised products.

In the case of investigational medicinal products, although the discovery of critical failures to comply will be recorded on the EudraCT database, this procedure should also be invoked when considered necessary by the reporting authority.

Exchange of Information on Manufacturers and Manufacturing or Wholesale
Distribution Authorisations between Competent Authorities in the European Economic
Area

Appendix 1: Request form for the exchange of information

COMPILATION OF COMMUNITY PROCEDURES

REQUEST FORM FOR THE EXCHANGE OF INFORMATION BETWEEN COMPETENT AUTHORITIES IN THE EEA (Appendix 1)

The competent authority of ....

requests the competent authority of ....
to confirm that:

Company name: ....

Site address: ....

....

tick box(es) as appropriate

| ☐ | has been authorised in acccordance with Art. 40 of Directive 2001/83/EC (Art. 44 Directive 2001/82/EC) |

| ☐ | has been authorised in accordance with Art. 77 of Directive 2001/83/EC (Art. 65 Directive 2001/82/EC) |

| ☐ | has been authorised in accordance with Art. 13 of Directive 2001/20/EC |

| ☐ | has completed the post-authorisation process validation plan submitted to support the application for... (product name, dosage form, strength, MA number) in accordance with scheme in the Notice to Applicants. The submitted plan for the validation is attached. |

| ☐ | has been inspected and found to be compliant with standards of GMP equivalent to those laid down in Directive 2003/94/EC and/or Directive 91/412/EEC. |

Reason for the request: ....

....

Name and signature of a responsible officer of the requesting competent authority

....

Date: ....

Appendix 2: Reply form in response to a request for exchange of information

COMPILATION OF COMMUNITY PROCEDURES

REPLY FORM IN RESPONSE TO A REQUEST FOR THE EXCHANGE OF INFORMATION
BETWEEN COMPETENT AUTHORITIES IN THE EEA (Appendix 2)

As requested by the competent authority of ....on ...../...../....., the
competent authority of...

confirms the following:

The company..

Site address..

....
tick box(es) as appropriate

☐ has been authorised in accordance with Art. 40 of Directive 2001/83/EC (Art. 44 Directive 2001/82/EC)
transposed in the following national legislation: .... under the
authorisation reference number ....

for the dosage forms/activities listed on the attached form (appendix 2A).
The company's legally registered address (where different) is:...
....

☐ has been authorised in accordance with Art. 77 of Directive 2001/83/EC (Art. 65 Directive 2001/82/EC)
transposed in the following national legislation: ....
under the authorisation reference number...
The company's legally registered address (where different)..
....

☐ has been authorised in accordance with Art. 13 of Directive 2001/20/EC transposed in the following national
legislation: .... under the authorisation reference number
....for the dosage forms/activities listed on the attached form (appendix 2A).
The company's legally registered address (where different) is:...
....

☐ Has/has not*(delete as needed) completed the post-authorisation process validation plan submitted to support
the application in accordance with GMP

for...

(product name, dosage form, strength, MA number) and in accordance with the scheme in the Notice to
Applicants.

Comments (where validation has not been completed
accordingly):..

☐ has been inspected on ....and found to be/not to be *(delete as needed) compliant with standards
of GMP equivalent to those laid down in Directive 2003/94/EC and/or Directive 91/412/EEC for the dosage
forms/activities listed on, and subject to any conditions identified in, the attached form (appendix 2A).

Name and signature of a responsible officer of the reporting competent authority

....Date:......................

The signing competent authority undertakes to inform the requesting competent authority of any subsequent change
that it becomes aware of affecting the information provided.

Exchange of Information on Manufacturers and Manufacturing or Wholesale
Distribution Authorisations between Competent Authorities in the European Economic
Area

Appendix 2A: List of dosage forms to be appended to Appendix 2

COMPILATION OF COMMUNITY PROCEDURES

Appendix 2A : Dosage forms relating to authorisation/manufacture found to be in compliance with GMP/relevant to exchange of information *(delete all details that do not apply and annotate boxes as follows T = total manufacture, P = partial manufacture, I = import)*:

Sterile products:

Liquid dosage forms (Large Volume Parenterals)
        - aseptically prepared ☐
        - terminally sterilised ☐

Liquid dosage forms (Small Volume Parenterals)
        - aseptically prepared ☐
        - terminally sterilised ☐

Eye drops ☐

Semi-solid dosage forms
Solid dosage forms   - solid fill ☐
                     - freeze-dried ☐

Non-sterile products:
Liquid dosage forms ☐
Semi-solid dosage forms ☐
Solid dosage forms
        - unit dose form (tablets, capsules, ☐
          suppositories, pessaries)
        - multi dose form (powders, granules) ☐

Biological products:
Vaccines ☐
Sera ☐
Blood products ☐
Allergens ☐

Other (describe: e.g. hormones, enzymes of human or animal origin, genetically engineered
products) ☐

Packaging only:
Liquid dosage form
Semi-solid dosage form
Solid dosage form

Laboratory Testing: Chemical ☐   Microbiological ☐   Other ☐

The following restrictions or clarifying remarks apply to the scope of this exchange of information:

....
....
....
....

ADDITIONALLY, FOR MANUFACTURERS IN THIRD COUNTRIES:

For use in man ☐ animals ☐ investigational medicinal products ☐

Tick boxes as appropriate.

Appendix 3: Exchange of Information... following the discovery of serious non-compliance at a third country manufacturer where co-ordinated administrative action may be necessary

COMPILATION OF PROCEDURES

Exchange of Information between Competent Authorities of the European Economic Area
following the discovery of serious non-compliance at a
third country manufacturer where administrative action may be necessary (Appendix 3)

1. Details of Manufacturing Site/ Products		
Inspected site(s):		
Activities carried out	*Manufacture of active substance*	☐
	Manufacture of intermediates	☐
	Manufacture of bulk substance	☐
	Manufacture of finished medicinal product	☐
	Investigational medicinal product	☐
	Packaging	☐
	Laboratory Testing	☐
	Batch Control and release(for shipment to EEA)	☐
2. Details of Inspection		
Inspection date(s)		
	First inspection	☐
	Follow-up inspection	☐
	Re-inspection	☐
Date and brief description of the previous Inspection, if any		
Scope of the inspection	*Product related inspection*	☐
	General GMP inspection	☐
	Other (please explain):	☐
Dosage form (s)	*(Attach appendix 2A if necessary)*	
Name/ Type of product(s)	☐ *human use*	
	☐ *veterinary use*	
EMEA reference number(s), if any		
Marketing Authorisation Holder (MAH)		
Importer (EU)		
Inspected area(s): (Were several production units are in place)	*Unit Nr:*	
	Unit Nr:	
	Unit Nr:	
	Laboratory ☐ *:*	
	Comments:	

Exchange of Information on Manufacturers and Manufacturing or Wholesale
Distribution Authorisations between Competent Authorities in the European Economic
Area

Appendix 3 *(Continued)*

List of deficiencies and observations (critical only)	
Proposed corrective action by company where available (for critical deficiencies only)	
Inspectors evaluation of the manufacturer's action plan and response to the inspection findings (critical only)	
Planned re-inspection	☐ *no*
	☐ *yes, in ....* *(Month, year)* *Type:* ☐ *routine* ☐ *follow-up*
Action taken/ proposed by Member State	
Additional comments :	
Name of responsible authority for inspection	
Phone Number	
Fax Number	
E-Mail	
Name of lead inspector (not mandatory)	
Signature of authorised person at responsible authority	
Date	

Please attachment the following if possible, together with appendix 2A and teleconference details if appropriate:

Products manufactured at site, if known	*Product /Dosage Form*	*Exported to following EU MS*
Human medicinal product(s)		
Veterinary medicinal product(s)		

Guidance on the Occasions when it is Appropriate for Competent Authorities to Conduct Inspections at the Premises of Manufacturers of Active Substances used as Starting Materials

London, 20 September 2006

EMEA/INS/GMP/313538/2006

Note: This document forms part of the Compilation of Community Procedures on Inspections and Exchange of Information. Please check for updates on the EMEA website (Inspections pages).

Guidance on the Occasions when it is Appropriate for Competent Authorities to
Conduct Inspections at the Premises of Manufacturers of Active Substances used as
Starting Materials

Guideline Title:	*Guidance on the occasions when it is appropriate for Competent Authorities to conduct inspections at the premises of Manufacturers of Active Substances used as starting materials[46]*
History:	*This document was developed as guidance for Competent Authorities to ensure a harmonised approach as to when inspections of active substance manufacturers may be appropriate based on the provisions of Art. 111(1) of Directive 2001/83/EC and Art. 80(1) of Directive 2001/82/EC as amended.*
Date of Adoption:	*September 2005*
Date of entry into force:	*1 October 2005*

Introduction

The legal basis for the regulation of medicinal products for Human and Veterinary use is determined by the Community Directives 2001/83/EC and 2001/82/EC, respectively. These Directives have been amended, correspondingly, by Directives 2004/27/EC and Directive 2004/28/EC to, inter alia, permit the inspection by Competent Authorities, under certain circumstances, of premises used to manufacture active substances.

The relevant sections from the amended Directives 2001/83/EC and 2001/82/EC are set out in Annex 1.

Purpose

The purpose of this guidance is to encourage uniformity of approach regarding the decision making process as to when an inspection of a company which manufactures or distributes active substances may be appropriate. Repackaging or relabelling of active substances carried out by a distributor are considered as manufacturing activities.

---

[46] When the term active substance is used in this document it should be taken to mean active substance used as a starting material.

Scope

The scope of this guidance covers the inspection activities of Member State Competent Authorities in relation to active substances that are used in the manufacture of human and/or veterinary medicinal products. This guidance applies to active substances manufactured inside and outside of the European Economic Area (EEA) (approximately 80% of active substances used in the manufacture of medicinal products within the EEA are manufactured outside of the EEA). The scope also includes activities carried out by distributors in line with the full definition of "manufacture of active substances used as starting materials" given in Annex 1 under Article 46(a) of Directive 2001/83/EC and Article /50(a) of Directive 2001/82/EC.

When a Mutual Recognition Agreement (MRA) is in place covering GMP for active substances, and where it is in accordance with the terms of the agreement, inspections performed by the MRA partner authority will take the place of inspections by the competent authorities of the EEA.

Principle

A Competent Authority must be able to satisfy itself that the manufacture and distribution of medicinal products has been carried out in accordance with the principles of good manufacturing practice and that the holders of manufacturing authorisations have only used active substances as starting materials which themselves have been manufactured and distributed in accordance with good manufacturing practice for active substances used as starting materials. Where it has grounds for suspecting non-compliance, the Competent Authority may carry out announced or unannounced inspections at the manufacturer or distributor of the actives substance(s).

> Article 46(f) of Directive 2001/83/EC and Article 50(f) of Directive 2001/82/EC oblige the holder of a manufacturing authorisation to use as starting materials only active substances, which have been manufactured in accordance with the detailed guidelines on good manufacturing practice for starting materials.

When an application for a marketing authorisation, or variation to change or add a new active substance manufacturer, is submitted, the applicant will be required to include a declaration from the Qualified Person of the manufacturing authorisation holder that the active substance(s) concerned is/are manufactured in accordance with the detailed guidelines on good manufacturing practice for starting materials.

It is expected that the holder of the manufacturing authorisation will base such a declaration on carrying out, or having carried out on his behalf, an audit of the manufacturers/distributors of the active substances concerned. Examination, by inspectors, of the audit programmes used by authorisation holders for conducting regular audits (every 2 – 3 years), including review of audit reports, is one of the primary means by which Competent Authorities will determine if manufacturing authorisation holders are in compliance with the above articles.

Where the Competent Authority concludes that a manufacturing authorisation holder has not fulfilled its obligations under Article 46(f) of Directive 2001/83/EC and/or Article 50(f) of Directive 2001/82/EC regulatory action may be taken against the manufacturing authorisation holder and where necessary, appropriate action in connection with products on the market.

In compliance with Article 111 of Directive 2001/83/EC and Article 80 of Directive 2001/82/EC the Competent Authority may carry out an inspection of an active substance manufacturer in order to ensure that a manufacturing authorisation holder has fulfilled its obligations under Article 46(f) and/or Article 50(f) of the above mentioned Directives.

Examples of when Inspection may be appropriate

The following is a list of examples of when the inspection of premises used to manufacture a starting material, which is, in turn, used in the manufacture of a human or veterinary medicinal product, may be required. The legislation provides for unannounced inspections but this is not expected to become routine practice. Member States are expected to reserve unannounced inspections for occasions where such action is appropriate.

1. Directly linked to EU Legislation

(Reference to Directive 2001/83/EC / Directive 2001/82/EC as amended)

1.1. When carried out by a Member State as part of the verification of the particulars submitted in support of an application for a marketing authorisation. This may apply in relation to marketing authorisation applications under national or mutual recognition or decentralised procedures and to application for variations to existing marketing authorisations (Article 19(1)/ Article 23(1))

1.2.   When requested by another Member State where the requesting authority provides a written request detailing why an inspection is necessary. (Article 111(1)/Article 80 (1))

1.3.   When requested by the European Commission where the Commission provides a written request detailing why an inspection is necessary (Article 111(1))/Article 80 (1)

1.4.   When requested by the European Medicines Agency (EMEA) in relation to the assessment of a product under the centralised system or in connection with matters referred to it in accordance with Community legislation (Article 111(1)/ Article 80 (1))

1.5.   When requested by the Commission or the EMEA on behalf of the European Directorate for the Quality of Medicinal Products (EDQM) in order to verify if the data submitted in order to obtain a conformity certificate conforms with the monographs of the European Pharmacopoeia (Ph. Eur.) (Article 111 (1)/ Article 80 (1)) (Res AP/CSP (99)4)

1.6.   When requested by the Commission or the EMEA on behalf of the EDQM where the latter suspects that there are grounds for suspending or withdrawing a conformity certificate (Certificate of Suitability) (Article 111(1)/Article 80(1) (Res AP/CSP (99)4).

1.7.   Where the competent Authority considers that there are grounds for suspecting serious noncompliance with the principles of good manufacturing practice referred to in Article 47/Article 51 (Article 111(1)/ Article 80(1) – see also 2.3 below. This may also have regulatory consequences for relevant manufacturing authorisation holders.

1.8.   Where there is disagreement between Member States on the conclusions from an inspection of a manufacturer of active substances to be used as starting materials for medicinal products (Article 122(3)/ Article 90(4)).

1.9.   Where an uninvolved Member State is requested by the Commission to participate in a re-inspection in another Member State (Article 122(3)/ Article 90)

1.10. When requested by the manufacturer of an active substance located on the territory of a Member State of the EEA. Such an inspection may, for example, be for export purposes Article 111(1)/Article 80(1).

1.11. When requested by a manufacturer of an active substance, which is located in a non European Economic Area (EEA) and non Mutual Recognition Agreement (MRA) country. In such circumstances, at least one holder of a manufacturing authorisation supplied by the active substance manufacturer shall be located in the Member State of the competent authority which is requested to carry out the inspection (Article 111(1)/Article 80(1).

1.12. Where an active substance manufacturer supplies to a number of manufacturing authorisation holders in two or more Member States, the choice of competent authority to carry out the inspection is left to that active substance manufacturer.

2. Other Examples

The following cases are examples for inspection triggers, where there is a suspicion of noncompliance with the GMP principles and guidelines in compliance with provisions of Article 111 of Directive 2001/83/EC and Article 80 of Directive 2001/82/EC. Examples 2.9 & 2.10 represent interfaces between manufacturing of the active substance and the finished medicinal product. It is therefore justified to include them in inspection schemes for medicinal products.

2.1. When analysis of a sample of an active substance used as a starting material carried out by, or on behalf of, the competent authority indicates significant non-compliance with the specification or suitability for use.

2.2. Following a report of a serious adverse reaction and/or recall of a medicinal product in which the quality of the active substance is implicated.

2.3. On receipt of information from another Competent Authority, based inside or outside the EEA, or other well-supported evidence, that activities at the premises are not compliant with the GMP principles. This may include premises located inside or outside the EEA. It may also include invocation of the safeguard clause contained in a MRA where the competent authority considers that it is imperative that an inspection of an active substance manufacturer located in the territory of an MRA partner be carried out.

2.4. Where there are suspicions regarding the authenticity of data, relating to an active substance. This would include data submitted in support of a marketing authorisation application, data provided on Certificates of Analysis or information on the identity of the original manufacturer of an active substance.

2.5. Where, during an inspection of a manufacturer of medicinal products, it is noted that there have been recurrent problems with the quality of individual batches of an active substance from a specific active substance manufacturer.

2.6. When recommended in an inspection report as a consequence of, or follow up to, observations from another inspection.

2.7. Where an inspection carried out on behalf of the EDQM reveals significant non-compliance with GMP principles, the competent authority may consider it appropriate to carry out a follow up inspection.

2.8. When a pharmacopoeial specification has been changed for significant safety reasons and there are grounds for suspecting that it has not been implemented by the active substance manufacturer.

2.9. When the active substance is a biological substance and the manufacturer is not subject to routine repeated inspections. Note: As the characterisation and quality of most biological substances is highly dependent on the production process, their manufacture is considered to be an integral part of the manufacturing process for the dosage form and should be subject to routine inspection.

2.10. When the active substance is presented as sterile and is to be incorporated aseptically during the manufacture of a medicinal product and the manufacturer is not subject to routine repeated inspections. Note: The sterilisation and subsequent aseptic handling of the active substance is considered to be part of the manufacturing process for the dosage form and should be subject to routine inspection. Steps preceding such sterilisation and aseptic handing, or when the substance is not intended to be incorporated aseptically fall under the guidance detailed in section 1 or the other parts of section 2.

2.11. As a measure to ensure that a manufacturing authorisation holder has fulfilled its obligations under Article 46(f) of Directive 2001/83/EC and/or Article 50(f) of Directive 2001/82/EC by virtue of Article 111 of Directive 2001/83/EC or Article 80 of Directive 2001/82/EC to ensure that the legal requirements governing medicinal products are complied with..

References

Directive 2001/82/EC as amended by Directive 2004/28/EC

Directive 2001/83/EC as amended by Directives 2002/98/EC, 2004/24/EC and 2004/27/EC

The Issue and Update
of GMP Certificates

London, 20 September 2006

EMEA/INS/GMP/313535/2006

**Published on Behalf of DG Enterprise and Industry
Directorate General by EMEA (European Medicines
Agency)**

Note: *This document forms part of the Compilation of Community
Procedures on Inspections and Exchange of Information.
Please check for updates on the EMEA website (Inspections
pages).*

Title of Form: *The issue and update of GMP Certificates*

Date of Publishing: *April 2007*

History: *First version*

Date of Adoption: *March 2007*

Date of coming into operation: *By 30 September 2007*

Note: *GMP Certificates are issued, where
appropriate, to manufacturers following an
inspection in accordance with Art. 111(5) of
Directive 2001/83/EC and Art. 80(5) of
Directive 2001/82/EC. They are also entered
into the Community database (EudraGMP) as
required in Arts 111(6) and 80(6) of the same
directives.*

1. *Introduction*

Art. 111 (5) of Directive 2001/83/EC and Art. 80 (5) of Directive 2001/82/EC as amended, require a certificate of Good Manufacturing Practice to be issued to the manufacturer within 90 days of carrying out an inspection if the manufacturer complies with the principles and guidelines of GMP as provided for by Community law. The GMP certificates issued, or the information indicating that a manufacturer does not comply, shall be entered into the EudraGMP Community database.

The requirement specifically refers to inspections referred to in Art. 111 (1) of Directive 2001/83/EC and Art. 80 (1) of Directive 2001/82/EC, as amended. It includes therefore inspections of:

- Manufacturers, importers and contract laboratories according to national and centrally organised inspection programmes

- Active substance manufacturers, in particular where there are grounds for suspecting noncompliance, carried out in accordance with the Community Procedure entitled "Guidance on the occasions when it is appropriate for competent authorities to conduct inspections at the premises of manufacturers of active substances used as starting materials", which includes requests by a manufacturer itself, member state, the Commission or EMEA. It also includes requests by EDQM on behalf of the Commission or EMEA as part of the certification procedure for monographs of the European Pharmacopoeia.

- Marketing authorisation holders in so far as compliance with Good Manufacturing Practice is concerned

- Manufacturers located in third countries,

The requirement applies regardless as to whether the inspections are unannounced, routine or requested by a Member State, the European Commission, European Medicines Agency, EDQM or manufacturer itself.

In addition where appropriate, and where the national competent authority chooses to do so, GMP certificates may be issued following inspection of manufacturers of investigational medicinal products for human use. In any case entry into EudraGMP database will be made to fulfil Art. 11(1)f of Directive 2001/20/EC.

This document is intended to give interpretation on aspects of responsibilities of the issue, renewal and update of GMP certificates.

2. Use of Certificates

GMP certificates are for the purpose of confirming to a manufacturer (whether for active substances or medicinal products) the overall conclusion of an inspection with respect to compliance with GMP. In some cases, particularly outside of the EEA, they may be used by applicants to support regulatory submissions. Within the EEA they do not replace confirmation of the holding of a manufacturing authorisation. The GMP status of third country manufacturing sites for medicinal products and active substances may be confirmed using the EudraGMP database or until this is fully operational, confirmed using the Community procedure for the exchange of information.

For active substances, the supporting document in regulatory submissions is the declaration by the Qualified Person of the manufacturing authorisation holder that uses the active substance as a starting material.

GMP certificates issued by EEA authorities are recognised within the framework of WHO and to fulfil obligations under the Mutual Recognition Agreements were agreed.

3. When GMP Certificates should be issued and EudraGMP database entry

3.1 Responsibility for issue of GMP Certificates

For medicinal products responsibility for issuing GMP certificates and placing entries into EudraGMP rests with the supervisory authority, including those certificates issued following inspections performed at the request of the Commission, EMEA, EDQM, Member State or an active substance manufacturer as well as inspections performed by another member state on behalf of the supervisory authority. If there is more than one supervisory authority for third country manufacturers then these authorities should agree on who will take on this responsibility but normally one of the supervisory authorities will lead the inspection and this one should take responsibility.

In the case of an inspection of an active substance manufacturer, as the concept of supervisory authority does not apply, responsibility for the GMP certificate and EudraGMP entry rests with the authority that carries out or leads the inspection.

Following each relevant inspection, a report in accordance with the Community format should be produced by the responsible inspector or inspection team, which should contain a clear statement as to whether or not the manufacturer complies with the principles and guidelines of GMP as provided for in Community legislation. Where this is the case, within 90 days of the last day of the inspection concerned, the supervisory authority should issue a GMP certificate in accordance with the Community format to the manufacturer that underwent the inspection. In the case of non-compliance see the relevant Community procedure.

Each certificate should include a reference that enables traceability within the inspectorate that issued it so that the inspectorate can respond promptly to enquiries regarding authenticity.

Duplicates of valid GMP certificates may be issued in response to a request from the manufacturer, or MRA partner authority in accordance with the terms of the agreement.

3.2 Circumstances where the issue of a certificate to a manufacturer may not be applicable (other than in cases of failure to comply with GMP).

If the aim of any particular visit to a site is not primarily to assess compliance with GMP and the issue of a certificate is therefore not foreseen, then this should be made clear to the concerned manufacturer at the outset.

It may not be appropriate to issue a GMP certificate following an inspection in response to an application for, or variation to a manufacturing authorisation, even if the outcome of the inspection is positive with respect to the application, particularly where approval is based upon plans and commitments rather than a direct inspection of facilities and operations.

Normally, an inspection is conducted in a single visit over a consecutive period of days but it may be split into a number of separate visits. Provided the subsequent visits occur within a reasonable period of time of the first visit, as decided by national procedures, the individual visits may collectively be considered as one inspection for which a single certificate will be issued within 90 days of the last day of the last visit. The manufacturer should be informed of this beforehand.

A GMP certificate is not issued to a third country manufacturer when the GMP status has been verified using the distant assessment procedure described in the Community procedure on co-coordinating the verification of the GMP status of manufacturers in third countries. A EudraGMP database entry is nevertheless made (see section 3.6).

Depending on national procedures, GMP certificates need not be issued to manufacturers of investigational medicinal products. Nevertheless EudraGMP entry will be required (see section 3.7).

3.3 Scope of individual certificates

The certificate should include all operations deemed to be GMP compliant as a result of the inspection. For large sites in the EEA this may not necessarily include all authorised operations as several inspections may be needed to assess all the authorised operations over a period of time as agreed in Community procedures.

Inspections performed at third country manufacturers are often particularly restricted in scope and provision is made for this in part 2 of the certificate format. For ease of database entry and to reduce the use of free text, the EudraGMP database contains standard phrases to cover the most common situations.

3.4 Responsibility for EudraGMP database entry

The supervisory authority may enter the details of the certificate into the EudraGMP before or at the time the certificate itself is issued to the manufacturer, or as soon as possible thereafter. Database entries will have a status of draft, current or withdrawn.

3.5 EudraGMP entry for GMP Certificates issued by MRA Partners

The information from GMP certificates issued by MRA partner authorities is, on the first occasion, input into EudraGMP by the requesting authority in the EEA. Once the necessary agreements are in place it is suggested that subsequent certificates for the same site are input directly by the MRA partner. In the absence of such an agreement subsequent certificates will continue to be input by the requesting authority in the EEA.

3.6 Distant Assessment

When the GMP status of a manufacturer located in a third country has been verified using the distant assessment procedure described in the Community procedure on co-coordinating the verification of the GMP status of manufacturers in third countries, no certificate should be issued to the manufacturer in question but an entry in the EudraGMP database should nevertheless be made by the supervisory authority indicating in the relevant field that the distant assessment procedure was followed.

3.7 Investigational Medicinal Products for Human Use (IMPs)

Directive 2001/83/EC does not make reference to the issue of GMP certificates following an inspection of a manufacturer of IMPs, however Member States may choose to do so. In order to facilitate the exchange of information on clinical trials Art. 11 of Directive 2001/20/EC requires a reference to inspections to be included in a European database and it has been agreed that the appropriate database is EudraGMP database for GMP inspections of manufacturers of IMPs. Therefore an entry should be made whether or not a certificate is issued to the manufacturer in question.

4. Non-compliance with GMP

A separate Community procedure deals with the handling of non-compliance.

5. Renewal and update of GMP Certificates

5.1   A certificate itself is not renewed, as it is a declaration of the status of GMP compliance at a particular point in time connected with a satisfactory inspection outcome. A new certificate will be issued following the next inspection, if appropriate. Entries in EudraGMP however require a different approach.

EudraGMP requires the Member State inputting new information to decide whether the new certificate replaces an existing entry for the site in question, in which case they must take action to withdraw the superseded information, or, whether the information is in addition to the existing information, in which case the information being supplemented should remain in the database. In the case of third country manufacturers with more than one supervisory authority it is possible that a different authority carries out the subsequent inspection but it is not possible for an authority to withdraw a database entry made by another authority. Therefore both authorities have to work together to maintain the database in order that superseded information is withdrawn by the supervisory authority that originally input it.

However, sometimes it will be necessary to retain some of the existing information if it is not superseded following a new inspection. This would happen, for example, when the most recent inspection does not cover everything covered by the previous inspection. In this case the following action is appropriate:

- Withdraw the existing certificate (or have the original issuing authority withdraw it) and re-issue it having removed the superseded information but retaining the original date of inspection.

- Issue a further new certificate with new information and the most recent inspection date.

5.2 Administrative updates and re-issue

An updated certificate may be issued to a manufacturer and input into EudraGMP by the authority that issued the last certificate at the request of a manufacturer when administrative changes occur that affect the details appearing on the certificate and where the supervisory authority agrees that a re-inspection is not required. An example would be a change in the name of the manufacturer. These new certificates will superseded the existing certificate but will maintain the original date of inspection, as an inspection will not have been carried out.

6. *Closure of manufacturing site*

Member states should take steps to ensure that when a site under its supervision ceases to operate, any GMP certificate is withdrawn from the Community database along with any manufacturing authorisation and noncompliance information.

Appendix

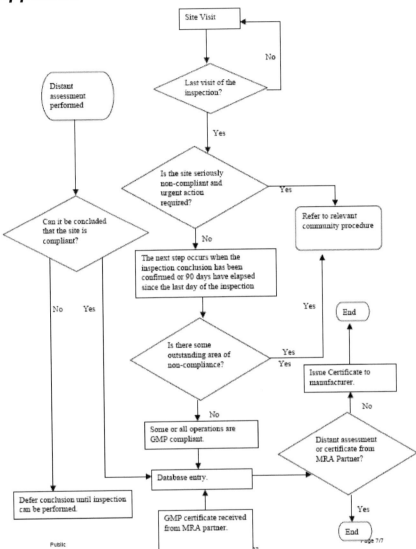

A Model for Risk Based Planning for Inspections of Pharmaceutical Manufacturers

London, 20 September 2006

EMEA/INS/GMP/313535/2006

Published in Agreement with the European Commission by EMEA (European Medicines Agency)

Note: *This document forms part of the Compilation of Community Procedures on Inspections and Exchange of Information. Please check for updates on the EMEA website (Inspections pages).*

This procedure is optional and shall be used as a model which will be refined with experience.

Title: *A model for risk based planning for inspections of pharmaceutical manufacturers*

Date of Adoption: *November 2007*

Date of entry into force: *April 2008*

Supersedes: *not applicable*

Note: *This procedure is optional.*

Section 4.4 includes proposals by ICH Q9 drafting group. Member States may use other descriptors for assigning the compliance factor referred to in section 4.4.4. Further categories may be defined as appropriate. The factors identified in section 4.4.3 may affect the compliance factor determined in section 4.4.4.

1. Introduction

1.1 According to directive 2001/83/EC, 2001/82/EC and 2001/20/EC, respectively, the Competent Authority shall ensure, by means of repeated inspections, and if necessary unannounced inspections, that the legal requirements governing medicinal products are complied with. The Competent Authority may also carry out unannounced inspections at the premises of manufacturers of active substances used as starting materials, or at the premises of marketing authorisation holders whenever it considers that there are grounds for suspecting noncompliance with the principles and guidelines of good manufacturing practice.

1.2 A risk based approach to inspection planning will enable the frequency, depth and breadth of inspections to be determined accordingly. This will allow flexible and effective administration, whilst maintaining a high level of patient safety.

1.3 Competent Authorities of the Member States need to develop a systematic and risk-based approach to make the best use of their surveillance and enforcement resources while maximizing the impact of those resources on the public health.

1.4   Each Competent Authority should have a written procedure that covers the preparation, realization and supervision of an annual inspection programme. This programme should ensure that the extent and frequency of inspections can be adhered to as planned. Sufficient resources must be determined and made available to ensure that the designated programme of inspections can be carried out in an appropriate manner.

2. Purpose

2.1   This document outlines recommendations for a risk based planning system according to which sites that fall under regulatory supervision are subject to inspection.

2.2   It is intended that each GMP Pharmaceutical Inspectorate uses the document as the basis for developing and implementing its own annual inspection programme.

2.3   Competent authorities are free to develop and/or use the most appropriate risk tool to achieve this aim based on the elements outlined in this document.

3. Scope

3.1   This procedure covers the field of inspection of manufacturers of medicinal products, investigational medicinal products, biological substances and sterilisation of active substances.

3.2   This procedure covers both human and veterinary medicinal products.

4. Procedure

4.1 Principle

Planning and scheduling of inspections is realized as follows:

- compile all relevant sites/facilities in a list

- Establish risk ranking (based on product risk and compliance factor) for each site

- establish the necessary expenditure of inspection time for each site

- establish the inspection frequency

- prioritize inspections by calculating individual inspection dates per site

- establish risk ranking

4.2 Inspections-site list

All sites/facilities that are subject to inspection are to be listed in an appropriate up to date list. This list could include the following information:

List of sites subject to inspection
• Name and address of inspectorate
• Name of the competent inspector
• Name and address of each site
• Dosage forms manufactured per site
• Number of deficiencies categorised according to the Definition of Significant Deficiencies laid down in the GMP Inspection Report - Community format
• Date of the last inspection per site
• Number of inspection days required per site
• Inspection frequency per site
• Date of the next inspection

4.3 Expenditure of time

The following table presents guidance values for the required inspection time per type of site. The type of manufacturing site is classified by the relevant dosage form and the manufacturing process, respectively. The risk ranking of the type of manufacturing site is based on the assessment of the risk severity, probability of occurrence and probability of detection with respect to product quality defects and process safety issues. This risk ranking assumes that critical processes and products (e.g. sterile products) would have a higher public health consequence than less critical products and processes; hence these products are given a higher weight.

Classification of manufacturing or importation sites according to the type of product/process		Overall inspection days
1.1	**Sterile Products**	
	1.1.1 Aseptically prepared (list of dosage forms) 1.1.1.1 Large volume liquids 1.1.1.2 Lyophilisates 1.1.1.3 Semi-solids 1.1.1.4 Small volume liquids 1.1.1.5 Solids and implants	**> 10**
	1.1.2 Terminally sterilised (list of dosage forms) 1.1.2.1 Large volume liquids 1.1.2.2 Semi-solids 1.1.2.3 Small volume liquids 1.1.2.4 Solids and implants	**> 8**
	1.1.3 Batch certification only	**> 1**
1.2	**Non-sterile products**	
	1.2.1 Non-sterile products (list of dosage forms) 1.2.1.1 Capsules, hard shell 1.2.1.2 Capsules, soft shell 1.2.1.3 Chewing gums 1.2.1.4 Impregnated matrices 1.2.1.5 Liquids for external use 1.2.1.6 Liquids for internal use 1.2.1.7 Medicinal gases 1.2.1.8 Other solid dosage forms 1.2.1.9 Pressurised preparations 1.2.1.10 Radionuclide generators 1.2.1.11 Semi-solids 1.2.1.12 Suppositories 1.2.1.13 Tablets 1.2.1.14 Transdermal patches 1.2.1.15 Intraruminal devices 1.2.1.16 Veterinary premixes	**> 4**
	1.2.2 Batch certification only	**> 1**
1.3	**Biological medicinal products**	
	1.3.1 Biological medicinal products 1.3.1.1 Blood products 1.3.1.2 Immunological products 1.3.1.3 Cell therapy products 1.3.1.4 Gene therapy products 1.3.1.5 Biotechnology products 1.3.1.6 Human or animal extracted products	**> 7**

	1.3.2 Batch certification only (list of product types) 1.3.2.1 Blood products 1.3.2.2 Immunological products 1.3.2.3 Cell therapy products 1.3.2.4 Gene therapy products 1.3.2.5 Biotechnology products 1.3.2.6 Human or animal extracted products	**> 1**
1.2	**Non-sterile products**	
	1.2.1 Non-sterile products (list of dosage forms) 1.2.1.1 Capsules, hard shell 1.2.1.2 Capsules, soft shell 1.2.1.3 Chewing gums 1.2.1.4 Impregnated matrices 1.2.1.5 Liquids for external use 1.2.1.6 Liquids for internal use 1.2.1.7 Medicinal gases 1.2.1.8 Other solid dosage forms 1.2.1.9 Pressurised preparations 1.2.1.10 Radionuclide generators 1.2.1.11 Semi-solids 1.2.1.12 Suppositories 1.2.1.13 Tablets 1.2.1.14 Transdermal patches 1.2.1.15 Intraruminal devices 1.2.1.16 Veterinary premixes	**> 4**
	1.2.2 Batch certification only	**> 1**
1.3	**Biological medicinal products**	
	1.3.1 Biological medicinal products 1.3.1.1 Blood products 1.3.1.2 Immunological products 1.3.1.3 Cell therapy products 1.3.1.4 Gene therapy products 1.3.1.5 Biotechnology products 1.3.1.6 Human or animal extracted products	**> 7**
	1.3.2 Batch certification only (list of product types) 1.3.2.1 Blood products 1.3.2.2 Immunological products 1.3.2.3 Cell therapy products 1.3.2.4 Gene therapy products 1.3.2.5 Biotechnology products 1.3.2.6 Human or animal extracted products	**> 1**
1.2	**Non-sterile products**	
	1.2.1 Non-sterile products (list of dosage forms) 1.2.1.1 Capsules, hard shell 1.2.1.2 Capsules, soft shell 1.2.1.3 Chewing gums 1.2.1.4 Impregnated matrices	**> 4**

	1.2.1.5 Liquids for external use 1.2.1.6 Liquids for internal use 1.2.1.7 Medicinal gases 1.2.1.8 Other solid dosage forms 1.2.1.9 Pressurised preparations 1.2.1.10 Radionuclide generators 1.2.1.11 Semi-solids 1.2.1.12 Suppositories 1.2.1.13 Tablets 1.2.1.14 Transdermal patches 1.2.1.15 Intraruminal devices 1.2.1.16 Veterinary premixes	
	1.2.2 Batch certification only	**> 1**
1.3	**Biological medicinal products**	
	1.3.1 Biological medicinal products 1.3.1.1 Blood products 1.3.1.2 Immunological products 1.3.1.3 Cell therapy products 1.3.1.4 Gene therapy products 1.3.1.5 Biotechnology products 1.3.1.6 Human or animal extracted products	**> 7**
	1.3.2 Batch certification only (list of product types) 1.3.2.1 Blood products 1.3.2.2 Immunological products 1.3.2.3 Cell therapy products 1.3.2.4 Gene therapy products 1.3.2.5 Biotechnology products 1.3.2.6 Human or animal extracted products	**> 1**
1.4	**Other products or manufacturing activity** (any other relevant manufacturing activity/product type that is not covered above e.g. sterilisation of active substances, manufacture of biological active starting materials (when required by national legislation), herbal or homeopathic products, bulk or total manufacturing, etc).	
	1.4.1 Manufacture of: 1.4.1.1 Herbal products 1.4.1.2 Homoeopathic products 1.4.1.3 Biological active starting materials	**> 3**
	1.4.2 Sterilisation of active substances/excipients/finished product: 1.4.2.1 Filtration 1.4.2.2 Dry heat 1.4.2.3 Moist heat 1.4.2.4 Chemical 1.4.2.5 Gamma irradiation 1.4.2.6 Electron beam	**>2**

1.5	Packaging only	

	1.5.1 Primary packing
	    1.5.1.1 Capsules, hard shell
	    1.5.1.2 Capsules, soft shell
	    1.5.1.3 Chewing gums
	    1.5.1.4 Impregnated matrices
	    1.5.1.5 Liquids for external use
	    1.5.1.6 Liquids for internal use
	    1.5.1.7 Medicinal gases
	    1.5.1.8 Other solid dosage forms
	    1.5.1.9 Pressurised preparations
	    1.5.1.10 Radionuclide generators
	    1.5.1.11 Semi-solids
	    1.5.1.12 Suppositories
	    1.5.1.13 Tablets
	    1.5.1.14 Transdermal patches
	    1.5.1.15 Intraruminal devices
	    1.5.1.16 Veterinary premixes
		> 2

	1.5.2 Secondary packing	> 1
1.6	Quality control testing	
	1.6.1 Microbiological: sterility 1.6.2 Microbiological: non-sterility 1.6.3 Chemical/Physical 1.6.4 Biological	> 2

The overall inspection days are guidance values and include the necessary time for preparation and report of the inspection and represent the total personnel expenditure (e.g. 10 overall inspection days equals in 2 inspectors inspecting for 5 days or 4 inspectors inspecting for 2½ days; preparation and report time included).

Depending on the

- type of inspection (full vs. part inspection),

- complexity of the site (size, variety of facilities),

- complexity of the manufacturing process (type and sequence of operations, process controls applied),

- the complexity of the product and its therapeutic significance and

- patient exposure

the required inspection time may be adjusted accordingly.

4.4 Frequency of inspections

4.4.1 Large companies may be inspected department by department, a full general GMP inspection being completed at least every five years. Generally the interval between inspections should not exceed 3 years as lack of continuity may give rise to lower awareness of current GMP or allow significant deficiencies to develop. The necessity to carry out immediate inspections e.g. due to product quality defects or significant changes of building, equipment or processes is not affected.

4.4.2 Companies representing a low risk and meeting the expectation of GMP at a high level do not have to be inspected as often as the ones that manufacture products or perform activities representing great risk and operate with great deficiencies. It should be stressed that the activities of the individual company (e.g. products and dosage forms manufactured, units and substances handled and personnel, premises and equipment involved in the manufacture) and its past record of GMP compliance should be taken into consideration when planning the frequency and duration of inspection. Accordingly a review of the observations arising from the last inspection including all deficiencies will form a major precondition for the subsequent decision on an adequate inspection frequency.

4.4.3 To define the frequency of inspections the competent authority should take into account, amongst others, factors such as:

- The agency's knowledge of the company (overall compliance status and history of the company or facility);

- Results of product testing by OMCL´s;

- Number and significance of quality defects (e.g. recall);

- Results of previous inspections;

- Compliance information from agencies/bodies outside the EU;

- Major changes of building, equipment, processes, key personnel;

- Experience with manufacturing of a product (e.g., frequency, volume, number of batches).

4.4.4 Generally the frequency of inspections can be categorized as follows:

Category	Description[2]	Inspection interval
Compliance Factor I Poor Compliance	The last inspection revealed critical and/or more than/equal to six (> 6) major deficiencies	1 year
Compliance Factor II Acceptable Compliance	The last two inspections revealed no critical and less than six (< 6) major deficiencies	2 years
Compliance Factor III Good Compliance	The last two inspections revealed no critical and major deficiencies	3 years

[2] Deficiencies are categorized according to the Definition of Significant Deficiencies laid down in the GMP Inspection report - Community format.

4.5 Calculation of the next inspection date

The calculation of the next inspection date results from the last inspection date and the inspectorate's risk assessment process.

4.6 Responsibilities and supervision

The responsibility for the compilation and supervision of an annual inspection programme should be defined within the GMP Pharmaceutical Inspectorate. A periodical review of the inspection programme should ensure that serious deviations from the time plan are noticed and corrective actions taken as necessary.

Forms
Used by Regulators

GMP Inspection Report - Community Format

London, 20 September 2006

EMEA/INS/GMP/313539/2006

**Published on Behalf of the European Commission by
EMEA (European Medicines Agency)**

Note: *This document forms part of the Compilation of Community
Procedures on Inspections and Exchange of Information.
Please check for updates on the EMEA website (Inspections
pages).*

Guideline Title: *GMP Inspection report - Community format*

History: *A new Community format for a GMP
inspection report has been established in
accordance with Art. 47 of Directive
2004/27/EC and Art. 51 of Directive
2004/28/EC amending Directives 2001/83/EC
and 2001/82/EC respectively. The new format
superceeds the format published in 1999,
upon which it is based.*

Date of Adoption: *April 2005.*

Date of entry into force: *1 October 2005.*

Content:
- *GMP Inspection report – Community format*
- *Definition of Significant Deficiencies*

Report Reference no.:		
Inspected site(s):	*Name and full address of the inspected site.*	
Activities Carried out:	*Manufacture of active substance*	☐
	Manufacture of finished product	☐
	Manufacture of intermediate or bulk	☐
	Packaging only	☐
	Importing	☐
	Laboratory testing	☐
	Batch control and batch release	☐
	Storage and distribution	☐
	Investigational medicinal products	☐
	Other _____	☐
Inspection date(s):	*Date(s), month, year.*	
Inspector(s):	*Name(s) of the inspector(s).*	
	Name(s) of expert / assessor (if applicable).	
	Name(s) of the Competent Authority(ies).	
References:	*Reference number of Marketing and / or Manufacturing Authorisations*	
	EMEA reference number(s).(If the inspection is an EMEA inspection).	

Introduction:	Short description of the company and the activities of the company. _For inspections in non-EEA countries,_ it should be stated whether the Competent Authority of the country, where the inspection took place, was informed of the inspection and whether the Competent Authority took part in the inspection. Date of previous inspection. Name(s) of Inspector(s) involved in previous inspection. Major changes since the previous inspection.

Brief report of the inspection activities undertaken:	
Scope of Inspection:	Short description of the inspection (Product related, process related inspection and/or General GMP inspection, reference to specific dosage forms where appropriate). The reason for the inspection should be specified (e.g. new marketing application, routine, investigation of product defect.
Inspected area(s):	Each inspected area should be specified.
Activities not inspected:	Where necessary attention should be drawn to areas or activities not subject to inspection on this occasion.
Personnel met during the inspection:	The names and titles of key personnel met should be specified (listed in annex).

Inspectors findings and observations relevant to the inspection; and deficiencies:	*Relevant headings from The Rules Governing Medicinal Products in the European Community, Good Manufacturing Practice for Medicinal Products Vol. IV. (Guide to GMP, Basic Requirements, relevant for scope of inspection).* *This section can link the findings to the deficiencies and be used to explain classification.* *The detail in the narrative of this section of the report may be reduced where a Site Master File acceptable to the reporting authority has been submitted to the Competent Authority.*
Headings to be used *New headings may be introduced when relevant*	Overview of inspection findings from last inspection and the corrective action taken. Quality Management Personnel Premises and Equipment Documentation Production Quality Control Contract Manufacture and Analysis Complaints and Product Recall Self Inspection
Distribution and Shipment:	e.g. Compliance with Good Distribution Practice
Questions raised relating to the assessment of a marketing application:	e.g. Pre-authorisation Inspections
Other specific issues identified:	e.g. Relevant future changes announced by company
Site Master File:	Assessment of SMF if any; date of SMF
Miscellaneous: Samples taken	

Annexes attached:	*List of any annexes attached*

List of Deficiencies classified into critical, major and others:	All deficiencies should be listed and the relevant reference to the EU GMP Guide and other relevant EU Guidelines should be mentioned. All deficiencies found should be listed even if corrective action has taken place straight away. If the deficiencies are related to the assessment of the marketing application it should be clearly stated. The company should be asked to inform the Inspectorate about the proposed time schedule for corrections and on progress.
Recommendations:	To the Committee requesting the inspection or to the Competent / Enforcement Authority for the site inspected.
Summary and conclusions:	The Inspector(s) should state whether, within the scope of the inspection, the company operates in accordance with the EU GMP Rules provided, where relevant, that appropriate corrective actions are implemented and mention any other item to alert requesting authority. Reference may be made to conclusions recorded in other documents, such as the close-out letter, depending on national procedures.
Name(s): Signatures(s): Organisation(s): Date: Distribution of Report:	The inspection report should be signed and dated by the inspector(s)/assessors having participated in the inspection.

2. Definition of Significant Deficiencies

2.1 Critical Deficiency:

A deficiency which has produced, or leads to a significant risk of producing either a product which is harmful to the human or veterinary patient or a product which could result in a harmful residue in a food producing animal.

2.2 Major Deficiency:

A non-critical deficiency:

which has produced or may produce a product, which does not comply with its marketing authorisation;

or

which indicates a major deviation from EU Good Manufacturing Practice;

or

(within EU) which indicates a major deviation from the terms of the manufacturing authorisation;

or

which indicates a failure to carry out satisfactory procedures for release of batches or (within EU) a failure of the Qualified Person to fulfil his legal duties;

or

a combination of several "other" deficiencies, none of which on their own may be major, but which may together represent a major deficiency and should be explained and reported as such;

2.3 Other Deficiency:

A deficiency, which cannot be classified as either critical or major, but which indicates a departure from good manufacturing practice.

(A deficiency may be "other" either because it is judged as minor, or because there is insufficient information to classify it as a major or critical).

Community Basic Format for Manufacturers Authorisation

London, 20 September 2006

EMEA/INS/GMP/313549/2006

**Published on Behalf of the European Commission by
EMEA (European Medicines Agency)**

Note: *This document forms part of the Compilation of Community
Procedures on Inspections and Exchange of Information.
Please check for updates on the EMEA website (Inspections
pages).*

Title of Form: *Community Basic Format for Manufacturers Authorisation[47]*

Date of publishing: *April 2003*

History: *A new Community format for a manufacturing authorisation was been established in accordance with Art. 47 of Directive 2004/27/EC and Art. 51 of Directive 2004/28/EC amending Directives 2001/83/EC and 2001/82/EC respectively. The new format superceeded the format published in 1999, upon which it was based. The new format which had been adopted in September 2005 was subsequently enhanced to facilitate EudraGMP database functionality.*

Date of Adoption: *April 2003*

Date of coming into operation: *by 31 December 2006*

Note: *Manufacturing authorisations are to be entered into the Community database (EudraGMP) as referred to in Art. 40(4) of Directive 2001/83/EC and Art. 44(4) of Directive 2001/82/EC.*

Content:

- *Community Basic Format for Manufacturers Authorisation*
- *Annexes 1 and/or 2 -Scope of Authorisation*
- *Annex 3 (Optional) -Address(es) of Contract Manufacturing Sites*
- *Annex 4 (Optional) -Address(es) of Contract Laboratories*
- *Annex 5 (Optional)-Name of Qualified Person*
- *Annex 6 (Optional) -Name of person responsible for quality control / production*
- *Annex 7 (Optional) -Date of Inspection on which authorisation granted*
- *Annex 8 (Optional) -Products authorised for manufacture/import*

---

[47] The authorisation referred to in paragraph 40(1) of Directive 2001/83/EC and 44(1) of Directive 2001/82/EC, as amended, shall also be required for imports coming from third countries into a Member State.

Community Basic Format for Manufacturers Authorisation[48]

1. Authorisation number

2. Name of authorisation holder

3. Address(es) of manufacturing site(s)

(All authorised sites should be listed if not covered by separate licences)

4. Legally registered address of authorisation holder

5. Scope of authorisation and dosage forms[49]   ANNEX 1 and/ or ANNEX 2

   (Separate Annexes for different sites should be used if not covered by separate licences)

6. Legal basis of authorisation

7. Name of responsible officer of the competent authority of the member state granting the manufacturing authorisation

8. Signature

9. Date

10. Annexes attached   Annex 1 and/or Annex 2

   Optional Annexes as required:

   Annex 3 (Addresses of Contract Manufacturing Site(s))

   Annex 4 (Addresses of Contract Laboratories)

   Annex 5 (Name of Qualified Person)

   Annex 6 (Name of responsible persons)

   Annex 7 (Date of inspection on which authorisation granted, scope of last inspection)

   Annex 8 (Manufactured/ imported products authorised)

---

[48] The authorisation referred to in paragraph 40(1) of Directive 2001/83/EC and 44(1) of Directive 2001/82/EC, as amended, shall also be required for imports coming from third countries into a Member State.

[49] The Competent Authority is responsible for appropriate linking of the authorisation with the manufacturer's application (Art. 42(3) of Directive 2001/83/EC and Art. 46(3) of Directive 2001/82/EC as amended).

SCOPE OF AUTHORISATION (delete the sections that do not apply)   **ANNEX 1**

Name and address of the site:

☐ Human Medicinal Products

☐ Veterinary Medicinal Products

AUTHORISED OPERATIONS

☐ Manufacturing Operations (according to part 1)

☐ Importation of Medicinal Products (according to part 2)

Part 1 - MANUFACTURING OPERATIONS

- authorised manufacturing operations include total and partial manufacturing (including various processes of dividing up, packaging or presentation), batch release and certification, importation, storage and distribution of specified dosage forms unless informed to the contrary;
- quality control testing and/or release and batch certification activities without manufacturing operations should be specified under the relevant items;

- if the company is engaged in manufacture of products with special requirements e.g. radiopharmaceuticals or products containing penicillin, sulphonamides, cytotoxics, cephalosporins, substances with hormonal activity or other or potentially hazardous active ingredients this should be stated under the relevant product type and dosage form (applicable to all sections of Part 1 apart from sections 1.5.2 and 1.6)

1.1	**Sterile Products**
	1.1.1 Aseptically prepared (list of dosage forms) 1.1.1.1 Large volume liquids 1.1.1.2 Lyophilisates 1.1.1.3 Semi-solids 1.1.1.4 Small volume liquids 1.1.1.5 Solids and implants 1.1.1.6 Other aseptically prepared products <free text>
	1.1.2 Terminally sterilised (list of dosage forms) 1.1.2.1 Large volume liquids 1.1.2.2 Semi-solids 1.1.2.3 Small volume liquids 1.1.2.4 Solids and implants 1.1.2.5 Other terminally sterilised prepared products <free text>
	1.1.3 Batch certification only

1.2	Non-sterile products
	1.2.1 Non-sterile products (list of dosage forms)
	1.2.1.1 Capsules, hard shell
	1.2.1.2 Capsules, soft shell
	1.2.1.3 Chewing gums
	1.2.1.4 Impregnated matrices
	1.2.1.5 Liquids for external use
	1.2.1.6 Liquids for internal use
	1.2.1.7 Medicinal gases
	1.2.1.8 Other solid dosage forms
	1.2.1.9 Pressurised preparations
	1.2.1.10 Radionuclide generators
	1.2.1.11 Semi-solids
	1.2.1.12 Suppositories
	1.2.1.13 Tablets
	1.2.1.14 Transdermal patches
	1.2.1.15 Intraruminal devices
	1.2.1.16 Veterinary premixes
	1.2.1.17 Other non-sterile medicinal product <free text>
	1.2.2 Batch certification only
1.3	**Biological medicinal products**
	1.3.1 Biological medicinal products
	1.3.1.1 Blood products
	1.3.1.2 Immunological products
	1.3.1.3 Cell therapy products
	1.3.1.4 Gene therapy products
	1.3.1.5 Biotechnology products
	1.3.1.6 Human or animal extracted products
	1.3.1.7 Other biological medicinal products <free text>
	1.3.2 Batch certification only (list of product types)
	1.3.2.1 Blood products
	1.3.2.2 Immunological products
	1.3.2.3 Cell therapy products
	1.3.2.4 Gene therapy products
	1.3.2.5 Biotechnology products
	1.3.2.6 Human or animal extracted products
	1.3.2.7 Other biological medicinal products <free text>

1.4	Other products or manufacturing activity (any other relevant manufacturing activity/product type that is not covered above e.g. sterilisation of active substances, manufacture of biological active starting materials (when required by national legislation), herbal or homeopathic products, bulk or total manufacturing, etc).
	1.4.1 Manufacture of:
	1.4.1.1 Herbal products
	1.4.1.2 Homoeopathic products
	1.4.1.3 Biological active starting materials
	1.4.1.4 Other <free text>
	1.4.2 Sterilisation of active substances/excipients/finished product:
	1.4.2.1 Filtration
	1.4.2.2 Dry heat
	1.4.2.3 Moist heat
	1.4.2.4 Chemical
	1.4.2.5 Gamma irradiation
	1.4.2.6 Electron beam
	1.4.3 Others <free text>
1.5	**Packaging only**
	1.5.1 Primary packing
	1.5.1.1 Capsules, hard shell
	1.5.1.2 Capsules, soft shell
	1.5.1.3 Chewing gums
	1.5.1.4 Impregnated matrices
	1.5.1.5 Liquids for external use
	1.5.1.6 Liquids for internal use
	1.5.1.7 Medicinal gases
	1.5.1.8 Other solid dosage forms
	1.5.1.9 Pressurised preparations
	1.5.1.10 Radionuclide generators
	1.5.1.11 Semi-solids
	1.5.1.12 Suppositories
	1.5.1.13 Tablets
	1.5.1.14 Transdermal patches
	1.5.1.15 Intraruminal devices
	1.5.1.16 Veterinary premixes
	1.5.1.17 Other non-sterile medicinal products <free text>
	1.5.2 Secondary packing
1.6	**Quality control testing**
	1.6.1 Microbiological: sterility
	1.6.2 Microbiological: non-sterility
	1.6.3 Chemical/Physical
	1.6.4 Biological

Any restrictions or clarifying remarks related to the scope of these Manufacturing operations

....

....

ANNEX 1 (contd)

Part 2 - IMPORTATION OF MEDICINAL PRODUCTS	
- authorised importation activities without manufacturing activity	
- authorised importation activities include storage and distribution unless informed to the contrary	
2.1	**Quality control testing of imported medicinal products**
	2.1.1 Microbiological: sterility
	2.1.2 Microbiological: non-sterility
	2.1.3 Chemical/Physical
	2.1.4 Biological
2.2	**Batch certification of imported medicinal products**
	2.2.1 Sterile Products
	2.2.1.1 Aseptically prepared
	2.2.1.2 Terminally sterilised
	2.2.2 Non-sterile products
	2.2.3 Biological medicinal products
	2.2.3.1 Blood products
	2.2.3.2 Immunological products
	2.2.3.3 Cell therapy products
	2.2.3.4 Gene therapy products
	2.2.3.5 Biotechnology products
	2.2.3.6 Human or animal extracted products
	2.2.3.7 Other biological medicinal products <free text>
	2.2.4 Other importation activities (any other relevant importation activity that is not covered above e.g. importation of radiopharmaceuticals, medicinal gases, herbal or homeopathic products, etc.)
	2.2.4.1 Radiopharmaceuticals/Radionuclide generators
	2.2.4.2 Medicinal gases
	2.2.4.3 Herbal products
	2.2.4.4 Homoeopathic products
	2.2.4.5 Biological active starting materials
	2.2.4.6 Other <free text>

Any restrictions or clarifying remarks related to the scope of these Importing operations

....
....

SCOPE OF AUTHORISATION (delete the sections that do not apply or use yes/no) ANNEX 2

Name and address of the site:

☐ Human Investigational Medicinal Products   for phase I, II, III clinical trials (optional)

AUTHORISED OPERATIONS

☐ Manufacturing Operations of Investigational Medicinal Products (according to part 1)

☐ Importation of Investigational Medicinal Products (according to part 2)

Part 1 - MANUFACTURING OPERATIONS OF INVESTIGATIONAL MEDICINAL PRODUCTS

- authorised manufacturing operations include total and partial manufacturing (including various processes of dividing up, packaging or presentation), batch release and certification, importation, storage and distribution of specified dosage forms unless informed to the contrary;
- quality control testing and/or release and batch certification activities without manufacturing operations should be specified under the relevant items;

- if the company is engaged in manufacture of products with special requirements e.g. radiopharmaceuticals or products containing penicillin, sulphonamides, cytotoxics, cephalosporins, substances with hormonal activity or other potentially hazardous active ingredients this should be stated under the relevant product type and dosage form (applicable to all sections of Part 1 apart from sections 1.5.2 and 1.6)

1.1	Sterile investigational medicinal products
	1.1.1 *Aseptically prepared (list of dosage forms)*
	1.1.1.1 Large volume liquids 1.1.1.2 Lyophilisates 1.1.1.3 Semi-solids 1.1.1.4 Small volume liquids 1.1.1.5 Solids and implants 1.1.1.6 Other aseptically prepared products <free text>
	1.1.2 *Terminally sterilised (list of dosage forms)*
	1.1.2.1 Large volume liquids 1.1.2.2 Semi-solids 1.1.2.3 Small volume liquids 1.1.2.4 Solids and implants 1.1.2.5 Other terminally sterilised prepared products <free text>
	1.1.3 *Batch certification only*

1.2	**Non-sterile investigational medicinal products**
	1.2.1 Non-sterile products (list of dosage forms) 1.2.1.1 Capsules, hard shell 1.2.1.2 Capsules, soft shell 1.2.1.3 Chewing gums 1.2.1.4 Impregnated matrices 1.2.1.5 Liquids for external use 1.2.1.6 Liquids for internal use 1.2.1.7 Medicinal gases 1.2.1.8 Other solid dosage forms 1.2.1.9 Pressurised preparations 1.2.1.10 Radionuclide generators 1.2.1.11 Semi-solids 1.2.1.12 Suppositories 1.2.1.13 Tablets 1.2.1.14 Transdermal patches 1.2.1.15 Other non-sterile medicinal product <free text >
	1.2.2 Batch certification only
1.3	**Biological investigational medicinal products**
	1.3.1 Biological medicinal products (list of product types) 1.3.1.1 Blood products 1.3.1.2 Immunological products 1.3.1.3 Cell therapy products 1.3.1.4 Gene therapy products 1.3.1.5 Biotechnology products 1.3.1.6 Human or animal extracted products 1.3.1.7 Other biological medicinal products <free text >
	1.3.2 Batch certification only (list of product types) 1.3.2.1 Blood products 1.3.2.2 Immunological products 1.3.2.3 Cell therapy products 1.3.2.4 Gene therapy products 1.3.2.5 Biotechnology products 1.3.2.6 Human or animal extracted products 1.3.2.7 Other biological medicinal products <free text >

1.4	Other investigational medicinal products or manufacturing activity (any other relevant manufacturing activity/product type that is not covered above e.g. sterilisation of active substances, manufacture of biological active starting materials (when required by national legislation), herbal or homeopathic products, bulk or total manufacturing, etc).
	1.4.1 Manufacture of: 1.4.1.1 Herbal products 1.4.1.2 Homoeopathic products 1.4.1.3 Biological active starting materials 1.4.1.4 Other <free text> 1.4.2 Sterilisation of active substances/excipients/finished product 1.4.2.1 Filtration 1.4.2.2 Dry heat 1.4.2.3 Moist heat 1.4.2.4 Chemical 1.4.2.5 Gamma irradiation 1.4.2.6 Electron beam 1.4.3 Others <free text>
1.5	Packaging only
	1.5.1 Primary packing 1.5.1.1 Capsules, hard shell 1.5.1.2 Capsules, soft shell 1.5.1.3 Chewing gums 1.5.1.4 Impregnated matrices 1.5.1.5 Liquids for external use 1.5.1.6 Liquids for internal use 1.5.1.7 Medicinal gases 1.5.1.8 Other solid dosage forms 1.5.1.9 Pressurised preparations 1.5.1.10 Radionuclide generators 1.5.1.11 Semi-solids 1.5.1.12 Suppositories 1.5.1.13 Tablets 1.5.1.14 Transdermal patches 1.5.1.15 Other non-sterile medicinal products <free text >
	1.5.2 Secondary packing
1.6	Quality control testing
	1.6.1 Microbiological: sterility 1.6.2 Microbiological: non-sterility 1.6.3 Chemical/Physical 1.6.4 Biological

Any restrictions or clarifying remarks related to the scope of these Manufacturing operations

....
....

ANNEX 2 (Contd)

Part 2 - IMPORTATION OF INVESTIGATIONAL MEDICINAL PRODUCTS	
- authorised importation activities without manufacturing activity	
- authorised importation activities include storage and distribution unless indicated to the contrary	
2.1	Quality control testing of imported investigational medicinal products
	2.1.1 Microbiological: sterility 2.1.2 Microbiological: non-sterility 2.1.3 Chemical/Physical 2.1.4 Biological
2.2	Batch certification of imported investigational medicinal products
	2.2.1 *Sterile Products* 2.2.1.1 Aseptically prepared 2.2.1.2 Terminally sterilised
	2.2.2 *Non-sterile products*
	2.2.3 *Biological products* 2.2.3.1 Blood products 2.2.3.2 Immunological products 2.2.3.3 Cell therapy products 2.2.3.4 Gene therapy products 2.2.3.5 Biotechnology products 2.2.3.6 Human or animal extracted products 2.2.3.7 Other biological medicinal products <free text >
	2.2.4 *Other importation activities* (any other relevant importation activity that is not covered above e.g. importation of radiopharmaceuticals, medicinal gases, herbal or homeopathic products, etc.) 2.2.4.1 Radiopharmaceuticals/Radionuclide generators 2.2.4.2 Medicinal gases 2.2.4.3 Herbal products 2.2.4.4 Homoeopathic products 2.2.4.5 Biological active starting materials 2.2.4.6 Other <free text >

Any restrictions or clarifying remarks related to the scope of these Importing operations

....
....

ANNEX 3 (Optional)

Address(es) of Contract
Manufacturing Sites

....

....

....

ANNEX 4 (Optional)

Address(es) of Contract
Laboratories

....

....

....

ANNEX 5 (Optional)

Name(s) of Qualified
Person(s)

....

ANNEX 6 (Optional)

Name(s) of person(s)
responsible for quality control

....

Name(s) of person(s)
responsible for production

....

ANNEX 7 (Optional)

Date of Inspection on which authorisation was
granted

dd/mm/yyyy

Scope of last Inspection

....

ANNEX 8 (Optional)

Products authorised to be manufactured/imported (in accordance with Article 41 and 42 of Directive 2001/83/EC and/or Article 45 and 46 of Directive 2001/82/EC, as amended).

....

....

....

....

Community Format for a GMP Certificate

London, 11 September 2007

EMEA/INS/GMP/313556/2006 corr

Note: *This document forms part of the Compilation of Community Procedures on Inspections and Exchange of Information. Please check for updates on the EMEA website (Inspections pages).*

Title of Form: *Community format for a GMP Certificate*

Date of publishing: *July 2006*

History: *The Community format for a GMP Certificate was established in accordance with Art. 47 of Directive 2004/27/EC and Art. 51 of Directive 2004/28/EC amending Directives 2001/83/EC and 2001/82/EC respectively. The format adopted in September 2005 was modified as a consequence of the enhancement of the manufacturing authorisation format adopted in May 2006. September 2007 correction to numbering in section 2.2.*

Date of Adoption: *May 2006*

Date of coming into operation: *By 31 December 2006*

Note: *GMP Certificates are to be entered into the Community database (EudraGMP) as referred to in Art. 111(6) of Directive 2001/83/EC and Art. 80(6) of Directive 2001/82/EC.*

(LETTERHEAD OF COMPETENT AUTHORITY)

Certificate No: _ _ _/_ _ _/_ _

CERTIFICATE OF GMP COMPLIANCE OF A MANUFACTURER[1]
Part 1

Issued following an inspection in accordance with Art. 111(5) of Directive 2001/83/EC or Art. 80(5) of Directive 2001/82/EC as amended or Art. 15 of Directive 2001/20/EC*

or

Issued under the provisions of the Mutual Recognition Agreement between the European Community and [MRA Partner].*

The competent authority of...*[Member State]* confirms the following: The manufacturer

.... Site

address...

....

Has been inspected under the national inspection programme in connection with manufacturing authorisation no. .... in accordance with Art. 40 of Directive 2001/83/EC/ Art. 44 of Directive 2001/82/EC/ Art. 13 of Directive 2001/20/EC* transposed in the following national legislation:

....*

or Has been inspected in connection with marketing authorisation(s) listing manufacturers located outside of the European Economic Area in accordance with Art. 8(2)/33(2)/19(3)/44(3)* of Regulation (EC) 726/2004* or Art. 111(4) of Directive 2001/83/EC/Art. 80(4) of Directive 2001/82/EC transposed in the following national legislation:

....*

and/or* Is an active substance manufacturer that has been inspected in accordance with Art. 111(1) of Directive 2001/83/EC/ Art. 80(1) of Directive 2001/82/EC* transposed in the following national legislation:

....*

or

Other (please

specify):...*

From the knowledge gained during inspection of this manufacturer, the latest of which was conducted on ...../...../...... *[date]*, it is considered that it complies with the Good Manufacturing Practice requirements[1] referred to in the Agreement of Mutual Recognition between the European Community and *[MRA partner]*/The principles and guidelines of Good Manufacturing Practice laid down in Directive 2003/94/EC[2]/Directive 91/412/EEC[2]/The principles of GMP for active substances[2] referred to in Article 47 of Directive 2001/83/EC / Article 51 of Directive 2001/82/EC.*

This certificate reflects the status of the manufacturing site at the time of the inspection noted above and should not be relied upon to reflect the compliance status if more than three years have elapsed since the date of that inspection, after which time the issuing authority should be consulted. The authenticity of this certificate may be verified with the issuing authority.

---

[1] The certificate referred to in paragraph 111(5) of Directive 2001/83/EC and 80(5) of Directive 2001/82/EC, as amended, shall also be required for imports coming from third countries into a Member State.

[2] These requirements fulfil the GMP recommendations of WHO.

Part 2

| ☐ Human Medicinal Products* |
| ☐ Veterinary Medicinal Products* |
| ☐ Human Investigational Medicinal Products*   for phase I, II, III clinical trials* |

1 MANUFACTURING OPERATIONS *

- authorised manufacturing operations include total and partial manufacturing (including various processes of dividing up, packaging or presentation), batch release and certification, storage and distribution of specified dosage forms unless informed to the contrary;
- **quality control testing and/or release and batch certification activities without manufacturing operations should be specified under the relevant items;**
- if the company is engaged in manufacture of products with special requirements e.g. radiopharmaceuticals or products containing penicillin, sulphonamides, cytotoxics, cephalosporins, substances with hormonal activity or other or potentially hazardous active ingredients this should be stated under the relevant product type and dosage form.

1.1	**Sterile Products**
	1.1.1 Aseptically prepared (list of dosage forms)
	1.1.1.1 Large volume liquids
	1.1.1.2 Lyophilisates
	1.1.1.3 Semi-solids
	1.1.1.4 Small volume liquids
	1.1.1.5 Solids and implants
	1.1.1.6 Other aseptically prepared products <free text>
	1.1.2. Terminally sterilised (list of dosage forms)
	1.1.2.1 Large volume liquids
	1.1.2.2 Semi-solids
	1.1.2.3 Small volume liquids
	1.1.2.4 Solids and implants
	1.1.2.5 Other terminally sterilised prepared products <free text>
	1.1.3 Batch certification only

1.2	Non-sterile products
	1.2.1 Non-sterile products (list of dosage forms)
	1.2.1.1 Capsules, hard shell 1.2.1.2 Capsules, soft shell 1.2.1.3 Chewing gums 1.2.1.4 Impregnated matrices 1.2.1.5 Liquids for external use 1.2.1.6 Liquids for internal use 1.2.1.7 Medicinal gases 1.2.1.8 Other solid dosage forms 1.2.1.9 Pressurised preparations 1.2.1.10 Radionuclide generators 1.2.1.11 Semi-solids 1.2.1.12 Suppositories 1.2.1.13 Tablets 1.2.1.14 Transdermal patches 1.2.1.15 Intraruminal devices 1.2.1.16 Veterinary premixes 1.2.1.17 Other non-sterile medicinal product <free text>
	1.2.2 Batch certification only
1.3	**Biological medicinal products**
	1.3.1 Biological medicinal products
	1.3.1.1 Blood products 1.3.1.2 Immunological products 1.3.1.3 Cell therapy products 1.3.1.4 Gene therapy products 1.3.1.5 Biotechnology products 1.3.1.6 Human or animal extracted products 1.3.1.7 Other biological medicinal products <free text>
	1.3.2 Batch certification only (list of product types)
	1.3.2.1 Blood products 1.3.2.2 Immunological products 1.3.2.3 Cell therapy products 1.3.2.4 Gene therapy products 1.3.2.5 Biotechnology products 1.3.2.6 Human or animal extracted products 1.3.2.7 Other biological medicinal products <free text>

1.4	**Other products or manufacturing activity** (any other relevant manufacturing activity/product type that is not covered above e.g. sterilisation of active substances, manufacture of biological active starting materials (when required by national legislation), herbal or homeopathic products, bulk or total manufacturing, etc).
	1.4.1 Manufacture of:
	1.4.1.1 Herbal products
	1.4.1.2 Homoeopathic products
	1.4.1.3 Biological active starting materials
	1.4.1.4 Other \<free text\>
	1.4.2 Sterilisation of active substances/excipients/finished product:
	1.4.2.1 Filtration
	1.4.2.2 Dry heat
	1.4.2.3 Moist heat
	1.4.2.4 Chemical
	1.4.2.5 Gamma irradiation
	1.4.2.6 Electron beam
	1.4.3 Others \<free text\>
1.5	**Packaging only**
	1.5.1 Primary packing
	1.5.1.1 Capsules, hard shell
	1.5.1.2 Capsules, soft shell
	1.5.1.3 Chewing gums
	1.5.1.4 Impregnated matrices
	1.5.1.5 Liquids for external use
	1.5.1.6 Liquids for internal use
	1.5.1.7 Medicinal gases
	1.5.1.8 Other solid dosage forms
	1.5.1.9 Pressurised preparations
	1.5.1.10 Radionuclide generators
	1.5.1.11 Semi-solids
	1.5.1.12 Suppositories
	1.5.1.13 Tablets
	1.5.1.14 Transdermal patches
	1.5.1.15 Intraruminal devices
	1.5.1.16 Veterinary premixes
	1.5.1.17 Other non-sterile medicinal products \<free text\>
	1.5.2 Secondary packing
1.6	**Quality control testing**
	1.6.1 Microbiological: sterility
	1.6.2 Microbiological: non-sterility
	1.6.3 Chemical/Physical
	1.6.4 Biological

2 IMPORTATION OF MEDICINAL PRODUCTS*
- importation activities without manufacturing activity
- importation activities include storage and distribution unless informed to the contrary

2.1	Quality control testing of imported medicinal products

	2.1.1 Microbiological: sterility 2.1.2 Microbiological: non-sterility 2.1.3 Chemical/Physical 2.1.4 Biological
2.2	**Batch certification of imported medicinal products**

	2.2.1 *Sterile Products*
	
	    2.2.1.1 Aseptically prepared
	    2.2.1.2 Terminally sterilised
	
	2.2.2 *Non-sterile products*

	2.2.3 *Biological medicinal products*
	
	    2.2.3.1 Blood products
	    2.2.3.2 Immunological products
	    2.2.3.3 Cell therapy products
	    2.2.3.4 Gene therapy products
	    2.2.3.5 Biotechnology products
	    2.2.3.6 Human or animal extracted products
	    2.2.3.7 Other biological medicinal products <free text>

	2.2.4 *Other importation activities* (any other relevant importation activity that is not covered above e.g. importation of radiopharmaceuticals, medicinal gases, herbal or homeopathic products, etc.)
	
	    2.2.4.1 Radiopharmaceuticals/Radionuclide generators
	    2.2.4.2 Medicinal gases
	    2.2.4.3 Herbal products
	    2.2.4.4 Homoeopathic products
	    2.2.4.5 Biological active starting materials
	    2.2.4.6 Other <free text>

Manufacture of active substance. Names of substances subject to inspection*:

....

....

Any restrictions or clarifying remarks related to the scope of this certificate*:

....

....

...../....../........ [date]Name and signature of the authorised person of the Competent Authority of
[country][3]

....
[name, title, national authority, phone & fax numbers]

(*): delete that which does not apply.

---

[3] The signature, date and contact details should appear on each page of the certificate.
EMEA/INS/GMP/313556/2006

Procedures Related to Centralised Procedures

Procedure for Co-ordinating Foreign and Community Pre-Authorisation Inspections during the Assessment of Applications

London, 20 September 2006

EMEA/INS/GMP/313574/2006

Note: *This document forms part of the Compilation of Community Procedures on Inspections and Exchange of Information. Please check for updates on the EMEA website (Inspections pages).*

Guideline Title: *Procedure for Co-ordinating Foreign and Community Pre-Authorisation Inspections during the Assessment of Applications*

Publisher: *European Commission Enterprise Directorate-General*

Date of publishing: *January 2001*

Note: *This Procedure is included in The Rules Governing Medicinal Products in the European Community The Notice to Applicants, Volume 2A, Procedures for marketing authorisation as Chapter 4.*

Content:

- *Pre-authorisation inspections (GMP inspections)*

- *Pre-submission notification by the applicant for a marketing authorisation*

- *Designation of an inspection team and preparation for the inspection*

- *Contacts with the applicant and the manufacturer(s) to be inspected*

- *Inspection and transmission of the report and check on the importer*

- *Submission of the final report to the Rapporteur and the EMEA*

Pre-authorisation inspections (GMP inspections)

The legal basis for pre-authorisation inspections of manufacturers of medicinal products in connection with the granting of a marketing authorisation by the Community is laid down in Article 8.2 of the Regulation, which provides that:

"Where it considers it necessary in order to complete its examination of an application the Committee may require the applicant to submit to a specific inspection of the manufacturing site of the medicinal product concerned. The inspection, which shall be completed within the time limit referred to in Article 6, shall be undertaken by inspectors from the Member State who possess the appropriate qualifications and who may, if need be, be accompanied by a Rapporteur or expert appointed by the Committee".

The EMEA has a coordinating role for these inspections whilst the responsibility for carrying them out rests with the Supervisory Authority which is defined by legislation as the Competent Authority of the Member State in which the product is either manufactured or imported, controlled and released for sale within the European Economic Area (EEA).

Member countries of the EEA, i.e. Norway, Iceland and Liechtenstein participate in the system of mutual recognition of inspections and quality controls of the European Union.

For applications where the manufacturer of the product is outside the EEA and where there is an operational Mutual Recognition Agreement[50] between the country in which the manufacturer is located and the EEA, the EMEA will inform the Rapporteur for the application and the relevant Supervisory Authority of the nature of the agreement and whether or not it covers pre-authorisation inspections.

Importation and batch release should be carried out in accordance with the guidelines in force. Where a product is to be manufactured outside the EEA and the applicant wishes to import and batch release it through more than one Member State (and hence there will be more than one Supervisory Authority), the EMEA will consult the CPMP and the applicant to identify a preference for one of the Supervisory Authorities to take on the responsibility for the inspection of the manufacturer. Taking account of this request, the EMEA will agree the responsibility for inspection with the Supervisory Authorities involved.

1. Pre-submission notification by the applicant for a marketing authorisation

In their notification of intention to submit (see section 3.1), applicants should mention the name (including contact point) and the address of the proposed manufacturer of the active substance(s) and finished product together with the proposed name and address of the site(s) in the EEA responsible for batch release of the medicinal product. In the case of a medicinal product imported from a third country the notification must also include the name and address of the proposed importer responsible for batch release (including the Member State in which it is located) and site(s) responsible for sampling and testing. Final manufacturing and batch release arrangements will have to be provided when submitting the application. The sequence of all different sites involved should be clearly described.

---

[50] The European Commission has negotiated Mutual Recognition Agreements with New Zealand, Australia, Canada, Switzerland and the USA. Negotiations are on-going with Japan.

---

2. Designation of an inspection team and preparation for the inspection

Once the application is received, the EMEA determines whether
or not the manufacturing, control, batch release and importation
site(s) concerned have already been inspected, by whom, and if
satisfactory inspection reports are available. Where a
satisfactory report is not available the EMEA contacts the
Rapporteur and Co-Rapporteur, and a decision is made
whether or not to ask the CPMP to make a request for an
inspection in connection with specific aspects of the application
or, in the case of manufacturers in third countries, for general
GMP compliance. Such request is adopted by the CPMP at day
90 or at the latest by day 120. For an inspection covering
specific aspects of the application, issues to be checked during
the inspection will be detailed in an attachment to the day 70
assessment report(s).

When the Supervisory Authority is not able to inspect in a third
country, the Rapporteur and the Supervisory Authority together
designate another Competent Authority as the "Leading
Inspection Service" for the inspection (this is the only difference
between EU and foreign inspections).

Each request for inspection must be adopted by the CPMP. It
should be pointed out that the inspections, where requested by
the CPMP, should be carried out within the 210 days set out in
the legislation for the scientific evaluation of the application and
that companies therefore, should be required to be ready for
inspection from the time of submission of the application and be
in compliance with EU Good Manufacturing Practice (GMP).
The EU Guidelines on Good Manufacturing Practise are
contained in Volume IV of the Rules Governing Medicinal
Products in the European Union. Manufacturers located in third
countries must comply with these guidelines. Manufacturers
located in third countries where there is an Operational Mutual
Recognition Agreement between the EU and the third country
involved need to comply with the GMP guidelines as contained
in the Mutual Recognition Agreement.

3. Contacts with the applicant and the manufacturer(s) to be inspected

Once the CPMP has requested an inspection and the
inspection team has been agreed, the EMEA notifies the
applicant that an inspection will take place, gives details of the
inspection team and asks for the inspection fees to be paid.

Payments for inspections are made in accordance with the decision on a scale of fees adopted by the Management Board under Article 53 (3) of the Regulation. For inspections outside the EU, travel costs are paid directly by the company in accordance with Article 5 (4) of Council Regulation (EEC) 297/95, as amended. However, one fee will be charged, at the rate mentioned in Council Regulation (EC) No 297/95, as amended, for each site inspected provided that only one manufacturing operation is carried out. Additional fees may be charged for activities on the same site that require a separate inspection and also for each contract manufacturing site and contract testing laboratory that requires to be inspected in connection with an application.

The inspectors make the arrangements with the manufacturer and fix an inspection date. In preparation of the inspection, the manufacturer(s) or the applicant may be asked to provide information about the site and operations to be inspected (the most convenient format for this information is a "Site Master File" in the format currently adopted by the European Community). The applicant may be requested to supply a copy of Part II of the application to the members of the inspection team.

Prior to the inspection, the Part II assessor liases with the inspection team on any points for special consideration during the inspection and whether or not any aspect of the manufacture of the starting material(s) is critical to ensure the quality of the finished product, in which case an inspection of the starting material(s) will be considered.

4. Inspection and transmission of the report and check on the importer

At the end of the inspection, the inspectors make a report of the main findings to the management of the site or company inspected.

A single inspection report is promptly drafted for each site or operation inspected by the inspection team.

The draft inspection report is sent by the inspectors to the management of the site or company with a request for comments on major factual errors, points of disagreement or remedial actions to be provided within 15 (calendar) days of receipt. The timing of any discussions or the provision of additional information will be agreed and communicated to the Rapporteur and the EMEA.

For imported products the relevant Supervisory Authority verifies the importer's ability to store, distribute, release and, unless there is an operational Mutual Recognition Agreement between the EU and the country where the product is manufactured, to carry out the controls mentioned in Article 51.1.b of Council Directive 2001/83/EC.

5. Submission of the final report to the Rapporteur and the EMEA

One month after transmission of the inspection report to the manufacturer, the inspection team send their report to the Rapporteur and the EMEA indicating whether or not the report has been agreed by the company inspected and, if not, the reason. A copy of the comments from the manufacturer is included. In all cases the inspection team will include their final conclusions.

This must be completed by day 180 of the assessment procedure.

Any further pre-authorisation inspections that are needed are coordinated by the EMEA.

****

Guideline on the Preparation of Reports on GMP Inspections Requested by Either the CPMP or CVMP in Connection with Applications for Marketing Authorisations and with Products Authorised under the Centralised System

London, 20 September 2006

EMEA/INS/GMP/313584/2006

Note: *This document forms part of the Compilation of Community Procedures on Inspections and Exchange of Information. Please check for updates on the EMEA website (Inspections pages).*

Guideline Title: *Guideline on the Preparation of Reports on GMP Inspections Requested by Either the CPMP or CVMP in Connection with Applications for Marketing Authorisations and with Products Authorised under the Centralised System*

Publisher: *European Medicines Agency*

Date of publishing: *--*

Content:

- *A Background*

- *B Procedure for Preparing Inspections Reports*

- *Appendix 1*

- *Appendix 2*

Background

1. In order to complete the assessment of applications for marketing authorisations under the centralised system the Committee for Medicinal Products for Human Use (CHMP) or the Committee for Medicinal Products for Veterinary Use (CVMP) may request that an inspection is carried out of the manufacturing site for a medicinal product in accordance with Articles 8 (2) and 33 (2) respectively of Regulation 726/2004 of the European Parliament and the Council.

2. Inspections may also be requested according to the provisions of Articles 19(3) and 44(3) of the same Regulation.

3. The results of these inspections should be reported to the EMEA and the CHMP and CVMP in accordance with the highest scientific standards.

4. In order to assure these standards the Board of Management of the EMEA and the representatives of the Member States of the European Union have agreed that inspection reports will be prepared in accordance with

guidelines that have been agreed by European Commission at the Working Party on the Control of Medicinal Products and Inspections.

5. This guideline has been prepared in accordance with this agreement and was discussed and finalised at the Ad Hoc Meeting of Inspection Services on September 3rd 1997 and implemented from November 13th 1997. It has been subsequently modified following discussion at the Ad-hoc meeting of GMP Inspection Services on February 18th and 19th 1999 and at the meeting of the Control of Medicinal Products and Inspections Working Party on March 25th 1999. A small revision to appendix 2 was agreed by ad hoc GMP Inspection Services in May 2005. This guideline should be read in conjunction with the terms of the standard contract between the EMEA and the Competent Authorities of the EU Member States.

6. This guideline does not apply to routine GMP inspections carried out by Member States of the European Union under Article 111 of Directive 2001/83/EC and Article 80 of Directive 2001/82/EC.

Procedure for Preparing Inspection Reports

1. Inspection reports will be prepared by the inspectors of the supervisory authority of the Member State for all inspections requested by either the CHMP or CVMP under the obligations of Articles 18 or 43 of Regulation 726/2004.

   (Note: Should a supervisory authority not be able to inspect in a third country, another competent authority may be requested to carry out the inspection)

2. The Inspectors of the supervisory authority may be assisted in the preparation of the report by either experts (for quality, inspections or other) or a Rapporteur appointed by either the CHMP or CVMP to take part in the inspection.

3. The EMEA requires the Inspection report to be in English. If the preliminary report is in another language, translation into English should be arranged by either the manufacturer or the applicant.

   In any case the inspectors will be responsible for ensuring that the report is completed in the agreed format. Translations should also be completed in the agreed format and should contain a cautionary statement as follows: "This report is a translation of the original text. For confirmation and clarification of the content, reference should be made to the original report".

4. The content and format of the report should be that described in Appendix 1.

5. The scope of the inspection should include a short description of the inspection (product-related inspection and/or General GMP Inspection). The reason for the inspection should be specified.

6. The report should record the evaluation of the manufacturing facilities/operations/systems, the quality control system and other aspects of the manufacturing activities in accordance with the agreed scope of the inspection making reference to the following:

   • the site master file (if available) for the site/facilities inspected

   • the European Community GMP Principles and Guidelines (Rules Governing Medicinal Products in the European Community Volume IV)

   • questions raised by the Rapporteur / Co-Rapporteur relating to the assessment of the manufacturing activities and/or control procedures

   • any other specific issues identified by the CHMP or the CVMP and/or the EMEA (e.g. reported problems, quality defects).

7. The inspection report should include a section giving a summary of the GMP deficiencies and other relevant observations (e.g. response to the Rapporteur's or Assessor's questions). All defects which will or may affect the safety of the product should be clearly stated. Deficiencies should be referred to in accordance with the chapter numbers and headings given in the European Community GMP Principles and Guidelines (Rules Governing Medicinal Products in the European Community Volume IV)

8. Additional appendices (e.g. Site Master File) may be added to the Inspections report, if considered necessary.

9. The draft inspection report (or at least the list of deficiencies) should be prepared as outlined above within 15 days of the completion of the inspection and sent to the manufacturer. The manufacturer should be asked to comment within a further 15 days. If a response is not received within this time the inspectors should record the absence of a reply and that the manufacturer did not choose to comment.

10. On receipt of comments on the draft report (within the allowed time) from the manufacturer the report should be finalised by the author(s) taking account, as necessary, the comments received.

11. When the report is complete the author(s) should prepare a summary of the inspection report for circulation to the scientific committee or other body that requested the inspection. This summary will follow the format given in Appendix 2 and should contain an overall conclusion as to whether or not the manufacturer is acceptable for either the proposed activities and/or the activities already carried out.

12. The inspection report should be finalised and sent to the EMEA and in the case of pre-authorisation inspections the Rapporteur and Co-Rapporteur within 40 days of the inspection.

13. In the case of a marketing application that is given an "accelerated" assessment the time allowed for reporting and finalising the inspection may need to be reduced significantly. In these circumstances the timetable for reporting the inspection will be agreed for each application with the Rapporteur/Co-Rapporteur, the EMEA, the inspection team, the applicant and the manufacturer.

14. The EMEA will check inspection reports received for adherence to this guideline and for their scientific content and overall quality. Reports that are found to be deficient, incomplete or below the required scientific standard will be returned to the authorities who were responsible for their preparation with a written explanation of the reasons for non-acceptance and proposed deadline for revision, for a re-inspection or other remedial action. This deadline for re-submission of the report will be set by the EMEA

taking account of the overall timetable adopted for completion of the assessment of the application

Appendix 1

Format for the preparation of GMP inspection reports requested by either the CHMP or CVMP in connection with applications for marketing authorisations and with products already authorised under the centralised system.

1. The Community format for GMP Inspection Reports should be used.

Appendix 2

Format of the CHMP/CVMP summary report on GMP inspections carried out under the centralised system.

1. Name of the product and pharmaceutical form.

2. EMEA reference number.

3. Name of the manufacturer/manufacturing authorisation holder.

4. Address and exact location/designation of the sites and production facilities inspected.

5. Name(s) of the Inspector(s) or/and "experts" participating in the inspection.

6. Date(s) of inspection.

7. Scope of the inspection.

8. Summary of the main steps/history of the inspection.

9. List of deficiencies and observations, which will or may affect the safety of the product.

10. a) Inspectors' comments on the manufacturer's response to the inspection findings (i.e. is the company's response acceptable?).

   b) Inspectors' comments on the questions/issues raised by the rapporteurs in the assessment report.

11. Conclusions on the acceptability of the manufacturer (are the manufacturing operations for the product in compliance with European Community GMP Principles and Guidelines?) for the product mentioned in the application.

12. Recommendations for further actions (if any).

Name(s) of Inspectors responsible for preparing the report

Organisations

Signatures:

Date ....

Delegation of Responsibilities for GMP Inspections for Products covered under the Centralised Procedure

London, 03 October 2006

Doc. Ref. EMEA/INS/GMP/392920/2006

Note: *This document forms part of the Compilation of Community Procedures on Inspections and Exchange of Information. Please check for updates on the EMEA website (Inspections pages).*

Title: *Delegation of Responsibilities for GMP Inspections for Products covered under the Centralised Procedure.*

Date of publishing: *October 2006.*

History: *This procedure was agreed in 2001 but had not been formally published. It has been reviewed for currency.*

Date of adoption: *September 2006*

Date of coming into operation: *Already in operation.*

1. Introduction

The Notice to Applicants states, "When the Supervisory Authority is not able to inspect in a third country, the Rapporteur and the Supervisory Authority together designate another competent authority as the "Leading Inspection Service" for the inspection".

Such a delegation of responsibilities is also covered in the Community procedure – "Outline of a Procedure for Co-ordinating the Verification of the GMP Status of Manufacturers in Third Countries":

"Where the Supervisory Member State is unable to verify the GMP status of any third country manufacturer(s) on the above basis it may request another EEA Competent Authority to carry out an inspection and to provide confirmation of the manufacturer's GMP compliance status. For centralised products this arrangement should be subject to obtaining the written consent of any other Supervisory Member States involved."

2. Procedure

The following procedure will be used for the delegation of responsibility for carrying out an inspection for centralised products in third countries:

2.1 EMEA will write to the Member State responsible for carrying out the inspection in the Third country (i.e. future Supervisory Authority) in line with the normal procedure.

2.2 The Supervisory Authority will reply to EMEA, formally stating that they are unable to carry out the Inspection.

2.3 EMEA will then write to the Rapporteur requesting delegation of the inspection to the Rapporteur or Co-Rapporteur Member State Inspectorate. The Rapporteur will confirm the replacement Competent Authority.

2.4 In the event that neither Rapporteur nor Co-Rapporteur Member State inspectorate can carry out the inspection, EMEA will write to one of the Member States Inspectorates who have indicated to EMEA an interest in taking on such delegated inspections, requesting them to carry out the inspection. The Rapporteur and future Supervisory Authority will be informed of the replacement Competent Authority.

2.5   EMEA will send the contract to the replacement Competent Authority. All correspondence relating to the logistic arrangements for carrying out the inspection will then be sent to the replacement Competent Authority.

2.6   The replacement Competent Authority will then carry out the inspection.

2.7   The replacement Competent Authority will be responsible for providing the report to the manufacturer who has been inspected and obtaining their comments and completing the report.

2.8   If the inspection findings indicate a need for urgent or non-urgent regulatory action, they must be discussed with the Supervisory Authority before finalisation so that any follow up action can be initially agreed.

2.9   The final report of the inspection will be provided to the future Supervisory Authority, together with copies of any follow up correspondence with the company.

2.10   The replacement Competent Authority will be responsible for providing the report to the manufacturer who has been inspected and obtaining their comments and completing the report.

        The replacement Competent Authority is responsible only for the carrying out of the Inspection and delivery of the completed report. Any follow up of the inspection required after the report has been issued and all future activities relating to the manufacturing site are the responsibility of the Supervisory Authority. It should be particularly noted that responsibility for entry of information into EudraGMP rests with the Supervisory Authority and agreement must be reached with the replacement Authority on how this task will be fulfilled.

        Where multiple products are sourced from a site outside the EEA and imported through different importers in more than one Member State, or where justified by the applicant, a product is imported and batch released through more that one Member State (and hence there will be more than one Supervisory Authority), the EMEA will consult the Supervisory Authorities involved in order to reach agreement on who will take responsibility.

Compilation History

History of Changes to the Compilation of Procedures

London, 11 April 2008

EMEA/INS/GMP/313589/2006 Rev. 8

December 2003	First published by EMEA on behalf of the Commission updating May 2001 version to include a new procedure for handling suspected quality defects, updated rapid alert procedure, addition of verification of validation to procedure and forms for exchange of information, and quality systems framework for EU inspectorates.
February 2004 (rev. 1)	Updated to include a new annex on investigational medicinal products to the procedure on the conduct of inspections together with a revised document on the training and qualifications of GMP inspectors. Both documents were developed in response to Art. 15(5) of Directive 2001/20/EC.
September 2004 (rev. 2)	Updated to include a minor change to section 5 on the procedure for handling rapid alerts and a consolidation of the procedure and various forms for the exchange of information. It includes a new form to be used in the event of an inspection performed in a third country with a negative outcome requiring co-ordinated administrative action throughout the Community.
February 2005 (rev. 3)	Revision to procedure on verification of GMP in third countries.

September 2005 (rev. 4)	In accordance with Art. 47 of Directive 2004/27/EC and Art. 51 of Directive 2004/28/EC amending Directives 2001/83/EC and 2001/82/EC respectively, revised Community formats for a GMP inspection report and manufacturing authorisation and a Community format for a GMP certificate were introduced. Guidance to Competent Authorities was included on when inspections of active substance manufacturers may be appropriate based on the provisions of Art. 111(1) of Directive 2001/83/EC and Art. 80(1) of Directive 2001/82/EC as amended. A small change to appendix 2 of the summary report for inspections conducted at the request of EMEA was also been introduced. The title of the procedure for handling suspected quality defects was corrected.
July 2006 (rev. 5)	An introduction was added together with a minor change to the procedure on rapid alerts arising from quality defects as well as enhanced formats for the Manufacturing Authorisation and GMP Certificate.
September 2006 (rev. 5 reformatted)	The individual documents of the Compilation were reformatted and arranged in order to facilitate individual download from the website. No changes were made to the main texts of the documents.
October 2006 (rev. 6)	Inclusion of a procedure, applicable to centrally authorised products, for dealing with the delegation of the performance of a GMP inspection by the Supervisory Authority to another Competent Authority.
March 2007 (rev. 7)	A procedure for the issue and update of GMP certificates has been added. The Content of the fabricator's/manufacturer's batch certificate for drugs/medicinal products exported to countries under the scope of a Mutual Recognition Agreement, and the Activity/decision diagram for inspection findings for applications under the centralised system, have been removed.
April 2008 (rev 8)	The Quality System Framework for GMP Inspectorates was revised to introduce a quality risk management approach following the implementation of ICH Q9 guideline.

Combined Glossary
and Index

Combined Glossary

A

Acceptance Criteria

Numerical limits, ranges, or other suitable measures for acceptance of test results. [Part II: Basic Reqs.]

Active Pharmaceutical Ingredient (API) (or Drug Substance)

Any substance or mixture of substances intended to be used in the manufacture of a drug (medicinal) product and that, when used in the production of a drug, becomes an active ingredient of the drug product. Such substances are intended to furnish pharmacological activity or other direct effect in the diagnosis, cure, mitigation, treatment, or prevention of disease or to affect the structure and function of the body. [Part II: Basic Reqs.]

Administrative Action

one of the actions described in section 6 of the Procedure for Dealing with Serious GMP Noncompliance or Voiding/Suspension of CEPs thus Requiring Co-ordinated Administrative Action. [GMP Noncomp. Proc.]

Air-Lock

An enclosed space with two or more doors, and which is interposed between two or more rooms, e.g. of differing class of cleanliness, for the purpose of controlling the air-flow between those rooms when they need to be entered. An air-lock is designed for and used by either people or goods. [Part II: Glossary]

Air Separation Plant

> Air separation plants take atmospheric air and through processes of purification, cleaning, compression, cooling, liquefaction and distillation separates the air into the gases oxygen, nitrogen and argon. [Part II: Annex 4]

API Starting Material

> A raw material, intermediate, or an API that is used in the production of an API and that is incorporated as a significant structural fragment into the structure of the API. An API Starting Material can be an article of commerce, a material purchased from one or more suppliers under contract or commercial agreement, or produced in-house. API Starting Materials are normally of defined chemical properties and structure. [Part II: Basic Reqs.]

Area

> Part of premises that is specific to the manufacture of medicinal gases. [Part II: Annex 4]

B

Batch (or Lot)

> A specific quantity of material produced in a process or series of processes so that it is expected to be homogeneous within specified limits. In the case of continuous production, a batch may correspond to a defined fraction of the production. The batch size can be defined either by a fixed quantity or by the amount produced in a fixed time interval. [Part II: Basic Reqs.]

Batch (or Lot)

> A defined quantity of starting material, packaging material or product processed in one process or series of processes so that it could be expected to be homogeneous.

Note: To complete certain stages of manufacture, it
may be necessary to divide a batch into a number of sub
batches, which are later brought together to form a final
homogeneous batch. In the case of continuous
manufacture, the batch must correspond to a defined
fraction of the production, characterised by its intended
homogeneity.

For control of the finished product, the following definition
has been given in Annex 1 of Directive 2001/83/EC as
amended by Directive 2003/63/EC: 'For the control of the
finished product, a batch of a proprietary medicinal
product comprises all the units of a pharmaceutical form
which are made from the same initial mass of material
and have undergone a single series of manufacturing
operations or a single sterilisation operation or, in the
case of a continuous production process, all the units
manufactured in a given period of time'. [Part II:
Glossary]

Batch Number (or Lot Number)

A unique combination of numbers, letters, and/or
symbols that identifies a batch (or lot) and from which the
production and distribution history can be determined.
[Part II: Basic Reqs.]

Batch Number (or Lot Number)

A distinctive combination of numbers and/or letters which
specifically identifies a batch. [Part II: Glossary]

Bioburden

The level and type (e.g. objectionable or not) of micro-
organisms that can be present in raw materials, API
starting materials, intermediates or APIs. Bioburden
should not be considered contamination unless the levels
have been exceeded or defined objectionable organisms
have been detected. [Part II: Basic Reqs.]

Biogenerator

A contained system, such as a fermenter, into which
biological agents are introduced along with other
materials so as to effect their multiplication or their

production of other substances by reaction with the other materials. Biogenerators are generally fitted with devices for regulation, control, connection, material addition and material withdrawal. [Part II: Glossary]

Biological Agents

Micro-organisms, including genetically engineered micro-organisms, cell cultures and endoparasites, whether pathogenic or not. [Part II: Glossary]

Blinding

The deliberate disguising of the identity of an investigational medicinal product in accordance with the instructions of the sponsor. [Comm. Dir. 2003/94/EC: Article 2]

Blinding

A procedure in which one or more parties to the trial are kept unaware of the treatment assignment(s). Single-blinding usually refers to the subject(s) being unaware, and double-blinding usually refers to the subject(s), investigator(s), monitor, and, in some cases, data analyst(s) being unaware of the treatment assignment(s). In relation to an investigational medicinal product, blinding shall mean the deliberate disguising of the identity of the product in accordance with the instructions of the sponsor. Unblinding shall mean the disclosure of the identity of blinded products. [Part II: Annex 13]

Blood

Whole blood collected from a single donor and processed either for transfusion or further manufacturing. [Part II: Annex 14]

Blood components

Therapeutic components of blood (red cells, white cells, plasma, platelets), that can be prepared by centrifugation, filtration and freezing using conventional blood bank methodology. [Part II: Annex 14]

Blowing down

Blow the pressure down to atmospheric pressure. [Part II: Annex 4]

Bulk Gas

Any gas intended for medicinal use, which has completed all processing up to but not including final packaging. [Part II: Annex 4]

Bulk Product

Any product which has completed all processing stages up to, but not including, final packaging. [Part II: Glossary]

Bulk Production Batch

a batch of product, of a size described in the application for a marketing authorisation, either ready for assembly into final containers or in individual containers ready for assembly to final packs. (A bulk production batch may, for example, consist of a bulk quantity of liquid product, of solid dosage forms such as tablets or capsules, or of filled ampoules).

Certification of the finished product batch: the certification in a register or equivalent document by a Q.P., as defined in Article 51 of Directive 2001/83/EC and Article 55 of Directive 2001/82/EC, before a batch is released for sale or distribution. [Part II: Annex 16]

C

Calibration

The demonstration that a particular instrument or device produces results within specified limits by comparison with those produced by a reference or traceable standard over an appropriate range of measurements. [Part II: Basic Reqs.]

Calibration

> The set of operations which establish, under specified conditions, the relationship between values indicated by a measuring instrument or measuring system, or values represented by a material measure, and the corresponding known values of a reference standard. [Part II: Glossary]

Cell Bank

> *Cell bank system:* A cell bank system is a system whereby successive batches of a product are manufactured by culture in cells derived from the same master cell bank. A number of containers from the master cell bank are used to prepare a working cell bank. The cell bank system is validated for a passage level or number of population doublings beyond that achieved during routine production. [Part II: Glossary]
>
> *Master cell bank:* A culture of [fully characterised] cells distributed into containers in a single operation, processed together in such a manner as to ensure uniformity and stored in such a manner as to ensure stability. A master cell bank is usually stored at - 70°C or lower. [Part II: Glossary]
>
> *Working cell bank:* A culture of cells derived from the master cell bank and intended for use in the preparation of production cell cultures. The working cell bank is usually stored at - 70°C or lower. [Part II: Glossary]

Cell Culture

> The result from the in-vitro growth of cells isolated from multicellular organisms. [Part II: Glossary]

Change Control

> A formal system by which qualified representatives of appropriate disciplines review proposed or actual changes that might affect the validated status of facilities, systems, equipment or processes. The intent is to determine the need for action that would ensure and document that the system is maintained in a validated state. [Part II: Annex 15]

Clean Area

An area with defined environmental control of particulate and microbial contamination, constructed and used in such a way as to reduce the introduction, generation and retention of contaminants within the area. [Part II: Glossary]

Note: The different degrees of environmental control are defined in the Supplementary Guidelines for the Manufacture of sterile medicinal products.

Clean/Contained Area

An area constructed and operated in such a manner that will achieve the aims of both a clean area and a contained area at the same time. [Part II: Glossary]

Cleaning Validation

Cleaning validation is documented evidence that an approved cleaning procedure will provide equipment which is suitable for processing medicinal products. [Part II: Annex 15]

Clinical trial

Any investigation in human subjects intended to discover or verify the clinical, pharmacological and/or other pharmacodynamic effects of an investigational product(s) and/or to identify any adverse reactions to an investigational product(s), and/or to study absorption, distribution, metabolism, and excretion of one or more investigational medicinal product(s) with the object of ascertaining its/their safety and/or efficacy. [Part II: Annex 13]

Comparator product

An investigational or marketed product (i.e. active control), or placebo, used as a reference in a clinical trial. [Part II: Annex 13]

Compressed gas

> A gas which when packaged under pressure is entirely gaseous at −50 0 C. (ISO 10286). [Part II: Annex 4]

Computer System

> A group of hardware components and associated software, designed and assembled to perform a specific function or group of functions. [Part II: Basic Reqs.]

Computerised System

> A system including the input of data, electronic processing and the output of information to be used either for reporting or automatic control. [Part II: Glossary]

Computerized System

> A process or operation integrated with a computer system.

Concurrent Validation

> Validation carried out during routine production of products intended for sale. [Part II: Annex 15]

Confirmation

> a signed statement that a process or test has been conducted in accordance with GMP and the relevant marketing authorisation, as agreed in writing with the Q.P. responsible for certifying the finished product batch before release. Confirm and confirmed have equivalent meanings. [Part II: Annex 16]

Contained Area

> An area constructed and operated in such a manner (and equipped with appropriate air handling and filtration) so as to prevent contamination of the external environment by biological agents from within the area. [Part II: Glossary]

Container

A container is a cryogenic vessel, a tank, a tanker, a cylinder, a cylinder bundle or any other package that is in direct contact with the medicinal gas. [Part II: Annex 4]

Containment

The action of confining a biological agent or other entity within a defined space. [Part II: Glossary]

Primary containment: A system of containment which prevents the escape of a biological agent into the immediate working environment. It involves the use of closed containers or safety biological cabinets along with secure operating procedures. [Part II: Glossary]

Secondary containment: A system of containment which prevents the escape of a biological agent into the external environment or into other working areas. It involves the use of rooms with specially designed air handling, the existence of airlocks and/or sterilisers for the exit of materials and secure operating procedures. In many cases it may add to the effectiveness of primary containment. [Part II: Glossary]

Contamination

The undesired introduction of impurities of a chemical or microbiological nature, or of foreign matter, into or onto a raw material, intermediate, or API during production, sampling, packaging or repackaging, storage or transport. [Part II: Basic Reqs.]

Contract Manufacturer

A manufacturer performing some aspect of manufacturing on behalf of the original manufacturer. [Part II: Basic Reqs.]

Controlled Area

An area constructed and operated in such a manner that some attempt is made to control the introduction of potential contamination (an air supply approximating to grade D may be appropriate), and the consequences of accidental release of living organisms. The level of control exercised should reflect the nature of the organism employed in the process. At a minimum, the area should be maintained at a pressure negative to the immediate external environment and allow for the efficient removal of small quantities of airborne contaminants. [Part II: Glossary]

Critical

Describes a process step, process condition, test requirement, or other relevant parameter or item that must be controlled within predetermined criteria to ensure that the API meets its specification. [Part II: Basic Reqs.]

Cross-Contamination

Contamination of a material or product with another material or product. [Part II: Basic Reqs.]

Cross Contamination

Contamination of a material or of a product with another material or product. [Part II: Glossary]

Crude Plant (Vegetable Drug)

Fresh or dried medicinal plant or parts thereof. [Part II: Glossary]

Cryogenic gas

Gas which liquefies at 1.013 bar at temperature below − 1500 C. [Part II: Annex 4]

Cryogenic vessel

A static or mobile thermally insulated container designed to contain liquefied or cryogenic gases. The gas is removed in gaseous or liquid form. [Part II: Annex 4]

Cryogenic Vessel

A container designed to contain liquefied gas at extremely low temperature. [Part II: Glossary]

Cylinder

>A transportable, pressure container with a water capacity not exceeding 150 litres. In this document when using the word cylinder it includes cylinder bundle (or cylinder pack) when appropriate. [Part II: Annex 4]

Cylinder

>A container designed to contain gas at a high pressure. [Part II: Glossary]

Cylinder Bundle

>A set assembly of cylinders, which are fastened together in a frame and interconnected by a manifold, transported and used as a unit. [Part II: Annex 4]

D

Decision maker(s)

>Person(s) with the competence and authority to make appropriate and timely quality risk management decisions. [Part II: Annex 20]

Design qualification (DQ)

>The documented verification that the proposed design of the facilities, systems and equipment is suitable for the intended purpose. [Part II: Annex 15]

Detectability

>The ability to discover or determine the existence, presence, or fact of a hazard. [Part II: Annex 20]

Deviation

>Departure from an approved instruction or established standard. [Part II: Basic Reqs.]

Drug (Medicinal) Product

> The dosage form in the final immediate packaging intended for marketing. (Reference Q1A). [Part II: Basic Reqs.]

Drug Substance

> See *Active Pharmaceutical Ingredient*. [Part II: Basic Reqs.]

E, F

Evacuate

> To remove the residual gas in a container by pulling a vacuum on it. [Part II: Annex 4]

Exotic Organism

> A biological agent where either the corresponding disease does not exist in a given country or geographical area, or where the disease is the subject of prophylactic measures or an eradication programme undertaken in the given country or geographical area. [Part II: Glossary]

Expiry Date (or Expiration Date)

> The date placed on the container/labels of an API designating the time during which the API is expected to remain within established shelf life specifications if stored under defined conditions, and after which it should not be used. [Part II: Basic Reqs.]

Finished Product

> A medicinal product which has undergone all stages of production, including packaging in its final container. [Part II: Glossary]

Finished Product Batch

with reference to the control of the finished product, a finished product batch is defined in Part 1 Module 3 point 3.2.2.5 of Directive 2001/83/EC2 and in Part 2 section F 1 of Directive 2001/82/EC. In the context of this annex the term in particular denotes the batch of product in its final pack for release to the market. [Part II: Annex 16]

G, H

Gas

A substance or a mixture of substances that is completely gaseous at 1,013 bar (101,325 kPa) and +15 0 C or has a vapour pressure exceeding 3 bar (300 kPa) at + 50 0 C. (ISO 10286). [Part II: Annex 4]

Good Manufacturing Practice

The part of quality assurance which ensures that products are consistently produced and controlled in accordance with the quality standards appropriate to their intended use. [Comm. Dir. 2003/94/EC: Article 2]

Harm

Damage to health, including the damage that can occur from loss of product quality or availability. [Part II: Annex 20]

Hazard

The potential source of harm (ISO/IEC Guide 51). [Part II: Annex 20]

Herbal Medicinal Product

Medicinal product containing, as active ingredients, exclusively plant material and/or vegetable drug preparations. [Part II: Glossary]

Hot –cells

> shielded workstations for manufacture and handling of radioactive materials. Hot-cells are not necessarily designed as an isolator. [Part II: Annex 3]

Hydrostatic Pressure Test

> Test performed for safety reasons as required by national or international guideline in order to make sure that cylinders or tanks can withhold high pressures. [Part II: Annex 4]

I, J, K

Importer

> the holder of the authorisation required by Article 40.3 of Directive 2001/83/EC and Article 44.3 of Directive 2001/82/EC for importing medicinal products from third countries. [Part II: Annex 16]

Immediate packaging

> The container or other form of packaging immediately in contact with the medicinal or investigational medicinal product. [Part II: Annex 13]

Impurity

> Any component present in the intermediate or API that is not the desired entity. [Part II: Basic Reqs.]

Impurity Profile

> A description of the identified and unidentified impurities present in an API. [Part II: Basic Reqs.]

In-Process Control (or Process Control)

> Checks performed during production in order to monitor and, if appropriate, to adjust the process and/or to ensure that the intermediate or API conforms to its specifications. [Part II: Basic Reqs.]

Infected

Contaminated with extraneous biological agents and therefore capable of spreading infection. [Part II: Glossary]

Inspection Report

Report prepared by the official representing the Competent Authority stating whether the company inspected in general complies with the Community GMP principles. [Conduct of Inspections]

Inspection

On-Site assessment of the compliance with the Community GMP principles performed by officials of Community Competent Authorities.

A general GMP Inspection covering general GMP aspects should be carried out before the authorization referred to in Article 40 of Directive 2001/83/EC and Article 44 of Directive 2001/82/EC respectively, is granted and periodically afterwards as required.

An inspection may be more product-or process-related when it focuses on the adherence by the manufacturer to the marketing authorization of a medicinal product and on the manufacture and documentation related to the product or to a specific manufacturing process. [Conduct of Inspections]

In-Process Control

Checks performed during production in order to monitor and if necessary to adjust the process to ensure that the product conforms its specification. The control of the environment or equipment may also be regarded as a part of in-process control. [Part II: Glossary]

Installation Qualification (IQ)

The documented verification that the facilities, systems and equipment, as installed or modified, comply with the approved design and the manufacturer's recommendations. [Part II: Annex 15]

Intermediate

> A material produced during steps of the processing of an API that undergoes further molecular change or purification before it becomes an API. Intermediates may or may not be isolated. (Note: this Guide only addresses those intermediates produced after the point that the company has defined as the point at which the production of the API begins.) [Part II: Basic Reqs.]

Intermediate Product

> Partly processed material which must undergo further manufacturing steps before it becomes a bulk product. [Part II: Glossary]

Investigational medicinal product

> A pharmaceutical form of an active substance or placebo being tested or used as a reference in a clinical trial, including a product with a marketing authorisation when used or assembled (formulated or packaged) in a way different from the authorised form, or when used for an unauthorised indication, or when used to gain further information about the authorised form. [Part II: Annex 13]

Investigational Medicinal Product

> Any product as defined in Article 2(d) of Directive 2001/20/EC. [Comm. Dir. 2003/94/EC: Article 2]

Irradiation

> *Gamma Irradiation*

> Two different processing modes may be employed: [Part II: Annex 12]

> (i) *Batch mode:* the product is arranged at fixed locations around the radiation source and cannot be loaded or unloaded while the radiation source is exposed.

> (ii) *Continuous mode:* an automatic system conveys the products into the radiation cell, past the exposed

radiation source along a defined path and at an appropriate speed, and out of the cell.

Electron Irradiation

The product is conveyed past a continuous or pulsed beam of high energy electrons (Beta radiation) which is scanned back and forth across the product pathway. [Part II: Annex 12]

Investigator

A person responsible for the conduct of the clinical trial at a trial site. If a trial is conducted by a team of individuals at a trial site, the investigator is the responsible leader of the team and may be called the principal investigator. [Part II: Annex 13]

L

Licence

For the purposes of this document, a licence is defined as an authorisation to manufacture or distribute medicinal products. [QS Framework]

Liquifiable Gases

Those which, at the normal filling temperature and pressure, remain as a liquid in the cylinder. [Part II: Glossary]

Liquefied gas

A gas which when packaged under pressure, is partially liquid (gas over a liquid) at −50 0 C. [Part II: Annex 4]

Lot

See *Batch*. [Part II: Basic Reqs.]

Lot Number

> see *Batch Number.* [Part II: Basic Reqs.]

M

Manifold

> Equipment or apparatus designed to enable one or more gas containers to be emptied and filled at a time. [Part II: Annex 4]

Manifold

> Equipment or apparatus designed to enable one or more gas containers to be filled simultaneously from the same source. [Part II: Glossary]

Manufacture

> All operations of purchase of materials and products, Production, Quality Control, release, storage, distribution of medicinal products and the related controls. [Part II: Glossary]

Manufacturer

> Any person engaged in activities for which the authorisation referred to in Article 40(1) and (3) of Directive 2001/83/EC or the authorisation referred to in Article 13(1) of Directive 2001/20/EC is required. [Comm. Dir. 2003/94/EC: Article 2]

Manufacturer

> Holder of a Manufacturing Authorisation as described in Article 40 of Directive 2001/83/EC[51]. [Part II: Glossary]

---

[51] Article 44 of Directive 2001/82/EC

Manufacture

All operations of receipt of materials, production, packaging, repackaging, labelling, relabelling, quality control, release, storage, and distribution of APIs and related controls. [Part II: Basic Reqs.]

Manufacturer/importer of Investigational Medicinal Products

Any holder of the authorisation to manufacture/import referred to in Article 13.1 of Directive 2001/20/EC. [Part II: Annex 13]

Manufacturing

production, quality control and release and delivery of radiopharmaceuticals from the active substance and starting materials. [Part II: Annex 3]

Material

A general term used to denote raw materials (starting materials, reagents, solvents), process aids, intermediates, APIs and packaging and labelling materials. [Part II: Basic Reqs.]

Maximum Theoretical Residual Impurity

Gaseous impurity coming from a possible retropollution and remaining after the cylinders pre-treatment before filling. The calculation of the maximum theoretical impurity is only relevant for compressed gases and supposes that these gases act as perfect gases. [Part II: Annex 4]

Medicinal Gas

Any gas or mixture of gases intended to be administered to patients for therapeutic, diagnostic or prophylactic purposes using pharmacological action and classified as a medicinal product. [Part II: Annex 4]

Medicinal Plant

Plant the whole or part of which is used for medicinal purpose. [Part II: Glossary]

Medicinal Product

> Any product as defined in Article 1(2) of Directive 2001/83/EC. [Comm. Dir. 2003/94/EC: Article 2]

Medicinal Product

> Any substance or combination of substances presented for treating or preventing disease in human beings or animals.
>
> Any substance or combination of substances which may be administered to human beings or animals with a view to making a medical diagnosis or to restoring, correcting or modifying physiological functions in human beings or in animals is likewise considered a medicinal product. [Part II: Glossary]

Medicinal Product Derived From Blood or Plasma

> Same meaning as that given in Directive 89/381/EEC. [Part II: Annex 14]

Medicated Feedingstuff

> Any mixture of a veterinary medicinal product or products and feed or feeds which is ready prepared for marketing and intended to be fed to animals without further processing because of its curative or preventative properties or other properties as a medicinal product covered by Article 1 (2) of Directive 2001/82/EC. [Part II: Annex 4]

Minimum Pressure Retention Valve

> Valve equipped with a non-return system which maintains a definite pressure (about 3 to 5 bars over atmospheric pressure) in order to prevent contamination during use. [Part II: Annex 4]

Mother Liquor

> The residual liquid which remains after the crystallization or isolation processes. A mother liquor may contain unreacted materials, intermediates, levels of the API

and/or impurities. It may be used for further processing.
[Part II: Basic Reqs.]

Mutual Recognition Agreement (MRA)

the 'appropriate arrangement' between the Community
and an exporting third country mentioned in Article 51(2)
of Directive 2001/83/EC and Article 55(2) of Directive
2001/82/EC. [Part II: Annex 16]

N, O, P

Non-return valve

Valve which permits flow in one direction only. [Part II:
Annex 4]

Operational Qualification (OQ)

The documented verification that the facilities, systems
and equipment, as installed or modified, perform as
intended throughout the anticipated operating ranges.
[Part II: Annex 15]

Order

Instruction to process, package and/or ship a certain
number of units of investigational medicinal product(s).
[Part II: Annex 13]

Outer packaging

The packaging into which the immediate container is
placed. [Part II: Annex 13]

Packaging

All operations, including filling and labelling, which a bulk
product has to undergo in order to become a finished
product. [Part II: Glossary]

Note: Sterile filling would not normally be regarded as part of packaging, the bulk product being the filled, but not finally packaged, primary containers.

Packaging Material

Any material intended to protect an intermediate or API during storage and transport. [Part II: Basic Reqs.]

Packaging Material

Any material employed in the packaging of a medicinal product, excluding any outer packaging used for transportation or shipment. Packaging materials are referred to as primary or secondary according to whether or not they are intended to be in direct contact with the product. [Part II: Glossary]

Parametric Release

A system of release that gives the assurance that the product is of the intended quality based on information collected during the manufacturing process and on the compliance with specific GMP requirements related to Parametric Release. [Part II: Annex 17]

Performance Qualification (PQ)

The documented verification that the facilities, systems and equipment, as connected together, can perform effectively and reproducibly, based on the approved process method and product specification. [Part II: Annex 15]

Pharmaceutical Inspectorate

The national body responsible for co-ordinating and carrying out GMP inspections, including inspections of pharmaceutical manufacturers and/or wholesale distributors. If relevant, this could include making decisions concerning the issue or withdrawal of establishment licences or authorisations for their activities, the issue or withdrawal of GMP certificates, providing advice and handling suspected quality defects. [QS Framework]

Pharmaceutical Quality Assurance

The total sum of the organised arrangements made with the object of ensuring that medicinal products or investigational medicinal products are of the quality required for their intended use. [Comm. Dir. 2003/94/EC: Article 2]

Pre-mix for Medicated Feedingstuffs

Any veterinary medicinal product prepared in advance with a view to the subsequent manufacture of medicated feedingstuffs. [Part II: Annex 4]

Preparation

handling and radiolabelling of kits with radionuclide eluted from generators or radioactive precursors within a hospital. Kits, generators and precursors should have a marketing authorisation or a national licence. [Part II: Annex 3]

Procedure

A documented description of the operations to be performed, the precautions to be taken and measures to be applied directly or indirectly related to the manufacture of an intermediate or API. [Part II: Basic Reqs.]

Procedures

Description of the operations to be carried out, the precautions to be taken and measures to be applied directly or indirectly related to the manufacture of a medicinal product. [Part II: Glossary]

Process Aids

Materials, excluding solvents, used as an aid in the manufacture of an intermediate or API that do not themselves participate in a chemical or biological reaction (e.g. filter aid, activated carbon, etc). [Part II: Basic Reqs.]

Process Control

> See *In-Process Control.* [Part II: Basic Reqs.]

Process Validation

> The documented evidence that the process, operated within established parameters, can perform effectively and reproducibly to produce a medicinal product meeting its predetermined specifications and quality attributes. [Part II: Annex 15]

Product Lifecycle

> All phases in the life of the product from the initial development through marketing until the product's discontinuation. [Part II: Annex 20]

Production

> All operations involved in the preparation of an API from receipt of materials through processing and packaging of the API. [Part II: Basic Reqs.]

Production

> All operations involved in the preparation of a medicinal product, from receipt of materials, through processing and packaging, to its completion as a finished product. [Part II: Glossary]

Product Specification File

> A reference file containing, or referring to files containing, all the information necessary to draft the detailed written instructions on processing, packaging, quality control testing, batch release and shipping of an investigational medicinal product. [Part II: Annex 13]

Prospective Validation

> Validation carried out before routine production of products intended for sale. [Part II: Annex 15]

Purge

To empty and clean a cylinder: [Part II: Annex 4]

- by blowing down and evacuating or

- by blowing down, partial pressurisation with the gas in question and then blowing down.

Q

QC Laboratory Inspections

On-Site assessment of the adherence to Good Quality Control Laboratory Practice is normally part of the GMP Inspection.

Contract QC Laboratories authorized according to Article 20(b) of Directive 2001/83/EC or Article 24(b) of Directive 2001/82/EC are also subject to these inspections.

Laboratory Inspection for compliance with GLP Principles is performed in accordance with guidelines given in the annexes to the Directive 88/320/EEC and is not part of this document. [Conduct of Inspections]

Qualification

Action of proving and documenting that equipment or ancillary systems are properly installed, work correctly, and actually lead to the expected results. Qualification is part of validation, but the individual qualification steps alone do not constitute process validation. [Part II: Basic Reqs.]

Qualification

Action of proving that any equipment works correctly and actually leads to the expected results. The word validation is sometimes widened to incorporate the concept of qualification. [Part II: Glossary]

Qualified Person

> The person referred to in Article 48 of Directive
> 2001/83/EC or in Article 13(2) of Directive 2001/20/EC.
> [Comm. Dir. 2003/94/EC: Article 2]

Qualified Person (Q.P.)

> the person defined in Article 48 of Directive 2001/83/EC
> and Article 52 of Directive 2001/82/EC. [Part II: Annex
> 16]

Qualified Person

> QP as described in Directives 2001/83/EC and
> 2001/82/EC. QP responsibilities are elaborated in
> Eudralex Volume 4, annex 16. [Part II: Annex 3]

Quality

> The degree to which a set of inherent properties of a
> product, system or process fulfills requirements (see ICH
> Q6a definition specifically for "quality" of drug substance
> and drug (medicinal) products.) [Part II: Annex 20]

Quality

> The totality of characteristics of an entity that bear on its
> ability to satisfy stated and implied needs. [QS
> Framework]

Quality Assurance (QA)

> The sum total of the organised arrangements made with
> the object of ensuring that all APIs are of the quality
> required for their intended use and that quality systems
> are maintained. [Part II: Basic Reqs.]

Quality Control (QC)

> Checking or testing that specifications are met. [Part II:
> Basic Reqs.]

Quality Control

> See Chapter 1. [Part II: Glossary]

Quality System

The sum of all that is necessary to implement an organisation's quality policy and meet quality objectives. It includes organisation structure, responsibilities, procedures, systems, processes and resources. Typically these features will be addressed in different kinds of documents as the quality manual and documented procedures, modus operandi. [QS Framework]

Quality System

The sum of all aspects of a system that implements quality policy and ensures that quality objectives are met. [Part II: Annex 20]

Quality Risk Management

A systematic process for the assessment, control, communication and review of risks to the quality of the drug (medicinal) product across the product lifecycle. [Part II: Annex 20]

Quality Unit(s)

An organizational unit independent of production which fulfills both Quality Assurance and Quality Control responsibilities. This can be in the form of separate QA and QC units or a single individual or group, depending upon the size and structure of the organization. [Part II: Basic Reqs.]

Quarantine

The status of materials isolated physically or by other effective means pending a decision on their subsequent approval or rejection. [Part II: Basic Reqs.]

Quarantine

The status of starting or packaging materials, intermediate, bulk or finished products isolated physically or by other effective means whilst awaiting a decision on their release or refusal. [Part II: Glossary]

R

Radiopharmaceutical

"Radiopharmaceutical" shall mean any medicinal product which, when ready for use, contains one or more radionuclides (radioactive isotopes) included for a medicinal purpose (Article 1(6) of Directive 2001/83/EC. [Part II: Glossary]

Randomisation

The process of assigning trial subjects to treatment or control groups using an element of chance to determine the assignments in order to reduce bias. [Part II: Annex 13]

Randomisation Code

A listing in which the treatment assigned to each subject from the randomisation process is identified. [Part II: Annex 13]

Raw Material

A general term used to denote starting materials, reagents, and solvents intended for use in the production of intermediates or APIs. [Part II: Basic Reqs.]

Reconciliation

A comparison, making due allowance for normal variation, between the amount of product or materials theoretically and actually produced or used. [Part II: Glossary]

Record

See Chapter 4. [Part II: Glossary]

Recovery

> The introduction of all or part of previous batches of the required quality into another batch at a defined stage of manufacture. [Part II: Glossary]

Reprocessing

> The reworking of all or part of a batch of product of an unacceptable quality from a defined stage of production so that its quality may be rendered acceptable by one or more additional operations. [Part II: Glossary]

Return

> Sending back to the manufacturer or distributor of a medicinal product which may or may not present a quality defect. [Part II: Glossary]

Requirements

> The explicit or implicit needs or expectations of the patients or their surrogates (e.g. health care professionals, regulators and legislators). In this document, "requirements" refers not only to statutory, legislative, or regulatory requirements, but also to such needs and expectations. [Part II: Annex 20]

Risk

> The combination of the probability of occurrence of harm and the severity of that harm (ISO/IEC Guide 51). [Part II: Annex 20]

Risk Acceptance

> The decision to accept risk (ISO Guide 73). [Part II: Annex 20]

Risk Analysis

> Method to assess and characterise the critical parameters in the functionality of an equipment or process. [Part II: Annex 15]

Risk Analysis

> The estimation of the risk associated with the identified hazards. [Part II: Annex 20]

Risk Assessment

> A systematic process of organizing information to support a risk decision to be made within a risk management process. It consists of the identification of hazards and the analysis and evaluation of risks associated with exposure to those hazards. [Part II: Annex 20]

Risk Communication

> The sharing of information about risk and risk management between the decision maker and other stakeholders. [Part II: Annex 20]

Risk Control

> Actions implementing risk management decisions (ISO Guide 73). [Part II: Annex 20]

Risk Evaluation

> The comparison of the estimated risk to given risk criteria using a quantitative or qualitative scale to determine the significance of the risk. [Part II: Annex 20]

Risk Identification

> The systematic use of information to identify potential sources of harm (hazards) referring to the risk question or problem description. [Part II: Annex 20]

Risk Management

> The systematic application of quality management policies, procedures, and practices to the tasks of assessing, controlling, communicating and reviewing risk. [Part II: Annex 20]

Risk Reduction

Actions taken to lessen the probability of occurrence of harm and the severity of that harm. [Part II: Annex 20]

Risk Review

Review or monitoring of output/results of the risk management process considering (if appropriate) new knowledge and experience about the risk. [Part II: Annex 20]

Retrospective Validation

Validation of a process for a product which has been marketed based upon accumulated manufacturing, testing and control batch data. [Part II: Annex 15]

Re-Validation

A repeat of the process validation to provide an assurance that changes in the process/equipment introduced in accordance with change control procedures do not adversely affect process characteristics and product quality. [Part II: Annex 15]

Reference Standard, Primary

A substance that has been shown by an extensive set of analytical tests to be authentic material that should be of high purity. This standard can be: [Part II: Basic Reqs.]

(1) obtained from an officially recognised source, or

(2) prepared by independent synthesis, or

(3) obtained from existing production material of high purity, or

(4) prepared by further purification of existing production material.

Reference Standard, Secondary

A substance of established quality and purity, as shown by comparison to a primary reference standard, used as

a reference standard for routine laboratory analysis.
[Part II: Basic Reqs.]

Reprocessing

Introducing an intermediate or API, including one that
does not conform to standards or specifications, back
into the process and repeating a crystallization step or
other appropriate chemical or physical manipulation
steps (e.g., distillation, filtration, chromatography, milling)
that are part of the established manufacturing process.
Continuation of a process step after an in-process control
test has shown that the step is incomplete is considered
to be part of the normal process, and not reprocessing.
[Part II: Basic Reqs.]

Retest Date

The date when a material should be re-examined to
ensure that it is still suitable for use. [Part II: Basic
Reqs.]

Reworking

Subjecting an intermediate or API that does not conform
to standards or specifications to one or more processing
steps that are different from the established
manufacturing process to obtain acceptable quality
intermediate or API (e.g., recrystallizing with a different
solvent). [Part II: Basic Reqs.]

S

Serious GMP Non-compliance

non-compliance with GMP that in the opinion of the
reporting inspectorate is of such a nature that
administrative action is necessary to remove a potential
risk to public/animal health. [GMP Noncomp. Proc.]

Seed Lot

Seed lot system: A seed lot system is a system according to which successive batches of a product are derived from the same master seed lot at a given passage level. For routine production, a working seed lot is prepared from the master seed lot. The final product is derived from the working seed lot and has not undergone more passages from the master seed lot than the vaccine shown in clinical studies to be satisfactory with respect to safety and efficacy. The origin and the passage history of the master seed lot and the working seed lot are recorded. [Part II: Glossary]

Master seed lot: A culture of a micro-organism distributed from a single bulk into containers in a single operation in such a manner as to ensure uniformity, to prevent contamination and to ensure stability. A master seed lot in liquid form is usually stored at or below - 70°C. A freeze-dried master seed lot is stored at a temperature known to ensure stability. [Part II: Glossary]

Working seed lot: A culture of a micro-organism derived from the master seed lot and intended for use in production. Working seed lots are distributed into containers and stored as described above for master seed lots. [Part II: Glossary]

Severity

A measure of the possible consequences of a hazard. [Part II: Annex 20]

Shipping

The operation of packaging for shipment and sending of ordered medicinal products for clinical trials. [Part II: Annex 13]

Signature (signed)

See definition for *signed.* [Part II: Basic Reqs.]

Signed (signature)

> The record of the individual who performed a particular action or review. This record can be initials, full handwritten signature, personal seal, or authenticated and secure electronic signature. [Part II: Basic Reqs.]

Significant Deficiencies

> *Critical Deficiency:*

>> A deficiency which has produced, or leads to a significant risk of producing either a product which is harmful to the human or veterinary patient or a product which could result in a harmful residue in a food producing animal. [GMP Inspection Report]

> *Major Deficiency:*

>> A *non-critical deficiency:* which has produced or may produce a product, which does not comply with its marketing authorisation;

>> or

>> which indicates a major deviation from EU Good Manufacturing Practice;

>> or

>> (within EU) which indicates a major deviation from the terms of the manufacturing authorisation;

>> or

>> which indicates a failure to carry out satisfactory procedures for release of batches or (within EU) a failure of the Qualified Person to fulfil his legal duties;

>> or

>> a combination of several "other" deficiencies, none of which on their own may be major, but which may together represent a major deficiency and should be explained and reported as such; [GMP Inspection Report]

Other Deficiency:

> A deficiency, which cannot be classified as either critical or major, but which indicates a departure from good manufacturing practice.
>
> (A deficiency may be "other" either because it is judged as minor, or because there is insufficient information to classify it as a major or critical). [GMP Inspection Report]

Simulated Product

> A material that closely approximates the physical and, where practical, the chemical characteristics (e.g. viscosity, particle size, pH etc.) of the product under validation. In many cases, these characteristics may be satisfied by a placebo product batch. [Part II: Annex 15]

Solvent

> An inorganic or organic liquid used as a vehicle for the preparation of solutions or suspensions in the manufacture of an intermediate or API. [Part II: Basic Reqs.]

Specification

> A list of tests, references to analytical procedures, and appropriate acceptance criteria that are numerical limits, ranges, or other criteria for the test described. It establishes the set of criteria to which a material should conform to be considered acceptable for its intended use. "Conformance to specification" means that the material, when tested according to the listed analytical procedures, will meet the listed acceptance criteria. [Part II: Basic Reqs.]

Specification

> See Chapter 4. [Part II: Glossary]

Sponsor

> An individual, company, institution or organisation which takes responsibility for the initiation, management and/or financing of a clinical trial. [Part II: Annex 13]

Stakeholder

> Any individual, group or organization that can affect, be affected by, or perceive itself to be affected by a risk. Decision makers might also be stakeholders. For the purposes of this guideline, the primary stakeholders are the patient, healthcare professional, regulatory authority, and industry. [Part II: Annex 20]

Starting Material

> Any substance used in the production of a medicinal product, but excluding packaging materials. [Part II: Glossary]

Sterility

> Sterility is the absence of living organisms. The conditions of the sterility test are given in the European Pharmacopoeia. [Part II: Glossary]

Sterility Assurance System

> The sum total of the arrangements made to assure the sterility of products. For terminally sterilized products these typically include the following stages: [Part II: Annex 17]

> (a) Product design.

> (b) Knowledge of and, if possible, control of the microbiological condition of starting materials and process aids (e.g. gases and lubricants).

> (c) Control of the contamination of the process of manufacture to avoid the ingress of microorganisms and their multiplication in the product. This is usually accomplished by cleaning and sanitization of product contact surfaces, prevention of aerial contamination

by handling in clean rooms, use of process control time limits and, if applicable, filtration stages.

(d) Prevention of mix up between sterile and non sterile product streams.

(e) Maintenance of product integrity.

(f) The sterilization process.

(g) The totality of the Quality System that contains the Sterility Assurance System e.g. change control, training, written procedures, release checks, planned preventative maintenance, failure mode analysis, prevention of human error, validation calibration, etc.

System

A group of equipment with a common purpose. [Part II: Annex 15]

System

Is used in the sense of a regulated pattern of interacting activities and techniques which are united to form an organised whole. [Part II: Glossary]

T, U, V

Tank

Static container for the storage of liquefied or cryogenic gas. [Part II: Annex 4]

Tanker

Container fixed on a vehicle for the transport of liquefied or cryogenic gas. [Part II: Annex 4]

Trend

> A statistical term referring to the direction or rate of change of a variable(s). [Part II: Annex 20]

Unblinding

> The disclosure of the identity of a blinded product. [Comm. Dir. 2003/94/EC: Article 2]

Validation

> A documented program that provides a high degree of assurance that a specific process, method, or system will consistently produce a result meeting pre-determined acceptance criteria. [Part II: Basic Reqs.]

Validation

> Action of proving, in accordance with the principles of Good Manufacturing Practice, that any procedure, process, equipment, material, activity or system actually leads to the expected results (see also qualification). [Part II: Glossary]

Validation Protocol

> A written plan stating how validation will be conducted and defining acceptance criteria. For example, the protocol for a manufacturing process identifies processing equipment, critical process parameters/operating ranges, product characteristics, sampling, test data to be collected, number of validation runs, and acceptable test results. [Part II: Basic Reqs.]

Valve

> Device for opening and closing containers. [Part II: Annex 4]

W, X, Y, Z

Worst Case

A condition or set of conditions encompassing upper and lower processing limits and circumstances, within standard operating procedures, which pose the greatest chance of product or process failure when compared to ideal conditions. Such conditions do not necessarily induce product or process failure. [Part II: Annex 15]

Yield, Expected

The quantity of material or the percentage of theoretical yield anticipated at any appropriate phase of production based on previous laboratory, pilot scale, or manufacturing data. [Part II: Basic Reqs.]

Yield, Theoretical

The quantity that would be produced at any appropriate phase of production, based upon the quantity of material to be used, in the absence of any loss or error in actual production. [Part II: Basic Reqs.]

Index

Good Manufacturing Practice (GMP) Guidelines

Design, 113, 117, 144, 278, 280, 319, 325, 376, 380, 383, 615
Design qualification (DQ), 325, 615
Detectability, 368, 615
Development, 367, 513, 655, 656, 657
Deviation, 166, 615
Deviations, 119, 130, 131
Directive, 1, 5, 8, 14, 18, 22, 23, 27, 28, 29, 30, 31, 33, 35, 36, 37, 38, 39, 52, 71, 85, 95, 103, 104, 105, 205, 221, 227, 233, 255, 256, 287, 291, 294, 296, 297, 298, 299, 300, 304, 305, 306, 307, 308, 310, 328, 338, 339, 387, 391, 392, 397, 399, 416, 426, 435, 438, 447, 452, 453, 466, 467, 469, 478, 488, 492, 493, 494, 502, 504, 510, 512, 518, 528, 529, 530, 532, 534, 535, 536, 540, 555, 562, 563, 573, 574, 575, 586, 589, 601, 602, 607, 609, 617, 618, 619, 620, 622, 623, 624, 625, 629, 630, 632
Directive 2001/20/EC, 18, 27, 29, 31, 35, 36, 287, 296, 297, 298, 299, 300, 306, 492, 493, 494, 510, 518, 536, 540, 574, 601, 620, 622, 623, 630
Directive 2001/83/EC, 8, 18, 22, 23, 27, 29, 30, 33, 35, 36, 37, 52, 71, 85, 95, 103, 104, 297, 304, 305, 328, 338, 339, 387, 391, 392, 416, 435, 438, 447, 469, 478, 488, 504, 510, 512, 518, 528, 529, 530, 532, 534, 535, 536, 540, 562, 563, 573, 574, 575, 586, 589, 602, 607, 609, 617, 618, 619, 622, 624, 625, 629, 630, 632
Directive 2003/63/EC, 27, 387, 607
Directive 91/356/EEC, 27, 28, 38, 304, 305, 416
Directives, 21, 22, 103, 104, 220, 227, 307, 402, 528, 530, 534, 555, 562, 573, 602, 630
Disinfection, 233

Distributed, 153, 354
Distribution, 2, 136, 137, 220, 398, 452, 512, 517, 558, 559
Distribution Procedures, 137
Documentation, 33, 63, 84, 120, 122, 124, 143, 163, 206, 217, 230, 244, 245, 259, 278, 283, 289, 304, 318, 322, 377, 406, 488, 491, 558
Doors, 186
Dose, 269, 278, 279, 280
Dosimeter, 195, 279
Dosimetry, 276
Drains, 59, 115
Drug (Medicinal) Product, 166, 616
Drug Substance, 164, 166, 605, 616
Eating, 56
Effectiveness, 7
Effluents, 205
Enforcement, 505, 559
Equipment, 57, 61, 117, 118, 119, 122, 147, 162, 188, 205, 215, 229, 231, 232, 236, 243, 252, 258, 289, 310, 320, 380, 391, 558, 622
Equipment Cleaning, 122
Equipment Maintenance, 117
Establish, 545
Establishment, 107, 207, 235
Evacuate, 251, 616
Examination, 530
Execution, 371
Exotic Organism, 390, 616
Expiration Date, 166, 616
Expiry, 141, 163, 166, 616
Expiry Date (or Expiration Date), 166, 616
Facilities, 61, 113, 136, 162, 320, 321, 324, 380
FDA, 1, 3, 426, 505, 655, 657
Fermentation, 107, 156, 158
Filling, 180, 183, 238, 243, 246, 292
Filters, 376
Finished Product, 84, 390, 616, 617
Finished Product Batch, 617
Flow, 245

558, 562, 582, 584, 585, 589,
590, 592, 596, 597, 619, 629,
638, 639
report, 398, 485, 499, 503,
552, 555, 589
Inspection report, 398, 485, 499,
503, 552, 555, 589
Inspection Report, 2, 479, 486,
504, 546, 555, 589, 592, 619,
638, 639
Installation Qualification (IQ),
144, 325, 619
Instructions, 63, 66, 67, 68, 69,
79, 87, 118, 123, 290, 291
Intermediate, 74, 78, 106, 136,
151, 167, 391, 620
Intermediate Product, 391, 620
Investigation, 190
Investigational medicinal product,
285, 287, 291, 300, 301, 556,
620
Investigational Medicinal Product,
285, 287, 294, 477, 487, 492,
494, 498, 501, 540, 620, 623
Investigations, 162
Investigator, 287, 621
IQ, 144, 319, 325, 619
Irradiation, 275, 281, 620, 621
ISO, 24, 176, 177, 178, 251, 368,
369, 370, 371, 376, 402, 403,
404, 409, 512, 612, 617, 633,
634
Isolator, 182
Key Personnel, 51
Label, 135, 383
Labels, 74, 77, 135
Laboratories, 152, 478, 493, 562,
563, 629
Laboratory Controls, 137, 163
Licence, 404, 410, 621
Lighting, 57, 116
Liquefied gas, 252, 621
Liquifiable Gases, 391, 621
Location, 336
Lot, 164, 165, 167, 387, 393,
606, 607, 621, 622, 637
Lot Number, 165, 167, 387, 607,
622
Maintenance, 61, 107, 116, 117,
157, 158, 245, 345, 515, 641

Management, 22, 23, 43, 44, 49,
107, 127, 154, 288, 310, 357,
360, 362, 365, 367, 370, 371,
372, 377, 379, 380, 382, 383,
405, 429, 441, 483, 487, 513,
514, 558, 585, 588, 631, 634,
655, 657
Manifold, 252, 391, 622
Manufacture, 91, 167, 175, 201,
211, 221, 222, 225, 241, 242,
255, 267, 269, 270, 275, 285,
307, 329, 389, 391, 549, 556,
558, 611, 622, 623
Manufacturer, 154, 165, 287,
354, 391, 613, 622, 623
Manufacturer/importer of
Investigational Medicinal
Products, 287, 623
Manufacturing, 1, 2, 18, 21, 22,
23, 24, 43, 44, 45, 46, 51, 52,
54, 61, 63, 66, 67, 68, 69, 73,
76, 93, 99, 104, 106, 153, 176,
211, 214, 220, 241, 285, 290,
291, 298, 307, 308, 310, 317,
322, 327, 328, 329, 337, 341,
349, 352, 391, 394, 397, 398,
410, 422, 452, 467, 478, 492,
493, 505, 506, 507, 512, 513,
517, 520, 536, 556, 558, 560,
562, 563, 574, 584, 602, 617,
622, 623, 638, 642, 656, 657
Manufacturing Formulae, 63, 290
Master Production and Control
Record, 123
Material, 105, 106, 107, 130, 164,
167, 168, 169, 392, 394, 606,
623, 626, 632, 640
Maximum Theoretical Residual
Impurity, 623
Medicated Feed, 624, 627
Medicated Feedingstuff, 624, 627
Medicinal Gas, 241, 623
Medicinal Plant, 391, 623
Medicinal Product, 1, 2, 9, 21, 29,
41, 43, 45, 175, 201, 202, 211,
221, 225, 255, 275, 285, 287,
294, 307, 328, 349, 352, 390,
391, 415, 431, 444, 477, 478,
487, 488, 491, 492, 493, 494,
498, 501, 531, 540, 558, 581,

362, 370, 372, 377, 379, 391,
417, 519, 520, 618, 619, 627,
628
Process Aids, 168, 627
Process Control, 130, 167, 168,
391, 618, 619, 628
Process Controls, 130
Process Validation, 144, 145,
320, 325, 519, 628
Processes, 76, 321, 364
Processing, 63, 66, 67, 68, 69,
78, 128, 189, 204, 213, 260,
281, 290, 291
Processing and Packaging
Instructions, 63
Product, 43, 47, 84, 95, 111, 166,
288, 290, 291, 297, 298, 304,
305, 326, 344, 368, 388, 390,
391, 431, 441, 444, 480, 487,
495, 496, 507, 557, 558, 590,
609, 616, 617, 620, 624, 628,
639, 640
Product Lifecycle, 368, 628
Product Specification File, 288,
290, 291, 297, 305, 495, 496,
628
Production, 34, 51, 53, 54, 55,
57, 58, 59, 61, 73, 83, 106,
110, 113, 117, 123, 124, 126,
128, 130, 134, 157, 158, 162,
168, 203, 204, 206, 213, 217,
229, 230, 234, 237, 245, 258,
267, 270, 291, 292, 313, 367,
382, 383, 391, 392, 558, 609,
622, 628
Production Area, 58
Production Record, 124, 126
Production Record Review, 126
Production Records, 124
Products, 3, 19, 21, 29, 41, 43,
45, 75, 80, 82, 158, 160, 175,
201, 202, 211, 219, 221, 225,
237, 255, 275, 285, 286, 287,
294, 304, 307, 324, 328, 349,
352, 354, 399, 415, 430, 442,
477, 478, 487, 488, 491, 492,
493, 494, 498, 501, 531, 540,
547, 558, 562, 581, 584, 587,
588, 589, 590, 595, 623
Programme, 83, 403, 514

Prospective Validation, 321, 326,
628
Protection, 214
Purchase, 154
Purge, 252, 629
QA, 108, 168, 169, 214, 630,
631, 656
QC Laboratory Inspections, 478,
629
Qualification, 143, 144, 168, 317,
319, 320, 325, 381, 392, 506,
511, 619, 625, 626, 629
Qualified Person, 44, 47, 49, 52,
71, 89, 91, 92, 93, 95, 96, 218,
219, 274, 286, 288, 290, 297,
298, 299, 300, 327, 328, 337,
339, 352, 353, 416, 435, 447,
463, 511, 529, 537, 560, 562,
563, 630, 638
Qualified Person (Q.P.), 328,
339, 630
Quality, 1, 2, 22, 23, 24, 31, 34,
43, 44, 45, 46, 47, 49, 51, 53,
54, 55, 60, 73, 75, 77, 81, 82,
83, 84, 85, 87, 96, 99, 107,
108, 111, 154, 158, 160, 161,
162, 168, 169, 175, 198, 208,
212, 214, 218, 238, 248, 261,
263, 264, 265, 270, 272, 288,
296, 297, 308, 310, 313, 342,
345, 357, 359, 360, 362, 365,
366, 367, 368, 369, 370, 371,
377, 379, 380, 382, 383, 391,
392, 398, 401, 402, 404, 409,
411, 415, 422, 425, 431, 437,
443, 444, 478, 483, 487, 488,
493, 507, 510, 513, 518, 531,
550, 558, 602, 622, 627, 629,
630, 631, 641, 655, 656
Quality Assurance, 24, 43, 44,
45, 55, 99, 168, 169, 175, 212,
263, 264, 265, 270, 272, 308,
310, 422, 510, 513, 627, 630,
631, 655, 656
Quality Assurance (QA), 168,
630, 656
Quality Control, 43, 44, 46, 47,
51, 53, 54, 55, 60, 73, 75, 77,
81, 82, 83, 84, 85, 87, 96, 169,
248, 261, 296, 313, 371, 391,

349, 351, 353, 354, 420, 490, 558
Sampling, 70, 85, 113, 128, 129, 131, 132, 147, 181, 261, 263
Sanitation, 116, 189
Schedules, 117
Seed Lot, 393, 637
Self-inspection, 37
Serious GMP Non-compliance, 465, 636
Severity, 370, 637
Sewage, 116
Sewage and Refuse, 116
Shipment, 558
Shipping, 288, 299, 304, 637
Signature (signed), 170, 637
Signed (signature), 170, 638
Significant Deficiencies, 546, 552, 555, 560, 638
Simulated Product, 326, 639
Solvent, 170, 639
Solvents, 150, 151
Specification, 84, 132, 171, 219, 288, 290, 291, 297, 305, 394, 495, 496, 628, 639
Specifications, 63, 65, 120, 121, 137, 191, 206, 213, 217, 259, 260, 289, 290, 291
Sponsor, 288, 300, 301, 640
Stability Studies, 383
Staff, 185, 206, 321
Stakeholder, 370, 640
Standardisation, 15, 309
Standards, 176, 370
Starting Material, 1, 2, 101, 103, 105, 106, 164, 394, 527, 606, 640
State, 1, 15, 17, 19, 35, 52, 261, 329, 351, 355, 427, 428, 429, 430, 431, 439, 440, 441, 442, 443, 453, 454, 455, 457, 458, 459, 461, 462, 463, 465, 466, 469, 486, 490, 492, 498, 499, 502, 504, 510, 514, 518, 529, 530, 531, 532, 536, 537, 540, 562, 563, 574, 575, 582, 583, 589, 596, 597
Status, 2, 497, 498, 509, 596
Sterilisation, 192, 193, 195, 233, 237, 549

Sterility, 344, 345, 394, 640, 641
Sterility Assurance System, 344, 345, 640, 641
Storage, 59, 113, 129, 136, 207, 235, 238, 243, 250, 258, 290, 351, 352, 382, 556
Storage Conditions, 352
Supervision, 466, 467
system
    open, ii
System, 3, 120, 165, 194, 272, 288, 326, 344, 345, 390, 394, 399, 411, 425, 427, 428, 429, 430, 431, 432, 439, 440, 441, 442, 443, 444, 483, 513, 587, 588, 602, 612, 631, 640, 641, 655
Tank, 252, 641
Tanker, 253, 641
Testing, 70, 86, 128, 139, 314
Theory, 371
Third Countries, 2, 398, 497, 498, 509, 596
Traceability, 153, 311
Training, 2, 54, 111, 367, 377, 398, 509, 512, 655, 657
Trend, 370, 642
Unblinding, 286, 608, 642
Validation, 76, 133, 140, 142, 143, 144, 145, 146, 147, 163, 171, 182, 189, 195, 271, 277, 292, 314, 317, 318, 320, 321, 322, 323, 325, 326, 382, 394, 506, 519, 611, 612, 628, 635, 642
Validation Protocol, 171, 642
Valve, 246, 252, 253, 624, 625, 642
Valves, 205
Vegetable, 390, 614
Verification, 2, 297, 398, 488, 497, 498, 509, 520, 596
Veterinary Medicinal Products, 221, 225
Vials, 198
Virus, 309
Warehousing Procedures, 136
Washing, 61
Water, 115, 188, 190, 246, 248, 505

About the author

Mindy Allport-Settle has served as a key executive, board member, and consultant for some of the best companies in the pharmaceutical and FDA-regulated industry. As CEO of PharmaLogika, Inc. since 2008 and over the course of her career, she has provided informed guidance in regulatory compliance, corporate structuring, restructuring and turnarounds, new drug submissions, research & development and product commercialization strategies, operational, project and contract management, and new business development. Her experience and dedication have resulted in international recognition as the developer of the only FDA-recognized and benchmarked quality systems training and development business methodology designed for regulated industries. Her education includes a Bachelor's degree from the University of North Carolina, an MBA in Global Management from the University of Phoenix, and completion of the corporate governance course series in audit committees, compensation committees, and board effectiveness at Harvard Business School.

About PharmaLogika

Since 2002, PharmaLogika, Inc has established itself as one of the world's premier consulting firms for Pharmaceutical, Biotech, and Medical Device companies across the globe. In so doing, it has earned the trust of executives in Life Sciences for its integrity, accuracy, and unwavering commitment to independent thought with regard to its products and services as well as those of its customers. Through www.PharmaLogika.com, its involvement in sponsored events, and personal references it has reached millions in print and online. Its mission, to provide flawlessly designed and executed products and services to startups as well as established industry leaders to facilitate their growth from discovery and clinical trial navigation to the commercialization and marketing of their products.

PharmaLogika consults with pharmaceutical, biotech, and medical device quality units to provide third party audits, training, pre approval inspections (PAIs), compliance remediation, and a portfolio of related quality and regulatory affairs products and services. Those products include but are not limited to Quality Assurance Forms, SOP and clinical templates, and the highly successful Integrated Development Training System.

Regulatory action guidance as well as quality systems guidance are delivered as part of its standard products and services. Through the use of highly skilled resources throughout the process, each offering is designed to enact a comprehensive quality systems approach in addressing Quality Assurance (QA) issues. The results insure a close adherence to current Good Manufacturing Practice (cGMP) standards.

PharmaLogika also has a Research and Development OTC line for human consumption that targets alpha 1-antitrypsin deficiency, Fibromyalgia, Restless Legs Syndrome, and Attention Deficit Disorder. A veterinary OTC is currently available that provides canine and feline oral debriding and cleansing agents as well as a stain remover and topical antiseptic. These products combine to provide a strong pipeline of both current and future deliverables.

PharmaLogika, Inc.

PO Box 461

Willow Springs, NC 27592

www.PharmaLogika.com

Other books available

Current Good Manufacturing Practices: Pharmaceutical, Biologics, and Medical Device Regulations and Guidance Documents Concise Reference

Course Development 101: Developing Training Programs for Regulated Industries

Compliance Remediation for Pharmaceutical Manufacturing: A Project Management Guide for Re-establishing FDA Compliance

Please visit www.PharmaLogika.com for additional titles

Need More Copies?

Order now at

www.PharmaLogika.com

or

www.Amazon.com

* Companion training materials and bulk discounts are only available at www.PharmaLogika.com

8845220R0

Made in the USA
Lexington, KY
07 March 2011